Rebel Heart

BEBE BUELL

with VICTOR BOCKRIS

Rebel Heart

An American Rock 'n' Roll Journey

St. Martin's Press

❧ New York

To all the "rebel hearts" in the world,
and for Liv, my mother, and Annie,
the three strongest and most loving girls I know

CONTENTS

Rebel
Heart

PROLOGUE

A Mother's Nightmare

One day in the spring of 1968, two weeks after my first boyfriend, Paul Cowsill of the Cowsills pop group, dumped me, my girlfriend Penny (an admiral's daughter) and I were walking along the boardwalk nearest Bellevue Avenue in Newport, Rhode Island. I wore low-cut hip-hugger jeans, a fabulous wide leather belt, and a tight little top. I had on a full-length magic purple coat, and my very long, wild hair was braided meticulously. Penny was a little more worldly and a couple of years older than I was, and she knew a lot about rock 'n' roll. As we were walking along, a big black Cadillac limousine pulled up to the curb, the electric window lowered, and an exotic-looking black man peered out at us and said, "Hey, girls, you wanna come with us to the show?"

The guy looked just like a pimp in any of the popular black exploitation movies I'd seen. My mind immediately raced to the conclusion that the Cadillac contained a big horrible pimp trying to pick us up! I couldn't believe my eyes. He was wearing a magnificently ruffled shirt and a big Spanish hat with a feather in it! I mean, he was all decked out to complete pimpdom in my imagination. So of course I wouldn't even look at him, no way! I just kept determinedly walking along, eyes facing forward. Meanwhile, Penny, who was a naughty girl, was chatting with him in what I thought was an inappropriately excited fashion, asking, "Well, where are you going?" She wanted to jump right in!

I started hammering away at her, crying, begging, pleading with her. Finally, I just about literally dragged her away from the car, hissing, "Penny! What are you doing?"

Looking extremely pissed off, she finally told the guy, "Well look, I can't go because my girlfriend won't come, so good luck!" And as the limousine purred away from the curb, she actually waved at it! Then she wheeled furiously on me, grabbed my hand, and, hardly controlling herself, spat out, "You jerk! You're not going to believe whose car you wouldn't get into!"

First, she marched me down to the local head shop and showed me this big 3-D black-light poster. Then she took me to the record store, where we bought *Are You Experienced?* "Wait till you hear this record!" she said. "This record will change your life! And you'll wish you'd gotten into that car!"

We went home and she played me the record and we cried for four hours. "See?" she said. "He was not a pimp. That was Jimi Hendrix!"

I cried all day and half the night, until I fell into a fitful sleep, hating myself for not getting into his car. I'm an idiot! I kept telling myself over and over again, like a mantra. I'm an asshole!

In the summer of 1970, when I turned seventeen, I discovered LSD. I'd had a somewhat disturbed childhood, but it was balanced by the enormous love my mother had for me, and the drive that she had to make our lives better and better. When I was a teenager, my stepfather was stationed in Camp Lejeune, North Carolina, where he had a big job as a commanding officer at the base there. The biggest mistake my parents made was giving me a beautiful blue Volkswagen convertible for my birthday. At first, I was frightened of LSD. I said so lots of times. But I went to parties where I watched my friends, who did really well in school, take it. They were nice kids. We all lived on the same military base and went to the base's school, which was the same as going to Catholic school. We were all looking for ways to get off the base and get into trouble. Then one night, everything just clicked—I had driven the Bug to Jacksonville Beach. We were all hanging out. This kid had just come back from San Francisco, and the word on the street was that he had the best acid—Orange Barrel Sunshine. The circumstances were right: He was an angelic hippie. I just looked into his eyes and said, "Okay, I am going to try acid now!" So finally, after having questioned it and being terrified, I just did it. And I will never forget it as long as I live.

It was the most amazing and fantastic experience. I was lying there, staring at a red-white-and-blue ceiling fan. The fan was in slow motion—the blades became totally individual. Oh boy! I thought. I stood up because I wanted to go for a walk, but everything was wrong. The acid was extremely hallucinogenic and powerful.

My gorgeous model mommy, 1952/BUELL
PRIVATE ARCHIVE

I went down to the beach and saw a man really far away on the pier, and I could see his fishing line! A friend of mine was lying on his side and I saw rows and rows of him in different colors. I went back home, and my Jimi Hendrix poster pointed at me like the one with Uncle Sam saying I WANT YOU! I think I thought of Uncle Sam because I was a military brat. I closed my eyes, then opened them, and Jimi Hendrix smiled at me. I thought, This is the best experience! On the other wall, I had the four head shots of the Beatles by Richard Avedon that came in the *White*

Album. They were designed to entertain you when you were tripping, and they were doing all kinds of things as I looked at them.

During my last two years of high school, 1970–1971, when I was sixteen and seventeen, was when I really started experimenting with psychedelic drugs. I mean, it was the seventies and I was a teenager. I was a mother's nightmare!

When you're going to school and you're living at home, you don't take acid during the week. No way! You take it on the weekends, when you can concentrate all of your energy on an uninterrupted exploration of inner space. However, taking acid in the same house occupied by your parents can be problematic. I had to be home by midnight, which was when I'd be peaking, tripping my brains out. On many occasions, I'd have to go into my bedroom, with the lights off, and lie down, pretending to go to sleep while I was flying. My parents were a universe away, but I could hear every word they said: "Do you think she's smoking pot?"

No! I'm tripping my brains out, guys!

There were times when I would be tripping in the living room, with my mother and father sitting right there. One time, a moth was flying around the room. "Mom, there's a big bird in the living room!" I called out. "We've got to get it out of here!" I will never forget the look on their faces.

I had unbelievably good trips. One night, I was really bored. I was high in my room, opened the window, and there was a tree. I pulled a leaf off the tree and it said, *Ouch.* That triggered some interesting questions. I started asking myself, Does a tree talk? The following week, my mother had the tree pruners there. I almost went into a seizure. They were going to do surgery on the tree without anesthetic! You can imagine how my parents must have felt about my sanity at this point.

On another occasion, I was driving down the street with my girlfriend Claire; we were tripping our brains out. She said something really funny, and I was laughing hysterically and trying to change lanes. Meanwhile, we had turned on the windshield wipers and were watching the trails of rain on the glass, which was like a whole other universe. I started to change lanes, when I heard an urgent voice in my head say, Bebe, look left! There was an enormous truck with a semitrailer barreling along at sixty miles an hour some five feet behind me in the left-hand lane. If I had turned left, I would have been creamed spinach.

I was dangerous and damn good-looking. I had acid and a car! And my mother always made sure I had the nicest clothes. She bought me the gorgeous purple wool maxicoat. She understood how I wanted to dress. I listened to a lot of Grand Funk Railroad. When I heard "Layla," I jumped to the phone to call the local radio station and was told I was the seventy-fifth caller. That was one of the first times I knew I had good taste. I knew what a good song was. I saw *Romeo and Juliet*, directed by Franco Zeffirelli, and *The Heart Is a Lonely Hunter* on LSD. These were life-changing experiences. I identified with being different and being trapped in a small town. I always identified with being the person who wanted to get out. Two of my favorite songs were "We Gotta Get Out of this Place" and "It's My Life" by the Animals. I'd march around the house in a tirade, and my mother would start saying, "Young lady!" We were living in a maze neither of us knew how to negotiate, let alone together.

In my senior year, I got into a lot of trouble, and I skipped school so frequently that I was not able to keep my position on the basketball team because of my grades. The important groups I listened to were Led Zeppelin, the Rolling Stones, especially their double album, *Exile on Main Street*, and Grand Funk Railroad. But I was in a lot of pain because I didn't get along with my stepfather, Major Lester E. Johnson. He was top dog on the base; therefore, everything I did was scrutinized. But I had good friends, I had my VW, and responsibility was not a priority. We were not told that if we did not get our shit together, we would not have a life. All we could think about was expanding our minds and getting out of school so we could be free to hang out. That was the main aspiration of our generation. Later, when people asked us what we did back then, our answer was, "We hung out." It was a style of life greatly influenced by Andy Warhol's films, like *The Chelsea Girls* and *My Hustler. Trash* in 1970 and *Heat* in 1972 were the big movies. The idea was to get to know who you were in a way that we thought our parents had never figured out. We were an exceedingly egotistical generation.

Right after I graduated and shortly before I went to New York, I ran away to Virginia Beach with my derelict friends, sleeping in people's cars. People would sneak me into their bedrooms, but I wasn't sexually active at all. I had lied to my mother and told her I was going to visit one of my best childhood friends in Norfolk, Virginia.

My parents caught me because I was going to this guy Steve's house. I usually ducked down in the backseat when I was driven around Norfolk, but this time I was sitting up, and my parents, by a twist of fate, passed me in their white Cadillac, which immediately screeched and turned around. I thought I was in a movie. We made a beeline to Steve's, but when I got out of the car, I saw my parents. The next thing I knew, my stepfather was chasing me; then he caught up with me and I was carted off to a hotel.

First, my mother wanted to make sure I was all right, and then, boy, did I get it! I was totally stripped of my whole costume by my mother. She was crying. She made me take off my hip-hugger jeans and leather belt, my hippie fringe vest with its purple beads, stash bag, and bracelets—everything was stripped from my body and destroyed on the spot! It was like being dishonorably discharged! There was no spanking or yelling, but they did check me for needle marks, which I felt was really an insult. "Mom, excuse me," I said haughtily, "but I'm not screwed up on hard drugs." In those days, parents thought even marijuana was horrifying.

We were transferred to Quantico, Virginia, over the summer. For the remainder of the summer I worked as a security person at a department store on the base. I had to keep an eye on people, which was crazy, because I was a master shoplifter! Teenage girls had to be in those days. How else would we make money for Viva lipstick and all that stuff? We'd make it, though—the People's Drugstore. "For the people, yeah!" Yeah, the revolution was becoming less political and more personal. The remnants of the hippie culture were wandering around like a ragged, defeated army. I never committed grand larceny; I just shoplifted lipstick.

I could still break my mom down and get her to buy me records. Moby Grape was big that year. And my mother took me to see the notorious Swedish film *I Am Curious (Yellow)* because I asked her to, and she wanted to see it, too. I have the same relationship with my daughter: We went to see *Showgirls* together. At least my mother realized that I wasn't normal, that she had given birth to someone who was going to make something of her life, and she wanted to give me every opportunity to make the most of this undirected energy that I had. She knew I wasn't going to play basketball or run off and get married to the doctor or the lawyer, so modeling was the logical next step. She knew I was dying to go to New York City, and she wanted to give me as much positive direction as she could. She thought the most lucrative career for a girl who was a nonconformist and who lacked direction was the modeling profession—it could provide the highest income. I certainly didn't want to go to college or conform.

My senior yearbook photo; one of the shots that went to Eileen Ford/BUELL PRIVATE ARCHIVE

In the months before I left for New York, there was a lot of tension and fighting with my parents. My parents fought a lot because my stepfather liked to drink. He was a scotch and rum man, but not in a redneck way; actually, my stepfather had a lot of poise.

I used to steal the Cadillac to go to D.C. My sense of direction is obscene. I can find my way to a big city—just give me a car and point me in the right direction. I'll find it! I found my way to Washington, got a parking space in Georgetown, the cool place to be in Washington. I met this guy with a fake English accent and English clothes. He lived with his parents in a big house in Georgetown. His name was Michael. He introduced me to some cool people and new music. I was given a test of fire before I went to NYC.

My mother couldn't understand what my desires and drives really were. And because of the times, what I was experimenting with and believed in were called "hippie ways." I wasn't Grace Kelly. My mother wanted me either to graduate with honors or to go to New York and be Lauren Hutton. She had a photographer in Washington take some photos of me; they were snapshots. My hair was long, a mane. My mother had read that that's what Eileen Ford was looking for. She sent her the pictures. She got a phone call within forty-eight hours, telling her to bring me to New York.

One of the pictures that went to Eileen Ford,
1972/BUELL PRIVATE ARCHIVE

CHAPTER 1

The Wild Child

1972-1973

I was raised at CBGB
Cut my teeth at Max's Kansas City
My soul is pure rock
Ain't never gonna stop.
   "NORMAL GIRL," LYRICS BY BEBE BUELL

I moved to New York to find the place where I would be happy, where I belonged, where my essence was. It was where I needed to be, where girls and guys like me were. This is where you went. This is where it was. I never had a desire to go to California. That's where the culture girls like the GTOs I'd read about in *Rolling Stone* went. Girls who wanted to be stars went to New York. I wanted to be a superstar!

In January 1972, I moved to New York City to begin my career as a model. I was five nine. I had been a star forward on my Catholic school's basketball team and I had the athletic, thoroughbred good looks of a Virginia aristocrat. I came from an aristocracy of invention. My mother, whose first husband—my father in name only—divorced Mom when I was two, had remade herself and, in

Early test shot, 1973/STEPHEN ANDERSON

particular, me. I was the perfect candidate for the University of Manhattan, because when I arrived, I was a blank canvas waiting to be painted into a masterpiece. I was under contract to the Eileen Ford Modeling Agency. All the top models of the era—Veronica Hamil, Susie Blakeley, Lauren Hutton—were there. The first person who tried to color me as she saw fit was Eileen Ford. I vividly recall walking into her office on East Fifty-ninth Street with my mother and sitting there full of expectations.

"You're a beautiful girl," Eileen Ford said.

"Thank you," I replied.

"You might have to have the bump in the middle of your nose fixed," she suggested.

"I have a bumpy male side and a smooth female side," I attempted to explain.

She thought that was crazy. I was horrified. She detected that I was not a big-city girl, and she invited me to spend a few days living in her Upper East Side town house with her family. A couple of other models were staying there. She went to the gym with me to see me in a leotard.

"You have a great body!" she enthused. I guess I was Eileen Ford's type, but I didn't like living at her house, because I felt that she was watching everything I did. I lasted five days.

My second week in New York, I moved to St. Mary's Residence, a Catholic Barbizon-type place between Second and Third Avenue on East Seventy-second Street—a residence along the lines of the Barbizon Hotel. The area was known by the local wolves as "the stewardess/model ghetto." The combination of hundreds of perky, naïve girls and their desire to make it drew some of the ooziest creeps in the city to the restaurants and bars that defined the neighborhood. I avoided them like the plague. My mother and Les Johnson paid my rent and gave me an allowance of fifty dollars per week. I had my own room with a bed, a dresser, and a closet. I shared a bathroom. There was no TV, but I had a radio. In the early seventies, my life revolved around the radio. It was God. It wasn't like it is now. The radio played very cool music. You could hear fantastic songs like "Gloria" and "Satisfaction" on the radio—real *music*. I listened to K-Rock when I woke up, when I was putting on my makeup or getting ready to go out to my appointments. I lived for rock and roll, which I got from the radio and *The Ed Sullivan Show*. The radio, records, and that TV show were the only ways to get your music when I was a kid.

I was on Eileen Ford's roster as one of her top-ten possible contenders. She was sure I was going to go the same way as Christie Brinkley, and in the beginning, I worked a lot. Being a successful model is a twenty-four-hour-a-day job. When you are not working, you take care of yourself: your hair, your nails, your skin, your weight, your posture, what you eat and must not eat, exercise. I loved fashion, but I soon realized modeling was not what I wanted to do. I wanted to express myself, and I couldn't express myself by modeling. I harbored a secret ambition to be a rock star. I was writing song lyrics in a notebook, and I kept reevaluating them. Rock 'n' roll was uppermost in my soul.

On my first assignment, while my mother was still in New York, staying at the Mayflower Hotel, I did a test with a photographer who tried to get me to take off my top. He said, "Oh! Let's take some beauty shots!" A lot of the typical clichés came alive for me when I started out. On a typical day, I would get up at 7:00 A.M., take a shower, have some juice and vitamins, make phone calls, get dressed, then go to the booking. How I was feeling would depend on the job. If I was doing bread-and-butter work like being photographed for a catalog, I'd be unhappy. But if I was doing a glamorous *Cosmopolitan* booking, I'd be excited, because I could perform for the camera. Then it would depend on the photographer. If I was working with somebody as great as Francesco Scavullo, I would be very inspired.

First, I would do "go-sees." If *Vogue* wanted me to do ten pages for them, the photographer would need to see me before booking me. If I was going to be meeting Richard Avedon, it was the greatest! I would walk into his studio and his assistant would greet me. There would be other models there. I would take a seat and wait my turn, then go in and show them my portfolio. They would look at it, then ask me a couple of questions. The next day, my booker would give me their response.

Modeling was a conservative business in 1972, but I was not a conservative girl. All the other girls would show up clean-cut and coiffed in chic slacks, sweaters, and loafers. I would arrive in platform shoes and glitter rock clothes with feathers hanging off

Modern Bride magazine; my first job, 1972/JOHN VIDOL

me, looking like I'd just rolled off the dance floor. I immediately got a reputation as the rock and roll model who didn't take it too seriously. I was the beautiful girl who didn't like to be on time and wouldn't put on an outfit if she didn't like it. This was bad behavior for a model, because you're being hired to model clothes you don't like. But I would cry until they made another model wear the tacky clothes.

When I was a young girl, just seeing my picture in a magazine or catalog was exciting. Being on the cover of a magazine was a real buzz. So I did get some ego satisfaction, because I got to express myself. It's not like it sucked; it just wasn't who I was. I didn't feel like I fit in with the other girls. We never had anything in common. They talked about their stockbroker boyfriends, or what they were reading. We weren't on the same planet. Meanwhile, my career started to take off. I worked mostly for *Brides* and *Cosmopolitan* magazines. I was starting to make sixty dollars an hour. The checks went to Eileen; then she'd cut me a check after taking the agency's 10 percent.

One day, I was going to lunch at Sixtieth and Third. Woody Allen was walking down the street. When he saw me, he did a double take. Fifteen minutes later, I was eating in one of those fishbowl restaurants, when he walked past and peered in at me.

"What is it about girls like you?" my girlfriend asked. "Why do famous people notice you?"

"I don't know," I said. "You tell me and we'll both know."

I didn't see anything in Woody Allen, but people constantly told me I looked like the young Mia Farrow, and I saw this karma of bumping into Woody Allen as symbolic of what was to come for me. Woody Allen and New York City were beginning to make perfect sense to me.

I had a similar experience with Salvador Dalí. There was a newsstand that sold international publications in the St. Regis Hotel on Fifty-fifth Street, just off Fifth Avenue. I was leafing through British *Vogue* one day when this majestic-looking man with a red cape kept looking at me. I realized it was none other than the legendary Dalí. He asked me if I'd like to go upstairs and have tea with him. On that first day, he introduced me to Amanda Lear! And he asked me what I was doing in New York City. When I told him I

British *Vogue*/CLIVE ARROWSMITH

was a model, he said, "Yes, but you've got something more. Do you want to be an actress?"

"I don't know," I said. "I'm open."

Dalí was surprisingly unkempt. His waxy mustache was dirty and gross and his clothes were tattered, but he was endearing. And I knew he wasn't trying to make a pass at me. That same day, I met Michael J. Pollard, the gnomish actor who had starred so memorably in *Bonnie and Clyde*. He was a drunken mess, but he was fascinating and articulate. Everyone sat around chatting. We had a beautiful tea.

I ran into Dalí a couple of times after that, and he always made me feel that I had a glow, something that made him want to know me and invite me to tea with his interesting, crazy friends. I kept having these glimpses of my fate, like Alice in Wonderland peeking into different rooms.

My first connection to the nightlife was through an entrepreneur named Richard. He was a polite young man I met through Eileen Ford. Richard smoked pot, but Eileen didn't know that. The worst we did was a little pot and a Quaalude. After I moved to St. Mary's, Richard would call to see if I wanted to go out dancing, and I started to frequent the uptown night spots. I met a lot of people through Richard, like the photographer Eric Bowman and the fashion designers Giorgio Saint Angelo and Halston. He also introduced me to the first gay man with whom I would form a lifelong friendship, the photographer David Croland. I met him backstage at a benefit for children with cancer, where I performed along with Alice Cooper and Shelley Winters. David was body-painting people. I had to stand there stark naked in a G-string while he painted me. He said, "You look like a nurse!" He painted one breast as a black baby and one breast as a white baby, and I vamped onto the stage in high heels with one "baby" in each arm. This marked my first stage appearance in New York and the beginning of a love affair with my gay audience. The situation was even more auspicious for me, since this was the same stage at the Academy of Music on Fourteenth Street where the Rolling Stones made their American debut in 1964.

One night, I went out with a boy I had met through another model. He was from Long Island and had too much money because his father was a rich doctor. He picked me up in his Cadillac from one of my "go-sees," so I had my portfolio with me. We were going to a party at Francesco Scavullo's house. We were driving along with his friends, who were smoking joints and popping pills. There was so much peer pressure involved with drugs in those days. They gave me a pill and put some amyl nitrate under my nose, and I threw up all over the beautiful interior of his car. When we got to Scavullo's, they all had to go to the kitchen to clean themselves up. They were so angry, they didn't want to have anything to do with me.

I didn't know you weren't supposed to drink on top of the pills. I was just naïve. A whiskey sour was a drink I heard people ordering on television, so I proceeded to drink a whiskey sour. The next thing I knew, my head was spinning out of control and I started to get paranoid and panic. I was sitting on a chair, clutching my portfolio, when somebody asked me perfectly politely if they could see my pictures. I went nuts, saying, "*No, no!*" I knew that I had to get to a bathroom. I found one off Scavullo's bedroom, locked myself in, and lay down on the cold tiles. I needed to have my face on the floor to stop the dreadful spinning sensation. It was a nice clean bathroom.

The next thing I knew, people were pounding on the door, shouting, "Darling, are you all right? Let us in!" I was so completely out of it, I had no idea that I had been on that floor for two hours. This was my first meeting with Francesco Scavullo, who was the most important fashion photographer in New York other than Richard Avedon.

Francesco and his companion-cum-assistant, Sean, scraped me off the floor and propped me up on his bed with pillows. Francesco asked me what I had taken, and everybody came over, fussing and wanting to know who had given me these drugs, what I had taken, and where I was from.

"I'm from St. Mary's Residence," I heard myself saying. Disembodied voices came at me as if in a dream. . . .

"What? Oh my God, we gotta get this girl outta here! She's jailbait!" Meanwhile Francesco, who was a kind man, got a cold rag for my head, assured me it would pass, and told me not to worry. "Just tell me what kind of pill," he said.

"Red," I said, and once again the voices started. "Oh, they gave her Tuinol!" someone said. "Oh, she took Tuinol and whiskey sours." Francesco held the wet rag on my head, gently scolding me. "Darling, if you continue to do things like this, it could be very bad for your career. How are you going to get up in the morning?"

I knew a lot of models who were far more messed up than I was that night, but it certainly wasn't the norm for me. However, shortly thereafter, it happened again.

On that occasion, it knocked me out for hours. When I woke up, it was 7:00 P.M. the next day, but I looked at the clock and thought it was 7:00 A.M. I got dressed, but when I walked out my door, it was dark. That was the first time in my life that I had no sense of time, and it was scary. This was before answering machines. I could not check my messages and find out who had been looking for me that day. Supposedly, people from the agency had been knocking on my door all day and I had slept through it all! I told Eileen Ford the truth—that somebody had given me a pill.

"What color was it?" she asked.

"Red."

"Oh my God," she said, "a Tuinol!" Then she started to lecture me: I was falling into the wrong crowd! These people were going to ruin my career, and my life! The next thing I knew, these people would be putting needles in my arms! I didn't know what she was talking about.

"I don't want to put needles in my arms!" I said. "I'm not like that!" It was the same battle I had had with my stepfather and my mother when I was in high school. I have never—and I want to put this on record—shot up in my life. I'm just not interested.

This concern about my taking drugs came from the fact that models were notorious for getting messed up on drugs. One of my earliest modeling memories is of this beautiful top model named Pola. One day, I went to a test shoot at Chris Von Wagenheim's studio. Beautiful Pola was almost completely passed out, sprawled on a chair, and people were working on every part of her—her fingernails, her hair, her makeup. There was literally drool running down her chin. I looked at her arms and saw the series of pinpricks made by needles and the makeup sponges trying to cover them. They were catering to her, knowing she was a junkie. Finally, when it was time for her to be photographed, they held amyl nitrate under her nose. I was standing in the middle of the makeup room. As soon as I smelled the amyl, I hurled all over the room. So they all jumped to the conclusion that I was on heroin! I'd arrived on time and was totally straight, but everyone was yelling at me!

A year later, I got a call from a friend who had been at that shoot. He told me Pola had died of a heroin overdose. When she overdosed, she fell onto her wrought-iron water-based heater. Nobody found her for three days. When they did, she had been boiled, and her dog had eaten part of her. Before that, she had been on the cover of *Cosmopolitan* and *Vogue*.

My secret desires were locked up inside of me. I didn't dare tell anybody what I really wanted to be. All I knew was that I wanted to be somebody. That somebody resembled Anita Pallenberg, Pattie Boyd, Marianne Faithfull, Jane Fonda, Brigitte Bardot, and Janis Joplin! Or at least resembled their essence. I don't know if the word *star* was embedded in my mind. I had discussed my desires to be in a band with the girls at St. Mary's Residence, but I might as well have been talking to the Stepford Wives. They knew me as somebody who would get all dressed up and head downtown on the Second Avenue bus to my doom. I always had fantasies of being some kind of artist. A performer, a "somebody." But I was afraid that people would laugh at me because I wanted to be famous.

Meanwhile, there was a lot of sexual energy crackling around me. People always wanted to have sex with me, instead of wondering what I thought or felt. That was painful. I wanted to be taken seriously as a viable commodity, not a piece of ass. Approval was really important to me. I think when you grow up without a dad, a man's approval is particularly important. I wanted someone to appreciate me for having a vision. I came to New York as a model, but I certainly thought I was going to be a hell of a lot more than that!

My life took a definitive turn when I met the rock 'n' roll singer-songwriter Todd Rundgren. He had started his career in the late sixties as the leader of a great hard-rock band from Philadelphia called Nazz. Now he was approaching the pinnacle of a brilliant solo career with the hit single "I Saw the Light." Richard Postrel introduced us one night when we stopped by Todd's apartment to drop off some tapes.

We pulled up in front of 206 East Thirteenth Street and Third

Avenue. It looked like a dangerous neighborhood in 1972: The streets were populated by pimps, hookers, and pool hustlers. "Wait down here," Richard said.

"Right!" I said. "Forget it!" Todd didn't have a doorbell, so Richard threw a coin up at his window. I thought that was cool, but when Todd stuck his head out the window and threw down a key, I almost shouted, "Richard, he has green-and-yellow-and-purple hair!" I'd never seen anything like it! Wow! I couldn't wait to get up those stairs. His building was a landmark brownstone. Inside, we mounted a stately staircase, but when Todd opened his door, I glimpsed the interior of an apartment that was the polar opposite of the building's nineteenth-century opulence. I'd never seen such a mess. It was as if Jackson Pollock had taken the props of a rock star's life—guitars, records, speakers, microphones, wires, wild clothes, rattlesnake-skin shoes, half-empty coffee cups, and take-out food containers—and smeared them around, abstracting the room with Todd's heavy-metal genius.

He looked like a cross between Bugs Bunny and Antonin Artaud. We looked at each other, and I fell madly in love with him; I was just nuts about him. On the way home, I drove Richard crazy, wanting to know everything about Todd, his girlfriends, his past, whom he slept with, whom he didn't sleep with, what he was doing. Richard told me all about Patti Smith and Sam Shepard. Patti had been Todd's girlfriend for a while.

Three days later, I got a call from my booker. There was a strange guy with green-and-yellow-and-purple hair sitting on the steps of the agency, waiting for me. She wanted to let me know in case I didn't want to see him. I zipped over there as fast as I could without killing myself, but when I got there, I acted all cool and spontaneous, like I was all surprised. "Oh, hi, what are you doing here?" I said.

"Oh, uh, actually, I was in the, uh, neighborhood," he replied, acting cool, too, like it was no big thing. "My dog, Puppet, had a little, uh, checkup today, and, you know, I had to wait for her for a couple hours, so I thought well, like I'd stop and hope maybe I ran into you."

We made plans to meet that night. When I got to his apartment, it was my turn to throw the penny up at his window. Being the ex–

basketball player I was, I got a hole in one, and Todd was impressed. We went out with a bunch of his friends and ended up at Max's Kansas City, which was the only downtown club of its kind in those days. It was famous largely for its clientele of artists and the Warhol people who populated its notorious back room. We ate dinner in the front room and everybody got drunk. I took a trip to the bathroom and peeked into the back room, which was lighted by a Dan Flavin red light sculpture. I thought, Hmm, this red room looks a lot better than the room we're in. I didn't understand the social structure of Max's at all. I sashayed back there with Paul Fishkin, who was the president of Todd's record label, Bearsville. We went back to our table and I told Todd, "I think we're in the wrong room. I think we're supposed to be back there."

"Well, that's if you want to hang out," he said, "but we're eating."

I could not stop thinking about Max's Kansas City, but nobody from St. Mary's Residence would go with me. My roommates were soap-opera stars and had to be up in the morning. They warned me I'd ruin my career if I went down there. Two nights later, I lied to the nuns, got dressed to the nines in platform shoes and a multicolored dress with a fake fur, and took the bus down Second Avenue to Irving Place. From there, I walked over to Seventeenth and Park and waltzed straight into Max's Kansas City's back room, having no idea of its reputation as a den of iniquity unlike any other restaurant or bar in the world. I was dying to be where I thought I belonged.

The first person I made eye contact with was Andy Warhol. He was stepping out of the men's room, and he immediately asked me, "Oh, who are you? I haven't seen you around before. . . ."

"My name's Bebe Buell, and I'm from Virginia!"

"Oh, are you, uh, a uh . . . debutante or something? Well, does your, uh, your mother breed horses or something?"

"No," I said, laughing, "I'm a model with the Ford Agency."

"Well, who knows you yet?"

"I don't know anybody, except I've met this guy Todd Rundgren. . . ."

"Oh, you can do better. Come sit with us! And we'll talk to you about everything."

I went over to his table, and that night I met Lou Reed; the editor of *Interview*, Bob Colacello; the stars of *Trash* and *Heat*, Jane Forth and Eric Emerson; the star of *Flesh*, Patti D'Arbanville; and the brilliant singer-songwriter and ex-leader of the Velvet Underground, John Cale.

"You look rich," Andy continued, eyes wide. "You look like you come from a really nice family. Where are you from?" I guess I looked a little groomed. Compared to them, I was wholesome. But I didn't know what to say to him, because Andy wasn't exactly vivacious, and he freaked me out by asking if I was a debutante. I think he just cared whether I had money. I couldn't figure out why he didn't just come out and say, Look, are you a rich kid? He'd say, "Oh, so, uh, you know, uh, that's a reeeeaaally nice Georgio Saint Angelo. . . . Where did you get that?"

"It's funny, because this girl I live with at St. Mary's Residence . . . she gets all these samples for free!"

"Ohhh . . . fabulous!"

Andy lost interest in me after a minute because I wasn't begging him to paint my portrait. I was thinking, So this is Andy Warhol. I had no idea Andy was gay. I had no idea what gay and straight meant. Andy didn't strike me as being male or female; he just struck me as being silver. He was Silver Guy! That was his aura to me. Everybody was straight to me, even gay people! I was introduced to gay culture by osmosis. I did not know that Bob Colacello was gay. I did not know that Lou Reed was bisexual. I did not know that all these people were hanging out, fucking one another. I had no idea of anything, but I was ripe, eager to learn, and to these people, I must have seemed tantalizingly fresh. I felt like a princess because everybody wanted to meet me. I didn't have to lift a finger walking into that room. It was like a magic fairyland to me. I immediately made friends. People were giving me their phone numbers. This was the seventies, and people were having sex in phone booths, but I always thought there were so many romances on that scene because of the lighting. Everybody looked red, and it seemed to help things along. I didn't get out of there until 4:00 A.M., so everyone's warnings about Max's having a negative effect on my career were correct. But I knew that I had found my world. It became my second home.

The second time I went to Max's with Todd, we all went back to

Todd's. I asked if I could put my head in his lap—because I was tired—and I fell asleep. I'd never heard his music. In the morning, when he went to play me "Black Mariah" from his new *Something/Anything?* album, the stereo blew up.

Two weeks later, I moved into Todd's apartment to take care of Puppet while he went on the road with Alice Cooper. We weren't lovers yet. We were heavy maker-outers and dry humpers. A week later, Todd flew me down to Miami, to the Playboy Plaza Hotel (a little omen of what was to come). Then we had mad sex. He was the first man I'd ever had sex with, and it was extraordinary. Now he was officially my boyfriend. I met Alice Cooper, but I kept asking, "Todd, are these guys going to think I'm a groupie if I'm with you?"

"Nah, Bebe," he replied, "you've got too much class."

Alice didn't take any drugs and was never into shagging groupies. You could go to him with your problems and he would be sweet and patient. His great loves were TV and Budweiser. I felt so sorry for the poor snake he used in his stage act, but Todd said, "Don't worry about it. The snake has been on the road for a long time. The snake drinks; the snake smokes; the snake has girlfriends. In fact, he gets laid more than any of us."

Shortly thereafter, I moved to Todd's apartment. I started to miss early-morning calls for modeling jobs. It was such an amazing environment, cluttered and packed with shoes, clothes, records, instruments, and tapes. There was a piano, and things were hanging everywhere. Todd had the most unusual wardrobe, because he was into English rock fashions before other American rock stars were. The apartment had a big front room with a kitchen and a bathroom, and also a hall and another big room, which was Paul Fishkin's room, but he was hardly ever around. Paul had this poor cat, Perry Como, which he kept locked in his room. Consequently, Perry was insane. As soon as everyone left and I was done singing in front of the mirror, I would try to talk to this cat. I would take Perry into our room, but Perry was so pissed off, he peed in Todd's favorite shoes, creating a horrible odor. Being eighteen, and unprepared for such emergencies, I shoved the offending shoe under the faucet and tried to wash it out, but then I had a wet leather shoe on my hands! Todd spent the next four hours trying to get the smell out by spraying Chanel No. 5 in them, but that complicated matters. Finally, they took Perry away and gave him a home—thank God! Because I was just insufferable about it! Paul Fishkin neglected that cat, and every time he walked through the door, I would go ballistic.

Bearsville Records was Albert Grossman's label. Albert had been Bob Dylan's manager in the sixties. He was in the movie *Don't Look Back*. Now he was Todd's manager. He looked like Ben Franklin on acid. Albert had a monster reputation. He could be very diplomatic and cool, but as soon as his judgment was questioned, a very different Albert would emerge and he would reduce the culprit to a pile of nothing with just one sentence.

Todd and Albert got along well. Once, we went to dinner at Albert's house. Todd and I sat there with Albert and the great white blues singer Paul Butterfield. Todd and I were both so thin, and we would sit there and watch these guys with huge stomachs eat. We took psychedelic drugs. I would hallucinate, and Albert was always Santa Claus to me. Some people saw him as an Indian chief; some people saw him as this person of power. To me, he was Santa Claus.

Albert adored me. But sometimes that caused conflicts, because he would defend just about anything and everything I did. I don't know how this affected Todd, but our relationship lasted for five years, and Albert did everything to keep me around. He treated me wonderfully; he always thought I had a spark and a flair. I also loved Jim Merlis, who was the press agent at Warner Bros., which distributed Bearsville. I would visit Jim and drive him crazy at his office, and I'd visit Paul Fishkin, who also had a small office at Warner's. Suddenly, I was all over the place, like a rock 'n' roll Ping-Pong ball! And I loved living like that.

Eileen Ford and I got along really well until I started going to Max's Kansas City every night, being a rock 'n' roll girl, not showing up at photo shoots, and sleeping through important cover tries. As a result of my preference for the rock life over the modeling world, I now had one angry mother, one angry agent, and some angry friends, all of whom thought of Bebe as a sweet virgin princess from Virginia living in a pink fantasy. I was now living in a crummy apartment in a hooker neighborhood with a rock-star boyfriend and going to that den of iniquity, Max's Kansas City, every night. And I was very definitely not a virgin.

The people at Max's were all older than I was. I was the baby. Liz Derringer—the wife of Rick Derringer, an outstanding guitar player, successful solo star, and supersuccessful producer, who was Todd's only true friend—was my best friend, and she was five years older than I was. Another friend was Alice Cooper's drummer's wife, Babette Smith. She was the same kind of model I was, a naughty model who didn't ever show up for work on time. Everybody thought that Babette and I looked like twins. Pam Turbov on the West Coast and then Jeanne Theis, who worked at Bearsville, also became dear friends. Jeanne and I bonded because I had a nemesis, Susan Lee, who was also part of the Bearsville crew. Jeanne would keep me posted on what was going on in the office when I wasn't around, and I think she felt protective, because she took me under her wing.

One night when I was first dating Todd, he was working at Moogy Klingman's loft/studio, Secret Sounds. Moogy and Todd brought Rick in to play guitar. When I got to the studio, there were a whole bunch of people there, including Bette Midler. "Come down to the baths; you're going to love my show," Bette said. So I went down to the baths, and I looked around and noticed that I was the only woman in the whole place. The Divine Bette was singing to a completely gay audience. That's when I realized how much I really loved and depended on my fags. My little army of gay friends started with my hairdresser, Eugene Seifker, who once famously cut two feet off my hair; Couri Hay and Bob Feiden, who were writers; and Wayne (now Jayne) County and David Croland. There were others, like Leee Black Childers, who really wanted to be one of my fags but wasn't allowed to be because he worked for Lisa Robinson, who was already the doyenne of the downtown rock press, and she hated me. Lisa exerted power over a number of rock writers and photographers by keeping them on the payroll of *Rock Scene* and other rock magazines. She ruled the roost, and Cyrinda Foxe and that crew either weren't allowed to be my friends or hated me as passionately as my gay friends loved me. (One of the great things about this scene was how passionate it always was.) Whenever he would get drunk, Leee Childers would pull me aside and whisper, "I really think you're fabulous, and if it was up to me, I would be worshiping at your altar!" The gay community was always kind to me, never called me names, never accused me of being a groupie! The gay community was more into asking, "Darling, what was he like in bed?" They loved my exciting life; they never judged it. . . . And another thing—in time, my fags would have power!

Another stalwart friend I met when I started living with Todd was the rock photographer Bob Gruen. His was a friendship nobody could put a dent in. Lisa Robinson could have told him I'd sold his dog at the corner bodega and he would not have believed her. Bob's one of my oldest and most loyal friends. Whether I'm living in New York or somewhere else, he's always been a part of my life. Friendship was a vital element of the downtown underground scene.

The backroom of Max's Kansas City undoubtedly contained a collection of the most subversive rock stars, poets, drag queens, painters, movie stars, drug dealers, drug addicts, sluts, photographers, and hustlers in the world at that time. It was a major experience just to sit there and take in the living theater that was happening around me. It was a pivotal place on the map of my life. I cut my teeth at Max's. Lou Reed was the daddy figure.

Todd, Bebe, and my dear Ron Delsner at the Palladium, NYC, 1975/BOB GRUEN

Debbie Harry had been a waitress at Max's before I first went there. She had brown hair, and I used to think she was so beautiful. "Why was she waitressing?" I used to ask. "She should be a rock star." She had charisma, too. She'd go up and dance, and she had something. She was shy and everything, but she had this light around her. There was another girl who was really pretty: Dory Weiner. I used to feel that maybe I should dance next to those girls. Patti D'Arbanville, who starred in Andy Warhol's *Flesh*, would come to Max's wearing blue jeans, a simple checkered shirt tied at the waist, and sneakers. Even without an ounce of makeup, she would be the most beautiful girl in the room. All of us hated her, because we would be wearing way too much makeup, way too many feathers, shoes we couldn't walk in, and this tiny little beauty would bounce into the room, making all the men salivate. When I got inspired by her and started doing the same thing, Andy told me, "You're the only person I know who makes the hippie look work."

I saw some of the best rock 'n' roll shows I have ever seen in my life at Max's. If you were lucky enough to catch one of the Dolls' brilliant gigs, it was indescribable. I think that everybody just needed to replace the Velvet Underground, as far as being our hometown band, and in 1972–1974, the Dolls were *it*. I think that one of the things that got me moving so much as the "It Girl" in New York was appearing in the backroom at Max's, not my modeling. Once I began making that my second home, my living room, and once I had started dating Todd Rundgren, I went there all the time, and I really became a part of the scene. *Interview* magazine started writing about me right away. They had a picture of Todd and me from a party that we went to in 1973, and it just all happened from that. And then there were pictures of us from the rock magazines and in the local papers. Lillian Roxane had written about Todd and me in one of her last columns before her death. I remember I had a battle from the very beginning because people spelled my name wrong. *Beebee* was the way they spelled it in *Interview*, like *Deedee*. And Lillian did the same thing. Lisa Robinson was the first person to spell in right, in *Creem* in 1973. So I already had visibility as a quasi-scene-maker pseudocelebrity: "Oh, she hangs out with Mick Jagger." When I walked in the room it was like a rock star had arrived, instead of a model. Girls wanted to use my hair-

brush because they thought Todd had used my hairbrush. And I am not fucking kidding. This would happen to me. People would steal things from me as souvenirs. By now, my notoriety preceded me. Whenever I would walk in, people would say, "Oh my god, there's Bebe Buell!" I was also a respected critic. Record companies were coming to me when I was nineteen and twenty and asking me who I would sign. I've always been someone whom people respect as a tastemaker.

To the press, I was Todd Rundgren's girlfriend. Stories would circulate. They tried to call me everything but a groupie. "Friend of the stars." "Filet mignon of rock." I think that in our incestuous circle and in the back room at Max's, people knew of my involvement with Mick. But at that point, there were no other girls who were in the same category as I was in terms of my success as a model; even Jerry Hall and Patti Hansen came three years after me. There was that dormant period in the early seventies when I was the only one of that breed out there. But I was cut from the cloth. And that's where I felt the most comfortable and happy.

Eileen got fed up. She believed I was on my way to becoming one of the biggest models in New York. I was a hair's breadth away, so she was pissed off at me no end. Sometimes I'd get a good night's sleep, but most times I wouldn't. In the beginning, I didn't fuck up as much, but after a couple of months with Todd, I really started to fuck up bad. I mean, it was just like . . . forget it! "If you do not cool out, I'm going to have your mother come and take you home," Eileen informed me. "You're running around way too much." Meanwhile, as I was trashing a career that would have made me rich, Todd was in his element. The early seventies was the domain of the singer-songwriter, and at Max's, we became a royal couple.

From the outset, I approached my relationship with Todd from the position of a muse. I believed being a muse meant not just inspiring specific songs but inspiring every aspect of the artist's life—how he dressed, where he ate, whom he chose to work with. I was there for the big changes. When I met Todd, he was at the beginning of a lucrative solo career. Everybody saw him as this prolific Elton John–like songwriter with pop sensibilities, plus a little bit of raunchiness left over from his hard-rock days with Nazz. He was the perfect combination of guitar hero, singer-songwriter, rock star. He had it all. I always kept him stimulated, and I kept him up on what was cool. I would bring stuff home and play it for him. Todd might have ridiculed me and teased me occasionally about my eclectic taste, but he never disrespected me. He would listen, take it in, and ask me what was cool about this or that.

About six months into our relationship, I persuaded Todd to trip with me on some very good mescaline I had gotten from Danny Fields. Todd had not taken any hallucinogenic drugs before this, being primarily a pot smoker. The result was the eclectic *A Wizard/A True Star*, which I thought was a masterpiece, though it didn't reach as large an audience as *Something/Anything?* In fact, after this trip, Todd never reached such a large audience again. I think I kept his feet on the ground and that if I hadn't been there, he would have gone even further into the stratosphere. But in retrospect, I also think that when you are someone like Todd, a mind-expanding drug doesn't necessarily do you any favors. It opens doors to secret places that you can't share, and I think that was what happened with Todd.

After we took mescaline, something changed in Todd. It made him start questioning what he was doing; he began thinking about karma and reincarnation. It was like the Beatles going through their guru phase, except that they were well established by the time they took off, and they came back. Whereas Todd was in his early twenties and just getting started on his solo career. And in some ways, he didn't come back.

We had a classic seventies relationship, with a lot of love and a lot of freedom to explore on our own. I didn't have much to worry about, because I lived with Todd and the rent was paid. So I had fun with whatever money I made. I bought clothes; I went to Max's and bought everybody surf and turf. I went to visit my mother, and I bought presents for my family. Todd was the man of the house. He was also a workaholic. He would always be doing something at Moogy Klingman's studio.

When Todd wasn't working, we'd go out to dinner, watch TV on the couch, and smooch. We had a fireplace, so we'd build a fire, smoke a joint, and talk. But sometimes there was really no talking with Todd. At those times, you'd just listen to him, which did not suit my independent, feisty personality. I would demand that he hear my side as well, and then Todd and I would work it out. We did spend five years together. There was a certain necessity for us to communicate, and there was a genuine friendship there, a genuine love. But he usually carried on a monologue when spouting his crazy ideas about videos and computers and extravagant stage shows. He had a scientific approach to everything; he really didn't believe in the unexplainable. Todd was into Einstein and Carl Sagan and Buckminster Fuller—he was a very big Buckminster Fuller fan.

"In the future, we're going to do everything on computers," he would say. Todd was a futurist. And I would just have to sit there and listen to all of his ideas.

Todd did drugs. He was experimenting. When I met him, he was smoking pot and he had dabbled in opiates. He loved hash oil. He went through a period of experimenting with cocaine. When he was going through his phase of wanting to try cocaine, he'd experiment with it in all different ways to see what kind of effect it would have on him; it was almost like a kind of intellectual study on the drug. We had this little marble table next to our round water bed, and when he was going through his coke phase, he wanted to keep a few lines right next to the bed so that as soon as he woke up he could bend over and do some coke. That lasted for a day or two. Todd was a dabbler. He would try a drug, and if he didn't like it, he would say, "Next." He never was obsessive. Sometimes I took coke, and sometimes I didn't, but I really didn't like coke. I didn't like the way it made me feel; it made me too anxious. It wasn't anything about being judgmental; I just didn't like the effect it had on me. I think all of us preferred Quaaludes. I tried them. I tried everything. And I tried some things too many times.

I cannot smell tequila, because if I do, I throw up. If I smell amyl nitrate, I will throw up immediately. I had drunk too many shots of tequila on an empty stomach in the past and made myself violently ill. I can't drink tequila or vodka, and I can't drink Courvoisier. When I had them, I got sick, and once something makes me sick, I can't go back to it. The only thing I'll go back to that hurts me is a man. With drugs, there's so much peer pressure involved. You're out with friends and they're drinking and taking shots. Maybe you didn't eat as much dinner as they did, and so you end up getting sick, but they don't.

I enjoyed pot the most. I started smoking it when I was fifteen, long before I met Todd. I've smoked pot regularly most of my life. I think it's a good thing—a tonic, a soother, an inspirer. I'm an advocate for the legalization of marijuana and the use of hemp, and I think it's ridiculous for marijuana to be put into the same category as drugs. I don't think it is a drug; I think it's a medicinal plant, so I don't put it in the same category.

Mostly, drugs were a way of life, part of the scene. It was like saying, Okay, what am I going to wear tonight? Oh, and I must stop and pick up my drugs before we go to the show. It was part of the planning of the evening: Are we going to trip? Are we going to smoke? In those days, you could smoke a joint in the middle of a club. Nobody gave a shit. But Todd was always the boss of the pot. I didn't really have access to it. If I wanted to smoke a joint, I'd go to Todd and say, "Are we going to smoke a joint?" I didn't go into the stash and roll joints.

In fact, it always upset Todd if I did drugs with somebody else. If I did drugs with somebody else, he would hear of it, and I think it made him worry that somebody would hurt me or take advantage of me.

When I was first living with Todd, David Johansen, lead singer in the New York Dolls, and Cyrinda Foxe, who went on to marry

Steven Tyler of Aerosmith and star in Andy Warhol's last film, *Bad*, had nowhere to stay, so we put them up for two or three weeks in the apartment on Thirteenth Street. She thought the apartment was really dirty. I had moved in but hadn't really Bebeized it yet. I came home one night and found that she had completely bleached and Ajaxed the bathroom. It looked like a shining saint. I mean, it was so white, and she was lying in a bubble bath, drinking champagne that wasn't hers, and she had my dogs in with her. I just thanked her. I couldn't believe it. She said, "Oh, I couldn't stand it anymore. It was filthy. I had to make it all clean."

One time, I was lying on our mattress on the floor in the living room, which doubled as our bedroom. David and Cyrinda came home a little late and they were going to sleep on the couch. I lay there pretending that I was asleep, but a streetlight was shining through the window and I could see everything. I could see David's little butt bobbing in the wind. It was perfect, because I was down low, so my viewpoint was cinematic, and voyeuristic. I watched the whole thing. He kept biting her, and she kept saying, "Not so hard. Don't bite me so hard." Another time, I was in a cab with David Johansen—we had never dated or anything—and he leaned over to kiss me. It freaked me out, because David had never made a move on me before, and when I rejected his kiss, he bit me on the ear as hard as he could, like a dog biting another dog. I screamed and pushed him away.

The day they left, I went to the closet to get a dress to wear to Max's. Cyrinda had tried on every dress in my closet and had ripped every single one of them up the back while trying to squeeze into my tiny size six outfits. She was at least a ten or twelve. Her butt was a little bigger than mine and we had very different frames. I never got a chance to say anything, because she was no longer living in the apartment. She had very meticulously put everything back exactly as it was.

I had one silver dress, the only one she didn't tear, and I had to wear it over and over and over again. Before she began to hate me, Lisa Robinson wrote in *Creem*, "Bebe looked beautiful in her silver dress that she wore again, and again, and again. And again. And again." God, what a bitch. I smelled it coming. I was going to be one of the girls Lisa didn't like. Cyrinda and Lisa, and that little clique of chicks, just didn't like me. I was a little too pretty, a little too tall, and a little too lucky. I felt right away that Cyrinda was not a happy person, that she had a nasty streak in her.

Todd did not have friends the way most people do. Rick Derringer was his friend, but I brought Rick and Todd together, because Rick's wife, Liz, and I were such good friends and we were always trying to get the boys together for dinner. Liz and I hit it off immediately. We instantly became Mutt and Jeff. She was the first girlfriend I had in New York, and she's still my best friend. Her best characteristics are loyalty and a true desire to have fun. She's a true rock 'n' roll spirit. She wanted to go to concerts and hang out! Shop! And go on vacations. We liked the same things. We didn't always agree on music, because my taste is a little tougher than hers. But we certainly had no problem getting into trouble together. We were beautiful young girls who had rock-star boyfriends who were making a lot of money. Either we found trouble or it found us.

One night, Todd and I were visiting Liz and Rick. We were all tripping. While the boys talked music, Liz and I decided to take a shower. We were in the shower so long, talking and laughing so hard, we actually turned lobster red. So we got out of the shower, but then Liz said, "Oh my God, I forgot to shave my legs! Let's shave ourselves." There was an electric razor there, and she said, "Let me just clean this, because Edgar [Winter, of the albino twin guitar maestros Johnny and Edgar] just used it." She shook the razor, but when she scooped out its contents, Edgar's whiter-than-white whiskers looked exactly like cocaine. I mean, in our altered state of mind, they looked exactly like coke! We immediately lost interest in shaving, ran into the kitchen, bright red and stark naked, got some aluminum foil, put the shaved whiskers in the foil, and folded them up into a small packet. Yelling to Todd and Rick that we were just going out to get falafel, we hoofed it over to MacDougal Street, went up to this guy who was standing on the corner, and said, "We've got the best cocaine in the world—twenty dollars."

"What do you mean, man?"

"Look!" Liz said. "Look!" And we handed him the packet.

He immediately gave us twenty bucks. We zipped off, picked up some falafels, then sprinted back to her place, laughing our asses off so hard, we almost fell over in the street. When we got home Liz sud-

Bebe Stardust–A Max's glitter child with no eyebrows, 1973/LYNN GOLDSMITH

denly said, "Oh my God, what if he recognizes us? We sold him albino whiskers!" This time, we did fall on the floor, screaming hysterically. Neither Todd nor Rick looked up from what he was doing. We were a totally involved bunch of maniacs.

To be honest, Todd was a little bit too serious for this brand of humor. I mean, he and Rick Derringer had the weirdest relationship. Todd was verbally abusive to Rick, and I always wondered how Rick put up with it. Rick was just so sweet and laid-back, he'd just say, "Oh, that's just Todd." He didn't care, but all of us who loved Todd would sort of dismiss it, say, "Okay, Todd. Todd is God! Right!" But after a while, it just got to be boring; he had the ego of fifty ships. And their little boats, too. He had just a *Titanic* ego. He was too argumentative, too much the captain of the debate team. I don't know if he got this argumentative streak from his father or from being too smart and not being able to tolerate anybody's silliness. I could never figure it out, because I was quite young. As serious, and sometimes pretentious, as he was, Todd was also really into having fun. He'd take me places I'd never been, like to an acupuncture party. Or he would take me to meet a guy who sat around and talked about the benefits of letting water drip on the middle of your head for an hour. He'd take me out to Indian restaurants. He really exposed me to a lot of great, wonderful, different stuff.

One of the things I really loved about him was that he never tried to make me feel like a little girl or stupid. He always treated me as very smart, and if I did anything childish—you have to remember that I was only eighteen when we met—he would say to me, "Bebe, you are smarter than that." He would never call me an

33

idiot. He was actually a very good father. Todd always told me that I wasn't schizophrenic—I was *twenty*phrenic.

On the home front, Todd could take apart a television and put it back together again, or fix a broken strap on a shoe in five minutes. I really love to clean house. When I get nervous, I vacuum. That drove Todd crazy. He made up a jingle about me: "Wipey Queen does everything." But when I'd been cooking and cleaning too long and looked in the mirror and saw myself one day middle-aged and in curlers, I got nervous. Then I had to put on a tight dress, go to some wild rock parties, and feel drop-dead gorgeous again.

Another reason Todd was so good for me was that he was perpetually on a spiritual quest. I would sit in the backseat of that quest and pretend I wanted to go to Max's instead, but I retained everything. Todd encouraged me, but to be up against a mind as intricate and complex as Todd's was often too challenging. At times, I felt as if my identity was nonexistent, because everything was about him, and when it did become about me, there was always a lack of interest on his part. And so when I met people like Mick Jagger, people who would try to bring out the part of my personality they considered warm, effervescent, and magnetic, I would embrace them.

That's why I started to run away from home a lot. I would leave the nest because "Daddy" never praised me. I created a father-daughter situation with Todd because of the lack of a father in my childhood. This guy, who was born in Upper Darby and had middle-class Philadelphia roots, had a real way of playing the father trip. When you combined that with the oddball genius intellect of a guy who wanted to have green and yellow streaks put in his hair, and then combined that with the imperfections of his looks, which always annoyed him but which I found devastatingly gorgeous, you got an extremely magnetic package. I just loved his big old teeth and his skinniness and his rock and rollness. Whatever I say about Todd as my story continues, don't forget he was—and is—one of the most important people in my life.

Back in 1972, I had no problem opening my fat mouth. My mouth has never been an obstacle. But there was that little thing inside of me that wouldn't let me form the words I wanted to say. I relied entirely on what everybody told me I should rely on: my beauty. That was a time when people just were not allowed to be completely wild. I was a wild child in the tradition of Jane Birkin or Marianne Faithfull. I thought that the way you got into this "boy's club" of rock stars was to be one of the cool girls, like Anita or Patti. I didn't know anything except what I'd read about the GTOs or the groupie culture of L.A. according to Pamela Des Barres. That was West Coast crap. I didn't dare tell anyone I wanted to be Mick Jagger, because I was afraid no one would let me be Mick Jagger. I wasn't lucky enough to find a Chris Stein like Debbie Harry did. I was with Todd Rundgren. Todd didn't allow for any Mick Jaggers in his house. He was the star; I was the decoration. My boyfriends were Svengalis; they were high-maintenance.

The first person who told me I had talent as a writer was Patti Smith. I showed her a poem, "You Needle/You Pin/You Prick." And then she started asking me to show her my poems. Todd introduced me to Patti. She was his girlfriend before I was. I liked her immensely. She told me, "You look like Anita Pallenberg, Nico, and Marianne Faithfull rolled into one cream puff, but you gotta cut your hair with the bangs and stuff." So I did. Then she tried to talk me into dyeing my hair white, but I didn't.

In 1973, I was most interested in being around as much creative energy and as many interesting people as I could. I wasn't trying to land a husband or have a perfect life. I was too young to know what I wanted. I hadn't completely found myself. In my deepest heart, what I wanted most was to be a rock and roll singer. In my thoughts and journals, that's what I expressed. And I was conscious of that, but I never had the courage to tell people. The only person I really talked to was Patti Smith. When I showed her my poems, she said, "Bebe, what is all this?"

"These are my little songs."

"Your little songs . . . What do you mean, 'little songs'?"

"You know." That was when we used to take hairbrushes and pretend they were microphones. We'd take a couple of hits of pot and we'd get off on being the Supremes.

When I started dating Todd, I couldn't understand his attraction to Patti. She looked like Keith Richards. How could he fuck Keith? I was drawn to her and intrigued. I was everything she liked. To her, I was the beautiful blond, blue-eyed angel girl. I was everything Patti liked and hated. If I had been a competitor, she would have loathed me. She gave me a chance because I was a nice kid, and that endeared her to me. I could be a pain in the ass, but I did look like some of her sixties English girl heroes. Also, I was Todd's girlfriend, and she wanted to keep him in her life and have a civilized relationship with him, so I think she felt she had to be nice to me. I think she knew that if she was nasty to me, the communication with Todd would be cut off. Patti had a very cruel streak. She could be flirtatious, inconsiderate about my young heart, which she stomped all over whenever she wanted to be close to Todd.

I used to drive Patti crazy. I'd go visit her every day. I would just show up on Twenty-third Street, where she was living with Robert Mapplethorpe and Allen Lanier. I'd arrive right after Allen had just fucked her, or when she was fixing one of her shrines, or when she was writing, but she'd always let me come in. Patti was my favorite person to go visit in the afternoon. We'd sit and talk, and she told me, "I really want to sing."

"So do I," I said. This was way before she started singing. We'd put on records like "Gimme Shelter" and sing them at the top of our lungs, trying to imitate the attitude on the vocals, trying to get it right in our throats. We'd stand in front of the mirror and sing, and Patti would say, "Yeah, this is how you learn how to sing." I had great times with her like that—she was really fun. Sometimes I would have pot with me, but Patti could not smoke a lot, because she was so crazy that after two hits, she'd be off in the stratosphere, man, telling me stories about Sam Shepard and rapping about her philosophy. I was so young and crazy, I would always go running to Patti every time I had a problem with Todd. But Patti still loved Todd a little, so it was hard for her to have this brat coming over to ask her for advice about him. She still had feelings for him, even though she was living with Allen. Sometimes I would catch Todd and Patti copping a hug or something, and I would get very teenage wasteland about it. I'd say, "How come you're messing with my boyfriend?"

"Relax," she'd say. "It's okay. Just cool out, little girl."

Todd and I had incredible sexual chemistry; we had sex all the time. We never had a lull. Todd Rundgren was an extremely middle-class, normal lover, but we had great sex. It was very straightforward and wholesome, a meeting of two souls who loved each other. Aerobics was not necessary. Our bodies would just meet, and it was wonderful.

My whole vision of what I found exciting in a man was shaped by the Rolling Stones, starting with Mick, then taking a different turn with Brian Jones and that whole new sixties essence of what a man was. The genius and the beauty of the rock and roll scene excited me to the point that, like any girl who wants a boyfriend or hopes she meets a guy someday, I was hoping that I could go out with someone like that. Somebody *cool!* So to end up with Todd, who had such a genius in that particular era for knowing what was going on, completed me. He confirmed that I had something that stood out, that people would notice me, and that I would somehow get pulled into this club—the cool club—and I was.

The problem was that everything was too easy—modeling, traveling, partying—and I forgot my original desires and beliefs. I started to fall into the pattern of going the route that was the most fun. And when I was young, I thought it would last forever. I thought that I would always be twenty-one and a size six and the flavor of the month. Certainly I wasn't as focused or driven at twenty-one as my daughter was. I was still trying to figure out stuff, like a clumsy colt stumbling around in my platforms. I would go from wanting to be a rock star one day to wanting to be Lauren Hutton on every *Vogue* cover the next. Or I'd want to be the perfect rock and roll wife one minute, then wish I were a mother. And— God help me—at one point, I wanted to be a music mogul. I had all kinds of desires and there were all kinds of obstacles to fulfilling them. I wanted to be a sexual, free-spirited Brigitte Bardot/Jane Birkin type, but inside I was a frightened little girl with sexual hang-ups that thwarted that ambition. Patti became a singer, but I didn't at that time, because I felt trapped by my beauty and the physical demands that were being made on me. People looked at her and they saw Keith Richards. People looked at me and they saw Barbarella. They wanted to put me in a plastic suit and Patti in trousers, and I was unable to voice my ambitions because I was scared. I thought people would laugh at me. That's why I wanted the Brian Jones types: I always wanted a man with brains—a genius, a tortured artist whom I could be Florence Nightingale to. That goes back to my George Sand and Lillie Langtry fixations. Lillie

Langtry said, "I'm Oscar Wilde's muse!" I knew that I had some destiny as a servant of the arts, but I also knew that I was an artist myself. But because of my problems with my parents and men, I was always on a quest to please. In the end, I wanted to make others happy more than I wanted to make myself happy. That would become my Achilles' heel.

CHAPTER 2

The Groundbreakers
1973

I'm cool
I'm cooler than cool
I'm the Queen of cool
I wrote the bible on cool
I wrote the book on cool
I wrote the rules on cool
   "COOL," LYRICS BY BEBE BUELL

I was never on a quest for sex itself. I'd rather kiss and pet for hours than hang from chandeliers. In fact, to me, sex is the hardest part of a relationship. I was always on a quest for rock 'n' roll. I'm getting tired of seeing women portrayed as predators who go out and hunt for gold. If that's what I had been, wouldn't I have married a really rich man and retreated to the country and had my five babies? Instead, I had such a pure love for that particular art form—rock 'n' roll music—that it became the emotional engine that drove everything I did. Since I have an ear for talent and a knack for organizing, I'm surprised it took me so long to officially become a manager.

I never had a free-love mentality. When I compare fidelity now with fidelity in the seventies, I know I could never live now the way I did when I was a kid. Infidelity now would be painful, whereas when I was living with Todd, I almost felt obligated to keep up with the boys. It put a considerable strain on our relationship, but it would have been totally uncool to admit jealousy.

One day, I came home from a modeling job and heard all this moaning and groaning and panting. I climbed up the staircase and caught Patti D'Arbanville sitting on Todd's lap. I was extremely upset and angry. Todd tried to explain that he hadn't been doing anything, that he'd been reading a book the whole time. Patti jumped up and said, "Let's go out," and she dragged me off, claiming she had come to the house to see me. Bullshit. I think she wanted to fuck Todd. She had seen us at some show and she definitely had an eye for Todd. She saw his big business and wanted some of it—he's famous for his huge penis. Patti introduced me to Jimmy Page that night. They wanted me to go off and party at the Plaza Hotel, but I wanted to go home so I could scream at Todd.

Todd was always fucking someone—he was one of the epic womanizers in rock history—but when I did it, it became much more of a big production. Of course, we were living in a society and world ruled by a double standard. There was still that belief that men could do it and women couldn't, and I wasn't buying that. And I think because of Todd's infidelity, and because of my inability to get a solid commitment from him, I was in a perpetual state of looking for another man.

There were always extrasexicular activities going on, and there were a lot of loft gatherings, where people tried to re-create the Warhol Factory feeling. Sometimes there'd be parties, and the Dolls or Eric Emerson's band, the Magic Tramps, would start playing. Eric, who starred in *Chelsea Girls* and *Heat*, two of Warhol's best films, could leap through the air like Rudolf Nureyev. He would wear Iggy Pop costumes but add sparkles and glitter to them. Iggy could contort, but Eric could fly through the air like a fucking bird. He could have been a big star, but he was so natural, he couldn't plug into the machinery of rock.

In terms of live music, this was the time of the New York Dolls, Alice Cooper, and David Bowie. The Dolls were just pure fun to see. I loved their sense of fun. In May, Todd produced the Dolls' first album because my girlfriends and I dragged him down to see their show. There were mixed feelings about that record, but I think Todd did the best job one could have done. The Dolls liked to have huge parties in the studio and they all had something to say about how the music should sound, as in "This isn't loud enough!" And I didn't help, because when I would show up, I would act just as teenaged and stupid as they did. It drove Todd crazy. He was always trying to get everything into the cohesive soup that a producer creates, but I would be right there with Johnny Thunders, screaming, "More guitar!" I didn't really understand how hard it is to make records. I thought it was supposed to be fun. Todd worked in a very serious manner.

Backstage with Todd at Three Rivers Stadium, 1974/RICHARD FEGLEY

The best thing about the rock scene in New York was the people. Apart from the bands, there were hundreds of people working as writers, photographers, agents, managers, producers, and gofers, as well as the girlfriends, who cared just as passionately about the music as the musicians and who poured all their energy into encouraging them. The musicians and Andy Warhol, who was an honorary rock star, were the stars of that scene. I did not hang out with people my own age. I tended to talk to people like Danny Goldberg, and Clive Davis, and Danny Fields. They all thought I was bright and adorable. They came to me and asked, "Bebe, what good bands are there? What's happening?"

A good example of this was how Todd Rundgren came to produce Grand Funk Railroad. This highly successful band was an unlikely candidate for Todd, despite their having a series of gold records. Rock writers hated them. There was nothing cool or chic about them. And they were in a serious slump after spending the majority of 1972 in litigation as a result of legal problems with their manager. In that sense, they presented a challenge. The catalyst for the deal was the dynamic photographer Lynn Goldsmith. Lynn, who became something of a legend herself later in the decade, was involved with the band and with Todd, whom I suspected she was bonking behind my back. She brought him the offer to produce what was essentially a comeback album. I also played a role in persuading Todd to do what would become a pivotal project in his career. Todd always called me his "cool meter." If I liked something, he paid attention to it, and I liked Grand Funk Railroad's songs. I thought they were fucking great! Shoot me, I just did: "I'm your captain, I'm your captain, and I'm feeling kind of sick." They were a power trio with a singing guitar player, Mark Farner. I didn't know any of them. I just loved the band. Between Lynn Goldsmith coordinating the meeting between Grand Funk and Todd and me begging on my knees for him to produce the album, he agreed. He was paid $150,000, which made him the highest-paid producer in the music industry. It also made him his first million when the band got a number-one single, "We're an American Band," and a gold album of the same name. He'll never admit it, but I really led Todd into that world. Yes, it was an enormous amount of money, but Todd was a stubborn person, and he didn't do things for money at that point. I don't know if he would have done Grand Funk if I had not begged, screamed, pleaded, and told him they'd been my favorite band in high school.

In the summer of 1973, Liz Derringer helped me look for a bigger apartment. We found a three-story town house at 51 Horatio Street for $600 a month. Todd was paying $150 for the Thirteenth Street apartment. When Todd came home from work the night we'd found the apartment, I gave him the full Lucille Ball treatment. First, I made his favorite dinner. Then I rolled him a big bomber of the finest pot, spoiling him to the nth degree. Then I commenced my campaign. "Ya know, honey," I began, "I think I found our dream house today."

"Really, Bebe," he responded, "what is it?"

"You're not going to believe this," I told him, launching into a detailed description floor by floor, then wrapping it up with the extra bonus that Richie Havens would be our next-door neighbor.

"How much, Lucy?" he asked warily, playing the role of Ricky Ricardo.

"Aaahhh, uuuuhhh . . . six hundred dollars!"

"*What?* Oh my God!" The pot was multiplying the amount in his head, but that was considered a ridiculously high rent in our world in 1973.

"Well, let's just go look at it," I begged. So we went to look at it, and of course Todd fell in love with the place.

"Well, you know," he rationalized, "I just made all this money for doing Grand Funk and I'm going to be getting a big check, and I'm getting ready to produce Hall and Oates next, so, all right, let's go for it!"

That place became our rock 'n' roll palace. It helped emphasize Todd's success. And of course it was effortless for him to pay for it.

In September 1973, as Grand Funk Railroad's "We're an American Band" soared to number one on the U.S. singles charts, we moved in. From the outset, Todd was rarely there. I was like a child left at Rock Disneyland, with access to all the rides. It was insane. I could walk around the terrace and knock on Richie Havens's window at any hour of the night and he would give me the biggest bud of the most gorgeous pot on earth. Plus, I never had to worry about anything practical, because Todd was the man of the house. Even though I was earning money, he paid our rent and the monthly bills.

We had two dogs and a South American raccoon. Todd got it from Ecuador. He came home with it one day and I was like, "Excuse me, who's this?"

"Oh, this is Kundalini."

"Oh really? Isn't that nice. . . . What the fuck is Kundalini?"

"I named him after kundalini yoga."

"Where the hell did you hear about kundalini yoga, Todd? Isn't it like that yoga where you can stand on your head for seven hours or something? Who taught you that?" (I found out later who had! It was his road manager, Susan Lee—more about her shortly.)

We used to have divine parties in our three levels of decadence: The top floor had two bedrooms, where everybody would go to have sex, and a bath. The mezzanine was where Todd and I had our bedroom, and there was a second little living room where Todd kept his piano. The first floor consisted of a kitchen, a dining room, and a living room with a fireplace. There was a spiral staircase connecting the three levels. People were everywhere, hanging off the staircases, strewn throughout the living rooms. God knows what went on in the bathrooms. Surveying my domain at the height of one of our successful nights, I was happily reminded of the movie *Beyond the Valley of the Dolls.*

Albert Grossman used to have his equally decadent and divine parties in tepees on his property up in Bearsville, New York, a mile or two up the road from Woodstock, which was Rock Central for the country-house set who had followed Bob Dylan up there in the 1960s. We would light a fire in the big tepee and there would be all kinds of psychedelic drugs, usually mescaline, bottomless bottles of booze, and marijuana galore. People would get really high and go sit in the tepee, where something spiritual was supposed to happen. It usually turned into people going off and fucking. The seventies had arrived!

The first time I caught Todd cheating on me was at one of Albert's tepee parties. I was tripping on mescaline, and I went into the kitchen. Albert had a cook named Cindy. She put an amazing amount of detail into her cooking. She was also very thin; everybody spoke of her as "the anorexic cook," which was kind of odd, but she had that Miss Christine (of the GTOs) look. Todd liked either pretty, wholesome girls who looked like me or girls like Patti Smith or Miss Christine, who had a twisted, skinny, unkempt, uptight look. He really went for those needy, anorexic, negative girls. When I caught him touching and kissing Cindy in the kitchen, it had a devastating effect because I was tripping. I tried to be cool and accept it, like an open-minded seventies girlfriend should. I spun around, fluttering and saying, "Oh, trippy, trippy," then flew off into the tepee, crying. Albert pulled me aside and asked what was wrong. I told him that Todd was fucking his cook.

"Yeah, the guys really seem to like Cindy" was Albert's classic response. Thanks for the sympathy, Al.

For a young girl, I was having to adjust to a lot of nonsense. My decadent partner and I were living the *Bob & Carol & Ted & Alice* lifestyle, but we were still very much a couple. I was expected to switch at the drop of a hat from being Mrs. Rock 'n' Roll to being Laura Petrie in *The Dick Van Dyke Show*. Todd would think nothing of coming home with an exotic animal, or going on the road for three months, leaving me with no staples, no way to know what I was supposed to do. He never gave me money, never! No way! The household bills would automatically be sent to his accountant, and I would have to live off whatever money I might pick up from small modeling jobs. Chris Stein would occasionally give me fifty dollars to be in one of the videos he and Anton Perich used to make in Anton's loft, which had been Andy Warhol's Factory from 1968 to 1973. I still had a couple of clients who hadn't completely abandoned me. Thank God for the catalog company Butterick. For some reason, they consistently kept me booked—twice a month. So I was able to make about a thousand dollars a month, which was ample pocket money.

As a matter of fact, I rarely had to spend money, because either I walked everywhere, balancing on a pair of platforms better than any other human being, or people would pick me up in their cabs or limos. When I would get to where I was going, I never had to pay for anything. I knew that Max's owner, the legendary Mickey Ruskin, liked me right away, because he leaned over to me and said, "Don't eat the chickpeas; you'll have no career." Mickey never made me pay for anything at Max's, and if I tried to pay, he would just give it back to me. Sometimes I would have a surf attack and buy surf and turf dinner for twelve people. Then I had to pay for it. But basically, I never paid for one drink in this city.

I saw a lot of drugs in the back room of Max's, and the rock scene was awash in drugs. I constantly got mixed signals from the modeling world, which left me with the impression that if I did heroin, it would keep me young and beautiful and I wouldn't age until I stopped, and I thought romantically, how Dorian Gray. If I actually did even one little drug in the seventies, I would get yelled and screamed at and told how stupid I was and that I was going to ruin my career! Now I'd say, What career? By 1973, I didn't have a career. I was Todd Rundgren's girlfriend; that was my fucking career, thank you very much. I liked to smoke pot, and these guys were doing one hundred times what I was doing. And yet they were warning *me* to slow down! I was also getting mixed signals about drugs from the rock world because I saw my heroes, and all these people whom I admired so much, being twenty-four-hour-a-day drug users. Every time I met somebody fabulous, from Lou Reed to Jim Carroll, I would discover they had been or were a junkie. I asked myself, How can these people be junkies and still be famous and rich and successful?

The drugs of choice when I first came to New York were more of the downer school: Tranquilizers, reds, Quaaludes, amyl nitrate, drugs that made the brain go to a dead place were big. That was frightening. People would drink and drink and start hitting these horrible substances, ingesting them or snorting them. I never saw much of the needle thing.

In 1972 and 1973, there was a lot of vomiting. I got really tired of seeing everyone I admired throwing up. It just got to be commonplace. I remember people puking in potted plants at big rock parties—just in passing. One time, John Bonham from Led Zeppelin was at a party that Atlantic Records had for them, and he just leaned over and puked into a potted plant and then carried on like nothing had happened. I was thinking, Jesus Christ! So that's how it starts. You know, like people losing their cookies and then reporting back for normal activities. I could probably describe what it was like to see everyone puke! When we had parties, I always had to deal with people puking in our house, on our furniture, in our bathroom; sometimes they couldn't help themselves. Once we were having a party after the Hall and Oates, Lou Reed, Al Green show at the Felt Forum, which was the strangest bill ever. That was back in the days when Lou used to simulate shooting up onstage. Dee

Dee Ramone threw up right on my blue corduroy sectional, which I later sold for a thousand dollars *because* he puked on it.

Another night, I ran into Michael J. Pollard in the back room at Max's. Everybody was picking on him because he was very screwed up on drugs or drunk. It was time to leave. Everybody was standing out in front of Max's and everybody had a ride home or they had cabs and ways to get home. He was just standing there by himself, so I asked him if he wanted to share a cab. In the cab, I was trying to have a conversation, trying to be charming. "Oh, you were so good in *Bonnie and Clyde* and what are you doing next?" I asked, but he was so out of it, he couldn't talk. Then he asked me to help him put the window down, but as I was leaning across him to try to roll it down, he hurled all over the interior of the cab. The driver was one of those old Jewish guys; he was pissed off about it but being sweet. We went into Michael's wallet to find out where he lived, because he still couldn't speak. I found out his address and I took twenty dollars to pay the driver.

Alice Cooper's girlfriend and her crowd were dabbling in the even scarier elephant tranquilizers. She was screwing Johnny Thunders while Alice was on the road, and I went over to hang out one day. I had become friends with her because Todd had opened for Alice on the road. I was not really aware of her intensity, but she was from Detroit, and I guess she had a pretty stiff stomach for hard drugs. She loved THC—that elephant tranquilizer crap was her drug of choice. She was a THC expert! I didn't know you were supposed to do only a tiny little pinch of it. She laid out a huge line for me. I don't know what I do to women. I wish I could put my finger on it. Maybe it was my innocence, maybe it was my love of life, or maybe it was a lot of things. She could have killed me. I called Todd on the phone as I was starting to die. I knew I was going to die in Alice's apartment because I was seeing angels with electric guitars. I called Todd and I told him, "Somebody gave me something bad."

"I'll be right there," he said. Their apartment was in the Fifties and he was coming from down around Twelfth Street. He zoomed there real fast. I remember him coming through the door. I was crawling on the floor. Johnny Thunders was there, and Todd said, "Bebe, what the hell are you doing with this crowd?"

He took me out on the pavement and stuck his fingers down my throat, making me throw up—once again, puking for progress. I just threw it all out of me. At times like that, Todd was so sweet. He was very concerned, and mad at Alice's girlfriend. He even called Alice on the road and told him, "You'd better take care of your mean little girlfriend, who purposely gave Bebe a horse tranquilizer and told her it was cocaine just to be mean; it could have killed her." I don't think I have ever been that messed up. That definitely beat the Scavullo floor. When you have a hallucination that involves angels, you know you're in trouble. When he got me home, he ran a bath, then he washed me and put me in my jammies. He said, "I don't want you taking these drugs."

Although Todd was only six years older than I was, I saw him as a father figure. He protected me, advised me, took care of me. The problem that arose early on, and which would finally become fatal, was that since he was on the road at least six months of the year, it was only natural that both of us would stray.

I knew Alice Cooper and the people in the back room at Max's on a social level, but when I started to become a person who was not always faithful, I became a connoisseur: Iggy Pop was my first. To me, the best band of that era, the band that blew everyone away, was The Stooges. I saw The Stooges upstairs at Max's, and that was definitely one of the ten best shows that I've seen. I just loved the sexual intensity and danger of the music. It was the opposite of Todd's music. It was so loud and so good and Iggy was so wild, everything a rock star is supposed to be. And it was devastating to see it. We had a great table: I was sitting with Alice Cooper, Todd, Jane Forth, Cindy Lang, and Eric Emerson, who was dressed exactly like Iggy that night—in some little bikini porn thing with glitter all over it. The whole crowd was there, and Iggy was brilliant, totally amazing. He started off the set with "Search and Destroy." All of a sudden, blood just started to pour out of this very neat little slice on Iggy's chest. He'd cut himself diving on glass. I just about died seeing that show.

A few weeks later, I was at a New York Dolls show, and Iggy smashed his head into something by mistake and was bleeding everywhere. Nobody else was helping him, so I ran up with this wet towel and wiped the blood off his head, and he said, "You really care." He was surprised somebody gave a damn about his head. Anyway, Todd and I went home, and I figured I'd never see Iggy again. The next day, Todd was going to San Diego to start a national tour, and I was upset because he wasn't taking me with him. He went out to get some socks, and while I was sitting there crying, there was a knock on the door. It was Iggy. I love it when surprises like that happen. I swear to God, this is where the brilliance of Iggy comes in. He was so totally screwed up the one time I told him my address, I never thought he would remember 51 Horatio Street in the condition he was in. And not only did he show up at the house the next day, pretending that he was there to see Todd, whom he'd never met in his life, but he looked amazing, like a sun-kissed blond beauty. Todd was not being nice to me that day because he thought I was acting too wild—going out too much, hanging out at Max's too much, going to see the Dolls too much. Todd came home to finish packing, and there was Iggy.

"I didn't invite him," I told Todd, but he didn't believe me.

"I just came over to hang out because you two are the nicest people I met last night," Iggy was saying. He's a charming man, and he knows it. "I like the fact that you don't do drugs and that you're just nice and you have a clean house. You wouldn't believe some of the places I've been staying. I haven't taken a bath in about three weeks. Can I borrow your tub?"

"You know he will steal from you because he's a junkie," Todd said, pulling me aside. "He'll walk off with half the house. You really shouldn't let him stay here. But I'm leaving now, I'm going to play some gigs, and I'm expecting you to use your best judgment in this situation."

I lived with Todd Rundgren for five years and we always fooled around with other people, but we didn't always talk about it or flaunt it. The irony is, when I first met him, fidelity was very important to me. I was so young, eighteen going on nineteen, and he formed a lot of my opinions about men and about relationships. That's when I realized I didn't stand a chance with my fidelity philosophy. My heart would have been in fifty thousand pieces, because he cheated on me from the very beginning. So when Iggy came over, I could tell that Todd was trying to be mature and cool and very seventies, but I still couldn't wait for him to get the hell

Backstage with Iggy at Max's–note the fresh stitches, 1973/LYNN GOLDSMITH

outta there. I was nuts about Iggy. I was completely wild about him. But it didn't start off passionate and sexy. We went to a movie, *Paper Moon*, then ate some hamburgers, but I couldn't understand why he kept passing out all the time. He was always falling asleep. David Croland came to visit when Iggy was there. Jim (Iggy) kept nodding out. When I said, "He's just tired," David got disgusted with me for being so naïve. "Bebe, he's nodding out, for Christ sake," he said; "the guy's nodding out in your house!" Despite the high incidence of drug use in the seventies, being a junkie still wasn't socially acceptable. I hung out with him for about two weeks, until he went on the road and Todd came home. It was never a mad affair, but I'll admit that I had a huge crush on Iggy. My mother met him and thought he was smart. She also thought he was weird-looking, but then, she thought everyone I brought home was weird-looking.

Iggy was a fling with feelings, and it could have been more if he hadn't been on drugs. He was adorable until he started to take drugs. Drugs were never a big part of my life, although I was exposed to them a lot. Iggy got so fucked up, but he was discreet about it: He never actually took stuff in front of me. And whatever he was doing he was hiding it well. I think he was just taking a whole lot of pills—Tuinol, Valium. He was always real laid-back—he was one of those kinds of guys. He would always have a big, hearty breakfast and be so enthusiastic and alive in the morning. But then, as the afternoon progressed, he would start with pills, and that would escalate; by three or four o'clock in the morning, he'd be comatose. You never thought he would get it together; plus, he never had any money. I was too vain and neurotic about getting old to get into the drug scene. Using heroin never crossed my mind; I'm so frightened of needles, I have to be drunk when I go for a blood test, which produces some strange results. I don't like cocaine, because it makes me feel like a chatterbox, and the next day I regret everything I said.

I was always very careful when it came to hard drugs, but I did snort a line of heroin once by mistake. This was with Iggy Pop in 1973. We went out for a huge Mexican meal, just the two of us, and later we were going to go meet up with our friend Ben Edmonds. Iggy is a real food whore (he *loves* eating) and we ate enchiladas, burritos, tacos, guacamole, hot peppers, jalapeños, and afterward—this was a classically seedy picture, which would probably give my mother a heart attack even now—Iggy had to take a piss. I was driving, so I pulled over. This was back when they had bathrooms in gas stations, and sweet little guys in uniforms would come up and clean your windshield.

"Come into the bathroom with me," Jim said. We got in there and he goes, "I've got a little treat. It's my birthday, a little treat," and he laid out some lines on the back of the toilet. I assumed it was cocaine, but I noticed it was a little brown.

"Jim," I said, "this burns. This is weird coke."

"It's not coke, Bebe," he said.

"Well, what is it?"

"Heroin, honey."

"Jim," I go, "I don't do heroin." I was terrified.

"How much did you do?"

"Just one line, a normal line, like a cocaine line."

"Well, don't do any more," he said, but he did it. So we got over to Ben's, and sure enough, half an hour later, I felt sort of high, but it didn't really hit me for another fifteen minutes. I felt light, as if I were floating, but then, all of a sudden, I started throwing up like you would not believe. I was on Ben's couch. They saw that I was going to be sick, and they yelled, "Get in the bathroom!" They didn't let me kneel down; they put me straight in the shower. I think they knew this was going to be a big problem.

"What did she eat?" Ben was shouting.

"Mexican!" Jim yelled. "Like you wouldn't believe how much we ate, man!"

I started puking my brains out, to the point that I was so sick, you could have given me a million dollars and I would not have done heroin again. Iggy took my clothes off. He was going to wash them, because I had literally thrown up all over myself. So I was sitting in the tub stark naked. I was puking and the shower was running, and Iggy was taking his hand and scooping up the vomit and putting it into a pot so that the drain wouldn't clog up. Then he took his clothes off and got right in the tub with me to hold my hair.

"What are you doing?" I asked him. "I'm going to throw up all over you."

"It's all right; it's okay, honey; I deserve it. Puke all over me if you want. I deserve it, baby. Just puke all over me." I threw up to the point where I didn't think there was anything left in me to throw up. I was dry retching and nothing would come out. It was just like "*Gguuurrrggghh*"; it was just horrible.

Then Ben piped up—and I'll never forget this as long as I live, it was so funny—"There's nothing left in there; it's time for the Pepto." So they gave me Pepto-Bismol and a Coca-Cola, and then I was fine. I puked so much, I remember Iggy telling the story for days afterward: "I've never seen anybody puke like that; it was unbelievable," he said. "I mean, there was enough puke there for twenty people. You should have seen her, man. She was puking and puking." It had come out my nose, my ears, my mouth. I'm surprised it didn't come out of my ass. After I puked Jim and I took a shower. He took all the puke and scooped it with the pot and flushed it down the toilet, nice and tidy. He's very tidy; when he wants to clean he's good. He washed my hair. Ben was washing my clothes in his stackable washer-dryer unit. They dressed me, and I remember feeling pretty good. All I know is, I didn't feel sick or bad anymore. Actually, I felt good because I still had the heroin in my system, but at the time, I thought it was the Pepto and the Coca-Cola that were helping. I never touched heroin again. I felt *so* good only for a brief time, when I was walking from the couch to the bathroom. I'd never been that high before, and I was thinking, If I wasn't sick, this would be the most amazing thing ever. I was very lucky—it didn't seduce me. I made up my mind that I was never going to touch that drug again! This was 1973. I was a kid, and this was all new to me. When I do something and it hurts me, I don't do it again. I'm not quite as smart with men, but I have always had common sense when it comes to drugs. I don't like cigarettes, either. I have an obsessive-compulsive personality, but I guess I don't have an addictive one. That's definitely what saved me.

As soon as Todd got home, he put his foot down.

At Max's, the big thing was to get your picture pinned up above the cash register for a week. Since I'd my fling with Iggy while Todd was on the road, I thought I would get away with it, that Todd would come home and everything would be normal. Then Todd and I went waltzing into Max's, and there I was above the cash register. I'd finally gotten my wish: In a big blown-up photo the size of a house, there I was with Iggy Pop, and Iggy was wearing Todd's denim cap.

My next extracurricular guy was David Bowie. I first met David at Max's. I was there with Todd and a group of people. David was with his wife, Angela, and they came over to our table. David said he thought I was very beautiful and so did his wife. He told me his name and introduced his wife, then asked me my name. I said, "I'm Bebe Buell, and this is my boyfriend, Todd Rundgren."

"I've heard of you. You're supposed to be pretty fucking smart," he said, looking at Todd.

"Yes, I am, and I hear you're supposed to be ripping me off," Todd said. David looked at him as if Todd was out of his mind. There was immediate friction between David and Todd. At the time, there was a glitter rivalry. I think Todd was very inspired by David's look. The most we'd ever seen of that look was with Alice Cooper and Marc Bolan, and the Dolls. David had a different way of delivering the whole package. It was more reminiscent of our

53

drag queens and our lovely Candy Darling. I think Jayne County—at the time she was Wayne County—had a lot to do with David cultivating his look. It seemed like Angela was the driving force behind David making challenging statements. David came walking in the back room in a beautiful blue suit, and he had that spiked red-orange hair. He was wearing a tie and everybody else was so scruffy. Angela had an incredible look—no eyebrows, white hair, and a giant feathered jacket. She took everything to the extreme. She was very tall and androgynous-looking.

The next day, my phone rang; it was David Bowie. Somehow, he'd found out where I lived and tracked me down. He invited me to go to Radio City Music Hall to see the Rockettes; then he wanted me to be his guest on a sight-seeing trip around New York City. He was sweet. He explained his relationship with Angela, which was a little puzzling. I hadn't been exposed to open marriages and bisexuality. I went shopping with him. He bought me a couple of pairs of shoes and a couple of dresses and some glitter paste-on stars. About a week later, we pasted the stars on our faces when I took him to see the Dolls. David picked me up in this huge limousine. "How do you pay for all of this?" I asked him.

"Oh, my manager pays for it," he said. David was very extravagant for somebody who had not yet made it on our shores. The Dolls were incredible, and David and I made out through the whole show. He had a big smile on his face in between kissing me. It made the papers and got all over town. That caused a scandal. I was still with Todd, but that kind of nonsense went on all the time with us. There was a lot of temptation.

For the whole week after David picked me out of the crowd and came over to say hello, everyone was talking about it. Andy Warhol would come over to me at Max's and say, "What was he like? Was he fabulous?" Everybody was curious. I felt like Grace Kelly for a week. We hung out for four days, visiting all the New York sights. David was like a little kid. He burst into tears when he saw the Rockettes at Radio City Music Hall. He called me at all hours of the night, asking me to come over and rescue him from one emotional trauma after another. He was staying at the Gramercy Park Hotel, and I would go rushing over there at four or five o'clock in the morning. Every time I got there, there would be someone leaving and someone arriving. He just had a trail of women coming in and out all the time. Our glam scene had more punk-rock resonance to it than the English scene.

The men I had affairs with and the music I listened to around the house were the opposite of Todd and his music in many ways, and I do think this sometimes fueled his creativity. David was a good example. Todd had never really glammed out before. He had multicolored hair and he dressed in fashionable English outfits— tight velvet suits and stuff. It was very English, like Pete Townshend. He never wore makeup or glitter. One night, I was at Max's with David. We were sitting with Alice Cooper, and I think Todd was starting to get a little jealous. Todd turned glitter rock star overnight, making a dramatic entrance into Max's Kansas City's back room to reclaim his territory. He walked in with feathers on his eyes and glitter. And he put this stuff in his hair and it was all shiny. He had on this silver lamé jacket that sparkled, skintight blue pants, and heavy black kohl eye makeup. He just came over to the table and sat down next to me, and David burst into tears.

"David, it's okay," Todd said. "I'm leaving to go on the road tomorrow. She's all yours."

"What do you mean, I'm all his?" I exclaimed. "David, would you please tell him we're not having sex?" But David just sat there crying.

"What the hell's going on here with you guys?" said Alice, who was sitting there, being very macho for a guy who carried a woman's name. "Smarten up!" Todd just turned around and walked out, and I chased him. And the feathers were falling off of him as he was walking.

"Todd, Todd!" I cried, picking up the feathers behind him as I followed him out.

In one of his performances, David wore an enormously wide pair of pants that looked like an accordion. Less than a year later, I took David to see Todd's show at Carnegie Hall, and Todd came out wearing the same pants. David just sat there looking at me, totally in shock, saying, "Bebe!" So there was definitely part of Todd that was influenced by Bowie because of me.

Todd and I finally managed to patch things up, and he got over the incident at Max's, but David was such a drama queen, he couldn't leave it at that. I was lying in bed with Todd at 4:30 one morning, when David called, weeping. I don't think he was crying over me; I think he was crying because he just did that a lot. He asked me to come over and read to him.

Jayne County and Leee Black Childers really groomed David, taught him all about drag queens and transvestites. He didn't know anything about that; he was a little folksy before they got their hands on him. Nor is Angela given enough credit for her influence. But people are always embarrassed by where they really get their inspiration. After hanging out for a couple of weeks, David and I decided that we might have sex, but then we both burst out laughing and ended up doing our makeup. He taught me a lot about makeup and fashion. He was the first man who ever painted my toenails for me. I don't think I was really his cup of tea sexually. I wasn't black and I wasn't weird. Sometimes sex just doesn't work.

Mick Jagger was my third extracurricular guy. I first met Mick at an Eric Clapton show at Madison Square Garden that Todd was invited to jam at in 1973. We were all congregating at the bar at the Plaza Hotel and then taking a fleet of cars over to Madison Square Garden. On the way there, Todd was teasing me: "Mick Jagger's going to be there. . . . Are you going to be like a silly little girl?"

"Possibly!"

And he gave me the Mick Jagger lecture—the same one he gave me when I later met Warren Beatty and when I met Rod Stewart. "Watch out for these guys! They'll just try to have sex with you!" Et cetera, et cetera. The typical fatherly lecture! Imagine! I was getting the typical fatherly rock and roll lecture from Todd Rundgren. I really didn't have any expectations. You could just feel rock in the air! It was fabulous! I was really in paradise that night, because Eric Clapton was somebody I adored from Cream and I thought he was a genius. It was wonderful to be a part of this energy, and it was funny, because everyone was really trying to embrace Todd, but his stubbornness and his "Toddness" prevented him from clicking with them. Todd was never one of the boys; he was never a "mate." He was a little too serious.

All I know is that when Mick Jagger walked in the room, my heart pounded harder than it's ever pounded and I felt the air leave my chest! I didn't know if Jagger was going to sing or just hang out.

He was just playing the little imp that night, running around and causing havoc with all the women there, flirting with everyone endlessly. As soon as someone's boyfriend would turn around, he'd go over and start in on them. Johnny Podell was there with Monica Podell. Mick ran over to Monica when Johnny walked away. He whispered something and touched her, and then he ran over to Neil Smith's wife, Babette, who was a fetching tall blond, and started telling her what he'd like to do to her. He was just going around and starting trouble. He thought nothing of having a bonk with someone in a bathroom, one of his favorite places for a quickie. As soon as he saw me, it was like, *Whooosh*, fresh blood!

Mick flirted with me unbelievably and told me I was pretty and that I should be with him and not Todd. But Mick says that to all the girls. He's like the little pixie who runs around causing trouble with all the females, and that's what I love about him—his boldness. He was relentless that night. He would come running up to me and say, "But you, I'd go to your house." All the others usually said stuff like "Come to my hotel." So that became a long-standing joke with us throughout our friendship, whenever he would show up at my house without calling first. The night I met him, we must have smelled rock and roll scent on each other. He just really liked me immediately, and I could tell it was genuine, because he wasn't being inappropriate like he was with the other girls. He wasn't touching or feeling me up. He was actually being boyish and shy and charming.

"I hear about you around town. All the boys think you're so beautiful, all my friends think you're so beautiful, so what are you doing with Todd?" was his introductory salvo. "So how is your relationship with Todd? Well, you know my friend so and so . . . you haven't been out with Jimmy Page? You must never date Jimmy Page!" He also kept telling Todd what a great ass he had.

"God, Todd Rundgren, you've got a great ass," he'd say, which was absolutely true, this being the height of tight-as-bejesus pants, which left nothing to the imagination. Finally, Todd threw a moody and we had to leave. All the way home, I got the "Be careful" lecture: "You should be careful about these boys; they do this to everyone. I know this is your childhood idol, but he wouldn't be acting like this if you weren't one of the hottest girls in town, and my girlfriend to boot. That helps, too." Todd's theory was that Mick liked a woman better if she had a boyfriend; that made it all the more challenging and fun. And perhaps there is a grain of truth in that. Whatever, I felt like Mick picked me, even though there were a lot of beautiful women available. I felt he wanted *me*. That night I met him, it was hysterical—he was just such a troublemaker.

Shortly thereafter, Mick did track me down. He called me at Horatio Street and took me to a hip Japanese restaurant on Thirteenth and Second called Mei, where we were sure to be seen. He turned me on to my first Japanese food and my first Indian food, and he taught me a lot about wine. He's self-taught, and he can talk about anything.

Mick wanted to sleep with me, but he didn't want to scare me. We ended up sleeping together in his suite at the Plaza Hotel. Mick is the sweetest, tenderest, nicest, most beautiful, considerate lover. He's aggressive, strong, and confident. He just wants you to have pleasure. Mick, Warren Beatty, and Jack Nicholson are like perfect practitioners of love. God put them on this planet to make love to women. They really take pride and pleasure at being skillful lovers. But I always found it a little generic being with Mick. There was no cosmic interaction: You just knew if you were going to make love with Mick, you were going to get a really concrete love session. You

Daryl Hall, Mick Jagger, and me peeking past Todd—backstage at the Felt Forum, 1975/CHUCK PULIN

knew you weren't going to walk away from it unsatisfied. But sex was not the dominant thing in our relationship. This was the beginning of a long, deep friendship.

Todd and I respected each other enough to keep our affairs discreet, and when one was over, we fell back into each other's arms. Then it was makeup sex galore, with Todd consistently competing to be the best lover. Believe me, when your boyfriend knows that you've been with Iggy Pop, David Bowie, or Mick Jagger, you're in for quite a shag.

The problem was that my dalliances were much more public than Todd's: I was going out with the biggest rock stars of the decade, whereas Todd was just screwing the prettiest girl in Iowa. Plus, we lived in a time of a double standard: My affairs were top-notch gossip, but nobody noticed my boyfriend getting a blow job in the back of a limo. The full seventies lifestyle meant that fidelity wasn't a big thing, and relationships tended to be much more open because of that. It didn't mean you didn't love your mate, but the person you kept house with might not necessarily be the one you traveled around the world with or had sex with. Todd was my mad scientist boyfriend, my anchor, who lived in between a pair of headphones in recording studios. I was a young wildcat who wanted to live out all my fantasies. Soon we became the poster couple for the classic "open" relationship of the 1970s.

In my first incarnation, I became famous as a result of my affiliation with Max's and rock and roll stars and my decision to put Max's above my career, which most people would find ridiculous today, but not then. That started happening around 1973–1974. People started noticing that I had an eye for talent. David Bowie and I were two of the three people who were upstairs at Max's the night Bruce Springsteen played a brilliant set at the piano. I went back and reported, "God, this guy I just saw the other night, Bruce Springsteen, he's incredible!"

The photograph that pinned my wild child image was a Bearsville picture, taken with Todd when we first started going out. It got used in 1973 by Lisa Robinson in *Creem* magazine. I looked about fifteen. In that photo, Todd's got his hand over my naked breast, which at the time was considered extremely risqué. I think that that image was created for me; it was not created by me.

To be ridiculed and picked on as much as I have been at one time or another but also to have been embraced and respected is a strange combination to live with. It gave me mixed signals. I already had very fucked-up signals from my nonexistent father, and then my next father figure, Todd Rundgren, made damn sure that every signal he sent was from outer space. So I was never given any concrete evidence of who I was.

Two of the prettiest stars on the New York turntable—Todd and Bebe, 1972/STEPHEN ANDERSON

CHAPTER 3

Riffs of Innocence
1973-1974

From sea to shining sea
There's not a soul who needs to rock like me
And from the mountain tops
You can feel my heart beat
"MOTHER OF ROCK 'N' ROLL," LYRICS BY BEBE BUELL

Things kept happening to me. In the spring of 1973, the young
rock photographer Lynn Goldsmith kicked off a series of events
that would change my life when she persuaded me to pose nude. It
all began when she came over to Horatio Street to do some infor-
mal portraits, bringing a superb bottle of Chianti, which we proceeded to imbibe with considerable gusto. I tried on various items
of Todd's and she started snapping away. Little by little, the photos
started to become more "artistic." Then, before I knew it, she was
saying, "Let's do some nudes." We were a little tipsy. There was nobody else in the house. I dropped the robe and the jacket that I was
wearing, and she started directing me firmly but quietly: "Stand
against the bare brick wall! Put on the purple top hat!" I felt comfortable with Lynn. She had a relaxing manner, much like a doctor.

One of the Lynn nudes that wowed *Playboy*, 1973/LYNN GOLDSMITH

Over the next three hours, she shot twelve rolls of color and black-and-white photographs.

When Lynn got the pictures developed, she called me and said, "Bebe, these pictures are astounding." She asked me to come up to her place on West Sixty-seventh Street to see them. She put the slides on a light box so I could look at a number of them at the same time. I was absolutely blown away. They were the most beautiful, powerful photographs I had ever seen of myself. I looked good naked. Lynn said she wanted to take some more. So I stripped again. I found it much easier to take off my clothes for a camera than for a man.

Never once during these two sessions did Lynn mention anything about publishing the photos, let alone in a men's magazine. But when she got the second set back from the lab, she called me again. "Bebe, I really think we should go to *Playboy* and *Penthouse*, as a team. A woman photographing a woman nude and getting these kinds of results would be a first. It could be historic," she said. The sexual scenario in the United States had exploded into a million pieces by 1973. Woman's liberation had shattered the classic American male image. Gay liberation had swept up the pieces. Meanwhile, with hard-core porn like *Deep Throat*, starring Linda Lovelace, and *Behind the Green Door*, starring Marilyn Chambers, the sex industry was going through the roof. The big magazines were battling it out for an audience of millions. *Playboy* was trying to stand by its clean-cut format, featuring a provocative interview with an intellectual like Norman Mailer, a somewhat refined, classic nude centerfold, and some first-rate fiction, whereas *Penthouse* supplied all that, too, but it went for the jugular by pushing the envelope on how much pussy it could show issue by issue, and winning. Lynn wanted to go to *Penthouse* first, because she was sure they would pay a higher price for her "historic" idea. I wasn't so sure. I said, "Lynn, that magazine shows way too much pussy. They are way too gross. I'm not into it." But Lynn had a tenacity, a boldness, an aggressiveness about her when she was as intensely focused on something as she was on this, and she talked me into "just meeting" the magazine's notorious editor, Bob Guccione.

I immediately felt that something was not right about the meeting when it took place in a hotel suite! I mean, *Penthouse* had an enormous office complex, and I didn't understand why we couldn't meet there. Then there was the hair. The hair on his chest, the hair coming out of his nose, the hair coming out of his ears. And the gold chains on the hairy chest, and the big seventies hairdo, which made his head look like a basket. I knew immediately that we came from different worlds. He reminded me of somebody you might have met wearing chain mail in a Roman arena, waiting to serve you to the lions. As soon as we met with Guccione, he asked me if I would step into the bedroom for a moment. Lynn waited in the living room. Guccione came in. He was swarthy and oily and wearing a loud shirt. "I have to see your body," he rasped.

"You already have," I replied. "You've got the pictures right here!"

"No, no, no," he said. "I need to see your body, because I need to see if you have any scars."

"Excuse me, you're looking for scars?" Suddenly, I felt as if I were in school again. "I'm fucking nineteen. I don't think you're gonna find any wounds on me, baby." I said, "Puleeze! I am not stripping for you! What, I'm gonna take my pants off on the floor here?"

"Well, this is the way I'm going to be photographing you," he replied. Suddenly, I realized he shot all the centerfolds. He had never considered using Lynn's photographs. Sneering at him, I dropped my jeans to my knees.

He said, "Honey, I need you to take them all off."

I was like, "Honey, this is it. Take a close look, because this is all you're gonna see!" and I let my jeans fall to my ankles. Then I pulled them up, zipped them shut, and walked back into the living room. If he had arranged to have a formal test shoot, I would have stripped completely, but to ask me to remove my clothing just so he could see my scars was ridiculous and insulting. It was obvious from the photographs that I didn't have a blemish on my body. I was a flawless young girl. Then he upset Lynn, making it clear that he was going to be taking the pictures, even though I hadn't even agreed to be photographed. "Oh, no, no, no," she said. "We want to do this as a team!" Such was the youthful dream of the seventies—that we would all unite to work for a better world.

"C'mon, Lynn!" I snapped, and we walked right out of there.

"So! How did it go?" she said perkily, chasing me down the hall to the elevator.

"We are not doing *Penthouse*!" I fumed as we stormed through the lobby. "No *Penthouse*! That's it!"

"What happened?" she said, sounding surprised.

"He wanted me to strip for him, Lynn!" I screamed.

"You're kidding!"

"No, I'm not. And trust me, he did not want you shooting the centerfold!"

"Really?" Now Lynn was getting upset again. "Really? But you pulverized him!"

I was getting confused. While I was trying to defend her interests as well as mine, Lynn sounded as if she was half-blaming me for "pulverizing" Guccione. Before we parted, however, she said she understood, but she wanted to know if she could go ahead and show the pictures to *Playboy*. She thought that maybe they would go for our act. Lynn was five five and tiny. In platforms, I was six feet tall, and I had long hair, long legs, and long arms, but somehow we fit together as a team, at least for the moment.

Before checking in with Lynn again, I went over to Patti Smith's apartment on West Twenty-third Street to check my perceptions about *Playboy*. Patti always held a firm view of these things.

"Bebe!" she exclaimed, launching into one of her enthusiastic panegyrics. "*Playboy* is America. It's like Coca-Cola. It's like Andy Warhol. It's like a Campbell's soup can. It's Pop Art!" Now she had me going. "Plus," she claimed, "all the best girls do it, Brigitte Bar-

At CBGB with Liz Derringer and Patti Smith, 1977/BOB GRUEN

dot, Ursula Andress"—she reeled off a list of names, some of which sounded as if they might have come from one of her poems— "Amelia Earhart, Isadora Duncan. Oh, do it, Bebe! You gotta do it. It's all-American!" she added, appealing to my basketball player's team spirit. "It's daring!" And then she gave it the requisite punk twist: "Plus, it would really be great to shove it up those fashion bitches' asses!" Patti had a love-hate affair with the fashion biz. On the one hand, she lived in a mental landscape decorated by *Vogue*, *Harper's Bazaar*, *Breakfast at Tiffany's*, with Audrey Hepburn wearing black and white. On the other hand, she knew none of the fashion magazines would have given her a foot in the door, and she harbored a deep-seated ambivalence for all the models who lived in the glamorous, unbreachable world of Madison Avenue chic.

This was a perfect example of the collaborative spirit of New York, which made it such a special place to live in the 1970s. Meanwhile, I was having fantasies about starting my own band. There was an enormous gap between the Ford Agency and punk rock. These were early days for punk. Patti had only just started singing.

But I didn't see why I shouldn't be the first model to bridge the gap. I thought modeling and rock 'n' roll suited each other. My role models were Anita Pallenberg and Marianne Faithfull. I saw myself continuing their tradition as rock 'n' roll models. Patti also showed me the *Playboy* layouts of Brigitte Bardot, Ursula Andress, and Linda Evans, which were all just beautiful. And she warned me that the longer I modeled, the harder it would be to make the transition to having a band. It was time to take a stand, and make my move.

Patti's brand of feminism was based on not being a victim. She thought women should be in full control of their faculties and take a rebel stand. I jumped on Patti's vision. People were constantly comparing me to Bardot and Mia Farrow, which gave me the idea to create my wild child image, which was so popular at the time, and I started to translate it into this beautiful Jane Birkin movie, which would, as I imagined it, be fabulously and sexily rebellious. When I walked into a room, I wanted to make the other models tremble, as if the Antichrist had arrived. I wanted to hear them whisper, "That's Bebe Buell. . . . She goes out with . . . the devil."

A week later, I got a call from *Playboy*. They had received Lynn's pictures all right, and then had gone straight over her head to me. A woman named Hollis Wayne, an editor who decided which girls got tested for centerfolds, was on the line from Chicago, Hugh Hefner's headquarters. "You are definitely the girl next door, wholesome *Playboy* material," she began. "But what we especially like about you is that you've got a famous boyfriend and you've got a certain celebrity status. We've never done somebody like you in our centerfold and we would like to bring somebody like you into our magazine for the 1970s." Then she started comparing me to Betty Page, Marilyn Monroe, Stella Stevens, and other famous centerfolds of the 1950s and early 1960s.

"I'm nothing like those women," I protested, but she continued as if she had not heard me, concluding, "We see you as potentially being somebody like that in the *Playboy* family."

"Lynn is going to be sooo happy!" I purred.

"Oh, no," Hollis quickly interjected. "This doesn't involve Lynn. Lynn will get a finder's fee. We will pay her five hundred dollars for bringing you to the magazine, but we never use outside photographers for our centerfolds." Suddenly, she was reading off the names of every great living photographer, from Helmut Newton to Man Ray, but she was fading in and out of my consciousness as I imagined how Lynn would react to this development. No doubt, it was not going to meet her approval. "But for you," Hollis was saying, "we would like to use a new photographer, Richard Fegley." Richard has since become one of the most famous photographers *Playboy* has ever had, but at the time, nobody had ever heard of him. Lynn was more well known, and I could hear her screaming about sexist pigs. However, the fact that they had thought this through to the extent of assigning me to a specific photographer really sold me on going with the *Playboy* philosophy (not to mention the five-thousand-dollar fee I would receive upon publication, enough pocket money in those days to last me for a year). I was taking off, but Lynn was not going to be part of the picture. . . .

Lynn did not react well. She has always been a person who screams and yells. She was manipulative and hard on me, and as far as she was concerned, I had betrayed her. She threatened to sue me. She really read me the riot act. She wanted to shoot this and she was being fucked over, she said. She felt we could have made history, a woman shooting a woman. Even though Bunny Yeager had done it first when she photographed Betty Page. What was I thinking? she asked. Didn't I care? What about sisterhood? A big battle ensued.

Playboy explained to me that Lynn had no legal hold on me and that they had every right to discover me via her photographs. All they had to do was pay her a finder's fee. And that they had no plans of making any fucking history with *her*.

Lynn was so pissed, she had to find a way to take it out on me. However, while Lynn was bonking Todd and they both thought I was unaware of their activities, Lynn made a tactical error, confiding in me that she was getting it on with David Cassidy (the teeny-bop sensation of the decade), whom she had met when she photographed him. And she, of course, swore me to secrecy. I wasn't to tell a soul, which gave me my opening.

"Isn't it funny," I casually mentioned one day to Todd, my seventies soul mate, "that Lynn is bonking David Cassidy." I will never forget the expression on Todd's face. Normally, he has the longest face in the world, like a rabbit's; but it suddenly got even longer and thinner. "What's wrong?" I asked, all innocent and surprised.

"Lynn told you that?" he gurgled.

"Yeah. She said they have wild sex and he's the kinkiest devil on earth."

"*What?!*"

This was my way of letting him know that bonkage was caught! That his bonkage was now out in the open.

This put my standing with Lynn on another level altogether. A week after my tête-à-tête with Todd, I received a letter that had been painstakingly typed on Grand Funk Railroad stationery. In it, Lynn screamed at me for spilling the beans about her affair with David Cassidy, and, by implication, for acknowledging I knew she was bonking my boyfriend, too!

It soon emerged that another girl Todd had been seeing just before he started seeing Patti Smith, and after he had been seeing Miss Christine, Marlene, was going to be a *Playboy* centerfold before me, if indeed I made the final cut. On our first trip to London, in the autumn of 1972, when we were falling in love, I'd discovered that Todd had seen Marlene again. Then I started talking to her on the phone, and she now told me she was going to be Miss April in *Playboy* in 1974.

Playboy flew me to Chicago to do the test photo session in September 1973. It was much like being a little princess. A limousine ferried me from O'Hare Airport to Hugh Hefner's mansion. I had been in many limousines with Alice Cooper and Todd, surrounded by thousands of screaming teenyboppers, but as we pulled up to the mansion, I felt with satisfaction that this was the first time I'd had a limousine specifically for me. That was a good feeling.

When I walked in, I was told I'd be staying in the Orange Room; then I was escorted there to freshen up before lunch. I had been invited to stay for three days. The *Playboy* people liked to get to know their centerfolds, so there'd be no skeletons rattling out of the closet when the pictures came out. *Playboy* was extremely aware of its clean, upstanding American image. Its girls were to be wholesome wenches. They didn't want any troublemakers.

Settling into my room, I was startled to discover that I was sharing a bathroom with the Green Room. Tiptoeing in, I found out that it was occupied by Tommy Smothers of the then hot and controversial comedy team, the Smothers Brothers. I could hardly get out of there before collapsing in hysterical laughter. I mean, if I had to share a bathroom with anybody in the world, it had to be Tommy Smothers? I spent a pleasant afternoon visiting the *Playboy* offices, meeting Hollis Wayne, a personable, effervescent woman, the photographer Richard Fegley, and my liaison in Chicago, Gary Cole. I filled out my data sheets and familiarized myself with the layout. This was a far cry from the Guccione incident. I had my own dressing room, a makeup artist, and a hairdresser. We were going to be shooting for two days. I had my work cut out for me.

After dinner that night, I hung out in the main room with Hefner and his Chicago girlfriend, Karen, who had the biggest breasts I had ever seen, and his pals. Barbie Benton, who lived in the L.A. mansion, was his official girlfriend. Hefner confined himself to smoking his pipe, playing Monopoly, and drinking Pepsi, clad the whole time in a pair of his famous executive pajamas. He treated me with courtly propriety, asking if I was going to be a centerfold, and when I said yes, he gave me a kind of surprised look. At the time, I didn't have anything like the kind of tits most Playmates had. He commented on my resemblance to Mia Farrow, who had recently starred in *The Great Gatsby*, but there was nothing lecherous about him. Unlike Guccione, Hefner chose the centerfolds from their photographs alone. It had been a long day, so after a brief dip in the indoor pool, I went to bed, falling asleep around 11:00 P.M.

At 2:00 A.M., I went to the bathroom, half-asleep, not noticing that the door to Tommy Smothers's room was ajar. Since the light was on, he must have seen me naked. A few minutes later, as I was settling down to go back to sleep, an almost stark naked man streaked into the room and took a flying leap onto my bed, landing next to me and announcing that he was going to make love to me!

"Oh yeah?" I snapped. "Well, first of all, I don't like men without hair, and second, I have a boyfriend in New York. His name's Todd Rundgren!"

"So?" he said, and tried to kiss me. I can only imagine he was under the impression that if he succeeded, it would be so wonderful that I would completely change my mind. At which point, I wrapped a sheet around myself, jumped up, reminded him, "No means No," and basically led him back to the bathroom by his ear. "You're going back to bed right now!" I scolded.

"Are you sure?"

"Yes!" *Slam!*

It was a lot funnier than it was frightening.

Richard Fegley and I worked on the test shots over the next couple of days. I felt that I was working in a completely professional situation, so I was very comfortable emotionally. Physically, however, it was the hardest work I have ever done except for shooting the actual centerfold. He shot endless rolls of film, and the way I had to contort my body and hold poses for minutes at a time was like doing yoga. Long hours of contorting your body are simply not as easy as they look. I did learn a lot about how to turn my waist at a certain angle to make it smaller, or stick my fanny out to make it look rounder, things that would stand me in good stead in the future.

Everybody imagined that a beautiful young girl staying at the mansion by herself was there for the purpose of getting screwed by Hugh Hefner and his pals. Nothing could have been further from the truth. However, there was one instance of nonconsensual sex during my stay there. On my second night, I couldn't sleep, as I was nervous about the following day's test shoot. You could get anything you wanted to eat twenty-four hours a day, so I called down to the kitchen and ordered Eggs Benedict. Immediately after eating a humongous plate of this delicious concoction, I started to bloat. I freaked out, imagining myself posing for the pictures looking like a stuffed pig. So I hit upon the brilliant solution of taking a late-night swim in the indoor pool. I dived in, naked as a jaybird, believing that I had the whole luxurious pool to myself. I was swimming and diving and twirling around, accompanied by Steely Dan singing "Rikki Don't Lose That Number." I was singing along at the top of my lungs and having a blast, until, in one of my acrobatic somersaults, I noticed a huge plate-glass window under the water on one side of the pool. *Hey, waaaait a minute!* I thought, and dived under again to take a closer look. Imagine my horror and dismay on beholding some fifteen people giving me their full attention, and then a standing ovation.

I will never forget as long as I live the creepy feeling that flooded through my whole being. During my aquatic romp, I had alternately touched myself, masturbated on one of the water shoots, and done a number of other things that you do when you are attempting to unwind and believe you are completely alone. I had never been so humiliated in my life. I'd thought I was having a Calgon moment, but it turned out to be a Kodak moment! Leaping out of the pool, shaking with rage, and throwing on my robe, I stomped down to the gallery and screamed at all of them at the top of my lungs.

Back in New York, I waited to hear if *Playboy* had chosen to photograph me for the centerfold. They really tortured me. They'd keep in touch, they told me. "Well, we haven't made a decision yet, but you're still in the running." It was like waiting to hear if you're Miss America or not—nerve-racking. Meanwhile, they flew me back to Chicago a couple of times to be in other pictorial layouts before the decision on the centerfold was made. My first appearance in the magazine was in a spread called "The Girls of Skiing." It had me kneeling down, wearing nothing but a wool hat and a pair of fuzzy boots, picking a marshmallow off a stick. I was supposed to be a skier in Vermont. And my next pictures were in a lingerie spread called "Sheer Delights."

I was still worried that Todd was going to see Marlene as the April centerfold and fall back in love with her and dump me! It sounds insane, but that's what I thought. Finally, Patti Smith persuaded Todd that I was prettier than Marlene. Patti was always real sweet to me. She was one of the first people to give me confidence. She said I had "a really risqué mouth," and she told me she'd jerked off to the "Sheer Delights" lingerie shots. I was flattered. Anyway, one day in January 1974, I was crying my eyes out, thinking that Todd was looking at pictures of Marlene and was going to dump me for her, when, two hours later, *Playboy* called to tell me I'd been picked to be a Playmate. I was so happy, I danced around the room.

The centerfold was shot in Manhattan. Physically, it was the single most difficult photo session I have ever done. We worked all day. I arrived at the studio around 8:00 A.M. and we worked until 10:00 P.M. that night. And in the interim, I was barely allowed to breathe. Fegley used a Hasselblad camera. His assistant inserted a different plate for each shot and I had to hold my pose in between the insertion and removal of several plates. Looking at the pictures, you get the impression that I am lying on a flat surface, but I was contorted on a short chaise lounge. They had me propped up in such a position that by the end of the session, I couldn't walk. I had been lying on my back, with one arm thrust behind my head, which was twisted around, while I had to prop one leg up in the opposite direction for hours. Houdini himself could have learned something from being a *Playboy* centerfold.

In late 1973, Todd put together a band called Utopia. To him, Utopia was not just a band; it was a way of life, a vision of what he wanted his life to be. In the years I was with him, he was making really good money as a producer. The Grand Funk Railroad success allowed him to

Playboy centerfold, 1974/RICHARD FEGLEY

make a living as a producer, but I think he also felt defiance toward the industry and the impulse to not give them what they wanted. I think he could have had huge commercial success with Utopia if he had been willing to compromise a little and do material that could have been marketed on the radio, but he refused to do that. I sometimes wonder if he didn't make himself inaccessible on purpose.

As much as I didn't like some of the concepts of Utopia, I did appreciate the band's performance strength. I was with him when he did a big show at the Tower Theater in Philadelphia. The band came out onstage in a huge spaceship he had built for the occasion, but everything blew up and Todd had to leave without doing the show. He was always one of those people who said, "Don't save any money. I want to spend every penny I've got on the show."

Todd was extremely inventive, but he had poor business sense and he wouldn't let anybody tell him what to do with his money. None of us ever said Todd wasn't arrogant, but arrogance is an understatement. I am sometimes arrogant. Todd was in his own world: Planet Todd. Records like *Oops! Wrong Planet* and *Ra* weren't commercially successful, but he was still very strong in the live arena. Todd could still pack a room, and when he played Los Angeles or somewhere hip, he always sold out.

In June, I flew out to L.A. with Todd and his band for the start of their West Coast tour. We checked into the Continental Hyatt House Hotel (known by rock 'n' rollers as "the Riot House"). Todd was at the zenith of his solo career with the *A Wizard/A True Star* album, which I had helped him choose the cover for by turning him onto mescaline for the first time.

We stayed at the Riot House for a week. Todd played two shows. On the off nights, we went to see Tim Curry in *The Rocky Horror Picture Show* and we went to the clubs. One night, we visited Brian Wilson at his house. Todd was a big fan and he had a lot of respect for Brian, but Brian was obviously really screwed up. When he got up to walk across the room, he tiptoed and made little dancing motions to sounds nobody else could hear. It seemed like there was a crazy guy inside him who had gone to a bad place mentally. Todd, Brian, Wolfman Jack, and I went to the Troubadour to see some friends perform. Brian, in a drunken stupor, tried to jump up onstage with the band. And the bouncers removed him very unceremoniously, throwing him right out of the club and onto the street. That really upset Todd. He felt that a fragile genius like that should be treated with love and attention. Todd couldn't tolerate John Lennon putting a Kotex on his head, because he just thought John was being an asshole, but Brian was really not well. Todd didn't abandon Brian when he got thrown out of the Troubadour. We went back to the house with him and he played piano in the sandbox and sang like an angel in a falsetto voice, but he would sing stupid lines, like "There's a zebra in my tree."

He was like a passionate sheepdog. He would grab you and hug and kiss you and be very hospitable, but I sensed there was tension at home. I could see that his wife didn't like all these parties at the house. She was there, but she'd disappear often. She spent a lot of time upstairs. There were a lot of drugs around, but we were just smoking pot. When Todd was not in the mood for drugs he didn't do them. I think he was so distraught at seeing Brian in this condition, he didn't want to encourage him by setting a bad example. He wanted to be somebody Brian could depend upon.

Two nights before Todd left for San Francisco, we went to a party. Richard Pryor was there. Everybody was stoned out of their minds and Todd kept telling me to mingle, but I just clung to him because I was nervous. I didn't know anybody. Everybody was looped; there were people fucking in the corners, so I kept close to Todd. He kept saying to me, "Look, give me some space. Why don't you mingle?"

"Mingle with whom? I don't know anyone."

"You'll be fine. Just go and talk to people." I kept catching him on the telephone, which gave me a bad feeling in the pit of my stomach. And the only other person who was paying attention to me was Richard Pryor, who was utterly gorgeous and charming. He might have been stoned, but he was a doll. Suddenly, everybody started jamming in the middle of the floor, beating on things and playing guitar; Richard was playing bongos and flirting with me. Of course, as soon as Todd saw that Richard was flirting with me, he changed his tune. "Come and sit over here next to me!" he said. And I thought, Oh Lord. One minute he's telling me to go off and be independent and mingle, and the next minute he's telling me to come sit next to him!

"Yeah. Now that you're done calling your girlfriends and you have all your dates, you want me to come and sit with you!" I told him.

Back at the Hyatt House the day before the San Francisco trip, Todd told me, "Tomorrow, I'm going to San Francisco on my own." I flipped out and we had a big fight. At first, I was perplexed. I was crying and begging to go. We fought all night. I kept asking him why I couldn't go. "Are you fucking somebody up there? Is that why I can't come?" I had expected to go to San Francisco at least and fly back to New York from there. He got up the next morning and they were leaving. The band had a gig that night. I

With the South American raccoon who flew
first-class with Zeppelin, 1974/RICHARD FEGLEY

was still crying and begging him to let me go with him. Finally, he
said, "Look, you've made enough money modeling, and you can
get home. You're a big girl. Take care of yourself." Then I realized
he must be fucking somebody in San Francisco. Meanwhile, he left
me stranded, without any money or a ticket back to New York. I
think in part he was pissed off, but he was also trying to teach me to
be responsible. I was making enough money that I did not always
need to be completely reliant on him. Todd taught me a lot about
independence.

I called our travel agent and Todd's manager's office, but neither
of them returned my calls, so I started to get paranoid, believing
that Todd had instructed them to cut me off. Maybe he saw it as a

test of character, but I was twenty and I had never been three thousand miles from home, barely knowing anybody, without a penny and with no idea how to get back to New York. I burst into tears in the hotel's lobby. The first knight to come to my aid was Levon Helm of the Band. He gave me a hundred dollars and told me not to worry because the Band was staying in the hotel. He said if I needed more money, I could look him up. He was a sweetheart, but unfortunately, not characteristic of the hotel's clientele.

Todd had left his South American raccoon with me. Some of the Kinks managed to get into our room, and one of them dangled it over the edge from our tenth-floor terrace, while another one tried to set fire to its tail. Rock decadence was turning mean. Televisions were flying out windows; motorcycles were roaring down hallways. There were also a large number of strange-looking young girls dressed up like Christmas ornaments rushing around, or just camping out in front of some rock star's rooms with their coolers and their radios. This was a new breed of groupie. They were about fourteen (sometimes twelve) and were aggressive. They were harsh on other females attached to their heroes. You could easily get tripped, kicked, smacked, or have your hair pulled.

I ran into Kim Fowley, Rodney Bingenheimer, and Michelle Meyer, who pretty much ran the L.A. rock scene's social life, and I asked them, "What the hell is going on? Why are you all here?"

"Led Zeppelin's coming in from the airport!" they announced. This was the first time I witnessed a Zeppelin invasion. The band was coming to L.A. to host the biggest party of the year, the launch of their record label, Swan Song. They were the biggest band in the world in 1974. Todd's worst nightmare was arriving! Suddenly, I didn't feel safe in the lobby, but I didn't feel safe in my room with the pissed-off coatimundi and his sharp little claws, either.

Around four that afternoon, I was on the elevator with Kim and Rodney, explaining my plight and crying hysterically, my big red face streaked with mascara, when the door opened and Jimmy Page stepped in, accompanied by Robert Plant and the Zeppelin's notorious road manager, Richard Cole. They had just checked in and were on their way to their rooms. Jimmy was wearing a pair of dainty black boots, crushed blue velvet pants, a beautifully ruffled Edwardian shirt, and a velvet jacket worthy of Beau Brummell. His pale, handsome face was framed by exquisite black ringlets. He looked like Sir Lancelot. "Haven't I met you before?" he inquired in the most gallant voice. "Didn't I meet you with Patti D'Arbanville in New York?"

"No!" I blurted out, not wanting to be recognized in such a terrible state but not knowing quite what to do. "It's not possible."

"Darling, what's wrong?" Jimmy crooned.

"It's none of your business!" I said in heaps of irritation. "Who the fuck are you anyway?"

"Don't you remember?" He smiled. "It's me, Jimmy. I met you with Patti D'Arbanville in New York."

"I know who you are." I snuffled into my handkerchief and ran off the elevator. (Kim later informed me that he had seen the recognizable glimmer of interest in my eyes, despite my tearful state, so she assumed it was okay to fill Jimmy in on my situation.) Getting my room number from Rodney, Jimmy split. Good. Because I was in no mood for rock 'n' roll shenanigans. I was in rock 'n' roll hell. There were crowds of vicious girls roaming the corridors of the hotel, emitting wild, unidentifiable noises. In my lonely room, I was accompanied by the by now-unreliable and potentially vicious raccoon. I felt so sorry for the poor thing. We did get along.

That night, I hung out with my friends. Shaun Cassidy, David Cassidy's younger brother, who was fifteen, didn't have anywhere to sleep, so I let him camp out on my floor. Iggy Pop and his girlfriend, Coral, slept in my other bed. And Steve Sachs, the big drag queen groupie, who was everybody's friend, slept with me in my bed, along with the coatimundi. So I had a full house that night. Iggy was fucking in the bed next to ours, so Steve and I had to put our pillows over our heads. And that made me feel a little jealous, because I still liked Iggy. Everybody was asleep when the phone rang around 5:00 A.M.

"Bebe, this is Jimmy."

"Jimmy?"

Even half asleep, I suddenly knew who the voice belonged to.

"Oh, okay. Yeah?"

"Oh, darling, I'd love for you to come down to my room and have breakfast with me. I'm very sad right now."

"What's wrong?"

"I've just come back from playing on a session with Joe Walsh, playing guitar on a song about his wife and child, who were recently killed in a car accident. Please come and join me for breakfast. I'm very upset and lonely."

"Well, I'm just going to come down in my pajamas," I responded. "I'm really upset, too, and I've got my South American raccoon with

Photo I took of Jimmy Page, 1974/BEBE BUELL

me." The animal was my pet, so I wanted to take it, but I hadn't forgotten my rock 'n' roll etiquette, and I also wanted to freak him out a little bit. You have to admit, going down to his room with an exotic animal was kind of cool.

"Bring the raccoon and come on down."

I arrived at his suite wearing a T-shirt and a pair of gauzy Indian pants. My hair was pulled back and I wasn't wearing makeup. I had never presented myself to somebody of Jimmy's caliber in this kind of unadorned state before.

"Come in, darling," Jimmy said, welcoming me with a bow. "Would you like some cocaine? Are you hungry? I've got a great idea. Why don't we give this fruit basket to the raccoon and put them both in the bathroom?" Now the raccoon was in paradise, with enough fruit for Jabba the Hut, and we proceeded to hang out, drinking mimosas, doing some lines, and comparing notes on our current problems. Led Zeppelin's manager, Peter Grant, arrived. Peter had been a wrestler. In retirement, he had put on an enormous amount of weight. He weighed about 450 pounds. No single chair would support him. He carried his weight with great authority, though. He had a kind of gangsterish charm that belied the fact that he was one of the toughest men in the business. He was an ex tremely effective manager, and if he liked you, he could be a great friend.

They talked about the Joe Walsh tragedy, with Jimmy acting out the sad drama. Then he said that, under the circumstances, "Bebe's been kind enough to join me for breakfast."

Grant sized me up approvingly, noting that he had seen several photographs of me. He asked, "How would your boyfriend feel about you being here with Jimmy?"

"My boyfriend dumped me!" I blurted out. "And he's in San Francisco with somebody else."

"No one's going to shoot my guitar player in the kneecaps, then?"

"No, no," I assured him, emboldened by the coke I'd done. "Anyway, Todd doesn't care who I go out with," which was surely one of the great understatements of my life.

"Yes, it seems we're both in a transitional phase, aren't we, Peter?" Jimmy responded sympathetically, oozing great charm. It was all so Spinal Tap, but I was so naïve! Meanwhile, Peter had to take a leak and was making his way to the bathroom, when I suddenly remembered the raccoon.

"Should we tell him about the raccoon?" I hissed.

"No!" Jimmy insisted as we did another line and waited.

"What the fuck!" The bathroom door bammed almost off its hinges as, with a great primeval roar, Peter shot out of it, spluttering, "I thought you two just met! *All right, Jimmy!* What the fuck have you been doing here?" We dashed to the bathroom and peered in at an incredible mess. There was shit smeared all over the walls, and it looked as if somebody had been engaged in a great life-and-death struggle—hence Peter's suspicion that we had been engaging in some torrid orgy. He had not spotted the raccoon. It was lying on its back in the middle of the bathtub, like a tourist with a big stomach, sunning himself on the beach orgied out but happy, because not only had it filled its belly but it had also taken a gargantuan shit and spread it around in retaliation for its treatment by the Kinks. Peter summoned the porter and had Jimmy moved to a fresh suite.

Around 8:00 A.M., I ended up going to bed with Jimmy. As soon as we got onto the bed, Jimmy performed oral sex on me. He told me I would sleep much better if I had an orgasm; otherwise, the cocaine would keep me awake, and I didn't want any of the Valium he was offering me. We were first awakened by a hysterical Lori Maddox trying to get into the room. She found Jimmy's new room, but the chain lock was on the door. I didn't know whether Jimmy had told her that he wasn't going to see her anymore because he wanted to be with me. Or if he had told Richard Cole to make sure she was kept away. I just remember the cacophony of some girl screaming, "*Jimmy!*" outside the door. Then Richard suddenly showed up and dragged her off in hysterics. Then around noon, Steve Sachs came banging on the door with Richard Creamer, a rock photographer, yelling, "Jimmy! They're coming to take Bebe's bags away; she owes fifty dollars on her room." Jimmy handed him fifty dollars and said, "Well, Richard, it's very simple. Get the bags and bring them here. She'll be staying with me." I was kind of shocked by his presumption, but I was also very happy. It looked as if Todd's test was backfiring on him! I felt as if I had been rescued.

I always found men who would save me from previous dilemmas. When I been thrown off one horse, there was always somebody who rode up on another one. It wasn't something I sought. And it wasn't somehing I wanted. But I found it. David Byrne says, "Be careful what you wish for, because you might get it." I would want it so bad. I would wish for it. I would wish for rock stars. I would wish for some adoration for myself. I wanted people to think I was a beautiful girl, that I dressed great, that I was smart and witty and had all the right answers, and that I knew all the rock bands, I knew the best songs that week. I relished the image of who I thought I was.

Jimmy said, "We're having a lovely party for our new record company at the Beverly Hills Hotel and I would love you to be my companion for the launch."

I said, "Okay!" I was thinking, Todd is doing his thing and I'm doing mine. An eye for an eye. Todd was not going to be coming home for a couple of weeks. I wasn't worrying. As a matter of fact, I was hoping he would find out. I became Jimmy's girlfriend for the week. I stayed with him and was never far from his side.

That night, we went to the Rainbow Bar and Grill for dinner.

Believe me, when I walked into the Rainbow with Led Zeppelin, I was part of royalty and every woman in that room wanted to rip my skin off my bones. This was when I began to get the reputation for being a groupie, which is something I fervently feel that I never was. At the time, though, most people thought I was Todd Rundgren's wife, yet here I was, flagrantly going out with Jimmy Page, as I had been seen in similar public situations with Iggy Pop and David Bowie. But there really was a set of complicated circumstances behind every single one of these liaisons, and it usually began with Todd's infidelities, which is what people could not have known, of course. On this occasion, however, I was trespassing on the groupie territory previously dominated by Lori Maddox, Sable and Coral Starr, and Pamela Des Barres, the cream of the L.A. groupies. They were baying for my blood. I never felt like I fit in with the crowd out in L.A., because I felt girls out there were a little bit cruder and a lot more hard-core. Girls would just go back to the hotel and have sex with anyone. I was always amused by them, but I never saw them as comrades or equals, or women I wanted to hang out with. I mean, I knew these girls. I knew Lori Maddox and Sable Starr. They didn't have many scruples; I never operated on that level. And it was difficult for me, because I felt I couldn't trust the girls in L.A. I felt they were always trying to fuck the men I was with behind my back, and they definitely were. I called them "the body snatchers." Rock-star snatchers is what they were.

I noticed that there was a lot of violence surrounding Zeppelin. Somebody came over to our table, and that irritated everyone. Richard Cole hit the guy with his elbow and he fell to the ground, next to his teeth. That was a very disturbing thing for me to witness, because I never thought that violence was part of rock 'n' roll. I thought that sex and liberation, feminism and strength and meshing of the sexes, hard work, drive, willpower, and goodness were what rock 'n' roll was all about. Violence is too easy—it has nothing to do with rock 'n' roll. But Peter Grant brought the gangster image to the rock 'n' roll scene, and he prospered. Richard and Peter Grant were not to be tangled with. They were rough players, and if you got in their faces, or tried to fuck with their band, or did anything to disrupt or harm any member of the band, you would get a knuckle sandwich. It was a little like hanging out with the

Mafia. Everybody hung out in a pack and catered to those boys and their whims. They were living every rock and roll cliché to the hilt. That night, Lori Maddox was being kept away by security guards. And it was made very clear to Lori—who was probably the most beautiful girl in L.A. and had given herself exclusively to Jimmy from age fourteen to sixteen—and Miss Pamela that they were history. They immediately bonded against me, thinking that I was an interloper from the East Coast who had come to steal their thunder. Jimmy was serious. When Lisa Robinson flew out to cover the party for her column and a friend of Jimmy's overheard her commenting on what a run-around chick I was and how I was cheating on Todd, Jimmy had words with her. For whatever reason, she has hated me ever since.

The Swan Song party at the Beverly Hills Hotel was the climax of my time with Jimmy. It was the biggest rock party of the year and superelite. As at Max's Kansas City, stars from all walks of life wanted to be part of it, the new celebrity culture. I met Groucho Marx, and I remember him telling me I was a very beautiful girl.

I was very attracted to Jimmy Page. He was my type—very dashing, very English, very Renaissance. He had that otherwordly, other-time vibe. If you fantasized about being a princess and having a prince come and sweep you off your feet and take you on horseback to his castle, Jimmy Page was Sir Lancelot. What girl wouldn't enjoy that fantasy, even if it was only for a week?

We went out to dinner at expensive restaurants every night. We went shopping. Jimmy liked to go to metaphysical/astrology book-shops. We spent a lot of time in bed. We stayed up all night, hanging out, doing drugs, talking with Robert, Peter, Richard, and their entourages. Sometimes, I would do a little cocaine; other times, I would say no. I think Jimmy found that refreshing. I overheard him telling Robert and Peter, "She's not a coke whore." There certainly wasn't any peer pressure to do coke. We listened to music with Robert Plant and Richard Cole, who was always there. Peter Grant was around a lot. This was their heyday, and I got along fine with all of these guys because they had been instructed to treat me very well. Mind you, I knew they could turn on me just as quickly as they could protect me. If Jimmy had said, Get her out of here; I've had enough, I would have been gone as brutally as Lori Maddox had been dismissed. I had no illusions about that. As it was, however, Jimmy didn't cheat on me or go out with any other girls for the time we were together.

We had a powerful sexual relationship. It was very beautiful. He never tried to have anything but completely straight sex with me, although he had one weird penchant. When he kissed me, he loved to spew his saliva into my mouth. It was odd. I thought of it as his way of coming in my mouth without coming in my mouth. Otherwise, we had the most wholesome sex imaginable. I think I fulfilled a fantasy—that of the innocent girl—for a lot of these guys, who had had the most experienced, used women on the planet. I think they saw something of the little girl in me, which they wanted to preserve as something precious, fragile, like a flower in an otherwise-bleak landscape. But Jimmy was never violent; he never tried to practice black magic. I never saw any of that.

Meanwhile, Todd was on the road, and by now, he was frantically trying to find me. I flew back to New York with Led Zeppelin and their entourage. They rented the entire first-class cabin of an American Airlines jet so the raccoon could fly with us. I got along tremendously with all of them. We had a party flying across America at 35,000 feet.

In New York, they checked into the Pierre. I opened up the Horatio Street house, and Jimmy paid to get the dogs out of the kennel. But I spent the nights with Jimmy at the Pierre. During the days, we went to art galleries and museums, but mostly we went shopping. Jimmy bought great quantities of shirts and jackets; occasionally, he would buy me a dress or a pair of shoes, and he also bought me a wonderful book on the Pre-Raphaelite painter Burne-Jones.

One night, he asked me to go back to the Pierre for a party and picked me up in his car. We arrived at the hotel, where there were about seventy-five girls sitting on the floor outside his suite, and there was no security. In my position, you would have to fear for your life with these girls around. Thank God I was tall, so most of them couldn't reach me. Jimmy held my hand as we stepped over their inert bodies as they sprawled in the corridor. They were parked and refused to budge, scared of losing their places. While one went to the bathroom, another would watch her place and make sure she didn't miss anything. The truth was, the pop stars of the day *loved* it. They probably insisted that the hotel let the girls stay, and the hotel probably didn't want to give up such generous customers. The guys loved stepping over the girls, having to fight their way to their rooms, murmuring, "Girls, girls, move aside, please," and all the drama that went along with it. They were all such drama queens.

By now, Todd had to have heard about what was going on. There was an information channel across the country when the bands were on tour. Their followers, particularly the groupies, had a hot line. I had my own spy system and would often receive calls from girls in faraway towns, who'd say, "You won't believe what that asshole did last night!" And then they'd joyfully fill in all the details. I was going everywhere with Jimmy and it was beginning to be accepted that I was his new girl.

We parted very romantically. I spent his last night in New York with him at the hotel. He had two suites at the Pierre, connected by an adjoining door. He used one suite for entertaining and the other to live in, because he was fastidious and he didn't like the reek of beer cans and drug paraphernalia, or getting the smell of cigarette smoke on his clothes. The next morning, I rode out to the airport with him in his limousine. Just the two of us went—he was meeting Robert on the plane. Jimmy didn't make a strong plea for me to go over to London, because he had Clapton's ex, Charlotte, whom he'd stolen from Eric, and their daughter, Scarlet, living with him, but he gave me the impression that that relationship was souring and he wasn't sure what its future was going to be. He left me dangling, but it was very romantic, and he told me he would call me.

I spent the summer in New York and Woodstock. Todd bought a house on Mink Hollow Road in the Woodstock area, near his manager Albert Grossman's place in Bearsville. In those days, Woodstock was a wonderful place to go because it had the tranquillity of the country without the boredom of being cut off from other people. Dylan had long gone, but a number of musicians and artists of all kinds populated the houses dotted around the picturesque countryside. Todd bought a tractor and threw himself into the "back to the earth" movement that was so popular in the early seventies, when everybody was trying to figure out what they were supposed to be doing. I acquired some farm girl attire, like a pair of bib overalls.

BOB GRUEN

Being in Woodstock did not interrupt Todd's workaholic agenda. Whether we were in New York or the country, I always had to compete with his music for his attention, and, in the immortal words of William Burroughs, "that's a rumble no one can cool." At the time it hurt me incredibly that Todd even refused to take off a couple of hours to take me out to dinner on my twenty-first birthday. Here is one example of what this lack of attention led to. Mick remembered the date, July 14, and he called me up with one of his Jaggeresque games: "If you could meet any three people, who would they be?" I wanted to say, Jimi Hendrix, Charlotte Rampling (a particularly hot British actress, who'd recently starred in *The Night Porter* with Dirk Bogarde), and John Lennon, but I was trying to impress Mick with my intellect, so I blurted out, "Einstein, Picasso, and John Lennon!"

"Well," Mick replied without skipping a beat, "two of those are going to be impossible, because they're dead. These are very difficult requests. But what about dinner?"

He took me to the best Japanese restaurant in New York, a hole-in-the-wall called Mei, which was fashionable among the punk rock set on the Lower East Side. He gave me a large bottle of Shalimar perfume (I still have the bottle, although, being a Chanel girl, I could never actually wear that floozy juice.) After dinner, I was happy on sake, and Mick told me we were going to visit a friend. We hopped a cab to an apartment building on Sutton Place, an exclusive neighborhood in the East Fifties, famous for housing, among others, Greta Garbo. When we got inside the building, the River House, which overlooks the East River, there was a man standing at the foot of the stairs, and he snapped a Polaroid of us. It wasn't until he took the camera away from his face and said in an unmistakable Liverpudlian accent, "How are you, mate? This must be the birthday girl!" that I knew I was meeting John Lennon. Mick is always portrayed as the flamboyant, selfish womanizer, the perpetual devil, but he really is a sweet, caring man. As I followed him into into the apartment John was sharing with Mai Pang, I was so moved, I was concentrating on not bursting into tears.

John was in his famous "lost eighteen months" period, and he seemed to be in great shape. He sang "Happy Birthday" to me on acoustic guitar, followed by a whole bunch of other songs. It seemed to me that John was trying to escape from reality. I thought he was trying to have as much fun as he possibly could. Perhaps he was under Yoko's instructions to go out and sow his wild oats and get everything out of his system. He was only twenty-eight when he got together with Yoko, who was eight years older.

He didn't seem to have much interest in talking to me. The

press had been reporting at the time that Todd and John had a rancorous relationship. Todd had publically lambasted John for the way he had behaved in L.A. the night of the famous incident when he heckled the Smothers Brothers at the Troubadour. Meanwhile, I was pissed off with Todd for refusing to take me out and spending all of his time recording his next solo album. So when we got to John's that night, I called Todd at the studio. I thought it would be interesting to rub it in his face. I said, "Guess where I am?"

"Where?"

"Mick and I are at John Lennon's apartment."

"You're kidding!"

"No. And I think you should say hello to him." I handed John the phone. He said hello and they had a little exchange. When John gave the phone back to me, I said to Todd, "What happened?

"Why did you do that?" he snapped. "Why did you put him on the phone like that?"

"I thought the two of you should speak to each other! It's ridiculous."

Afterward, John said to me, "It must be difficult to live with him!" Then he started vividly recounting a recent UFO sighting. "Didn't I see a UFO, Mai?" he inquired eagerly, describing how it hovered by their terrace, which overlooked the East River, before buzzing away. I thought the whole thing was fascinating. This was one of my favorite subjects anyway and I really wanted to get into it. I had heard that other people had reported this same sighting, which made me wonder if the story might really be true. Why would John make it up? But Mick was in an altogether different place. He wanted to kiss everybody and was rolling around. "C'mon, Mick!" John barked. "Leave the girl alone. Can't you see she wants to listen to the UFO story?"

"Fuck the UFOs!" Mick shouted. "Let's all have some sex!" Horrified by that thought, Mai jumped up and cried out, "Let's all go to Chinatown!" Whereupon, despite the fact that Mick and I had just come from a Japanese restaurant and I would have much preferred to stay in their cozy apartment, we all ran out into the street, jumped into a cab, and sped downtown.

In the restaurant, John started eagerly challenging me to take the opportunity of my birthday to define who I was. "Well, who are you?" he kept saying, but in an encouraging, friendly way. Mai didn't seem to like the way he was going about it.

"John!" she admonished him. "John, stop it!" But he was adamant.

"No, no," he said, "let Bebe speak. She's a bright girl. Let her say what she feels." Turning to me, he went on prying: "Do you see yourself as part of Todd? How d'yer see yerself?"

John and I were having powerful eye contact, but I was terrified that I was going to say something stupid. I sure as hell didn't want to say something stupid to John Lennon on my birthday. People have different ways of finding themselves, and they dabble in different things. Because I was beautiful, I didn't have to be a waitress or a go-go dancer. I did upscale modeling, and made enough money to have fun. But I wasn't preparing for the future, starting up retirement accounts, which the girls do now. I was able to coast on my beauty. At that age, you don't realize that beauty doesn't last forever. And even when you're young, people keep telling you that you're not young anymore. When you're twenty-one and someone tells you you're not young anymore, it's devastating. That's a terrible signal to send to somebody. Plus, that night I was piss-drunk, and I was thinking, Ohhhh shit, when Mick, who'd stage-managed the whole event, stepped in.

"I think I know who Bebe is, John," he said in measured tones. "You know how you're walking along the street and there's a crack in the pavement, and there's a little flower coming up through the crack, and you wonder how the hell did it get there and how will it survive?"

The lump in my throat was about to burst, but I was still scared John was going to be sarcastic, because he was like that. I was afraid he'd say, Yeah, but flowers get squashed, but the conversation bubbled on pleasantly. John Lennon's eyes—oh man, if he wasn't special, then I'm insane. He was definitely a fallible and imperfect man —an idiot when he drank, and an absolute child when it came to discussing UFOs, or anything unknown. He was absolutely unattractive sometimes when he drank. But there was something about his perpetual quest for goodness that set him apart from people like Todd Rundgren, who, in my opinion, just pretended to be on a quest. John Lennon truly was. And he emanated a childlike purity. After hanging out with him that night and Todd scolding him on the phone for putting a Kotex on his head, I remember thinking that Todd had let me down spiritually and that someone like Lennon would not. Even though he was a Beatle, he continued to be like a salmon swimming upstream. What was beautiful about John was his patience. He was intolerant of stupidity, but he had a bit more patience for people's questions. Todd could sometimes be intolerant, cruel, and ruthless. He delivered his ideas, no matter how profound, in such a badass way that it was hard to benefit from his knowledge. His self-importance got in the way. He called himself "a futurist," but he scared me. With John Lennon, you felt you could be an imperfect person and still have an intelligent conversation.

I thought, This night is too good to be true. I have "Happy Birthday" sung to me by John Lennon. I have Mick Jagger saying I am a flower growing up through the sidewalk. I started to cry. What I love most about Mick is that he really did think of me like that, as a blossom. And that's what rock 'n' roll celebrates—the individual blossom that manages to grow through the concrete.

Mick and I hung out with David Bowie many times. Mick was worried because David was doing so much cocaine that he would hallucinate. One time, we were at his suite in the Sherry-Netherland Hotel and he asked us if we could see the angels flying outside the window. He made us go and look. "Don't you see them?" he said. "They're flying around."

"No, I don't, David," I replied.

"Well, maybe you just can't see them. Maybe I'm the only one who is meant to see them."

"Maybe," I said. "Maybe you've been chosen, because I don't see them." Mick was diplomatic all the way, though. He didn't like to mock David, because he still liked to have fun with him. They used to love to pick up beautiful black girls and take them back to the hotel and have mad sex with them. As a matter of fact, one of the times I was stupid enough to pick up my phone at 4:00 A.M., it was them calling me. Mick was saying, "We've got gorgeous black men here, and we're waiting for you."

"Oh! I'm going to take all of you on? Sounds just like me, doesn't it, Mick!" And I hung up. He called back again. It just went on and on, like the famous Warren Beatty stories of how he would call women in the night and whisper, "Hello . . ." That was Mick, too. So finally I just had to take the phone off the hook. That kind of thing happened when Todd was on the road.

David, Mick, and I went over to John's one night. We took a taxi, just the three of us. David wanted to take somebody along for protection, but Mick said, "Oh, darling, don't be ridiculous!" David was so paranoid—he was at the height of his cocaine psychosis. He had been exposed to a lot more drugs and insanity since I had hung out with him in 1973. But it was always a pleasant experience for me to see him. Mick and Bowie were mates. They would act very androgynous with each other.

The person who was always happiest to see me was John. I always felt very welcome and embraced by him. He liked either the Yoko look or the Bardot look, so I was his type. He wasn't competitive with Jagger, but he gave me a lot of attention and tried to hear what I was saying more than Mick did. Mick would often not hear the females in the room when the boys were around. When the men were talking, it was as if they were going into another room to have cigars and cognac after dinner; the women were definitely left out. But John wasn't like that. He was attentive to the women and interested in the female viewpoint, and he appeared to be interested in the things I would say, whereas Mick would just ignore me. So John made me feel very special.

On that particular night, John was attentive to me, but Mick and David stayed in the corner. I thought Mai seemed like John's housekeeper. Even though they were romantic, putting their arms around each other, exchanging little kisses now and then, she did not have the aura or physical presence of a girlfriend. Sometimes, after we left John's, Mick would bend my ear. "Oh, he still loves Yoko. He's not going to stay with Mai. This is all very temporary," he'd say.

We all sat on the bed and the floor together. There wasn't a lot of furniture; it wasn't a big apartment. It was a little penthouse; you had to go up some stairs to get to it. When we all said good-bye that night, John would do his *ta-ta* dance, twirling around in a little two-step. He was a funny creature, always doing a Marx Brothers routine. He was a combination of a man who wanted to be really knowledgeable and informed but also be the class clown. It always seemed as if he was covering a lot of pain.

When he and Yoko got back together, I got one of the towels they sent out. It said JOHN AND YOKO TOGETHER AGAIN. Then in the eighties, I became friends with Julian Lennon.

In September 1974, Todd was scheduled to do a publicity tour of London, Amsterdam, and Paris. He was going to do back-to-back interviews and photo sessions all day in each city to publicize *A Wizard/A True Star,* and he wanted me to be in all the pictures with him. We flew to London and had a beautiful suite with a river view at the Savoy Hotel. But unfortunately, I had been naughty and called Jimmy's office, letting him know that I was going to be in London at the Savoy, but not mentioning Todd. We were sitting down to breakfast in our suite and the eggs had just been served when an enormous bunch of flowers arrived with a card from Jimmy. Todd took my plate of scrambled eggs and threw them at the wall. Then he gave me his Jimmy Page lecture for the umpteenth time. "He's bad. He's evil. He's dark. He's the devil. He's got a woman and a kid. Once he gets tired of you, he'll retire you. Soon you'll be too old for him." So I promised right there and then that I would never see Jimmy Page again.

On our way back to New York after whirlwind visits to Amsterdam and Paris, we stopped in London again. Derek Taylor, a wonderful man who was the head of the Warner Bros. publicity department, had all this press laid on. Todd was the darling of the British rock press at this time. He and Derek were quite a pair on the publicity trail. But Jimmy had an indescribable allure, a pull on me. I had promised Todd that I would never see him again, but as soon as he went off to do some press and I was left at the Montcalm Hotel, I immediately called Jimmy up, and he talked me into coming around.

I called Derek and Todd at the studio and told them that I would meet them later that evening at the Speakeasy. I said I was going to go off and see some of my girlfriends from Models One. They were going to a press dinner, which I had been expected to attend. I told Todd that I really wanted to go and see these friends of mine, but I promised that I'd meet them later. What I didn't know was that Todd and Derek had bragged about me all day to the press and everybody was going to the Speakeasy that night all revved up to meet me.

I literally ran out of the Montcalm Hotel in a flimsy white dress and a pair of sandals; I didn't even take a purse with me. That's how Jimmy can get you going. I just wanted to see him. I got to Jimmy's house and we drank some champagne. At that age, I always did things spontaneously, never giving anything much thought. I was not thinking of the repercussions, because I didn't think I was going to get caught. I hadn't been there for fifteen minutes before we went to bed. I kept saying, "Jimmy, Jimmy, I've got to be at the Speakeasy at eleven." That's when I think he drugged me. I think we made love, but even that isn't clear. I don't know what happened after that. I am almost positive he put something in my drink. Maybe he wanted to push the envelope and end my relationship with Todd. He knew I was cheating, of course. He knew I was in London with Todd. And he knew that I was sneaking out to see him. But in Jimmy's defense, he never attempted to use a whip on me, never hurt me sexually, never tried to do anything weird to me. I do not know that side of him. When I hear the legends and myths, I'm always perplexed. I was Guinevere and he was Sir Lancelot and Todd was King Arthur. We had a whole little act down. And I really thought Jimmy loved me. I thought there was something there.

The next thing I knew, I woke up. When I realized it was the next day and that I had never shown up at the Speakeasy, the bottom fell out of my stomach. I panicked and called Derek Taylor. He screamed with relief. "*Oh my God! Where are you? We thought you were dead!* We've got the police looking for you! Where have you been? You didn't take your purse. You didn't take your clothes. . . ."

"Oh my God!" I exclaimed. "I went to see Jimmy and I fell asleep." I told Derek everything. I knew he wouldn't tell Todd. Derek said, "Oh my God, he must have drugged you. He must have put some Valium tablets in your wine. Bebe, you better get yourself over to the hotel, because I know Todd is leaving you here. . . ."

Jimmy knew I had called Derek, so he asked what had happened. "Can I help?" he said.

And I just moaned, "Oooohhh, I gotta get outta here. He's leaving me here!"

"Well, so what if he's leaving you here?"

"You don't understand. I have a life. I have a house." I was freaking out because I was so confused. I said, "How did this happen? Jimmy? How did this happen?"

"I don't know, darling. You fell asleep. I just thought you were tired."

"But I can't remember falling asleep," I said, starting to get even more upset.

I literally leapt up and put on my flimsy white dress. I didn't even put my shoes on. I sprinted downstairs, got a minicab, and rushed to the Montcalm, crying hysterically all the way. All I had on was this white see-through, flowing angel dress. An emotional heap of passion, I could have stepped right out of a Pre-Raphaelite painting. Jimmy has a strange hypnotic power. Sometimes I wonder if spewing his saliva into my mouth was his way of invading my whole being, because I was definitely at his beck and call. As I was pulling into the roundabout of the arch in front of the Montcalm, I saw Todd getting into a car and driving up and away. I leapt out of the cab and ran after the car, screaming, "*Todd, Todd, Stop, Stop! Aaarrrggghhhh!*" He stopped the car and I begged him, "Please, let me explain. Don't leave me!"

"Where have you been? We've been worried sick. The police have been looking for you. There's an APB out. . . ."

"Well, I'm here now."

"You have just twenty minutes to tell me what's going on, because I'm catching an airplane back to New York." He got out of the car and we went into the hotel. My bags were still in our suite. He had paid for my room for that day. He hadn't done a Continental Hyatt House hit on me.

I told him what had happened, and he cried. Todd never cried over Iggy or Mick, but he cried over Jimmy because he realized that I really liked Jimmy. Todd and I hurt each other a lot like that all the time. Todd was five years older than me, but I was too young to know better. We were all so young. I was trying to push Todd into giving me a marriage commitment, asking for fidelity. But Todd was afraid to give me that because of my actions. We had been creating a vicious circle, an eye for an eye. Which never works. Even though the Bible says it's legitimate, whenever you get into that syndrome, there's no end to it—it's like the infinity symbol. Todd and I cried and screamed and professed our undying love for each other that day in our suite at the Montcalm Hotel. He begged me never to talk to Jimmy again. He apologized for his infidelities and dalliances. I told him, "What's good for the goose is good for the gander," and he said, "I'm sorry; I'm sorry." I promised I would never do it again.

Todd said, "Bebe, if I'm going to stay here for another day, I need to go up to the Warner Bros. offices and straighten out some leftover matters." Which was fine with me, because I wanted a bath. I was a mess. He said, "I want you to stay in this room. I do not want you to leave the room." He had the hotel cut the phone off, and he took the key. All of which I humbly and thankfully agreed to. Anything to get into a hot bath.

But when Todd walked out that door, I became like a girl who needed her heroin. I threw on my clothes and went down to the lobby to call Jimmy and tell him what had happened and see what he would say. He told me I couldn't come back to him unless I was going to stay with him. Before I knew what I was saying, I told him that I would stay with him for a couple of days. He accepted that, even though my better judgment—the part of me that really loved Todd Rundgren, that from the depths of my heart really wanted to go and do the right thing with Todd—told me not to do it. I was propelled by some unstoppable force to betray him, ten minutes after swearing to him that I wouldn't get in touch with Jimmy. I couldn't stop myself. Maybe it was the music. Maybe it was his satanic Edwardian quality. Maybe it was the medieval Sir Lancelot vibe. I didn't know and I didn't care. I just wanted to be with Jimmy. In fact, I don't know how I waited for another twenty-four hours.

Todd wanted us to leave the next day, but I told him I wasn't ready to leave London. I said I wanted to stay for a couple of days and work out some stuff. Todd had this theory that Jimmy was evil and that he was good. And I was the virgin angel sacrifice in the middle of this duel between the two powers. He felt that Jimmy collected women and that once Jimmy had wooed me away from him and dominated me completely, I would become yesterday's news. Realizing what had happened, Todd very reluctantly gave me my airline ticket, two hundred pounds, and his blessing to go ahead and do what I had to do.

When I went back to Jimmy, he was a vision in a beautiful white suit. He got an erection, which I couldn't help noticing. He looked at me and said, "See what you do to me? You make me so hard."

Basically, we spent the whole time in bed, making love, talking, eating, and tripping our brains out on some very good mescaline. When you're tripping, an erection looks even larger than it is; it takes on a whole other dimension. I was afraid to have sex with him for a minute, because I was hallucinating that his penis stretched to the other side of the room. I needed to pull myself together and realize that it was an average-size penis.

Jimmy was very sexy. I think that he was having fun, enjoying a very pure exchange with a woman. I was different. Most of the women he knew were wilder and expected the macabre from him. I think if a woman had wanted her ass spanked and her hair pulled, he would gladly have delivered. If a woman had wanted to be beaten with whips, he would have obliged. If a woman wanted a cigarette put out on her chest, he would have done it.

On the second night I was there, he took me out to dinner. We traveled in a chauffeured Town Car to a famous Indian restaurant, where we had an excellent meal and wonderful wine. Jimmy had a real knack for keeping people at a distance when he was in public. It wasn't because people didn't know who he was. I think it was because they were genuinely afraid that he was Satan, that he had some sort of evil allure. People would not approach him because they were genuinely afraid that he was in cahoots with the devil. Mick Jagger is supposed to be Lucifer, but people never act that way around him. He gets a lot of "Hey, it's Mick Jagger. Hi!" I never saw that happen to Jimmy Page. Furthermore, unless it was a good-looking girl, Jimmy would act oblivious when someone was having a conversation with him. If some testosterone-driven guy came running up, saying, "Oh my God! You're my hero," he would just look straight ahead and not even acknowledge the person.

Around eleven o'clock one night, when we were tripping, we went into the large garden at the back of his house to look for fairies. If I hadn't known any better, I would have thought there were a couple out there, because I heard the bushes rattling and figured maybe there were some frigging fairies out there. At one point, he said, "Oh, I think there's one over there," and then this

95

man walked up to us. He was dressed all in black and had silver hair. He said, "Is Mr. Harris here?"

Jimmy explained that Richard Harris no longer lived in or owned the house.

Then later, something happened that made us both realize our relationship wasn't going to work. Jimmy wanted me to make breakfast. He said, "Why don't you go down to the kitchen and make breakfast for me." He wanted to see if I could cook. I was a great cook, but I was still inhibited and embarrassed at this point and I didn't think my breakfast would be up to par. So I went down and pretended to make breakfast, but I had the cook make it. The cook ended up telling Jimmy that I hadn't cooked it. So that didn't go over. He said to me later that night, when the cook made us dinner, that he knew that I hadn't made the breakfast.

Jimmy said I had to either stay with Todd or go with him. I had to make up my mind. I couldn't keep going back and forth. He said, "Stay here with me." He had several houses. The guy was incorrigible. I think he wanted the mother of his child, plus the child, to stay in the Plumpton, Sussex, house. And he was going to put me up in the London house, which was an extraordinarily beautiful one. Each room had a theme. His bedroom, for example, was the Butterfly Room; every surface was covered by large paintings of butterflies. He was feeling me out to see if I could graduate to official girlfriend status. If I had done things a little differently, I probably could have graduated to the next permanent position.

After two days, I kissed him good-bye. I figured that he had a lot to work out with his relationship and I had a lot to work out with mine, although I wasn't quite sure what would happen.

I ran home and told Todd, "I love you. He's too weird. I'm happy to be home." But there was still that weird Jimmy pull. I don't know what it is, but there's something extraordinary about that guy.

Later that month, Todd and I went to one of Albert Grossman's tepee parties and Todd fucked the goddamn anorexic cook, Cindy, again! But Todd was always fucking someone. So because of Todd's infidelity and my inability to get a solid commitment from him, I was always looking for another man.

CHAPTER 4

In the Court of the Rolling Stones 1974

I know you're bored baby
Tired baby
Don't give it all away
You know he's gonna find out about you someday
   "BORED BABY," LYRICS BY BEBE BUELL

When I got back from that trip to Europe with Todd, I really had my hands full. Todd had been right to fear Jimmy: Of all the men I saw in these years, Jimmy Page was the only one I was seriously considering leaving Todd for. Nobody in their right mind would have left Todd for Iggy Pop in his drug-induced state. I was not in love with David Bowie, nor he with me. He had a wife and a career. And while Mick was my childhood idol, I was never in love with him. Jimmy, on the other hand, was regal and otherworldly, like a person from another century. He was a lot like Henry VIII, only a lot more handsome, and Jimmy was slim, of course. He had a medieval attitude—not macho, but manly. The image he projected was: "I would stab—not shoot, but stab—any dragon for you."

If I could have been Jimmy Page's girlfriend, I would have been. If Jimmy Page had asked me to leave Todd, I would have. But in the end, he didn't.

Jimmy started bombarding the house with phone calls again when Todd was in the studio or on the road. The last phone call he made was absolutely frantic. He said he needed my date, place, and time of birth. Jimmy was big on astrology and he wanted to do my chart. I gave him the information, and he stopped calling me abruptly. I think he discovered I had a Mars-Venus link with Mick or something like that. And now, after fencing over the phone with Jimmy and maintaining my scene with Todd, I had to contend with Mick, who chose this moment to pursue me in his grand way. I mean, it was just beyond comprehension at that point. And it got back to Jimmy that I was hanging out with Mick. That was the kiss of death for Page. There was an incredible rivalry between them, as they had obviously slept with a lot of the same women. Mick always used to say to me, "Do not sleep with Jimmy Page."

And Jimmy used to say to me, "You slept with *Mick?*"

"Rubycon"—the point of no return.
Mind expanding music from Tangerine Dream.

rubycon
by
tangerine dream

On Virgin Records and Tapes.

Back in New York, I was in my element. The *Playboy* centerfold was about to come out. I was the "It Girl" at Max's Kansas City, where I would go every night and where everybody knew I was a Ford model but that I preferred being the wild child, someone who ran around with Alice Cooper, Todd, and Bowie. Nineteen seventy-four was the peak year for the rock 'n' roll couple. Cindy Lang and Alice Cooper,

Rick Derringer, Todd, me, and Liz Derringer "double dating,"
1975/BOB GRUEN

David and Angela Bowie, Jerry Hall and Bryan Ferry, Mick and
Bianca, Todd and me. The golden age of the rock couple had begun
with Patti and George Harrison in the sixties. Now it was reaching its
apotheosis, as I discovered when I became ensnared in Mick Jagger's
net that fall.

Mick was a traditional Englishman when it came to marriage.
He wanted Bianca to stay home and take care of their daughter Jade
while he did what he pleased, which turned out to be seeing a lot of
me, among others. Mick had become a constant in my life. We
were true friends. In fact, he had become one of my best friends and
he called me from everywhere all the time. I adored him. And I did
look forward to being with him sometimes. So when he called me
in September and asked, "Bebe, where have you been?" I pretty
much knew what was coming once he heard the answer.

"Oh God, Bebe, not Jimmy! Next it's gonna be Rod Stewart!"
Another one who ruffled his feathers. They ruffled each other's
feathers. They were always vying for the same pussies. So I went to

99

dinner with Mick, and I think he saw that I really liked Jimmy. He could also see that this feeling was different—that I might be in love with Jimmy. On the other hand, I think he wanted to get me alone and make love to me again. Mick has subtler ways of dealing with the competition. He's a sexual competitor.

I saw Mick several times that September and October. On one occasion, he took me over to the Sherry-Netherland, which is just across the street from his favorite hotel, the Plaza. We were going to visit David Bowie and the British singer Dana Gillespie. Shortly after we arrived, they brought out their ben-wa balls and wanted to have an orgy! I lost it, but Mick just laughed it off. He said, "C'mon, darling, we're leaving." As we left, he chided David and Dana, saying, "You two should know better! This is not for Bebe." And once again, I felt felt protected, which is one of the most important emotions for me. I don't want to disappoint anybody reading this book, because I'm sure in every other book you've read about them, Jimmy Page and Mick Jagger are described as sexual deviants. But with me, I swear that sex was really romantic, normal, nice, and sweet.

On another occasion, I was driving upstate to our house in Woodstock and stopped to visit Mick at the Plaza on the way. Mick begged me to stay with him. "I've got to go," I said, "I've got to get back to Todd." But Mick wouldn't stop kissing me and he kept saying, "I want you to stay. We'll make love; we'll eat strawberries."

"I can't make love," I told him. "I've got to go."

"But Bebe, I love you!"

"*What?*"

This just came out of left field, as far as I was concerned. I'd never heard him say that before. I'd heard "I adore you"; "Isn't she charming?"; "Isn't she delightful?"; "She's a daisy coming up through the cracks in the cement." But I had never heard "I love you." He actually confessed: "I want you! I don't want to be with Apples!" (Appolonia was a European model with whom he was having an affair at the time, a well-publicized one.) It was obvious that his marriage to Bianca was a sham, but she still had the ability to hurt him. I think there was genuine love there, but I think they were hell-bent on one-upmanship. Bianca was truly a Latin; she wasn't going to allow him to get the best of her.

Apart from Todd, I felt the most comfortable with Mick. I could go over, walk in the door, take off my clothes, put on a Plaza Hotel robe, put my feet up, and Mick would rub them. We were like an old couple, but we weren't. He had a handful of women, about five of us, his wife included, and I was one of his favorites. If I'd had wanted the relationship with Mick to be more, it could have been. Liz Derringer tells me that's true, because he told her that he loved me. He said that he didn't know if he would ever be able to stop making love to other women but that he could see us being boyfriend and girlfriend. I could have graduated to an official lover. (The way the Stones run their camp is much like the royals.)

As I got to see a lot of him, I discovered the private Mick was just what I thought he would be: brilliant, articulate, and very sane—in control of his mind and body and extremely charismatic and powerful. Furthermore, his truly international penis sported itself in trousers better than any other penis I have ever known. Above all, he was fun. He'd come up behind me at a party when I didn't know he was there and whisper, "I'd come to your house." He was charming, and all my friends told me that he really loved me.

One time, he showed up at Horatio Street at 4:00 A.M. I saw his footprints in the snow leading up to my door and I thought as I looked out the window, Holy shit, those are Mick Jagger's footsteps leading to my door! He transported me to Wonderland. You could smell the crisp scent of Christmas in the air. I called down to him, "What are you doing here?"

"I've got some yogurt," he called up. Who else could get away with a line like that? Mick never took limos to get around New York except when he was with Bianca. He just loved walking the streets of this very walkable city.

Mick has absolutely zero prejudices; he loves girls of all kinds and colors equally. He's beyond categories. I loved him dearly, but I realized that I would never want to be his official girlfriend, because I could not have handled the constant public persona. I knew it would make me lose touch with myself, lose who I was becoming, and I did not want to disappear just as I was beginning to find out who I really was.

Mick demanded a certain chic of his women. Before we went out, if he didn't like what I was wearing, he would send me back to put on another outfit. He always kidded me about my platform shoes. If you had a dress and you couldn't find the right shoes to go with it, you called Mick. He bought me dresses, flowers, and expensive perfumes. He would fly me to meet him on his private plane. He would think nothing of spending five hundred dollars for wine at dinner. But he also spent hours looking for bargains. Mick's a genius with skin. He always knew what creams to use, and he often shared his beauty products with me. He'd say, "Let me look at that, Bebe," and then he'd produce a jar and start massaging the contents into my skin. He told me how to steam my face, what herbs to use. No woman on earth knows more about cosmetics than Mick does.

Bianca was very sweet to me. She would clutch my hand and ask me to sit next to her at parties, referring to me as "Mick's little friend," which was amusing, since I was two inches taller than her husband and a good six inches taller than she was. Bianca was always complimentary. I used to clip my nails very short and paint them bright red, which wasn't considered fashionable. She said how chic they looked. That was typical of her: she always complimented me on my hair, my clothes. She tried to make me feel like a million bucks. Of course, by doing all this, she was also saying to Mick, Go ahead and have your little girlfriends; it doesn't bother me.

What was really wonderful about being with Mick and the Rolling Stones was that they brought with them a whole world of magic. At the time, Led Zeppelin and Alice Cooper were just as popular and impressive as the Stones, but the Stones possessed one thing the others did not: the ability to maintain distance and approachability simultaneously. And backstage, they always made you feel like the Queen of Sheba. They had beautiful food and the best wine and alcohol. They brought a certain elegance to the rock 'n' roll party. And if you were one of the beauties they wanted to be around, they treated you wonderfully. Doors would just swing open like the wind.

The November 1974 issue of *Playboy* hit the stands in mid-October and blew up my life. I was prominently identified as Todd's girlfriend in the accompanying article and photo captions. Mick was also mentioned as a friend of ours, who "called regularly from Montauk," where he used to stay at Andy Warhol's estate. That annoyed Jimmy Page no end. The centerfold made me the most sexually desirable girl in rock 'n' roll, but, simultaneously, it also flushed my American modeling career down the toilet, taking with it the countless hundreds of thousands of dollars I could have earned. Eileen Ford could not be appeased. I picked up the phone one day and heard her say acidly, "You wouldn't do lingerie for three hundred dollars an hour, but you'd go buck naked!" This was the beginning of a forty-five-minute diatribe about loyalty and betrayal, which she concluded by firing me.

"You could have made millions!" she claimed. It took me some time to forget that, because she was probably right. I could have done *Sports Illustrated*. I could have gone all the way. In my defense, I did not think that doing *Playboy* would all but rule out any grand possibilities in modeling in the United States. I also had no idea that if I did the centerfold, everybody would take it for granted that I had had sex with Hugh Hefner, or that it would be like a gauntlet thrown down before every rock star, all of whom now felt as if they had to conquer me sexually.

The shadow the *Playboy* centerfold cast over my life was deepened by a scandal that erupted around Hugh Hefner the month that issue came out. His top female aide, a bright, personable woman, whom he relied upon greatly on a daily basis, had become involved with a man who was trafficking in cocaine without her knowledge. The authorities seized upon the opportunity to harass anybody standing for sexual freedom, and the FBI put Hefner under surveillance. As the heat mounted, the aide committed suicide. In all the time I worked for *Playboy* or stayed at the mansion, I never saw drugs or heard of drugs being used, but Hefner was shattered, and the incident cast a pall over the *Playboy* empire during the mid-1970s. Then, as if the November issue of the magazine was not cursed enough, the girl on the cover, Claudia Jennings, died in a horrible car crash on the freeway out in L.A. a couple of years later. She had been a real little spitfire, a B-movie queen, hung out with the Rolling Stones, and partied with the best of them. So the issue became "historic" for all three of us.

In retrospect, I believe I sabotaged my modeling career because

I knew I would never be happy as a high-fashion model, no matter how much money I made. At the time, relations between models and rock stars were rare. *Après moi le déluge*, as they say, but the bottom line is, I wanted to be accepted as a rock 'n' roll person. I wanted to be Billy the Kid in skirts and live the life of a maverick. As it turned out, it would be some time before I achieved this goal, but at least I had taken a major step in that direction.

Playboy sealed my fate, and it did so by presenting a sexual image of me that had nothing to do with rock 'n' roll and which I was not capable of living up to. I was not Edy Williams, the well-endowed B actress in Russ Meyer pictures, who dressed revealingly and made a spectacle of herself every time she entered a room, throwing her arms up in the air in a universal embrace. *Playboy* brought me great visibility and a great sexual image, but it once again forced me into being somebody I wasn't. People thought I was a highly charged sexual creature, when in fact, it takes a lot to stimulate me. I can turn it on and off like a light switch, but that centerfold made everybody want to engage in sexual intercourse with me. Which was difficult for me, because sex is not the biggest thing on my agenda—perhaps because of Catholicism, or perhaps because of the things that happened to me as a child. Another thing about me that upsets men is that I am always shy about my body. I'm schizophrenic like that. Put a camera in front of me and, *whoosh*, off will come everything, but, to this day, if I'm walking around the bedroom and somebody else is there, I still wrap sheets around my body.

To keep a rock 'n' roll man intrigued, one must be athletic sexually, and I think a lot of my flirtations and my flings were short-lived because I was never able to perform to capacity. That became the central struggle of my life. Everybody automatically assumed that I was tenacious, wild, uninhibited, liberated, all the things I wasn't. Despite all the brouhaha, I was still just a repressed little Catholic schoolgirl.

Todd's reaction to the *Playboy* explosion was pretty reasonable. At least he was prominently featured, so that made him look good. But of course he was also aware of it being like a red flag, which would incite all the rock bulls to take a run at me.

Todd and I stayed together through many more ridiculous ups

and downs. Todd would always be fucking these nondescript road tramps, whereas I would be fucking major icons, but even that was a double-edged sword. I really thought that I was the only girl they desired. Todd constantly explained to me that the more I did this, the more I would be labeled a groupie, even though he was the one who was always telling me I *wasn't* a groupie, that I had too much class.

The Wilhelmina Agency snapped me up when Ford dropped me. Wilhelmina devised a brilliant comeback strategy. Explaining that Europeans had much less puritanical tastes than Americans, she sug-

gested I move to London for a few months and work in England, France, and Italy. This offer dovetailed with my heart's desire when Jimmy Page suddenly started calling me again, requesting that I join him in London. *Playboy* had paid me five thousand dollars for the centerfold, enough money to make it possible for me to do pretty much whatever I wanted. To make matters even more perfect, Todd was planning to travel on a six-week spiritual quest to India, leaving

FRANK LAFITTE

me free to play out my fate without being concerned he'd hear about it. When Peter Grant sent me a cable on behalf of Jimmy, officially informing me that Page was going to be in London during November and would like to see me, I cabled back, announcing my imminent arrival. Telling Todd that I was going to be modeling in London for several weeks, I took off for the first time on my own, full of the greatest expectations.

From the outset, the trip provided the perfect script for *A Hard Day's Night*–style comedy. Peter Grant had instructed me to telephone the Equinox bookshop on arrival in London. I phoned from New York to make sure they knew I was arriving and spoke to the bookstore's manager, Eric, who very politely said, "Just come to the store. We'll sort you out, and then you'll go out to the country."

As soon as I actually got to the bookshop, Eric explained that I could not stay there, although Jimmy owned the shop and a comfortable apartment above it, because Charlotte, the mother of his child, was going to be staying there!

"What?" I said,

"Jimmy has given her the boot," he explained.

"For me?" I inquired humbly.

"Well, it doesn't quite work like that," Eric replied.

"What do you mean, Eric?"

"Well, something happened last night. . . ."

"What happened?"

Then the story came tumbling out: "Chrissie and Ronnie Wood were out in the country visiting Jimmy and Charlotte for the weekend, and Jimmy and Chrissie have pissed off together!" he explained in that charming way the British have of using the terminology of bodily functions as shorthand. He continued the story, like a child trying to explain something he does not understand. "After all the drink and drugs, Chrissie and Jimmy pissed off down the hill to the boathouse, where they were caught bonking! Woody woke up, to be greeted by a hysterical, disheveled Charlotte running up the hill to let Woody know what was happening."

At that point, it appeared that Charlotte thought she was going to piss off with Woody. She went to Woody's house after Woody had invited her there, saying, "If they're going to piss off down the hill, let's you and me just piss offf to my house and let them sort this out." Back at Woody's, however, Woody and Charlotte did not click in any way. Now, as a result, Woody was missing a wife, Charlotte was banished to the bookshop with Jimmy's daughter, Scarlet, while Jimmy and Chrissie stayed at the country house in Plumpton, Sussex. And Eric was now telling me as decorously as possible to piss off out of it. (Jimmy did not speak to me for many years. In retrospect, I suspect he had been on a slow boil since I'd left him in London the previous September. Furthermore, on hearing of my several recent encounters with Mick, and with the release of *Playboy*, which emphasized my relationships with Todd and Mick but not him, he had decided to take his revenge by leading me to think that I was going to have a wonderful time with him while Todd was in India.)

I suddenly thought of my father protector, Derek Taylor! Derek had taken a shine to me earlier that fall, and I just adored him. He made me feel safe and protected. After bursting into tears at the complete absurdity of what was happening, I called Derek from the bookshop. Upon hearing my voice, he immediately said, "What have you done now, child?"

The British rock world is a very small one and Derek seemed to know exactly what was going on before I had even tried to explain it. "Come on up to the office," he said. "It'll be fine." Derek really catered to his stars, and because I was Todd Rundgren's girlfriend, he always took good care of me. I also think he thought I was a bit of a spitfire. He was one of the people who said to me, "You have so much star quality. Why do you give so much of what you've got to these guys? Why don't you just tell them to piss off and go off and do your own thing?" Many people said that to me, but at that point, I was too young to understand it. I was from a generation that didn't think that far into the future. We thought opportunities would always exist, that we would be fifteen forever.

I took a cab to the Warner Bros. office and ran up to Derek's office. He greeted me with wonderful open arms. He lighted some incense, gave me a cup of the kind of tea only the British know how to make, and requested that I tell him the story. After I'd brought him up-to-date with the Jimmy Page saga, he said, "Hold on a minute, dear. I think I can solve your dilemma."

Half an hour later, Ron Wood tumbled into the room, and after introductions had been made and we'd compared notes and expressed mutual sympathy, he graciously invited me to stay at his house. Mindful of what had just happened to Charlotte when she'd tried to stay there, and not wanting to take part in this game of musical chairs any longer than necessary, I sniffled, saying that that would not be necessary, thank you very much, since I could afford to pay for my own hotel.

"Why would you want to stay in a hotel when you can stay in the

Wick?" Ronnie responded. (At the time, unbeknownst to me, his house was British Rock Central. The Stones were trying to find a replacement for Mick Taylor, who had just announced that he was leaving the band after five years of brilliant work. Keith had actually moved into Woody's gamekeeper's cottage, purportedly to avoid the policemen who had staked out his Cheyne Walk townhouse, although actually, he was trying to work Woody into the band.) Typical of Ronnie, he never mentioned anything about this, explaining the house's pedigree to me instead. He had bought it from the British actor Sir John Mills, father of Hayley. My ears perked up. Hayley Mills had had an enormous influence on me, along with millions of other kids in the 1960s, by appearing in a few sentimental movies—from *Pollyanna* to *The Parent Trap*—for Disney, which had made her an enormous star. Looking remarkably like Mick Jagger in his 1963 incarnation, she had released in me the desire to become a professional rock 'n' roller by playing the guitar and singing "Let's Get Together" in *The Parent Trap*. When Woody told me I could stay in Hayley's room, I smiled for the first time that afternoon. As Derek ushered us out of his office, he admonished Woody: "Take care of her. She's a nice girl, and her mother will be checking in."

As we drove out to Richmond Hill in Woody's Jaguar, he entertained me with stories about the house and its antecedents. As we drove up the Wick's driveway, I saw what looked from the front like a surprisingly small house. Two columns framed a red door. But when I walked in, I began to see its true dimensions. It stretched back some distance to beautiful rambling gardens. There was a huge entrance foyer dominated by a bright black-and-white-checkered floor. To my right, two doors opened into a comfortably furnished library. Straight ahead, another set of double doors led into a living room. To my left, a grand staircase carpeted in royal red led upstairs.

Hayley's bedroom was not large, but it was comfortably furnished with wall-to-wall carpet in hunter green and an antique double bed. Near the bay window was a comfortable seating area. The bathroom was twice as big and featured a large deep bath. After I had unpacked, taken a bath, and changed, Woody took me out to dinner. We got along like the proverbial house on fire. Both of us loved telling and listening to stories, and between us, we had enough to fill an anthology. After dinner, we went to Tramps, London's equivalent of Max's, where we ran into Rod Stewart and Angela Bowie, both of whom drove back to join us at the Wick. When we got back, I went upstairs and changed into my pajamas, because by now the long day, jet lag, and emotional trauma had taken their toll and I was ready to crash. I was frantically trying to contact Todd, which was impossible, since he was en route, but by now I was feeling like a real asshole, having made another big mistake in trying to run off with Jimmy. I'd done something horrible and I wanted to make amends. I knew I wouldn't be able to rest until Todd had forgiven me. I left messages for him at Albert's office in the States and made sure Derek got a message through to him that I was staying at the Wick, anything to emphasize that I wasn't with Jimmy. When I went back downstairs, Mick Jagger, Keith Richards, Ron Wood, Rod Stewart, and Eric Clapton were in the library, drinking, talking, and smoking. I thought I had died and gone to heaven. Keith gave me a big hug and mumbled affectionately in his inimitable manner, "How's it going, man? How's Todd doing?"

Mick gave me a big hug. Woody said, "Ooooh, she came to see James, and James is with Chrissie!" and they all started cracking jokes.

But Mick said, "I told you about him, didn't I? Didn't I tell you he's a devil? You're just not kinky enough for him, not weird enough. If you'd been weirder, you'd be the one at Plumpton now."

"What do you mean!" Woody half-choked, half-screamed. He was trying to laugh, but it hurt him horribly that Jimmy had done that. I think he felt awful. But now he could see that I was exhausted.

"Go on up to bed, dear," Woody told me, and I gratefully followed his instructions. In Hayley Mills's magic bedroom, I slid gratefully between the embracing covers, wearing a very down-home pair of plaid pajamas. I settled into the luxurious double bed like a fairy princess.

Just as I was slipping away I heard a rustle and felt a body snuggling up behind me as I lay on my side. Who's that?" I whispered urgently.

"It's Woody. I've just come for a cuddle and to make sure you're all right, dear," he said. Hospitable blokes, the English, I thought, murmuring, "Okay." And he cuddled, making no attempt to interfere with me, but finally I had to ask him to leave. I wanted to be alone! And he shuffled off.

What seemed like an hour later, I heard another rustle and felt a body snuggling up behind me. "Who's that?" I whispered again, not knowing what to imagine.

"It's Mick. I've just come for a cuddle."

"Okay," I said. And he cuddled, but his desires were quite clearly less innocent than Woody's. Mick wanted to have sex! I said, "I'm tired, darling; I've got to go to sleep; puleeeze go upstairs!"

"It's cold up there," he whined. "I don't like it up there. It's freezing up there. Please, Bebe, please." But after all I had just gone through, I didn't want him there. I was too cranky and emotionally used up, I didn't want sexual comfort, and I was ravenous for sleep. Finally, he reluctantly shuffled off.

I was almost asleep when a third person knocked lightly on the door. "Hello, dear, can I come in for a cuddle?"

"Which one are you?"

"It's me, darling, Rod."

"Oh God! Go home to Dee!" I told him (Dee Harrington was his beautiful model girlfriend) and he evaporated.

Alone at last, I couldn't help wondering how many girls in my position would have turned down three of the most attractive men in my world in one night.

I was the first one up in the morning, since my body was still on American time. In fact, I was well rested, to the point of being truly curious as to what kind of a wild and woolly place I had ended up in. So I climbed cautiously out of bed and started to explore. Woody's room was right across the hall from mine. I decided to start there first. I crept in. Woody had a bed that looked as if it was large enough to accommodate an entire rock band, but as I approached it and peered in, I came upon just one tiny little person lying there, Angela Bowie. Uh-oh, I started thinking. What happened here while I was sleeping? So I said, "Angela! Wake up!" I'd only met her once, briefly. "Angela, where are all the boys?" I whispered. "Where is everyone?"

"I don't know," she said. "When I came to bed, everyone disappeared." My first thought was that they hadn't wanted to sleep with her. "Aren't you Todd's girlfriend?" she asked. "What are you doing here?" I realized that I didn't have an answer for that one. Her chest looked like a man's. I have never seen a woman with such an androgynous look. She resembled a beautiful alien. I envied her, because I had to carry around my balloons. Meanwhile, she put her sleeping mask on, muttered something in her fake British accent, and went back to sleep. I pressed on.

I looked everywhere. I went down to the studio—nobody. I ran into the kitchen—empty. I walked into the living room. I couldn't find them anywhere. Finally, I asked Woody's manservant, "Where do you think everybody is?"

"There's a room at the top," he told me sotto voce. "Why don't you try the top?" I climbed the stairs to the third floor with mounting anticipation. I opened the door to what was definitely a secret room, and there were Woody, Mick, Keith, Rod, and Eric, all in a row, passed out, a big blanket covering them. Woody came around momentarily and, with his perfect comic timing, whispered, "Darling, you've got to climb in with us. She'll be after you in a minute!" And then everybody started laughing. They were acting like a bunch of little schoolboys. None of them had wanted to have sex with Angela, but I don't think a single one knew how to turn down a sexual advance. They told me not to let her know the room existed and to give her some tea and get rid of her.

I went back to find Angela, who wasn't going to let me have an easy time of it. "Darling, where did you stay last night?" she asked, her voice dripping sarcasm.

"I've got my own room," I said

"Who did you sleep with in it?" she asked.

I bristled. "Nobody. I don't want to sleep with anybody. I miss Todd. I love Todd."

"Oh, yeah, sure, darling!" she replied, insulting me. "Yeah, right!" putting on her fake British accent. But basically, she was just jealous. Mick had told me their monster single from *Goat's Head Soup* ("Angie") was not about Angela. It was about David!

———

I spent the entire month of November living in Woody's magic
mansion. I adored staying in Hayley's room, but I soon gravitated
toward sleeping on one side of Woody's eight-foot-wide bed, because it was next to the only phone on the second floor. Todd would
call me occasionally at odd hours, and I wanted to be able to answer
the phone before anybody else did and he got too many wrong
ideas. Woody and I soon developed a close relationship as brotherly
mates and enjoyed our time together immensely. The only time
there were any sexual shenanigans in that bed was one night when
Mick jumped into bed with us. At first, it was very playful, like
an adolescent wrestling match. I was wearing pajamas, Woody had
on some leopard-style underwear, but Mick, being the ringmaster
of the sexual romp, was naked. With my back to Mick, I was snuggling toward Woody, when Mick reached around to touch me and
touched Woody's willy by accident. We all leapt into the air.
Woody screamed, "Oh my God, you touched my cock!" Mick
was screaming, "Get the Valium!" I ran away from both of them,

heading upstairs, where I ended up spending the night with Mick.

Normally, we'd wake up every afternoon around 5:00 P.M. Woody's man would bring in the tea and toast and we'd discuss our plans for the night—specifically, where we were going to go for dinner. Then I would repair to Hayley's bathroom for my glorious bath. Sometimes, I'd take long bubble baths and hold court. It was Mick who especially loved to come and talk to me while I was having a bath. He'd perch on a stool and we'd have wonderful long conversations. It gave me the idea of having an interview show where I would interview people from the bath. Every time I took a bath, I would get more visitors than a store window. But the best thing about living at the Wick was how I was treated as one of the boys. It was just loads and loads of fun. Woody kept me in stitches most of the time.

We'd get dressed, rendezvous with Keith and whoever else was around—Mick was often there—for a cocktail before departing en masse to one of London's fabulous restaurants. Sometimes, we'd visit clubs, but we'd usually reconvene at Woody's, where they had everything they wanted, including a recording studio in the basement. The Stones were recording parts of *It's Only Rock 'n' Roll*. Woody, David Bowie, and Mick recorded the title track there one night. Woody was one of the few people to have a VCR at that time, and we watched tons of movies. Everybody would gather for *Monty Python's Flying Circus* and *The Benny Hill Show*, the two comedy shows most popular with the rock establishment. An enormous amount of time was spent lying around the elegant library on beautiful Moroccan cushions, smoking pot, drinking, and having fascinating conversations. Since they could never go shopping without being mobbed, people would come around to show them various clothes and measure them for their orders. I never saw cocaine while I was there, but then, I wasn't into drugs. Drugs were a lot different in England. People smoked pot and hash with cigarettes. So I hardly ever smoked, because I didn't smoke tobacco. And for some weird reason, the cocaine they got in England was always a hell of a lot better than the blow we got in the States. During the month I lived at Woody's, I was surrounded by a lot of mayhem, but I didn't participate in much of it. I would drink my cabernet—everybody teased me about my red wines. I remember Mick bringing me this gorgeous bottle of five-hundred-dollar wine—a 1950s vintage—when I was staying at the Wick. Mick did not just dole out money. He's not like that. I've watched him give cabdrivers fifty-cent tips, which is upsetting, but then I've also seen him turn around and give a woman selling flowers on the street a fifty-dollar bill, telling her to go feed her babies. You never know which Mick you're going to get. Mick never handed me money. He gave me presents instead.

I always looked to Keith as the head of the family. The sensible one, the wise owl, because he always had wisdom, logic, and common sense about all things, in spite of his "I don't care" attitude about everything. This was the time in his life when he was somewhere between being the beautiful Keith and the ravaged Keith. He had a prominent black tooth, but he was still skinny and had a great rooster haircut and a smooth, angular face, which wasn't all lined like a map of the moon yet, and he always wore black kohl around his eyes. He was a pirate, but when people would get excited, he'd say, "Oh, oh, don't get so fucking excited. It's ridiculous. Mick is such a drama queen. Everybody calm down. Just do another line and shut up!" He was perennially laid-back and understanding. I would be on the phone all the time, because I had telephonitis. Woody would get upset, and I remember Keith saying to Woody, "Well, what do you expect! She's twenty-one! Of course she's gonna be on the phone all the time! Leave her alone. She's a child. Let her talk on the fucking phone."

"I forgot," Woody admitted. "She *is* twenty-one, isn't she?"

"Yeah!" exclaimed Keith. "She's gonna talk on the phone! Don't worry about it!" It was almost as if he had been protecting me since I was ten years old. And I, in turn, loved being the girl Keith would consult about his daily problems: Which gun should he carry? Which knife should he sharpen? "What do you think of this scarf, Bebe?" he'd ask. These were the tough decisions a girl helped a Rolling Stone make in the world of rock 'n' roll.

I was going through this period when I was questioning spirituality, because Todd was going through a really intense period, a spiritual quest, and he was reading books about chakras and the seven rays of Buddhism, reincarnation, and Zen. And Keith was well versed in this area—brilliant, in fact. He was open to all types of cultural interpretations of the spiritual realm. He told me all about the Mayans and the pyramids and we discussed the mystery of Stonehenge. Keith had a theory that the Bible was really a series of fairy tales.

"How's Todd doing?" he would ask me. "What's he up to?"

"Oh, well," I'd say, acting vague because I didn't know very much about the subject and was on my guard. "He's fine. He's in India."

"That's nice, but how do you feel about it? Are you going to any of these meetings and retreats with him. Are you interested?" Once, when he overheard me making a flippant remark about Todd's quest at a party, he was on my case like a shot. "How dare you criticize somebody who is on a spiritual quest!" he demanded. He appeared to be so angry with me, I was on the verge of tears, but then he explained to me gently that you shouldn't criticize something you don't know anything about and don't really understand.

Everybody seemed to revere Keith, perhaps in part because they knew what the public then was not aware of—that he was the musical genius behind the Rolling Stones, that the band's sound, their songs, came primarily from him, although Mick was the only one who appeared to be able to unlock them successfully. Mick is one of the greatest performers of the twentieth century, but he is also a little boy, very childish, egotistical, and flamboyant. Whereas Keith is the voice of wisdom and experience, and he has the wear and tear of an old warrior about him.

I really loved Keith, and he treated me like a jewel. One time when we all arrived at a party, Mick just got out of the car, but Keith got out, twirled and extended his hand to help me out, then twirled back and executed a complex bow that would have put him in good standing alongside Sir Walter Raleigh. I remember thinking, Jesus, that was gorgeous. He had class, and he was a little more considerate of women, of their feelings and opinions, than Mick was.

One night, we were driving to a party at Robert Stigwood's in Keith's Bentley. Keith was at the wheel, and Ronnie, Mick, a girl called Beatrice, and I were in the back. Keith was a very good driver. He was a bit flippant with the one-finger steering and the knee driving, but he inspired trust. Near Woody's house, there was a rotary, and when Keith came to it, he drove around it three or four times. He kept going around and around and around like a delighted child.

"Oh, Keith, stop it," Mick was saying. "Take us to the country!"

"But I love to go around the roundabout," Keith said, laughing. "Just one more time." So he continued driving around, and sure enough, the flashing blue light of a police car suddenly appeared behind us. It was then that I discovered how much I really was one of the boys. Before the policeman could reach the car, everybody transferred the contents of their pockets to Beatrice's (she couldn't speak English), but nobody attempted to give anything to me. We pulled over, and the officer asked Keith, "Why do you need to drive around the rotary so many times?"

"I was pointing out some very important locations to the two young ladies in the car," Keith indicated airily, despite the fact that it was pitch-dark outside.

"Well, why didn't you just stop?" the young officer asked.

"Ah, that's not really in my nature," Keith retorted. "I like to keep moving." It was a lovely Keith Richards kind of answer, considering he invented the idea of the rhythm guitar as sex, but I thought, That's it—we're dead now. Then he added that he was attempting to explain to the young French girl what a roundabout was, because they didn't have them in France.

"What do you mean, they don't have them in France?" the policeman responded, losing his way now. "Every country has them. It's just a rotary, Mr. Richards. Perhaps, sir, you've been abusing substances."

Keith dismissed this notion with feigned surprise. "Of course not." he said. "I wouldn't be driving if I had."

Keith can act so sincere, and he just charmed the policeman out of pursuing the offense, which wasn't really an offense anyway.

"Well, Mr. Richards, please be on your way. Please go to your destination."

"Oh, yes, sir, immediately," Keith replied, and without batting an eye, he started the big car up again and we sped off to Robert Stigwood's house, where there was a wild party for Eric Clapton's birthday in full swing.

It was as elite a party as the Swan Song party in L.A. had been, with the curious absence of any females other than myself, Beatrice, and Pattie Boyd, the woman Eric Clapton had written "Layla" for. George Harrison had written countless songs for her, and every

English rock star I encountered, except Keith, appeared to want to be with her. Woody was madly in love with her. Mick couldn't understand why she went to bed with George Harrison, Eric, and Woody but wouldn't go to bed with him! Stigwood was gay, so he had his own crowd, but I wondered about the rest of them. I mean, Patti was with Eric. Were the rest of them all gay?

Patti took one look at me and whisked me off to the bathroom for a summit conference. "So, are you sleeping with Woody?" she began.

"No," I said. "Well, I am sleeping with him, but we're not, like, sleeping together."

"What do you mean by that?"

I could see that she was fond of him. It was interesting. Mick had told me how he lusted after her. Eric almost killed himself over her. Woody, who had had an affair with her, claimed she was the ultimate girl. I saw her in *A Hard Day's Night* when I was eleven, and I thought she was the ultimate rock star's girlfriend. And here I was, finally sitting opposite her, and I realized that she was just a normal woman—one who had very large breasts. That was another thing that was very shocking. I was thinking, Pattie Boyd has these really large tits, but she has this tiny little body. Then I thought, That's the key—the Barbie Doll body.

One night, Woody went up to Birmingham to play a gig with the Faces. I was in the house alone, watching a movie on his VCR in the library. The phone rang on several occasions, but every time I answered it, the caller would hang up. Finally, the doorbell rang, and it was the police.

"Are you Miss Buell?"

"Yes, sir, I am."

"What are you doing here?"

"I'm a houseguest."

"Well, Mr. Wood's wife has called our police department and asked us to inform you that you are a trespasser and you are to leave the premises."

I said, "Officer—if that is what they call you over here—I want to tell you that's not the truth. Mr. Wood's wife has run away with Jimmy Page. She's calling you, telling you to have me removed, but I am not even having an affair with her husband. I'm just a houseguest. She's trying to create a disturbance and cause trouble for me." He laughed in an "I get the picture" way. Then I added, "Mr. Wood will be home around three or four A.M." He continued to insist that the police had been informed I had broken into the house. I said, "Officer, look at this house; it's a fortress. Where would I possibly break in? And don't you think that after finding me here, Mr. Wood would have told me to leave?" Then I took him upstairs and showed him my room. Woody killed me for that.

"What you bring 'im into the house for?" he asked me later.

"Because I wanted him to see that I had a room!" He wasn't snoopy. He wanted to see my passport, because I had a six-week visa and he wanted to see how long I'd been here. Then he asked me for my return ticket.

The chemistry between Mick Jagger and Keith Richards was like that between siblings, yet Mick always had a great amount of respect for Keith. He always responded to things he was saying; he would allow Keith to have more opinions than anyone else in the room; he made excuses for Keith if he ever got fucked up; and he covered for Keith. Sometimes, Keith would nod off and just fall asleep on the couch, and Mick always said, "Just leave him alone. Let him be." Mick had accepted Keith for who he was. Sometimes, Keith would be sleeping during a conversation, or you'd think he was sleeping, and then he'd suddenly say, "Nao, nao, you're wrong about that," and then he'd go back to sleep again. And we would think, Huh? Everybody thought he was asleep, but he still heard everything. He once said to me, "You know that conversation Mick and you were having the other night, you were really right about that point you were making."

"You heard that?" I asked.

"Yeah, you know, Mick never treats women right." And we launched into a conversation about Mick's bad treatment of women.

I never saw Mick lose his temper with Keith. I noticed that Keith sometimes lost his patience with Mick. Mick would say something and Keith would interrupt him. "Oh Gawd! Please, dear." It was as if they were married: Mick was the woman and Keith was the man.

Mick didn't like arguing with Keith, because Keith was always so much nastier and so much better at it. "Oh, just shut up, Mick! What the fuck do you know anyway!" he'd say. He was always reminding Mick that he came from an ordinary middle-class family. "Oh, yes, we're so street-smart, aren't we, dear! Yeah, right, Mick! You know so much about it, don't you, you fucking middle-class idiot! Yes, we had to suffer as children, didn't we, Mick!"

When they were writing songs, however, they were equally attentive to each other. Mick would say something like, "Nao, nao naooo, it's like this." Then Keith would say, "Ooooohhh, ooohhh, you mean, na na, na." It seems crazy, but they communicate like this and they understand each other perfectly. Mick was always willing to try something, suggest something. Keith had a way of simplifying things sometimes, whereas Mick would not keep things simple as far as the music went—the way the words were delivered, or the way the melody went, or the way the chorus would come in, or the way the bridge would meet the words.

Mick took it upon himself to give me some personal tutoring. For instance, if we were going out to dinner, he might tell me, "Make sure you suggest we order the Château Rothschild 1947, because I know that menu, and it's the best bottle of wine on the menu. I want you to study the menu and then say, 'Oh, let's get this one,' but make sure everybody at the table hears you." He would just love it when I would do that sort of thing. We used to have wonderful talks about life and metaphysics and books. Mick never thought I read enough. He would tell me everything a book was about so that I could have a really good conversation. One of Mick's favorite things to do was to plan our conversations for those dinners. He would coach me to say a particular thing, which I'd do. It would often be about something nobody would have expected me to have an inkling about. Or he'd teach me a couple of lines of French and then he'd respond in French when I used them.

Beatrice, the French girl he was keeping around, just irritated the hell out of me. I was always ribbing Mick, saying, "Jesus Christ, you'll fuck anything, won't you?"

"She's pretty, Bebe," he'd reply.

"Yes, she's pretty, but she's brain-dead!"

"Well, what do I need her brains for? I've got you to talk to and

her to fuck! So it's fine. And you're both named Beatrice."

"I am *not* named Beatrice; I'm Bebe!"

I was always very combative, so he respected me. He liked independent women.

After four weeks, Todd called me from the outskirts of Calcutta and told me he was going back to the States and he thought I should return home. He didn't think it was healthy for me not to be getting proper sleep. I think he felt that I was being irresponsible by not taking my job seriously, and that I would probably regret it at some point in my life. He said, "You might be having a lot of fun now, but you're going to look back on this and wish you had done something else." He would always give me that teacher advice, like a ruler across the back of the hand.

I flew back to New York at the beginning of December, happily refreshed from my month in the charmed circle of the Rolling Stones.

I hadn't done any modeling on the '74 trip. Oh my God! It was very naughty of me! I did not handle things well, and when I got back to New York, Wilhelmina was as angry with me as Eileen Ford had been. She scolded me intensely, but after a brief cooling-off period, she was willing to give me another chance. The U.S. advertisers were still so uptight about the *Playboy* centerfold that I could only work for sexier magazines like *Cosmopolitan* and *Viva*. This made me so angry that, for the first time, I decided to take my modeling career seriously, just to show them what I could do.

CHAPTER 5

Bebe Takes Off
1975-1976

Money, money, money machine
Don't want to stop
Till I see some green
I'm your leopard cash machine
Yeah! I'm still a creem dream
   "MONEY MACHINE," LYRICS BY BEBE BUELL

In the summer of 1975, the Rolling Stones rented Andy Warhol's twenty-five-acre compound in Montauk, at the end of Long Island, overlooking the Atlantic Ocean. They were going to rehearse there for a summer tour of the United States. One Friday afternoon, right after I had done a job for *Cosmopolitan* magazine, Mick had a plane pick me up in Manhattan and fly me out to the nearby East Hampton airport so that I could spend a week out there.

It was nice in every way, but it was a little boring, too, because the estate was perched on a steep rocky cliff leading down to the sea. There were no beaches. The estate was far enough away from the town that the band could play at maximum volume at 4:00 A.M. without disturbing the peace. But apart from the wonderful experience of watching the band rehearse and entertaining Mick when he would summon me, there was nothing else to do. I don't even remember if there was a TV. I was also puzzled at first by what I was doing there, because Mick wasn't sleeping with me. He was clearly having problems with Bianca at that point. There was turmoil in their relationship, and when he wasn't singing or planning the logistics of the tour with his accountants and managers, he would bend my ear, complaining about the way Bianca treated him. After a phone conversation with her, he would often be in tears. Mick is a sensitive, sweet man, and she had the power to humiliate him in a way no other woman ever did. After his relationship with Bianca, I think he was determined never to let a woman have that crucial power over him again. That's one reason Jerry Hall had to put up with so much misery. There was an endless battle of egos between Bianca and Mick because of all the press attention given to their physical similarities. People felt that Mick was so egocentric that he could only fall in love with another version of himself. Whatever the case, they apparently had to challenge each other all the time. Meanwhile, it was rumored Mick was having an affair with the socialite Barbara Allen, who was staying at Dick Cavett's house, which was a few hundred yards away over the dunes. He was always wandering off to see her. I remember thinking, Why would he fly me out here and want me to stay if he's interested in somebody else? Then I recalled his words at the Wick: "I've got you to talk to and her to fuck." So I had to accept the fact that he simply liked my company—I know he adored my energy.

There was a main house, where everybody congregated to eat and work, and there were a number of small hutlike cabins for sleeping. Elton John came to visit once. So Elton had one hut, Mick had another—everyone had a little hut. On another occasion, Billy Preston, who would be a major contributor to the Stones' next album, *Black and Blue*, came to visit. He was a lot of fun. I loved watching the rehearsals most of all. The band had changed. They had recently lost Mick Taylor and they had a new guitar player—at last, Ronnie Wood was in the band. And drugs had clearly changed the creative energy in and around the band. I mean, if your musical pulse in the band is a heroin addict, that's going to take a toll on the band's energy. Ron Wood is a follower, not a leader. He's a sidekick,

Jack the Lad. I got to see the Stones play in a small room, the living room in Montauk, which was a unique experience. I got to hear some of the best Stones concerts on earth. Not to mention the bickering and the discussions that went along with it, and I got to see the relationship between Keith and Mick in action. Mick's so much like the long-suffering, tolerant wife who occasionally loses her cool with his sailor husband. "Oh yes, darlin', are we going to go off and be pirates today, then?" Keith is the man, the pirate naughty boy, who speaks in a language only Mick understands: "Oh grrr, oh wrrr, Mick, rrruuh, rrruuh, dit dit."

"Well, you're right, darling," Mick would respond. "Forget it. There's no arguing here." Those were really wonderful moments. But because of Keith's condition at the time, his availability, his moods, a lot of things had to be done around him. When Keith was in bad shape, he'd sleep. He was never one of those people who had a hypodermic needle hanging out of his arm. I never saw things like that. I would just see him falling asleep. There was never drool on his jacket. He was a ravishingly beautiful man.

I would just have to sit there and be completely quiet, and Mick would occasionally ask me what I thought. He'd keep me up all night sometimes. He'd be chattering all night, and I'd be tired. He played all kinds of games. He'd tap me on my shoulder; I'd turn, and he'd be over there. I felt like I was hanging out with a little prankster. Finally, I would be reduced to pleading. "Please, let me go to sleep now. Let me tell you one more time how sexy that is, but then I'm going to bed," I'd say. Sometimes, Mick would put on my underwear and come dancing across the room. Why do all Englishmen want to wear your underwear? I have not met an Englishman who did not want to take my underwear, even Elvis (Costello). He always wanted to wear it, too. But my underwear was usually too small for their cocks.

The scene out at Montauk that summer was pretty healthy. They weren't such bad guys; actually, they were really sweet and really fun. It was the women and one or two of the assistants and hangers-on who were obviously messed up on drugs. I knew instantly I was not supposed to ask questions about one guy who appeared to be particularly close to Keith. I knew there was something going on there, but I didn't want to know what. I didn't want to know anything that journalists would be able to ask me questions about. I would regularly say to Mick, "What I don't know won't hurt; I don't want to know that stuff." Nobody ever did heroin in front of me, and cocaine use was discreet. As a matter of fact, Mick would get angry with people who offered me drugs.

The other women who visited were Fran Lebowitz, whose brand of humor appealed to Keith, and Lisa Robinson. They'd both been covering the New York waterfront for so long, a rivalry was bound to fester and grow. I just loved Fran. She was cool.

I visited twice during the six weeks the band spent preparing for their biggest tour yet. It was to include a forty-foot-long phallus (created, one can only presume, on a mescaline trip), which would explode from the floorboards and lift Mick up off the stage like a great white whale. Once, I stayed for five days; another time, I went for a long weekend. Todd was on the road. I'm sure it would have bothered him if he had known that I was once again frittering away my days consorting with their Satanic Majesties, so I didn't tell him. He was off doing his thing, so I was off doing mine. And to be perfectly honest, I'm sure that every moment I spent with the Stones, and the other rock stars I had intimate relationships with, benefited me in all sorts of ways I'm probably putting to use right now playing in my own band. I wasn't a groupie or a bimbo. I had my eyes and ears wide open.

After a week, I got tired of it, and I told Mick, "I want to go back. I'm bored." And so Mick flew me back to the city.

By then, I had my own country house to retire to. Todd had bought the place in Lake Hill, just up the road from Woodstock and Bearsville, on Mink Hollow Road. Over the years, he would expand his estate into a compound that included a state-of-the-art recording studio, rehearsal spaces, and a video studio. This was well before MTV changed the way we look at rock music. As with everything he did, Todd went all the way. However, I refused to let Todd become antisocial after he moved upstate. I felt if I wasn't in Todd's life, he would be a bear in hibernation and no one would ever hear from him again. We still had the Horatio Street house, and I made sure that if we got invited to anything cool, he went. I said to him, "I am not going to let you rot up here in the country with your nose in a computer!" He put a million dollars into that huge video complex before videos were popular. It just sat there for a long time, not making any money. And in those days, a million dollars was a *hell* of a lot of money.

Albert Grossman lived in Bearsville, so being in Lake Hill brought us into more regular contact with him. What I loved most about Albert was that he got it. There was no "camp" prejudice with Albert. He knew how much of an asset I was to Todd. "What are we going to do with you?" he used to say to me. "You're a star, but what can we make you do? You're a star! But what are you?" Albert thought Todd dressed better because of me and that I kept him going because he was so competitive. When I would get a crush on other men, it would keep Todd going as an artist. Every time I had an affair, Albert took me to lunch, I swear to God! "Well, this is good for two more albums, thank you!" he'd say, jokingly. He was not quite as fat as Peter Grant, the mountain man manager of Led Zeppelin, but Albert could be very stern and solid, and he talked in a big brick voice!

Everbody thought I was more than a model. Why didn't it ever dawn on anybody then to put me in front of a rock 'n' roll band? I was a lunatic and I had a horrible reputation—it was a perfect job for me!

In between visits to Mick out in Montauk, I had one last memorable encounter with Jimmy Page. We spoke on the phone one day—he was in London and I was in New York—and at the end of what seemed like a brief, lighthearted conversation, he told me that he would send me a sign that night at midnight. Being three thousand miles away and not as caught up in his web as I had been in London, I did not give it much thought. Later that afternoon, my girlfriend Jeanne Theis and I drove up to Woodstock. Todd was away, and we spent our time talking over dinner and listening to music. Around 11:30, we started guessing what Jimmy's sign was going to be. Would he send somebody to the house with a message? Or would it involve another phone call? We were sitting in the small dining room when, on the stroke of midnight—I swear—we heard a crash upstairs. It could only have come from the bathroom. Rushing up there, we discovered that the large antique wood-framed oval mirror that had been carefully hung above the sink had been hurled a good ten feet across the room and lay shattered at the edge of the sunken bathtub. Without further discussion and as if of one mind, Jeanne and I scooped up our bags, bundled the dogs into the back of the car, and took off like a bat out of hell, driving all the way back to New York, not stopping until we'd reached the sanctuary of Horatio Street. To this day, I have absolutely no idea what force could have propelled the twenty-pound mirror clear across the room, although it did cross my mind that Kenneth Anger had been in the basement of Jimmy's house when I spent those two magic days with him the previous year. At the time, he gave me a proud tour, even though Jimmy had made it clear that the basement was off-limits. He said Kenneth was working down there and I wouldn't want to go down if I knew what was going on. When I returned to Woodstock in the daytime, the first thing I did was have the house exorcised, following the instructions of a friend who knew all about demonic possession.

Three months later, in the fall of 1975, I returned to London. This time, however, I really needed and wanted to get some serious modeling work done, so I made a point of not calling the Wick. The problem with knowing the Rolling Stones as I did is that once you walk through the looking glass into their world, it's such a magic place that leaving it doesn't make sense, but staying in it can only lead deeper into Wonderland, until you lose your way.

I joined an agency, Models One, and moved into a lovely flat the agency had arranged for me to have. It was in one of the loveliest parts of London, Sloane Square. I shared it with another model, Ulla Kivimaki. I still did some rock 'n' roll stuff, like going to the Speakeasy or having dinner with Mick, but I made a conscious effort to try to be the good Bebe and really think about myself. One night, I took Ulla to the Speakeasy, where Jeff Beck came up with this immortal comment: "You could never tell your mother you didn't fuck a girl with the name Ulla." From October to December, I went back and forth between London and New York, in search of my career.

This time, I was lucky enough to team up with one of the great British fashion photographers, Clive Arrowsmith. He was very much in the mold of David Bailey, but a true original, with a fine eye and a great work ethic, and he was loads of fun. He was *huuuge* in the fashion industry. He and Bailey shared all the *Harper's Queen*

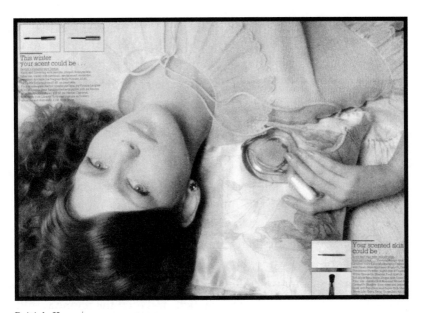

British *Vogue*/CLIVE ARROWSMITH

covers. Clive was a really cool guy—Welsh, in the John Cale vein. He had been married three times and had several children. I was twenty-two; Clive was thirty-five. I moved out of the Sloane Square flat and into a tiny, cheap room at the ultracool Portobello Hotel, which would become a key location in my London life in the 1970s. Clive was in his prime, and we did great work together for *Harper's Queen* and British *Vogue*. He was the first premiere fashion photographer to make a point of using me regularly. He legitimized me as a high-fashion model in England and the rest of Europe. Clive was an extremely attractive, fantastic person and there was a part of him that loved music. He could play guitar and sing; he was friends with George Harrison because they were both into Hare Krishna. Clive was the Richard Avedon of London. I remember once when he was photographing me for *Vogue:* I was lying on my back, with my hair spread out on a pillow, and as he would come over to adjust things, I felt myself becoming extremely drawn to him, the way you might fall in love with your doctor or psychiatrist. Clive created an entirely new image for me, one of sophistication and elegance—qualities that I possessed naturally because of my upbringing, but which I had rebelled against because of my rock 'n' roll desires.

Clive looked a lot like Todd—he had the same haircut; he was thin and tall and very rock 'n' roll. He was even a guitar player. Sometimes work is the greatest aphrodisiac. We had such a good and successful time together that I started falling in love with Clive. I moved out of the Portobello Hotel and into his fashionable Knightsbridge duplex. Dating a top fashion photographer was pretty glamorous, especially in the seventies, when London was still swinging.

People started to look at my beauty differently, seeing me through Clive's eyes. Clive saw me as a long-necked Grace Kelly with high cheekbones—as a much more refined beauty than I saw myself. When I moved in with him, I discovered that, if anything, he was more of a lunatic than your average rock 'n' roll star. Everything was cool for a while, but soon the strong pull of the Rolling Stones began seeping into our bedroom like some viral mist. We would be cozily asleep in Clive's big bed, and then the phone would ring at 1:00 A.M., and it would be Mick, demanding that I join him at some glamorous party or at Tramps. I would dart out of the house and hurry across town. This began to grate on Clive's nerves. I don't know if I was completely on his wavelength. I do know that I was constantly susceptible to distractions. If anybody from my rock and roll life called me and wanted me to go to Tramps or to this or that party, I would just leave Clive sitting in the house. I was just too far into my rock and roll world, and I don't know if anybody could have calmed me down at that point. I think Clive loved me and would have married me. And my feelings for him were very real, but his world was just so far away from mine. He was very religious, very into Krishna. He was much more into George Harrison than into Mick Jagger. I remember going with him to meet George for an Indian dinner once. It was certainly not like going out to dinner with Ron Wood or Rod Stewart. Clive and George talked about Krishna all night. I was intrigued by the whole Krishna business, but of course I had been exposed to many bouts of metaphysical drama and spiritual tirades by Todd. Clive was always praying, doing his beads, and chanting in front of a little shrine in his apartment. It soon became apparent that Clive and I did not have a big future together. He realized that I was not going to settle down and be a Krishna wife. Then he met another model, whose name was Karen. We were doing a booking together. I was in London only for a stint; I didn't even know if I wanted to live in London full-time.

It soon came time for me to return to New York, brush myself off, get back together with Todd, and try to be a good girl all over again.

Todd knew everything, of course. He always acted like he didn't know, like he didn't care, and I thought I was getting away with it. But he always knew. He loved me anyway. He was so many things to me—my father, my lover, my best friend, my mentor. Todd and I had a strange destiny. It's hard for me to explain or figure out, but it lasted five years. And it was obviously important enough for both of us that when I came back from this big modeling trip to London, I really decided that I wanted to be exclusively with him and that I wanted to settle down.

At the beginning of 1976, we decided to have a baby, and I quickly became pregnant. In March, I miscarried. This was my second pregnancy with Todd. Very early in our relationship, in 1973, I'd gotten pregnant, but I'd had a miscarriage then, too. That had been upsetting, but Todd thought I was way too young to have a baby and that I wasn't really sure what I wanted, so we both looked upon that miscarriage as a blessing in disguise. It came very quickly—after just a month. He did have to take me to the doctor for a D & C, the same things that they do in an abortion. The 1973 miscarriage wasn't so much traumatic as it was sad and scary.

The miscarriage in 1976 was a very big deal, though, because I had geared myself up to go ahead and have a baby with Todd, believing that this would seal our union. The miscarriage happened in our house up on Mink Hollow Road. I was lying on our water bed, watching a movie with a girlfriend, when I began to bleed. I stood up, and the blood was rushing out of me. I ran to the bathroom, stood in the tub, and started screaming. "Call Todd!" I yelled to my girlfriend Jackie. He was in the studio, and it took him fifteen minutes to get back to the house. Jackie was shrieking; we were both freaking out. I didn't want to get blood everywhere. I didn't stop screaming until Todd got home.

I felt so sorry for Todd; he was trying to calm me down, saying, "Bebe, wrap a towel around and under you." He was doing his best to keep calm. They rushed me to the hospital in Kingston, twenty minutes away. I spent the night there. The doctors told me the baby was still alive, that I had not lost the fetus, but they said that the chances of me being able to keep the pregnancy were not good. They recommended that I get a D & C, as they felt that this would not prove to be a healthy pregnancy. Todd and I were devastated.

Three months later, in June, we were going through another one of our spells of having a great time together. I was being a really good girl. I was going out to the country house, making candy apples, cooking big beautiful dinners, keeping the house really clean. I wasn't running around or hanging out with my friends as much. I was really putting a lot of energy into Todd, and he responded to that. I think the middle-class boy in him liked it.

Every Jerry Lewis telethon weekend, around Labor Day, Todd would have a party up at the house in Lake Hill. The telethon party consisted of an entire weekend when everybody and anybody came over to our house and tripped. Flamboyant and fun Joel Torne-benie, who is dead now, prepared the drugs. He would make this honey and psychedelic brew down in Mexico and then bring it across the border. The Albert tepee parties and Todd's telethon weekends were classic examples of 1970s ritualistic drug taking. People never knew what was in Joel's brew, because it looked and tasted like honey. He would let it sit and ferment for a year. It consisted of honey, as well as hunks of magic mushrooms and things of that nature. If you put this honey on your cereal or in your tea, or even just took it by the spoonful, as Todd would do, and ate it or spread it on toast, you were toast!

Later in my life, people questioned why I chose to stay with Todd over other rock stars, pointing out that they all used drugs. My answer was always that Todd took mind-expanding organic drugs. He wasn't into destructive and addictive chemicals.

Todd was always on that quest to find himself, but he somehow had time to fuck every woman on earth, too. I think he's right up there with Jack Nicholson and Warren Beatty. That behavior really influenced my opinions about relationships and men, and my belief that women have rights and should be able to fuck whomever they want. Why can't I date Mick Jagger, Todd Rundgren, Steven Tyler, and David Bowie all at the same time if I please? I wondered. Doesn't that mean I have good taste? Isn't it better than fucking every single person who moves? I had some scruples, after all.

Speaking of scruples: Mick called me up in the summer of 1976 because he wanted me to listen to the sequence of the songs on *Black and Blue*. He invited Liz Derringer and me up to the Plaza to listen to the album.

He asked us which songs we liked best, and when I picked mine, he said with a tinge of disappointment, "You've just picked the most obvious one. Don't you like the one that's just a bit different?"

"What do you mean?" I asked. "They're all typical Stones songs to me." Then we got into one of our typical debates. He asked me again what songs I liked, and he took my opinion extremely seriously. He turned to Charlie Watts and said, "Well, Bebe is a girl, and this is what *she* thinks: This is kind of standard Rolling Stones." Then they had an conversation about the music and included me in the discussion. It was fun.

Charlie's opinions were always vague. Whereas Keith and Mick would sit there and go at it. Woody would make jokes and pour drinks and make everyone happy. After he joined the Stones, it was very interesting to watch their collaborative effort. I tried to figure out how they got any work done. Somehow, they did manage to. Mick was so meticulous. He would hear things that none of us could hear. "You're slightly off-key there," he might say about a passage that had sounded just right to the rest of us.

The Stones created the prototype for the rock and roll lifestyle; bands like Led Zeppelin were sloppy seconds. I was teased a lot because I wasn't using drugs. Keith even made jokes about that sometimes. I remember one time when I was visiting Atlantic's recording studio and Faye Dunaway was there—this was when she was married to Peter Wolf—and I thought she was so charming, fabulous, and delightful. Everybody was doing blow, and I remember someone saying, "Would you like some?" and Keith said, "Don't ask her, because she'll just say no, that she'd much rather have a joint." He'd call me Mary Pickford—that line was always very funny. "Come here, Mary," he'd say. And I'd say, "Mary?" "Mary Pickford," he'd reply. I always thought that was endearing. I certainly was not known as a druggie, although I might have been known as the serial dater. There were very few people who knew how smart I was about music, which was difficult for me, and then word started to get around that I had good taste. "Bebe says it's cool, so maybe we should take a look at it," someone would say. I felt like Mrs. Rock 'n' Roll.

I was once at a table at some restaurant in New York with Mick Jagger, Jimmy Page, Rod Stewart, Ron Wood, and Eric Clapton. At this point, I had dated both Jimmy and Mick, and Rod fancied me big-time, but I hadn't snogged him, so there was a flirtation going on. Woody had a little crush on me from when I had stayed at the Wick. So there was a lot of tension: Everybody just wanted me dead. I swear to God. I felt like Lillie Langtry, because I was the only woman sitting at this table. Woody felt very territorial, because he thought of me as his little girl, and he was keeping an eye on me. He pulled me aside and whispered, "You know, you can't date all of us."

"Why?" I said. "You guys date all of us. What's the difference?"

I had gone to the restaurant with Mick and Woody, but Mick was mad at me. He said, "I know Jimmy's going to be there and I know that you are going to want to run off with him, but you better not do that." "Why? You're going to be with Bianca!" I shot back at him. Bianca was planning to join us later. At one point later in the evening, Warren Beatty and Jack Nicholson showed up. They were all fighting over me. They kept getting up and going off to talk among themselves. I just felt at this point there might even be wagers—I wasn't sure where I was going to end up that night! It was hysterical. It was also the first time I felt that beautiful sexual energy with Rod—when he was still cool, before he became an asshole, when he was still "Jack the Lad" Rod. We left the restaurant to go to a club. I was sitting in the back of the cab, and all the men were seething at me, but nobody wanted me to leave, either! Mick was in the front, Woody was next to him, Bianca, who had joined us, was next to Woody, and Rod, very boyishly and friskily, slid next to me. He smelled so good. And his hair was huge! He just reeked of rock star! It was almost as if he practiced more than all the other boys. He was so fucking good at it. "So, I hope you don't mind getting stuck next to me!" he said.

"Well, at least you're talking to me!"

"You're getting all the boys crazy! Tell me the truth, darling. If you could pick, which one of us would you go home with?"

"Jimmy!"

"Jimmy! Why Jimmy? He'll just want to sit around and talk about Satan all the time."

Behind one another's backs, they would say funny, competitive, silly things, but with affection. I always found it quite amusing that Mick named his son James.

Men are so curious! "Did you sleep with him? What was it like? How was he as a lover?" they'd ask me. A lot of men wanted to know how Mick was in bed. But more than sexual performance, it was Mick's essence that was important, that security that made you feel you were in good hands when you were with him. He is almost a textbook version of a perfect lover, because you can be pretty much assured that anything you thought anyone would do to you, he's going to try it. So nothing comes as a surprise. Other pop stars, in their moments of vulnerability, after a couple of hits on a joint and alcohol, would want to know about each other. I have had more conversations about genitalia and performance with other men than I have with other women.

Young models dating rock stars is expected these days. Back then, however, there were fewer women who actually had the stamina or personality to hang out in the rock circle. Plus, I think the rock 'n' roll guys in those days were much pickier about the women they hung out with—Marianne Faithfull, Sara Dylan, Jane Asher, Anita Pallenberg, Linda McCartney, Yoko Ono, Heather Daltry. These were remarkable women.

By mid-1976, things were looking up for me across the board. Even Wilhelmina seemed pleased with me. I was looking forward to doing some serious modeling in New York as a result of my success in Europe. *Cosmopolitan* booked me constantly. I should have known it couldn't last, but under no circumstances could I have imagined that my whole life would be irrevocably changed in the next six months.

By the late summer, Todd's road life with his band Utopia was cutting into his life at home, and I didn't like it. I was absolutely certain he was getting it on with his road manager, Susan Lee. She had been part of the Bearsville crew from the outset, but I had never paid much attention to her. She was a dark, stocky woman, and I felt she was flaunting herself at Todd, presenting herself as some kind of spiritual soul mate. I never imagined they'd have sex because, frankly, she was hardly Todd's type. She was large-breasted and had a moon face. Why would a tall, thin Playmate feel threatened? I was naïve. When you're young, you only sweat the lookers. To me, Susan was obviously using her self-assurance and nurturing hippie Earth Mama aura to manipulate Todd. She was so good at that, she had even won me over sometimes. I enjoyed our long talks. I admired the way she'd go up to people and give them one of those long, earnest est-style hugs, the way she'd massage your back. It was all part of that touchy-feely brand of hippie spirituality, where everybody talked about how much they loved you, when, in fact, they might not like you at all. But the fact that Susan and Todd were almost constantly on tour together was not groovy. Nor was her calling our house fourteen times a day when they were off the road. Insiders whispered to me that she had become obsessed with Todd. I knew of their shared "spiritual" bond because of his experimentations with TM, kundalini and tantric yoga, and past-life regressions. There was nothing particularly lofty about the way she'd sit around an L.A. hotel pool topless, with her legs spread and no underwear on. What religion was that? I started to realize that Susan was determined to undermine my place in Todd's world.

When I confronted Todd about Susan, he stonewalled me or denied it. "Come on, Beeb, give me more credit than that." I should have—for being a good liar, that is. Instead, I accepted that some vaguely metaphysical New Age bond existed between them. How could I compete with that? I was not well versed in that arena, which I found threatening. But I assumed my bond with Todd, coupled with the sexual and emotional energy we had together, would prevail. I was just a kid going up against a sophisticated ex–psych major a good eight years older than I. She knew what buttons to push and how to provoke tension between Todd and me. But when I started asking around among band women and the crew, I didn't like what I was hearing. I was being slyly ousted, but I still couldn't wrap my head around the idea that Todd would trade me in for Susan Lee.

Susan brought things to a fever pitch in August 1976, when Todd played the prestigious Knebworth Festival in England, sharing the stage with Mick and the Stones. Susan really worked me over, making me feel insecure and alienated, as if Todd and I were on our last legs. I felt vulnerable—and ripe for reprisal.

Mick was on Todd's case from the moment we arrived. He started playing his favorite game, teasing Todd by saying, "You better hold on to your girlfriend, Todd! I'm a bigger star than you are! I'm going to nab her." When Todd was performing, Mick would keep it up. He was shouting out, "Oh, Todd, what a cute ass you have!" Todd got frustrated and angry. I became so flustered, I lost my backstage pass, but Paul and Linda McCartney took me past the guards and into the backstage area, where I could watch the Stones.

Linda and I had met a couple of times socially—at the club of the moment, in New York or London. I always loved that woman. She was so fantastic, a divine, sweet, fabulous woman. I met Paul for the first time at Knebworth. Linda introduced me to him before the show started. Paul was awfully nice. In fact, everybody was. Linda made everyone she came in contact with feel important; there was just something special about her energy. She never acted jealous or threatened, and she was supportive. When you looked at Paul and Linda, you could see they were a couple, and you couldn't imagine one without the other. Jack Nicholson was also at Knebworth. I wanted to get to know him, but everybody, from Mick to Todd, kept me away from him. In the middle of an instrumental break in the Stones concert, Mick danced over to the side of the stage, winked at me, and pinned his pass on my blouse. Can you imagine him thinking about me in the middle of entertaining 200,000 people? He was so adorable.

Immediately after Todd and I got back from Knebworth, I flew out to L.A. with Liz and Rick Derringer for a CBS Records convention. Rick was with Columbia, and so was Aerosmith, and Rick opened for them at the convention. Rick was a member of the Edgar Winter group and a solo star ("Rock 'n' Roll Hootchie Koo"). Aerosmith had just had a big hit with "Dream On." After the show, Liz introduced me to Aerosmith's lead singer, Steven Tyler, also known as "the poor man's Mick Jagger," because of a remarkable resemblance in their lips. Liz had gone to high school with Steven. I wound up sitting with him and his then girlfriend, the extraordinarily gorgeous fifteen-year-old Julia Holcolm. Sitting next to him, I felt like lightning had struck. I had first met Steven at an outdoor concert in Boston three years earlier. Aerosmith had been considering Todd as producer for their next album. It was raining and muddy in Boston, and I wasn't dressed for inclement weather. Young girls often tend not to wear enough clothes. Todd screamed at me, calling me prissy because I didn't want to walk across a plank above a muddy ditch backstage. I wanted to stay behind, but Todd kept beckoning me across. Steven observed this tense exchange and impulsively leapt into the breach. Strutting over like Zorro, he deftly lifted me up and carried me across the plank. Todd had been pissed that my prissy fit commanded such attention.

Now, we were schmoozing our way through various parties at the lavish CBS convention. Aerosmith was huge: Their current album, *Rocks*, was their biggest hit yet. Both Steven and I felt an undeniable spark, an animal magnetism from the get-go, even though—or perhaps because—Steven knew I was with Todd. Julia was hanging on Steven's arm, and I was mostly hanging with Liz and Rick Derringer. They were like my rock and roll Cleaver parents, and they took care of me when Todd wasn't around. With Rick's success producing and playing with Johnny and Edgar Winter, they had tons of money. Liz was my best friend, and she spoiled me rotten. Julia was stunning, but she had recently had a devastating lost pregnancy and she and Steven were going through a very rough spell. For once, I was the older woman, even though I'd just turned twenty-three. Steven did note that he and I were the only ones wearing leopard skin that night.

Back in New York, Steven started phoning me at 4:00 A.M. At first, he was playful and flirtatious, but always totally wired. He'd taunt me with comments like "Are you still with that asshole?" My connection to Todd had always been karmic, spiritual, almost incestuous. He was the overbearing father and I was the rebellious daughter. With Steven, the connection was more primal. Todd had his pompous, rigid, extremely opinionated, combative side. I once insulted him by calling him "a closet debate team captain," putting him down by saying, "Go back to high school and get it out of your system!" So when Steven Tyler, that rock and roll knight in shining leopard, roared into my life and swept me off my feet with his grandstanding displays of rock-star chivalry, it was exactly what the doctor had ordered. The timing was perfect.

In August, after what had mostly been a beautiful summer with Todd, I found out through various channels that the runt *was* experimenting with kundalini and tantric yoga. I was still very much a rock 'n' roll girl. I was much more into God and aliens than I was into Hindu religion, even though I did believe in reincarnation and the journey of the soul, et cetera. I wasn't quite ready to hold one position for more than ten minutes while I was fucking. Okay, I wasn't there yet; my self-control wasn't that good—I don't think I could have sat still for more than two minutes back then. At the time, it made me snap because I was just so tired of the competition. I felt that to maintain some semblance of self-respect, I had to go out and pop another big rock star every time Todd would bonk some backseat babe in Boise—*an eye for an eyelash*—*and I was getting tired of it.* It was grating on my nerves. I just wanted to settle down and have a nice regular life at the movies. Men want their women to be good little girls who never do anything, while they get to be pirates and do *everything. And it never changes.* Hopefully, some of the women reading this book will pick up some tips and *change things!* Women make up over half the population on the planet, and this totally unbalanced scenario is way too tired. People talk about wanting to change things, so how about changing this old hat double standard? Let's get together, yeah, yeah, yeah. But how many relationships are as together as Paul and Linda McCartney's was? They treated each other as equals in the grand adventure of life. The irony is that if only men could see their way through to fidelity, they would have much better lives, too.

I continued to seethe about Susan. Even though I had had my fair share of infidelities, Todd and I had always gotten back together. But there was something about this relationship with Susan that really pissed me off. I hated her. I was a young, angry rock 'n' roll girl. I was tired of the battle of the wills and egos when I was around Todd and Susan. I was fed up with the denials, the sniping, the rumors spinning off the road. I was tired of Susan's swagger, which suggested she was levitating with my man. I was looking for a fairy-tale escape route. I wanted marriage, a family, security. I knew I was never going to get them with Todd.

One night, I was lying in bed with Todd, when the phone rang at 5:00 A.M.

"So, have you broken up with that asshole yet?" Steven began.

"I'm in bed. Todd and I are sleeping. You'll have to call me tomorrow."

"I'm coming in for the fight. What are you doing tomorrow?"

"I've got to go to the dentist."

"Oh, really, who's your dentist?"

"Dr. Krankheit."

"Oh, yeah, up there on Fifty-seventh."

"No, no. Fifty-sixth Street."

"What number?"

"I've got to go back to sleep!" I hung up.

"Steven Tyler's been calling you quite a bit, Bebe. Have you been calling him?" Todd asked.

"Uh, well, sometimes."

"Well, what's going on?"

"Well, Todd, why don't you tell me what's going on with Susan?"

Suddenly, a dead silence blanketed the room. Then we swept it under the rug and went back to sleep.

The next day, I went to the dentist. When I came out of the dentist chair, and walked to the reception area to get my things, I saw the leopard-skin knight in shining armor sitting there. Adorable— it was still early in the day, and he hadn't gotten fucked up yet.

"You are one tenacious boy," I mumbled out of one side of my mouth.

He was charming, together, and quick-witted. We walked all over town. He looked beautiful. I'm sure he wasn't 100 percent sober, but he was certainly more sober than he would be by midnight. We finally went down to Liz's to hang out. After we ate, I could see that he was getting antsy because we didn't have any drugs. I watched as his mood changed, but I was still kind of naïve. Now I would know exactly what was going on. But back then, I just thought he was itching to get to the fight.

The plan was for him to call me at Liz's after the fight. Todd had split earlier that day for Woodstock, and I didn't feel like going home and being alone. I thought it was kind of weird that Steven'd left so abruptly. I didn't hear from him for hours and hours, and I was getting a little sad. Finally, Liz and I decided to try to get some sleep. Then Steven called. It was 4:00 A.M.

"Come and get me. I'm fucked up."

"What's the matter?"

"Well, I'm with all these big basketball players and I'm conked out of my skull. You've got to come get me!"

I found out where he was; then I rushed over there. He was slumped in a chair like a Raggedy Andy doll. I hefted him up and carted him out of there. I didn't even look around to see who was in the room. When we got back downtown, Liz gave us her bed. She slept on the fold-out couch downstairs. That was the first night I spent with Steven. He certainly did come to life, for a man who had needed help to get himself home. Mind you, when I'd gotten him back to Liz's, I had thrown him in the shower, and cleaned him up, then made him drink some tea. Soon after that, he started giggling and calling me a "little mommy." I was a little mommy all right. *Bang! Zoom!* To the moon, Steven! He probably got me pregnant that night.

With Steven in Sunapee, New Hampshire, September 1976/BUELL PRIVATE COLLECTION

We fell madly in love. When we woke up the next morning, we knew it. He asked me to go with him to Sunapee, New Hampshire.

In the fall of 1976, Steven Tyler was riding high on the crest of Aerosmith's first wave of success. There were several things about him that I found extremely attractive. He was beautiful, he had a lot of style—both in the way he dressed and the way he courted me—and he was full of fun. He had the kind of innocent joy about life that successful people possess. And he was very rich. All these things made being with him constantly exciting. For example, when he said he wanted to fly up to his estate in New Hampshire, I didn't realize he meant in his own plane. Mick had flown me to Montauk on a chartered plane, but Steven was the first man who flew me off my feet.

Flying in his little four-seater private plane was the scariest ride of my life. The pilot, the great R&B singer and songwriter Bobby Womack, Steven, and I were on board. Tell me how we got there! They were all doing blow, including the pilot. He was a pilot/ au pair/houseboy, whatever. Totally had his shit together. I don't know how he did it, but he did. Trust me, you do not want to fly in a small plane with Steven Tyler. The plane was being kept high by more than its wings. Being confined in a tiny area with a person who had the energy of fifty wild ponies was terrifying.

"I wanna sit in the back! No, I wanna sit in the front now!"

He just couldn't sit still.

The next four days consisted of Steven driving me around in his Porsche, in between doing mountains of cocaine. When we made love, I felt that we connected on some level that was above anything I had experienced. But after a day or two, I saw dark terrain ahead. He was doing lots of drugs with musician buddies. At one point, I put my foot down.

"Could we just not do blow for once and go look at antiques and get a nice dinner out somewhere?" He gritted his teeth and gave me a mocking glare. "We're in the country," I went on. "There are beautiful restaurants, flea markets, antique dealers, fabrics, wallpaper, and carpets to look at and pick out, shops to visit."

I not only couldn't deal with hard drugs; I couldn't even face taking the pill. It made me puffy and, as a model, puffy was the last thing I needed. Of course, we were risking the ultimate Puff by not taking birth control. Sure, I had a diaphragm, but who had time to fuss with that? I was surprised that Steven finally made an effort to clean up his act for the remainder of the week. We were in love and we were going to be together. I intended to leave Todd, and Steven said he had left Julia, that it was over. We made love all the time. Our mornings began with Steven being romantic, tender, and very generous about my sexual needs, without expecting me to return the favor. I'd never known a man as enamored of pussy as Steven was. Our lovemaking felt powerful, purposeful, somehow meant to be. He was robust, funny, and sexy. We had lots of passionate, intimate times together in bed. I had a mystical hunch we had been brought together by some higher power—and that there would be a glorious outcome to this mating ritual. The idea of being apart suddenly seemed unimaginable.

When Steven asked me to accompany him on Aerosmith's six-week European tour in the fall, I said yes. It was much more than just wanting to hang out with him; something inside told me we had already conceived a child.

We flew to Boston and then went to Steven's carriage house in Brookline. He assured me Julia had already packed and was now headed back to her parents' home in the Pacific Northwest. I was looking forward to a night of togetherness, but I was greeted by far more togetherness than I'd bargained for. Julia was still there, holed up with a girlfriend, and in terrible shape. She was sobbing, stoned, disoriented, and hysterical over leaving Steven. As awkward as the situation was, I was neither angry nor offended. Instead, my heart broke for this young girl. She was crushed. I'd been there, done that, and knew what she was feeling.

I asked Steven to leave us alone so we could talk. Maybe it was my maternal hormones beginning to kick in, but I found myself adoring and protecting Julia. I held her in my arms for twenty minutes, comforting her as she sobbed. This was hardly the smooth mutual parting of the ways he had described, saying she was too young and needed to go out and get a life. He was playing a little too fast and loose with the two of us, having figured out that the truth would have caused me to back off. Even a year after the lost pregnancy, Julia was deeply saddened and shaken. She seemed lost. But there we were. Julia took the bedroom; Steven and I took the huge living room sectional.

I kept a diary of our time together that fall of 1976. A few entries from the beginning of the diary reveal my state of mind:

SATURDAY, OCTOBER 2: *Steven's house is going to be gorgeous when he gets it together. I still love Todd, but I know he's not right for me. Steven's perfect for me, and I am so in love and my stomach hasn't stopped butterflying since we've been together. The only obstacles in our way are: Julia on his end, and Todd on my end. I've finally fallen in love with Steven, OH MY GOD! Not since Jimmy Page have I felt this way for anyone besides Todd.*

It's going to be hard for us both, harder for me because Julia is in Portland with her parents. He's already laid the law down to her about me, but I haven't said a word to Todd. I spoke to him on the phone tonight. I tried so hard to be the best for Todd, but it just isn't my dream of a relationship. Steven gives me the affection and attention that Todd doesn't know how to give. Help me, God! I am going through this very important change. I'm hopelessly in love with Steven. I know this is my mate. Thank you, God! We made beautiful love this afternoon when we woke up.

MONDAY, OCTOBER 4: *Steven broke up with Julia tonight while I'm on the plane going back to New York. Leaving Steven was horrible, but it was my own choice. Julia is in Boston as of this morning. I must get back and talk to Todd about all of this. He must know, because this isn't just an affair; this is real. I've got to get to Europe. I must be with Steven for the tour. And I'm going to do all I can to pull it off. I know this is the man I am going to marry.*

When I got home, I had just enough time to grab my passport, pack some things at Horatio Street—and unload the news on Todd, who was up in Woodstock. When Susan, who happened to be visiting, picked up the phone, that sealed the deal. I asked for Todd. "I'm going to London for a while to model," I announced. Todd deserved at best a half truth, and I threw him one. The sound of Susan's voice seriously diminished whatever guilt I might otherwise have felt.

TUESDAY, OCTOBER 5: *Back to New Hampshire to be with Steven. When we got back to the house, we talked about me going to Europe.*

WEDNESDAY, OCTOBER 6: *I think I'm going to London with Steven and I'll work while he works. Things are getting so bent out of shape. I don't want Steven's and my love to be killed by all this ugliness and bitter feelings.*

THURSDAY, OCTOBER 7: *Steven and I made love twice tonight, and it was perfect. I couldn't help reflecting how fast going from the photographer Clive Arrowsmith to live Aerosmith was changing my life. I told Todd I was going to Europe with Steven, but I had decided that I was going to go as far as London and model while he did all the rest of the tour.*

SATURDAY, OCTOBER 9: *Jeff Beck at the Academy of Music. Dinner with Steven at an Italian restaurant. Confrontation with Julia. Shit hits the fan. Leave for Europe with Steven.*

MONDAY, OCTOBER 11: *In London. We slept until around 6:00 P.M. and then went down to the hotel to rehearsal. Then we went to the Speakeasy at four in the morning. When we got back to the hotel, we made love three times, all but once in the afternoon, when we woke up.*

THURSDAY, OCTOBER 14: *Steven played Scotland. TODD CALLED. UH-OH!! Sixteen days pregnant? Because I'm already feeling weird. Told him about pregnancy. Weird conversation, called again, and we had a beautiful talk. All is well. Todd truly loves me.*

FRIDAY, OCTOBER 15: *Steven is acting very weird. I miss Todd! Ha ha ha. MY PERIOD BETTER START! We went shopping at Harrods.*

SATURDAY, OCTOBER 16: *Drove to Birmingham with Steven for the gig, talked about my being pregnant and he said he wanted the baby.*

SUNDAY, OCTOBER 17: *Hammersmith Odeon. Great show. Party afterward with lots of noisy people and photographers, but so fun. Queen was there. Bob Gruen got lots of pictures. As for New York—spoke to Todd. Not so good.*

Aerosmith wasn't a big band in England, and there was a little backlash against them. After they closed their Hammersmith Odeon show with "Helter Skelter," they were accused of ripping off the Beatles. We had a couple of fights, one of them in public, which got into the British press after Steven destroyed his dressing room at Hammersmith. One time, he was looking at the deli tray backstage, discovered that the turkey wasn't fresh, and the whole food table ended up on the ceiling. "What do you expect? We're in England, you asshole," I screamed. I made him get on his hands and knees and pick up every speck of food. And he did it, too.

The first time I saw Aerosmith in concert, I was already dating Steven. I remember thinking that he was a very powerful performer, much like Iggy Pop, much more agile than Mick. He could do flips and back bends and other things I'd never seen Mick do. Mick was more burlesque, more vaudeville. Steven was a lot more animalistic, a lot more physical as a performer. He really gave it his all. He could do cheerleader moves like flips, leaps, all kinds of exciting, wonderful things, which I don't think many people could duplicate. Steven Tyler loves performing, and I could see that sheer joy. He was grateful to be alive, to be up there, to have this opportunity. I thought that was absolutely touching. I'm getting really bored with this "just rolled out of bed" look. I like my pop stars to dress well and have some serious attitude. I don't like all this "Here's my new flannel shirt." What's wrong with a little eyeliner? I think glamour is part of what makes rock 'n' roll exciting fun, and if you don't have that, then go back to your day job. I am absolutely bored stiff by bands that look like Guided by Voices. They're about as sexy as an old brown shoe.

I thought Aerosmith were more like the Yardbirds than the Stones. I don't think Aerosmith sounds anything like the Stones. First of all I think they're much more into blues, much more gritty, not that the Stones aren't gritty, but it's a different type of grit; it's more of technical grit.

"Back in the Saddle Again" is one of my favorite songs. "Sweet Emotion" is one of the greatest songs, and "Dream On" is a wonderful rock anthem. It's one of those kinds of songs that everybody in the audience participates in. I love live performances, where songs can bring the audience into a unified motion where they are all doing the same thing. I've seen Aerosmith audiences, when they play "Dream On," light so many lighters that it looks like the place is going to go up in flames. Steven gets his fuel from whatever the audience is giving him. I think most performers do that. I know that if my audience is not there I feel very naked, and you need that feedback in order to really give it all out.

Steven's partner in the band was Joe Perry—Keith to his Mick. Elyssa Perry was getting very jealous because I was becoming the queen bee of the band. Elyssa hated me from the minute she saw me. I thought she was a real witch—she told a lot of lies about me. This made Joe Perry very leery of me. He thought I had too many boyfriends and that I'd hurt Steven. Joe was old-fashioned and protective. He came up to me early on and said, "Listen, Bebe, don't hurt Steven, or you're not gonna come out of this smelling like a rose."

We went to see Paul McCartney's band Wings at Wembley. Steven was impressed that I knew Paul and Linda. We had a great time. Linda gave us some great Thai stick. I asked her if it was okay to smoke pot when you were pregnant and she said yes. When Steven and I went backstage at the Wings show, I talked to her about how I hated it when people called women groupies, and she said, "Oh darling, please, I've slept with every one of the Rolling Stones! You just can't let their jealousy affect you!" She tried to show me how you had to laugh it off, saying, "Oh my God, you wouldn't believe how I behaved in the sixties! I was far from an angel, my dear!"

In London, I always felt like a star. I was getting a lot of attention in the press, and so was Steven. They thought I was the cat's pajamas just for doing a saucy layout in a magazine. I got two years of press out of that just because I was a pretty girl, a model, and at that point I was getting published in British *Vogue* and *Harper's & Queen*, but I'd also been in *Playboy*, and I was dating pop stars. It was news to them. "Naughty Bebe Buell is in town. What pop star will she snag this week?" was a typical line. In England in 1976, I started to become a celebrity under my own steam. I had a wild child, independent, naughty-girl image because I did what I wanted. I dated whom I wanted. If anybody said anything negative to me, I'd say, "Go fuck yourself." But I also had that sweet, soft side of me that

145

European tour, fall 1976–I discovered I was pregnant in Belgium/BUELL PRIVATE ARCHIVE

was hurt and cared what people thought. I wanted to please everybody, would go out of my way to be effervescent and nurturing, because I wanted to correct the bad impression of who I was.

Steven and I were a hot combination. The charisma meter went out of control when we stood side by side. We were both powerful people and we had a similar aura: I was the wild child, the nude serial rock star dating wildcat. He was the crazy, wild, leopard-clad, badass, Mick Jaggeresque American rock 'n' roll singer. People really did look at me as a girl who was more like a guy. I had just been there a couple of months earlier with Todd, so people were asking, "What is it with this girl?"

After a week in London, the band was ready for the German leg of the tour. I was blue and was having wild mood swings. That should have told me right then what was up. "I don't want to stay here without you," I told Steven. "Beeber, are you pregnant?" he asked. The evidence was starting to add up even in his drug-addled mind. "I'm sure I'm not," I replied. Then Steven talked me into doing the entire tour. Flying to Germany, I threw up all over the road manager, and everybody in the band was whispering, "Oh no, poor Bebe has gotten into the heroin!" On the way from Germany to Brussels, I threw up in the plane. I was pregnant and I was sick.

In Germany, I was strip-searched because Steven had carried a knife on the plane. They turned me over to Helga, the customs agent from hell. She took me into a small back room and made me take off all my clothes. I couldn't stop crying. She could have cared less as she checked inside my vagina and my butt. I was humiliated. In Germany, I threw up right in the band manager's lap again.

By the time we hit Amsterdam, Steven was bouncing off the walls on cocaine. Meanwhile, even the smell of jet exhaust would send me into a massive hurl. I was craving beef stroganoff and orange juice. Elyssa—bossy, loud, mean, vengeful—decided I definitely was not gonna be part of the family, and I felt she started this huge conspiracy against me. It was easy to paint me into a corner and gossip about me, to hang tags on me, to manipulate me. It didn't help that I was such a nice girl. That just infuriated the jealous people even more. There was a lot of envy and jealousy surrounding me at that point. I really didn't stand a chance. It was a difficult situation for everyone involved. Steven and I had been seeing each other for only three weeks when I discovered I was pregnant, yet we already had an extremely strong, telepathic, psychic, sexual relationship.

There were other major changes. Once our two-week honeymoon was over, and he had pried me free of Todd, Steven underwent a frightening transformation on drugs. He was really crazy and stoned or drunk all the time. I had fallen in love with Dr. Jekyll and now I was pregnant by the maniacal Mr. Hyde. And I was absolutely not in love with Mr. Hyde, who could be one scary motherfucker.

At first, I wanted to marry Steven, but it did not take long on the road to discover that I was way out of my depth dealing with his almost daily, life-threatening drug addiction. We discussed marriage. If he'd asked me to marry him, I would have, but he didn't ask. I thought this was my fairy tale, but Steven was like a mutiple-personality case. He'd come down off drugs and apologize five hundred times a day—which did give me hope. Part of him—his inner middle-class Steve Tallarico side—desperately wanted to be a happy family man with a big house and babies all around. Then he'd toot up and turn into Mr. Hyde on tour, blitzing through London, Paris, Düsseldorf, Munich, Frankfurt, Bonn, Berlin, Brussels, and Stockholm in a reckless whiteout of Peruvian marching powder. Drugs also revealed Steven's bratty, condescending arrogance and cruelty. When he was under the influence, he had a way of barking orders to underlings that pissed me off.

Given my extreme hormonal surges, one effect of all this ugliness in close quarters was that life with Todd was beginning to seem downright calm and stable. I missed the familiarity and coziness of our city and country homes. My body was looking for a cave in which to go build my birthing bed. It was dawning on me that I was not likely to find it at 5:00 A.M. in Düsseldorf with a heavy-metal madman named Steven Tyler. My deepest concern was my unborn baby's welfare. I had seven months to go and was a long way from home. My hormones were in overdrive, my survival instincts were shrieking, and I had to stay out of harm's way. It was less about living with the sperm donor than about with reuniting with a potential nesting father. That meant going home.

What made it even more complicated was that on a good day, Steven could be charismatic, charming, outrageous, and utterly gorgeous. We did have some wonderfully tender moments. He gave me his pinkie diamond ring to wear on my ring finger when we were unable to find a more perfect one in Zurich. He bought me a chic fox coat before it was politically incorrect to wear fur. There was some kind of weird paternal instinct at work in Steven. But drugs made him insane. I witnessed juvenile flipouts in city after city but was never any closer to mortal danger than having to duck turkey meat flying my way.

Steven released his demons through his banshee stage act and by beating up on Joe Perry in their absurd sibling rivalry. I never un-

"Born to Breed." Bebe and Steven–Paris, France, 1976/CLAUDE GASSIAN

derstood those two. They'd wrestle, one or the other immobilized in a headlock, and really beat the crap out of each other, but neither ever look bruised or maimed. One minute, they were drawing blood backstage, and the next minute, they were back-to-back at a microphone, acting like they were madly in love.

On Halloween, which we spent in Paris, we visited a gynecologist, who confirmed I was pregnant. I was overjoyed but also overwhelmed. I gave Steven a big long hug before leaving the office. It was clear by then that I had fallen in love with two Stevens—one straight, the other stoned. "Beeber," he said, "you killed a bunny today. The rabbit done died and you're having a baby. And this baby better not come out with a long head. Bebe, that baby better not have droopy eyes and a long face." It was a cruel joke at Todd's expense. We sat down with a calendar and realized it would have to be a scientific marvel for it to be Todd's baby. I hadn't had sex with him for a month before sleeping with Steven. I was pregnant by Steven, case closed. It was like being hit by lightning.

Todd was in Woodstock when I called to break the news. We had been speaking more regularly ever since I saw how crazy

Steven was getting. "Is it mine or his?" he asked matter-of-factly, steeled for the answer. "I don't know how it could be yours," I said diplomatically. "How far along are you?" he asked. "I guess it could be mine, right?" I told Todd I hoped it was his baby, because I didn't want a baby with a crazy man. "Well, maybe it's not worth the risk. Have you considered an abortion?" I felt lost and unsafe. And I was fed up with turning to Todd and getting Susan on the line. Susan couldn't resist weighing in as well, offering advice (abortion) rooted less in Earth Mama sisterhood than in naked self-interest. I was outraged. She told me I was too young and immature to raise this baby. What she meant was that she dreaded my baby would become a precious lifelong link to Todd—thus blocking her visions of utopia. I didn't need a transatlantic phone line to hear jealousy from viperish females. I prayed that maybe Steven wouldn't be so crazy after Europe. I prayed for my baby to be born with Todd's blue eyes. I had never felt so torn and shaky.

Soon the back-stabbing gossip kicked in. Elyssa Perry, guided by a competitive-bitch streak and jealousy over my insider's position with Steven, planted thoughts in his fevered mind about the baby not being his. She figured she could best get to him by naming Ritchie Blackmore, Deep Purple's ace guitarist, as the rumored daddy. Ritchie was a friend—no more—and I'd seen a show or two of his that year. But hey, I'd played bingo with Muhammed Ali, too, so maybe I was carrying *his* baby. I was trapped in a world of merciless, twisted misogyny from both sexes, where if you were a tall, good-looking blond model, then to know a man was to swing from a chandelier with him—whoever he was.

It was like the *Playboy* scandal and losing my reputation all over again. Most people just figured I had run off with Steven, learned I was pregnant by Todd, and planned to run home to the daddy. I did not want my baby to grow up fatherless. I'd never had a father while growing up, and that was a palpable undercurrent. I had hormones guiding me one way and my heart and soul pulling me the other. I was beginning to feel there was no way out.

Steven acted as if he believed the rumors, but he knew the truth. He knew we hadn't been apart one second from the day we got together. I'd have had to have been like Mick, a midnight rambler, sneaking to the Bois de Boulogne to get laid, for the baby not to be

150

Steven's. Everyone's efforts to claim this baby was someone else's were thoroughly demeaning. It was illogical and deluded even to consider anyone else as the father. I felt targeted, the Yoko Ono of Aerosmith. Sadly, Steven wasn't making any sweeping promises when it came to giving up drugs. I could never be his partner on Planet Aerosmith.

November 1 was Steven's last gig in Paris. We made beautiful love that day and went to a party after the gig. I was carrying a child and needed rest, and I wanted to go to sleep at midnight. Steven and Joe both came charging offstage and wanted to do coke and swig booze all night. I not only couldn't abuse substances; almost any substance abused me. I had stopped drinking vodka and smoking pot. Even smoke from a secondhand cigarette made me vomit.

The next day, everybody was supposed to go back to Boston. I had to be back in the States for an appointment with the dentist. We were to fly back to America on the Concorde. Steven and I would then separate at the airport in New York and he would fly up to New Hampshire, where he could exorcise the tour demon and clean out. I stopped off for a day or so in New York, where I met with Todd at our favorite hangout, the Mexi-Frost restaurant. I wanted to explain why I was staying with this man, even though his drug insanities led me to seek comfort from Todd. Todd was crushed, baffled. We both burst into tears.

When I got back to Sunapee, I found that Steven had been trying to stop snorting mountains of cocaine. I have to give him credit for trying, but he just couldn't pull it off. His behavior grew even more erratic, more bizarre, and truly frightening. He would lock himself in the bathroom and get high. Twice, he had violent, terrifying drug-induced seizures. The first time, after shutting himself in the bathroom for a long time, I heard tapping against the door, as if he were locked inside and trying to jiggle the door open. But it was a hard, insistent sound—he was either kicking or banging his head against the door. When I got the door open, I saw him on the floor. His eyes were rolling back in his head, his tongue was hanging out, and his leg was jerking involuntarily in spasms, his foot knocking against the door. I freaked out and called the road manager, Henry Smith, who lived up the street.

"He's convulsing. He's seizing. Get here now!"

"Bebe, listen to me," Henry said calmly. "You have to get a pen or a pencil and hold his tongue down, because he could swallow it."

Steven was gone. His eyes rolled back in his head and his skinny body trembled uncontrollably. Henry arrived, made a call, and a mysterious man with a black bag materialized, shooting Steven up with something. A voice inside me whispered, Bebe, you're in this way over your head.

The next day, Steven was sitting up in bed having soup and being his charming self. He didn't remember anything from the seizure, but he swore that his brush with death was a wake-up call and he knew that it was indeed time to kick cocaine. By nightfall, he was loaded again.

The second seizure, which ended with Steven being rushed to a doctor's office, was my cue to leave. I figured he'd probably be dead in a year, at the rate he was going. It was life or death for me, too, but I had no choice. I needed to be sane, grounded, and surrounded by positive, healthy energy. I loved Steven deeply, but my survival instincts were taking over. Todd still represented a flight to safety, to the accepting daddy I'd never had. Whatever. I didn't care. I had to get out of there. "I'm really scared," I whispered to Todd over the phone. "Help me get out of here. I have to get away from this guy."

CHAPTER 6

Todd to the Rescue
1976-1977

You better hide, baby
Better think of another way to get your kicks
Cuz while you're busy messing up
She's earnestly copping some licks
"BORED BABY," LYRICS BEBE BUELL

Steven and I were supposed to go on vacation in Hawaii, but I decided to run. "Can I borrow your plane today?" I asked Steven. "Todd's not in Woodstock, so I'd like to go and get some stuff and my dollhouse." This was a prized gift from Todd, a custom-built pink-and-purple Victorian dollhouse. "Sure," he said. As he watched me pack, he asked, "Why are you taking so much stuff with you?" I finessed an answer about checking what clothes I had at my country house, what I needed for Sunapee, what I wanted to leave there. He shrugged. As the small jet lifted off the tiny landing strip, I felt a wave of relief. I had survived. When the pilot landed in Newburgh, New York, I was met by an employee of Todd's. I turned to the pilot and announced, "You can fly back up without me. I'm staying here."

"No way I'm returning without you," he insisted. "I'll get fired." It was a harsh way to end it, but I had a life growing inside me that represented all the accumulated madness of the previous three months. This was my moment of truth. I had to make a choice, be as strong as I could and dig in: "Well then, you're going to get fired. Because you're going to have to leave me here. I'm going home."

Steven, clearly in a drug-hazed state of denial, called at 1:30 A.M.

"Beeber, have you got too much stuff? Do you need a truck to bring it all back?"

It was painful to break the news that I was gone for good. I doubt anyone had ever delivered Steven an emotional blow like that. After all, he had dumped a girlfriend for me, I was carrying his baby, and now I was running for cover with Todd. I reminded him of his many broken promises.

"I don't have a problem," he pleaded. "I can stop anytime I want."

"Fine," I said before hanging up. "Clean up your act and then call me."

It was amazing to me that Todd was still decent enough to open the door and take me in. We were both clearly in denial, except that I could no longer button the top button of my snug-fitting model dresses and was now sporting trendy maternity wear. The first thing I said was, "Todd, this isn't your baby. Are you sure you can handle this?" And he said, "Don't ever say that again." We made a pact that he would be the father and raise the baby as his own and we wouldn't tell anyone.

There was a part of me that really wanted the baby to be Todd's, and I actually brainwashed myself into believing I was carrying Todd's child, because I desperately wanted everything to be normal and safe. Todd and I both wanted the baby to be his. I wanted to will myself into the fertility-science record books. I had seven sonograms to try and somehow prove it was Todd's baby, prove that a Rundgren sperm had somehow lived inside me from August through September, and fought off billions of Tyler-sperm rivals before fertilizing my egg. I believed Todd genuinely loved me, and that he also felt some responsibility for me because he had been a major influence in my life. But it was more than that. The pregnancy and miscarriage I had had with Todd in March was what solidified our relationship and now caused him to step in and be responsible for me. But I also think the possibility of my having been impregnated by another man enraged Todd and hurt his ego. That was another reason he really wanted people to think that it was his baby. So after he decided that he was going to be the baby's father, we both simply pretended he was and stopped talking about it. Despite our pact and the nurturing pledges to back it up, life with Todd was still full of unresolved tensions. There was a lot of anger. Todd wasn't pleased about the embarrassment that I had caused him. And there was always that doubt in everyone else's mind as to whose baby it was. Most people thought I had run off with Steven, then discovered I was pregnant by Todd, and had gone back to the dad. There was another crop of people who knew it was Steven's, of course. And then there were the damn fools who didn't think either one was the father.

Meanwhile, Todd was on the road throughout most of my pregnancy. It was a confusing time. Steven and I saw each other a few times during the pregnancy, and I told him the baby was Todd's. But Steven always knew Liv was his child. I made love with Steven because Todd was on the road and I wanted to be with the father of my child, but at the same time I knew I couldn't really be with him.

I used to pray every night that the baby's eyes would be blue, because Todd and I had blue eyes; Steven's eyes were brown. And boy, as it turned out, did she have blue eyes. Let me tell you—they were bluer than blue! I think God overcompensated: He threw in some sapphires.

"I'm so happy to be back with Todd in my home again," I wrote in my diary on November 19. "I am three months pregnant now and I feel very good about it. Steven was not a mistake; it was definitely a necessary experience. He's a very sweet, wonderful man and one of the best friends I will ever have, but I am still so glad to be back with Todd. Poor Steven is so fucked up on drugs. I learned a lot, but I also learned that my days of affairs are over, and Todd is my man for the rest of my life. I love you, Todd."

Todd's lifestyle was governed by seventies rock standards. Yes, he did drugs, but never anything addictive. He experimented with

Eastern mysticism, but he wasn't a space cadet; he screwed around, but he always came home; he partied, but he was never abusive or self-destructive. And no matter how fickle and ambivalent I was, he remained patient and accepting, even when he was on the road. Todd Land felt like a sane and safe place to be pregnant in. I was living in places I knew—Horatio Street and the warm, cozy house on Mink

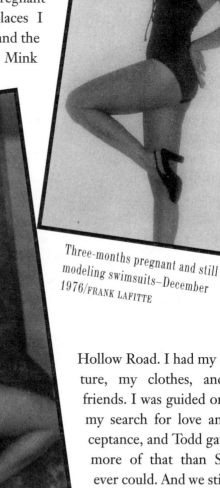

Three-months pregnant and still modeling swimsuits—December 1976/FRANK LAFITTE

Eight-months pregnant self-portrait in the mirror/BEBE BUELL

Hollow Road. I had my furniture, my clothes, and my friends. I was guided only by my search for love and acceptance, and Todd gave me more of that than Steven ever could. And we still had our adventures.

On November 25, I became so sick that Todd sweetly carried

the TV upstairs to the bedroom. I was half-asleep when I heard the front door slam shut downstairs and footsteps pounding up the stairs. I nervously kept my eye on the doorway. At that instant, Susan Lee burst through the door, stomped up to the bed, and began spewing bile about me being the most despicable creature on earth! How dare I get pregnant with another man's baby and ask Todd to take me back! I guess she realized that Todd was not going to let her take my place. Sick as I was, I sprang to my feet and screamed, "Get your hands off me!" As she lunged for me again, Todd rode in on a white horse with trumpets blaring and pulled her off of me. Todd threw her out of the house and fired her on the spot. This was two days before Utopia's Japanese tour kicked off.

Between Christmas and New Year's Eve, when I was three months pregnant, Todd took me to London. While I was there, I worked for British *Vogue*—I was posing for just a head shot, so I didn't need a flat stomach. While Todd toured, I went to see a specialist, Dr. Saree, to try to determine the exact day I got pregnant. This doctor did sonograms and could pinpoint conception dates. Of course, I found out that there was just no chance I was pregnant by Todd. I always knew in my heart the baby was Steven's—you always know when you're the mother.

I stayed at the Montcalm Hotel in central London. I was experiencing horrible morning sickness, puking all the time, sick as a dog. Keith Richards happened to be at the Montcalm with his six-year-old son, Marlon. This was right after Tara, his third child with Anita, died. It was an awful time. Marlon wasn't going to school, and he had little supervision. Keith was very depressed; he just sat on the couch doing drugs most of the time. Other times, he and I would lie on the bed for hours and chat. Keith was always trying to teach me about philosophy, hoping to enlighten me about what Todd was going through—about the spiritual quest he was on. Sometimes Keith would fall asleep mid-sentence, but I was used to that.

I would go down and take Marlon to the park, because the child was just dying for some exercise. I started spending more and more time there. I never had an affair with Keith, but I remember falling asleep in a chair with Marlon in my arms, rocking him and holding nim. My maternal instincts were kicking in. I had a very special connection with Marlon. I looked a little bit like his mother, so maybe there was something comforting about me. Anita was in Switzerland at the time.

One day, I was sitting in Keith's suite. Marlon was asleep in my arms, the TV was blasting, and Keith was nodding out on the couch. He was wearing cutoff blue jeans, and as he began to nod, he started to get an enormous hard-on which started to peek out of the bottom of his shorts. Suddenly, I was glad that Marlon was asleep. Now I could just watch this Eighth Wonder of the World. It was amazing. I don't think anybody realized it, because Bill Wyman usually grabbed the honors in this department, but Keith was the member of the Rolling Stones who was particularly well endowed. He was impressive to say the least. Oh my God! He had a hard-on parallel to his knee for a solid twenty minutes. Then, as his erection started to subside, it ducked perfectly back under his jeans. Many men are incapable of achieving even the slightest tumescence under the influence of drugs—that's one of its many curses. Keith clearly had no such problems. I just sat there smiling, reflecting what a blissful moment I was sharing with him. Unfortunately, that was the sum total of my sexual contact with Keith Richards.

Keith had the leadership qualities of a warrior. Even when he was barely able to talk, he could still organize a departure or an entrance. There would also still be awful moments when he'd be passed out cold with a junkie girl on either side of him, which was heartbreaking to watch, but he would wake up eventually. I found him extremely interesting, because there was this part of me that had a massive crush on him and wanted to know him more, get under his skin. Yet I was terrified by his ability to ingest drugs. Unbelievable.

I stayed in London through the first half of January while Todd toured Europe with Utopia. I moved out of the Montcalm, because I didn't want to be alone all the time. I accepted an invitation from John Phillips of the Mamas and the Papas and his wife, Genevieve Waite—I had met them through Mick—to stay with them at Glebe Place. They were so sweet, and their house was very comfortable, but the longer I stayed there, the more I realized that their whole life revolved around drugs. The room I stayed in was huge and had several ornate couches. It was very beautiful. I had a lovely big cushion to sleep on. They still had a huge Christmas tree up, and I would sleep in there with the Christmas tree. I remember that on my first morning there I was awakened by the sound of breaking glass. Tamberlaine, their very young son, was so bored, he was taking the balls off the Christmas tree, throwing them to the ground, and stomping on them, cutting his feet in the process. I jumped from my bed and said, "What are you doing?" I panicked. I washed his feet and got the glass out with tweezers while he sat there very patiently. The poor kid was crying out for attention, and this was the way he got it. I remember being so mad that I went to John and Genevieve's bed and I screamed and yelled at them. I remember slapping John. He jumped up and he went, "Why are you smacking me?"

"Because you're a fucking pig. You'd rather sleep and get high than take care of your child!" Then John, who was a really sweet, good man, snapped to. "All right!" he said, getting up. But I was outraged. Wait a minute, I thought. I am not a fucking maid. Who do these people think they are that they can lie around in bed, neglect their child, and have their houseguest end up being the one who takes care of everything?

Mick Jagger bopped in and out at Glebe Place, claiming that I was actually carrying his baby. This was right when Keith was getting ready to go on trial for possession of guns and drugs. It was a difficult time, but Mick could see that I was uncomfortable there. He actually took me to San Lorenzo for lunch one day and said, "I want you to get out of there." I didn't want to leave, because I didn't want to leave Tamberlaine alone. I adored Genevieve and John, but they were extremely fucked up and there were a lot of equally fucked up people dropping by. There was a lot of behavior that was not good for me at that point because of my condition, and I wasn't interested in partaking in it.

My visit to Glebe Place was memorable because Mick made love to me there one night. This was the first time in my life that I had an orgasm without clitoral stimulation. To this day, I don't know why, but it was a lovely experience, although I suffered at that time, feeling guilty about what I was doing. I was hanging out with three men, Todd, Steven, and Mick. I had been with Steven, then left him and returned to Todd. I was pretty much officially Todd's woman, and yet here I was, back fooling around with Mick again. He felt there was a glimmer of a chance that this child I was carrying might be his. I spent a lot of time with Mick when I was pregnant. It seemed he really wanted the baby to be his. I had them all fighting over who was the father. It was insane. I kept saying, "Mick, it can't be yours," because we hadn't made love at the time the baby was conceived. I couldn't tell Mick whose child it was. He knew I had hung out with Steven. And he teased me mercilessly, saying, "Why do you want to hang out with him when you've got me? I'm the real thing. What do you want the fake Mick for when you've got the real one?" I don't think it ever dawned on Mick that the baby was Steven's. Never. At that point, Mick and I were so close, such good friends, I mean just so fond of each other, I felt so comfortable and safe with him. It had been months since I had felt that. I was in dire need of some tender loving care and he certainly gave it to me.

I stayed only four or five days at Glebe Place, because I just could not deal with what I saw going on there. With John and Gen on the nod day in and day out, only vaguely aware of anything, I once again found myself taking care of the children while mom and dad slept. It was one of the most horrible scenes I'd ever experienced.

On January 17, I joined Todd in Paris. We made the most beautiful love, but then I had a pretty hard night with him. We had a silly fight at dinner, but later we had a real discussion right in front of Roger, his keyboard player, before we all went to bed. It hurt me, and I was very frightened, because I needed him so. After we argued and got it all out of our systems, Todd was very tender and sweet with me. I stayed with him for the rest of the tour, going to Amsterdam, Brussels, and London. I must have been in a completely schizophrenic state of mind. My diary is full of passionate descriptions of beautiful sex with Todd, followed by cryptic notes. Maybe it was because I was so tired all the time that I didn't know what I was writing, but if it was automatic writing, that just makes it more telling.

I returned to London again in March. This time, Todd was off on another one of his spiritual quests, so I stayed on my own at the Portobello Hotel, which was the closest thing London had to New York's Chelsea Hotel in those days. I stayed there because that's where the modeling agency said I could get a small, affordable room for myself. So I got one of the "coffin rooms," where the sink and shower were all one and the bed was tiny, but I could afford to live there for a month because they gave me an extended rate. It was just perfect for me. I spent my time modeling and hanging out with my punk-rock friends, some of the most fabulous people in London.

Patti Smith came to town and stayed at the Portobello, which soon became punk rock headquarters. That was when I found out she was bonking Paul Simonon of the Clash. They were very cozy. Every night, I would go down to the basement to have dinner, and the troops would roll in: the Clash; Patti and her band including J. D. Daugherty, who was a particularly good friend; Sid and Nancy. Everybody popped in. I was hanging out with many of them right before they became famous. Chrissie Hynde and I became fabulous friends. She called me Bardot. "You remind me of Brigitte Bardot. You remind me of all the great beauties," she said. She had just recorded her first single with Nick Lowe, "Stop Your Sobbing." She sang it for us for the first time in the bar at the Portobello. We all thought it was amazing. She had the best female voice in rock 'n' roll I'd heard in years. She was just so special and so English, even though she was an American girl from Ohio. She was one of those ballsy chicks who'd gotten on a plane and went to London, just like Jerry Hall went to Paris and I went to New York. While I let love rule, Chrissie didn't let relationships rule. The only guys Chrissie dated were the ones she was working with in bands.

When I went back to America after that trip, I took a copy of "God Save the Queen," by the Sex Pistols, back with me. I sat Todd down in the middle of the floor of our living room in the house on Mink Hollow Road and said, "All right! I'm going to play you the future." He was excited. I played it, and he burst out laughing. He said, "It's Chuck Berry with a bad singer." I said, "Todd! You're not embracing the attitude! You're not embracing the freshness! This is what we need right now after all these years of excess, of Led Zeppelin and huge expense accounts. This is what we need!"

"This is not music," he told me with his usual arch perception; "this is just fashion. Now everybody is going to run around with their hair spiked up and holes in their faces. I did this when I was eighteen with my first band." So then we got into a big fight about the lineage of Woody's Truck Stop, Nazz, and all that Philadelphia rock history and Todd's Upper Darby roots.

Todd really seemed to enjoy showing me off when I was pregnant. When I was almost eight months along and big, in May 1977, he took me to L.A. for Utopia's tour out west. I got to show off my glorious belly and cleavage in a sexy Oscar de la Renta number at a record-industry bash for Todd at Carlos and Charlie's on the Strip. Tom Petty was introduced to me, and he said, "Bebe, you look radiant." Pregnancy clearly agreed with me. But as the weeks ground on, it became increasingly apparent that Todd and I were just another couple of beautiful people going through the motions. And Steven wasn't going down without a fight. He still knew how to push my buttons.

When I returned to Horatio Street from L.A., Todd was still on the road. Steven came by and I made a fire, which he found amusing, since it was the end of May. Steven rubbed my tummy and talked sweetly as we sat by the fireplace. After a melancholy attempt to get back with Julia, he explained, he had had a couple of new girlfriends, but he still missed me. He claimed to be clean of drugs, although it was obvious to me that he had gotten coked up in preparation for his visit. Suddenly, Steven fell to his knees, burst into tears, and begged me to take him back! When I said a condition of my coming back was that he had to give up drugs, he flatly refused! I was so pissed, I lashed out. "It's not your baby anyway," I screamed. "I got the dates all mixed up when I figured out the timing! I've been pregnant longer than I thought." Steven was so high, so angry, and so upset, it was impossible to tell how much he grasped. But a look of pure madness flashed in his eyes. Then he went into an Elvis Presley routine, heavy with cornpone concern: "Is he treating you well? Are you making love with each other?"

"Well, we're not making love, because he's never here."

"Well, Beeber, you can't go through a whole pregnancy and not make love." Suddenly, we were in each other's arms. In the light of the fire, it was one of the most deeply intimate moments I've ever shared with a man. Steven made it through to 5:00 A.M., but then he split to reup his stash.

We got together on several other occasions, but each time after our intimate encounters, Steven was completely incapable of giving up drugs to make a life with me. Each time we parted, I felt a little more used, a little more alone, as if slivers of my heart were being sliced off with each meeting.

My last two months of pregnancy were the toughest. It turned out that when I was seven months pregnant, while I was seeing Steven, Todd was in Texas with the new woman in his life, Bruce Springsteen's ex-girlfriend a tall, slender redhead named Karen Darvin.

Ready to go into labor–June 30, 1977, NYC/BUELL PRIVATE COLLECTION

When Todd played Texas, Karen was in Dallas mending her broken heart with her parents. However, she not only felt up to seeing Todd's Utopia show; she mustered enough energy to go backstage and put the wounded-bird touch on Todd. Something clicked between them. I later discovered that after Dallas, their torrid affair played in several other Texas cities. Naturally, I suspected nothing, since Todd was covering his tracks with dutiful calls and flights home for a few days here and there. It was one thing to be drifting; it was another thing entirely to be screwing around on me seriously in my last trimester, when I needed him most! Todd and I were not together that much during the last months of my pregnancy because he had already met the woman with whom he would end up having two sons. I think he had fallen genuinely in love with Karen, just as I was genuinely in love with Steven. The bottom line was that both Steven and Todd chose to manipulate me through my pregnancy, rather than giving me the TLC I needed. The saddest part was that I loved being pregnant. It should have been the happiest, most joy-

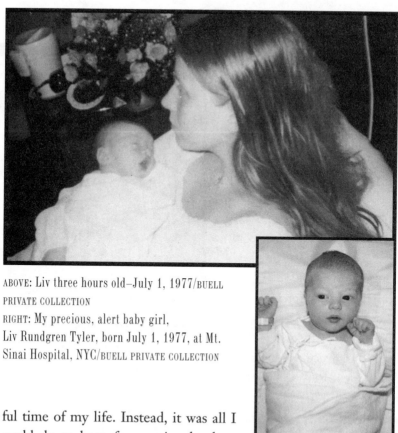

ABOVE: Liv three hours old–July 1, 1977/BUELL
PRIVATE COLLECTION
RIGHT: My precious, alert baby girl,
Liv Rundgren Tyler, born July 1, 1977, at Mt.
Sinai Hospital, NYC/BUELL PRIVATE COLLECTION

ful time of my life. Instead, it was all I
could do to keep from going bonkers
while sheltering myself and the baby
growing inside me from the reckless,
hurtful indulgences of the two men staking their claims as her
father. I remember once whispering to the kicking child in my
womb, "Kick once, sweetheart, for Todd, and if it's Steven, kick
twice." Liv was one step ahead of them even then: She kicked me
three times. I thought that was the best answer—perhaps the only
one.

I gave birth to Liv at 6:00 A.M. on July 1, 1977, at Mount Sinai
Hospital in New York City. Throughout the labor, Todd was totally
supportive; as I delivered Liv, he was right at my head, coaching
me, then cutting her umbilical cord. It was the most extraordinary,
profound, and physically excruciating time in my life. Afterward, as
I lay drained, exhilarated, sobbing with bliss at the exquisite newborn in my arms, Todd leaned close and whispered good-bye, saying he had stuff to do. Looking up, I gave him a twisted smile.

Thank goodness my mom was there to support me. If my labor had gone on any longer, I might have thrown Todd off his schedule. He left the delivery room and hoofed it over to a nearby hotel, where he had temporarily parked Karen for his convenience. The next day, I called everyone I knew to help me locate him, becoming so agitated and hysterical in the process that I had to be sedated. Finally, he staggered into the maternity ward at 7:00 P.M. on July 2, claiming that he'd been wandering the streets, drinking, smoking pot, and hanging out with friends in celebration. He apparently left out one little activity—and it wasn't passing out cigars. Todd had been with another woman. I'll never forget how Todd, whose name was on Liv's birth certificate as her father, bent over to hug me, because I picked up an alien scent, and my inner female voice screamed, *I smell woman!*

As I lay in the hospital for the next three days, my head swam with confusion over what we were all doing, what was going to happen next. Todd and I were still both in denial, pretending Liv was our baby. God only knows what we were doing. In his cruel, fumbling way, Todd was trying to be loyal and live up to his obligations

Leaving Mt. Sinai Hospital with Todd and four-day-old Liv–July 4, 1977/CHUCK PULIN

and promises and do the right thing. But he was doing it all wrong. Although I could not know this yet, Todd was already head over heels in love with Karen and merely in over his head with me. But what was I supposed to do? I had cut off any other paths of escape. I had laid down the law with Steven: As long as he did drugs, we had no future. I had become reliant upon Todd because we shared a past. And now I had my newborn baby girl to look after. By Independence Day, I was feeling utterly trapped. Todd picked me up from the hospital on July 4 and we drove upstate. As soon as we settled into familiar surroundings, things seemed wonderful and secure again—for about an hour. Then Todd said he was leaving for the city, that he had business to tend to. I was so immersed in motherhood, I still didn't get it. And if I had gotten it, I'd have been way too focused on my newborn's health to do much about it. But the truth was, Todd was heading right back to Karen.

One day when I returned to New York, I ran into Anita Pallenberg, who had her son, Marlon, with her. We talked for an hour. I told her about the controversy that surrounded my pregnancy. "Oh, darling, you wouldn't believe what went on when I was pregnant with Marlon." She laughed. "When I named him Marlon, everybody thought he was Marlon Brando's. But all you have to do is look at the jaw." And I laughed, because it was true—one look at Marlon and you knew he was Keith's child.

Shortly after Liv was born, I had a powerful urge to show off the baby to her daddy. I had talked to him about Liv by phone, but I thought it was time they got to know each other. I found out the band had use of a suite at the Ritz for some Aerosmith meetings, so I went there. When I knocked at the door, Henry Smith cracked it open and asked coldly, "Bebe, what are you doing here?"

"I want to see Steven."

"You can't see Steven." I saw Steven behind Henry, and when he spotted me, he came to the door.

"Beeber, what are you doing here?"

"I want to show you something. Your baby!"

"I thought you said it wasn't my baby." I pulled back the little blanket and held her out so he could get a good look at her. She had on a hat and baby sweater. "Look at her," I whispered. "Who else's baby could she be?"

I watched as he gazed into her gorgeous little face and they made eye contact. A look of wonder came over Steven.

"Okay," he whispered, "come on inside." We walked back to one of the bedrooms and he closed the door, asking Henry to guard the door. I placed the baby down on the bed between us and we wrapped our arms around her warm little body. We had tears in our eyes.

"Look at her lips," Steven said softly. "I can give up drugs for this. Everything's going to be beautiful again." She never made a peep as Steven and I slowly removed our clothes and made love, with our baby sleeping right next to us. We both felt we had to put our egos aside and do what was best for our child, but by the end of the afternoon, Steven had scored his next stash.

I found myself in a very difficult position. There is a certain amount of envy involved when you are a rebel soul and a woman who's not afraid to be one of the boys. Plus, being an unwed mother was not as fashionable then as it is now. Liberated women who took their clothes off and wanted to be as sexually free as a man were not common. There was no Madonna yet. So in the late 1970s, there was not the acceptance of free spirits that there is today.

A few weeks before Liv's birth, Todd had decided to give up the house on Horatio Street. He was gone or upstate so much, it made little sense to hold on to it. So when we were in town together, we'd stay at the Mayflower Hotel on Sixty-second Street and Central Park West. One day, Steven came into town and I visited him again at the Ritz. I dropped Liv off for a couple of hours with yet another player in this circus: Todd's mom, Ruth Rundgren, who was in town to visit her granddaughter. Steven met me at the door of his suite in a Clinique facial mask. He kept nodding out with this thick mask on, and I joked that he'd never get it off. After we had made love and were enjoying the delicious afterglow, Steven sat up, threw me a smirking grin, and asked, "So, Beeber, who's the redhead with Todd?" I was stunned. Talk about breaking the spell!

"What do you mean, 'who's the redhead?' What redhead?"

"You know, the one who was hangin' on to him at the show we did in Ohio last week. Tall, skinny redhead. They were definitely together. I thought you should know." My heart sucked into my stomach.

With Todd's then girlfriend, Karen Darvin—my replacement, 1980/MARCIA RESNICK

Given the powerful postpartum baby blues, the tricky emotions attached to being intimate again with my baby's father, and the sudden revelation of Todd's secret lover, I was flip-floppping out. It was more than I could handle. I walked out of the hotel and headed west along Central Park South for the Mayflower. I went up to our room and confronted Todd. He vehemently denied everything. Now I wondered if Steven had been kidding me. Maybe he'd decided to fuck with my head. If so, he had succeeded, because my head was spinning. I didn't know what to do to get my bearings. Meanwhile, Todd was furious about my seeing Steven. He did not want Steven to have any parenting privileges and refused to acknowledge him as Liv's father. I was being pushed around by a pair of powerful egomaniacs. There was no end to the mind games these two could play on me. Meanwhile, Steven must have passed out with his Clinique mask on. Because when I got back to his suite at the Ritz an hour and a half later, after confronting Todd about *"la grande rouge,"* the mask had hardened so completely it took me twenty minutes to chisel it off. At this point, I was hysterical, and

Steven was jumping up and down, saying, "You cannot just keep running back and forth. Now she's Todd's child."

I convinced Steven to get a blood test, so that we could confirm his paternity and have some kind of closure. Steven actually did go and get the blood test. I had to go and get Liv's little toe poked, and I was crying so hard because my daughter had never cried before. It turned out that she had my blood type: B positive. DNA tests weren't available in those days, so we still had no proof of paternity. Although we all knew, none of us were dealing with reality at all. We all sank deeper into denial and the fact was, Liv even looked something like Todd.

Liv's spiritual journey is very interesting to me because of the fact that she has these two fathers. One's a spiritual father, one's a biological father, but she could physically be by either of them. There are parts of Liv that do favor Todd's mannerisms—the way her eyes are, which makes me realize that parenthood goes way beyond biological connections.

Liv is a Cancer, with Cancer rising. Todd and I are both Cancers. That's a karmic thing, which I will never understand completely, but I try to accept it as the way things were meant to be. Liv's karmic connection to Todd, to Steven, and to me has profoundly changed all of our lives. Obviously, I was meant to survive the most emotionally turbulent, confusing year of my life in order to bring Liv into this world.

To his credit, Todd made an attempt to maintain peace between us by suggesting we take a holiday together, something we had never done before. "Let's go to Disney World," he suggested, "then to Saint Martin. Let's give ourselves a vacation and patch this up."

Despite the allure of an exotic getaway, things got ugly fast. Though Todd had never revealed an abusive streak, he now proved himself capable of inflicting great emotional harm. The first time we made love after Liv was born was in a hotel near Dulles Airport on our way south. I asked him what it was like to be with me again. What I needed was his reassurance that I was still sexy, beautiful, feminine.

"No man," he said, "is ever going to want you again, now that you've had a baby." How could he say something so heartless and cruel? I thought. What shreds of self-esteem that remained now vanished. Where was I supposed to go?

Once we got to Saint Martin, I found the smoking gun when I came across a "Wish you were here" love letter written to *la grande rouge*. I didn't need a French lit degree to figure out that Todd's steamy missive was written to the redhead Steven had spotted in Ohio.

"I want that fucking letter!" Todd screamed as soon as I brought it up, and he came after me. I refused to tell him where I'd hidden it. Enraged, he threw a glass of wine in my face. This was his first physically aggressive act in our five years together. Now it was Todd's turn to tear a hotel room apart: He looked everywhere for the letter, but he failed to check under the mattress. Todd suggested flying home alone and leaving me behind.

"No way," I said. We flew back together, but we checked into separate rooms at the Mayflower. By the time I dropped my bags and tried to phone him, his line was busy. He was obviously explaining to *la grande rouge* about why he hadn't written. As we drove to the country the following day, I sensed things were ready to explode, and the end was near. I was getting scared. For the first time, Todd seemed capable of real fury, and I was losing it myself.

The next day, I went to see Steven. Our relationship was really important to me—I wanted to marry him. We were cut from the same cloth, two peas in a pod. I truly cared about him and I believed he was worth one last shot. This time, I asked him point-blank if he could make the choice between our family and drugs, between reality and fantasy. Steven mulled it over, then shook his head and flatly replied, "No."

Once more, Todd put his foot down. "You get your fucking ass home now," he bellowed over the phone. "Do not go sniffing around Steven Tyler. We made a decision. You bring the child and yourself home now."

He sent his manager, Eric, over to the Mayflower with a car and demanded that I get my ass back to Woodstock, where he'd already gone, so I did. But as soon as I got home, he told me that he was breaking up with me and that he had already rented an apartment for Liv and me on Fifty-eighth Street, a place he and Patti Smith had picked out. That was a shock, because I didn't even know that he was still hanging out with Patti. But I was glad that she was the one who had helped pick out the apartment because I knew that she would at least pick one out that had light. My relationship was over; I mean, it was so over. When we finally officially broke up in September 1977, "our" baby was two and a half months old.

I had exactly five hours to pack up five years of my life. I left the place on Mink Hollow Road for the last time, riding shotgun in a beat-up old car belonging to one of Todd's roadies. As the car swung out onto the road, I saw a shiny black limousine, sunlight sparkling off its long, sleek hood, purring toward the house. Inside, behind one lowered smoked glass window, I caught a fleeting glimpse of the tall, skinny redhead reclining in the back. Todd was bringing his *grande rouge* up to Mink Hollow in style.

I had been banished from the kingdom. I felt like Anne Boleyn. Liv and I were heading to New York and the one-bedroom apartment Todd had rented for us on West Fifty-eighth. We were embarking on our own private journey. Liv was the one whose unconditional love would give me the courage to find my own way.

CHAPTER 7

A Real Double Duchess
1977-1979

Into land of up and down
Into island of in and out
Jungle make me scream and shout
Jungle make me scared.
"JACUZZI JUNGLE," LYRICS BY BEBE BUELL

The Fifty-eighth Street apartment was in a doorman building between Sixth and Seventh avenues. It had a bedroom, a big living room with a bay window, a kitchen, and a bathroom. It was a brand-new apartment, with all the latest appliances, to accommodate a brand-new life. Liv's crib was in my bedroom, where I slept alone.

Some people felt that's what I deserved, but the way that Todd and I broke up was extremely painful. I had issues of abandonment anyway, as well as father issues, and I really felt that I was being discarded. Emotionaly confused, I regretted my decision to go back to Todd and wished that I had stayed with the father of my baby. Maybe I had made a mistake. Can you imagine what I must have been feeling? I suppose I should have been happy to be alive, and thankful that Liv was a perfect baby, and I was, but that wasn't the point.

Going on incredibly powerful rock 'n' roll tours and then returning home is always deeply disorienting for musicians, let alone their entourages. I now felt a similar disorientation. One day, I was touring Europe with the number-one band in the world; the next, I was a single parent living alone on a small income, changing diapers. It was a mind-bending transition. To make matters worse, very few people knew our secret. Not being able to tell the truth about who Liv's father was forced me to live through a period of extreme alienation and isolation.

I spent many hours crying, because I was so torn between the stability of Todd Land and the passionate world I had inhabited all too briefly with Steven. I still had this great love for Steven—after all, we had created a child together—but I wasn't able to share anything with him. I wasn't so much torn as ripped.

After settling into the apartment, the first thing I did was to try to resurrect my modeling career. Three years after the fact and despite my now being a mother, the *Playboy* stigma still limited the kind of work I could get in the United States. I found this unbelievable: It was the seventies, after all. I did a lot of *Cosmopolitan* bookings. Apart from that, I tried to be a good mother and get on with my life.

One day when Liv was a few months old, I was visiting Liz Derringer at her Thirteenth Street apartment. Mick called and said, "I'm coming over to see my child." Mick and Woody dropped by. Mick looked at Liv and crowed, "She's mine. Look at those lips!" Then he said, "Okay, you've proved to me that you're a mother. Now put her away." I'll never forget that as long as I live. Some people did think she was Mick's baby, and Mick did nothing to discourage their opinions, introducing me as "the mother of one of my illegitimate children" whenever the opportunity arose.

We laughed and reminisced throughout the afternoon. When they were getting ready to leave, I said that I wanted to go with them. I could tell that Mick didn't really want me along, but I didn't get that many opportunities to have fun, so I insisted. Liz said she would take care of Liv for a couple of hours, so we left. It turned out they were going over to John Phillips and Genevieve Waite's place in the city to pick up Keith.

As soon as we walked into their big apartment on the Upper

West Side, I noticed that something was wrong. The place was unkempt. There was dog shit and child's feces on the carpet; it was really awful. I went into the bathroom, where I found blood on the walls and needles in the sink. It was a hellhole. John and Genevieve were totally fucked up. They were so out of it, they didn't even notice what was going on around them. The dishes hadn't been washed; obviously, nobody bathed, because the place stank. Keith was crashed out on the couch, with a sleazy girl on either side of him. Mick was producing a solo album with John, and he and Ronnie wanted to make sure that everybody was okay and to get Keith out of there. Now I understood why he hadn't wanted me to come. This was the underbelly of the Rolling Stones during Keith's long heroin habit.

I heard a baby crying, so I followed the sound down a corridor, into a bedroom, and up to a giant bed. A tiny baby was lying in the middle of the bed with pillows around her. Her diaper hadn't been changed. I rolled her over. She was lying on a hypodermic needle. Being a new mother, I was particularly sensitive to this new baby. For an instant, I lost my mind, but I gently sponged the baby and cleaned her up. She lay there looking at me as if to say, "Who are you?" She looked so happy now. After I changed her diaper, I went downstairs, found formula, and fed her.

Back in the living room, Mick was saying, "Keith . . . Keith . . . come on; come on! Come on, darling; let's leave. Come on, baby." We finally got Keith out of there. Woody stayed to look after the baby until somebody showed up to baby-sit. Mick, Keith, and I, as well as the two sleazy chicks, left in Keith's limo. When we got to Mick's house, Keith immediately lay back down with one junkie girl on either side and fell asleep. Mick asked the two girls to leave.

"Well now, darlings, I think you need to go. I'd like Keith to get some rest."

"Noooaw, we dooonn waaannnaa—"

"I think it's really time to leave now," he said a little more insistently. "It's bedtime." After they left, Mick turned and began to ascend the stairs to his bedroom. It was late at night. Halfway up the staircase, he turned to me and said, "Would you like to join me?"

"You know I've got to get back to the baby. I told Liz I'd be back in two hours."

"Oh, that's right. You are a mother now, aren't you? Yes, the mother of my illegitimate daughter." Mick couldn't stop taunting me.

Steven and I had a little affair again that fall. It was an intimate oasis in an otherwise-arid time for me. He brought Liv toys and played with her, and we made love. Shortly thereafter, he became involved with Cyrinda Foxe, who was getting divorced from David Johansen. Steven ended up marrying her in the summer, 1978, so I didn't see him for quite a while, which was really difficult. I was afraid that Steven was going to die at any minute and that Liv was never going to get to know him. Ever since the spate of rock-star deaths from 1969 to 1971, the rock press had kept a ghoulish list of the next rock star most likely to die. For years, Keith Richards had been number one on the list and Lou Reed had been number two. Now Steven eclipsed both of them. In December 1978, Steven and Cyrinda had a daughter, Mia. It seemed so ironic that, of all people, Cyrinda could publically be the mother of his daughter, while I couldn't be. And that Liv now had a half sister she couldn't even know. They were only eighteen months apart.

If it had not been for everything that had happened, I would probably not have responded to a call I got from Rod Stewart in November of 1977. However, when Rod heard that Todd and I had finally broken up, he had his assistant and publicist, Tony Tune, call and invite me to dinner.

"If Rod wants to see me and take me to dinner," I told Tony, "he has to call me himself."

"I'd love to have you come meet me at the hotel for dinner, downstairs in the dining room," Rod purred over the phone three minutes later. British rock stars have a way of making everything sound so gallant, it's hard to remember that, for the most part, it's all a game. But I was lonely and blue, so I accepted.

Looking forward to an empathetic tête-à-tête with Rod the Mod, I dressed carefully and demurely. Imagine my astonishment on arriving at Rod's hotel and discovering myself standing in front of a group of British photographers and journalists all screaming, "Rod! Bebe! This way! Look this way, darling! Bebe! Rod!"

It turned out that Rod was announcing his next album, or his next tour, or his next haircut. My life, I realized in a flash, had become a publicity stunt! I thought I was going to an intimate dinner with an old mate, one who knew I had just broken up with Todd and had a baby to care for. I was distraught, and suddenly I had to be "on" for this big brouhaha. I was extremely upset, but I knew right then that if I was going to see Rod Stewart, if only as a friend, I was going to be part of a publicity campaign emphasizing his rock 'n' rollness. That event got plastered all over the British papers and in international publications, from *Rolling Stone* to *Le Monde*.

Rod wasn't in favor with the British press at the time, because of the Britt Ekland business. They were angry at him for dyeing his hair blond. He wasn't that fun guy in the Faces anymore; he had become an eccentric millionaire and Tiffany lamp collector, whose fans couldn't relate to him anymore. He was looking for Bebe to give him back his street credibility. I roughed up his image, which was what everybody wanted. Frankly, I don't think Rod was as aware as his handlers were of my role at this turning point in his career. But because of the state I was in, and against my better judgment (though I don't dislike Rod), I had an affair with him.

The best thing about Rod was that he could always make me laugh. Plus, being with him was over the top glamorous. After I was dumped by Todd, my confidence was at a low ebb. To his credit, it was Rod who said, "Hey! You're beautiful! Get back to work. Don't waste it." He really pushed me to keep modeling. He could be sweet. We liked each other sexually and had a real fondness for each other. However, looking back today on my behavior during that period of my life, I consider going out with Rod to have been an act of total insanity on my part. I would never have dated Rod Stewart had I not been in as much pain as I was from being replaced by Todd. Rod Stewart is a dangerous person if you're a woman. If you go out with him even once it's plastered everywhere, and for some weird reason, he's always been able to use women to get attention. He gets something from being with anybody who's in the public eye. It's part of his persona; he's always gone out with women who attract the press. He wants that. But when I saw him in action his methods were always damaging to the girl in question.

Evening Standard

London: Wednesday January 11 1978

SIX HELD IN £500,000 HEROIN RAID

Rod changes partners again

SALE OF TWO CENTURIES NOW ON
25%-50% REDUCTIONS!

Evening News

LONDON: MONDAY FEBRUARY 6 1978

DEATH TO 200 TIMS

Blast alert in West End shops

Trouble for Bebe

DO YOU KNOW THESE GIRLS?

If you do, see the

From Liverpool
From Birmingham
From Southampton

How Moon made me mad, by miserable Marcy

THE LATEST: Bebe. Picture: VICTOR CRAWSHAW

Anna's set to make news!

MP joins plea over wheeli

Insult

KILLER SON'S FINAL TORMENT

Day Ketchup Kid saw red

In November and December, Rod went on a U.S. tour. I flew to a couple of dates with him. I took little Liv to the Rhode Island concert. I must say that Rod, unlike some of my boyfriends, was always receptive and sweet about accepting my daughter. He never made me feel uncomfortable if I wanted to have her along, but he was also the first man who made me feel really used. On one occasion during that tour, he called and said, "Come over to the hotel. I want you to meet my friend Gary Glitter." I got over there, and it turned out that what he really wanted was for me to pose for pictures on his arm, pouring champagne with Gary Glitter. For Rod, women were more like ornaments than companions. What bothered me about the whole thing with Rod was that I was made to look like this blow-up glamour girl bimbo, which I wasn't. Take the fur coat caper: Tony Tune said to me, "Oh, wear this fur coat to the airport." I didn't expect twenty photographers to come out of the woodwork. I don't even like fur, yet a picture of me in a fur coat was circulated all over the world. Tony loved to create situations that would get Rod press attention. He'd make Rod's dates angry so they would end up in the headlines the next day: ALANA THROWS CHAMPAGNE ON BRITT! He's a real troublemaker! Tony later wrote a book, in which he said he delivered me to Rod as a gift-wrapped package with a big red bow around it. That was the last straw. They were literally trying to package me as a bimbo—I was one of the first girls that word was applied to.

There's no way I can put a good face on it. Rod was phony posh, which I despise. Of course, he could also turn around and be wonderful. I just hated the people he hung out with. Every night, we went to the poshest restaurants, wearing the poshest clothes.

Our affair lasted for three months. I spent Christmas with my family in Maine, where Liv was staying with my first cousin Annie. This was the beginning of a jet-set period in my life, during which I was constantly traveling, while Liv stayed in Maine. I was twenty-four when this started and Liv was five months old. All I knew was that I had come to New York to make it. In five years, I had gone from being a model to a rock star's muse. There was no denying that, and I was not about to walk away from it. Meanwhile, my heart and head were spinning like tops. I knew that Liv was the most important person in my life, but I also knew that if I gave up on find-

ing out who I was try-
ing to become and
making a living out of
being it, I wouldn't
have a life to give her. I
wouldn't be any good
as a mother, either.

I haven't mentioned
my family much in my
story so far, but now is
the perfect time, be-
cause Liv's babyhood
was one of the crucial
times when they came
through on every level.
I had two particularly

With my sweet chubby baby–delicious!! Liv's
first Christmas, 1977/BUELL PRIVATE COLLECTION

strong women who brought me up and with whom I was always regularly in touch, my mother and my cousin Annie, who was ten years
older than I was. Despite all the bumps and bruises, caused as much
by the social revolution of the sixties and seventies as by our own individual personalities, I knew not only that they would be the best possible people to take care of Liv while I was on the road but that they
would welcome the opportunity.

For the first three years of Liv's life, she spent more time with
them than with me and I realize that this makes me vulnerable to
being called a neglectful parent for this reason, but nothing could
be further from the truth. My mom, Annie, and I worked out a way
of bringing Liv up within our extended family. When I was on the
road, I always made a point of returning home to her for all the important holidays—Christmas, Easter, her birthday, Halloween, and
so on. Many times, I wept as I looked at the photographs of Liv that
I carried with me on my travels.

If I had followed this course as a man, people would applaud me
for building the strongest support system I could. We were, after
all, rock 'n' roll people. We didn't lead normal lives. We lived on
the road. We were discovering a new way of being through the
music and making it up as we went along. I mean, who did I have as
a role model as a rock 'n' roll mother? Anita Pallenberg! Bless her

heart. By the time I sat down to write this book, I felt completely vindicated for making the choices I did.

In late December 1977, Rod flew me over to England to spend the post-Christmas season with him and his parents in an enormous mansion outside of London. He left me there one night to meet up with another girl he had flown in. The drummer of the Who, Keith Moon, had been a pal of mine ever since Keith Richards tried to set us up on a date in 1976. When Moony saw this poor girl with Rod at a party that night, he tore into her in my defense. I found out about this bizarre mess when I read about it in the headlines the next day.

I spent New Year's Eve in Saint Martin, at a place called La Samana. This was the in place to be in the Caribbean. I took Liv and traveled with some friends, but there was no romance involved. It was a much-needed New Year's vacation. Peter Frampton was there, Lee Radziwell, and some of the Kennedys and their children. Dustin Hoffman and his wife took care of Liv on the beach for me so that I could go off and do things, and Liv played with the Kennedy kids, which was cool. One night, somebody gave us some Quaaludes. We were drinking champagne, and I decided to dive into the pool. I was so disoriented that I dived into three feet of water at the wrong end. I did a beautiful deep dive and proceeded to hit the top of my head on the bottom of the pool. My friend, Mark, pulled me out. Little did I know that those kinds of accidents can lead to paralysis, that I was the luckiest person in the world. I was taken to the hospital, where I spent the night. When X rays were taken, the French doctor said, "You have a leeetle thing on your—"

"*What!*"

I finally went to a chiropractor in New York. It turned out that two of my small vertebrae had been pushed to within a fraction of a millimeter of each other.

I was back in London for Rod's birthday in early January. We had a nice dinner to celebrate; then he went on to Rio de Janeiro. A week later, in mid-January, he called and asked me to join him. I flew from London, then had a four-hour stopover in Frankfurt. The only other person in the first-class lounge on the London–Frankfurt leg of the journey was Frank Zappa. We struck up a conversation, during which he told me exactly what was going to happen to me if I continued on to Rio to join Rod. By the time we reached Frankfurt, he had invited me to join him and his band, which was flying tourist-class, at their hotel. While I was there drinking champagne alone, Zappa seriously tried to persuade me to join them on the road and forget all about Rod. Zappa was a very straight guy. There was nothing romantic about his interest in me. He had been responsible for putting together one of the first all-female rock bands in the United States, the GTOs, and it's more than likely that if I had taken his advice, I would have found myself singing in a band much sooner than I did. On the other hand, I would never have met Elvis Costello, who remains to this day one of the most important influences on my life. I really enjoyed my stopover with Frank Zappa, who was a wonderful, charming, and intelligent man. Everything that he told me would happen if I continued on to Rio to join Rod happened exactly as he'd prophesied.

Rod and I were not in love, but our affair was very much in the public eye, so when he kept flirting outrageously with a countess and all these other women in Rio, I started to get uptight. Rod had

With Rod Stewart in London, 1978/BUELL
PRIVATE COLLECTION

one habit that particularly upset me. He always tried to make me feel like a stupid little girl, while the rest of them were all *très* sophisticated. In fact, they were ten years older, but they weren't more sophisticated. I had more sophistication and style than all of them combined. They were a bunch of wanna-bes. The countess was constantly hiking up her dress to reveal the perfect triangle-shaped bush. Basically, I didn't fit in, and I felt uncomfortable. I thought they were all the biggest phonies. I wanted to go see Steve Jones and Paul Cook of the Sex Pistols, who were in Rio with their manager, Malcolm McLaren, having just come off their sensational U.S. tour. They were recording a record with Ronnie Biggs, the guy who had pulled off a big train robbery in Britan back in 1963. That sounded interesting. I was *bored*.

I can't say I never had fun with Rod's friends, but he could be vicious and cruel, and in the end, he turned on me because I was not going along with everything on his agenda. I, in turn, became bitter and no fun—and that's hard for me to do. Finally, I think I insulted Rod. He retaliated by taking away my Concorde ticket. I called my mother and told her what he'd done. I miraculously got my ticket back the following day, and I took the next flight back to London, where I had a booking with *Vogue*. Once again, Tony Tune had tipped off the press, because by the time I got off the Concorde at Heathrow Airport, thirty photographers and reporters were there to greet me. I was completely unprepared. Rod's people were afraid that I was going to get off the plane and say that I had had it with this fuddy-duddy and had had the worst time! But I was so naïve, I got off the airplane wearing jeans and no makeup, and I hadn't prepared a statement.

"Bebe, how do you feel about breaking up with Rod?" the reporters screamed.

I wish I had said, Oh God, I know, darling, what an idiot! I'm so thrilled about the breakup. If I had watched more episodes of *Dynasty*, I could have done my Alexis Carrington routine, but at this point, it was a shock. "He has given her the boot," his publicist was quoted over and over again as saying. It was my first contact with the paparazzi on my own. "I don't know what you're talking about," I yelled back. "What do you mean? *What do you mean?*"

By four o'clock in the afternoon, I was on the cover of every newspaper in England and on TV. ROD AND BEBE SPLIT UP! the headlines ran. It was news to me. Once again, I thought, What am I, a publicity stunt? How insulting! This was all absolutely new to me. I went down to the newsstand in my hotel to buy a Cadbury's fruit and nut bar, and I saw myself on the front page of five newspapers. When I gave the man my fifty pence, he recognized me. I went to a soothing dinner with my friends John Frieda, the hairdresser, and his wife, Lulu, the pop singer. When we came out of the restaurant, we were greeted by a dozen photographers. It was the first time I had ever been exposed to such a huge amount of publicity.

In the end, I think the three-month affair with Rod had a dual effect: On one level, it was convenient for Rod and cleansing for me. On another level, though, what he ended up doing to me made me more afraid of men than ever. After Rod, I didn't want to see anybody. If you're a female, Rod Stewart's the kind of person who is much more fun as a friend than as a lover. Though he's amusing, intelligent, and witty, I do consider him my big mistake. I have a rule that I don't get emotionally involved with a man unless the potential for love is there. I never felt that way about Rod. He's somebody I'd like to forget.

When I lived at the Portobello Hotel during my previous visits to London, I'd made friends with the punk-rock staff. When I checked in this time, I was concerned that they were going to hate me for dating Rod Stewart and selling out. When I came back from Rio, they hung up a dartboard with Rod's face on it in the basement bar and all my rocker friends would go down there and play darts, and we'd try to hit him in the eye. It was loads of fun. One girl bartender who had befriended me on an earlier visit took me to see Adam & the Ants, X-Ray Spex, and the Sex Pistols. My Portobello girlfriend was a die-hard punk. She had piercings through her cheek and the whole bit. She was a great girl, the nicest person. When Patti Smith came to play London again, her band stayed at the Portobello. This time, we hung out with the Clash. The height of punk, 1977–1978, was a wonderful time to be in London. It was really fun. I was always able to slip into the London scene, which I loved and wanted to be a part of. That's where I felt the happiest and most comfortable. The punk rockers were my natural friends, and they were the people I became most familiar with.

One night, I went to a show; the kids were riding pogo sticks—*boink, boink, boink.* This one little punk-rock guy with a giant blue spiked Mohawk and pierced face, totally hard-core, saw me standing there. He whispered to his friend and they went and got me a chair. He stood it over to the side and said, "Hey, stand on here. Then you can see. We'll watch out for you." It was so sweet. I thought, Oh my God, I'm like a little queen. I went and stood on my chair. I got to see the whole show and kept out of the crowd. Polite punk rockers. They just thought I was the coolest thing on earth. That was really fun, and that's why I always return to London—I feel safe there.

Back in New York, I took a break between February and June 1978, concentrating on how to get through the day. Todd was particularly kind to me at this point. Maybe it was because his song "Can We Still Be Friends"—which was about our relationship—had just come out and was one of his best and most successful songs in some time. He paid my rent and gave me enough money that I could just rest for a while. I needed to. My parents were worried about me; in fact, everybody was worried.

It was the first time I had not been in almost constant motion since 1974. I needed to rethink everything. The first part of my life was clearly over. I could not go on giving myself so completely to these men. Liv had to come first now. But to take care of Liv, I had to take care of myself.

In early June, I flew out to the West Coast to see if I could establish myself as a model or possibly as an actress in L.A. Thank God I had a close-knit, supportive family; they encouraged me

My dear friend, Pam Turbov, who introduced me to Elvis Costello in the summer of 1978 in Los Angeles/BEBE BUELL

as I tried to get my life together and get my career jump-started. Todd rented me an orange Camaro with an eight-track stereo system. At least I have a ride, I thought. Now my girlfriend, Jeanne Theis, who was working for Robert Stigwood, came back into my life. She had a great little house in Laurel Canyon, where I stayed for nothing. Now I would give Los Angeles a whirl. I had an agent, Mary Webb Davis. I was getting a few small modeling jobs here and there. I was also meeting directors, doing the whole movie thing. I was thinking about getting a band together and performing. I never expected that almost as soon as I landed, I would get swept off my feet again, higher than I could ever have dreamed of.

One night, another one of my L.A. girlfriends, Pam Turbov, said, "Listen, I wanna go to Hollywood High tonight because there's a really cool show—Mink DeVille, Nick Lowe, and Elvis Costello."

Anticipation was in the air that night. Nick Lowe was great. Mink DeVille had that flamenco dancer chic, if you fancy being ravished by a matador. Everybody was turned on, and Pam and I were pressed up against the stage like two excited little kids. When the lights first hit Elvis, it was astounding. They lit him from underneath, so that he would look almost frightening—the shadow of his glasses was pronounced. He stood there with legs spread, his toes locked in, wearing horn-rims. I looked up and gasped, "Oh my God. I can't believe it." He was the most handsome man I had ever seen. There was a hot buzz in the air. It was just like an Elvis Presley movie. This Elvis looked right at me and sang to me the whole night. Elvis looked thirty-five when actually he was twenty-four. And he had this non-ability on the guitar that made fabulous screeching noises. It was just too much; I thought I was gonna die. It was really good, truly pure, and brilliant.

Afterward, Pam said, "Let's go back and say hello."

I was too scared to meet him. I said, "We're outta here. We're going to see the Runaways."

"Why won't you go back? I want you to meet Jake Riviera. You'll love him." She was trying to get me a nice respectable boyfriend and she thought I would like Jake.

Later, we went to the Whiskey. As we were sitting there, I felt somebody staring at me. It was like a fifties movie. I panned the room, and there was Elvis with this beautiful black girl. When Elvis stares, he isn't flirty—he drills you. Pam told me he was really anti-woman and anti a lot of things, so I was afraid of him. Then the girl started staring at me, too.

"What are you looking at?" I said.

"Oh, I'm sorry," she said, "but you're just so pretty."

I felt like a jerk. Elvis smiled this giant grin. "Elvis, I'd like you to meet Next Year's Model," Pam said.

I immediately felt comfortable with him. He reminded me of Humphrey Bogart—he had the same sophistication and sweet toughness about him—the kinda guy you'd never expect to fall in love with a girl and be delicate, but he was. The next day, I had some photos to do, so I said good night. As I was turning around to leave, I accidentally smashed him right in the face with my drink, knocking his glasses off.

"Oh, I didn't need that face anyway," he responded. He was great. When Elvis smiles, you know he really means it, because he doesn't crack one very often. He's real surly. He's just got a lot on his mind. The next day, I got him to smoke pot. We drove around all day, laughing. I'm sure his handlers immediately thought I was having a horrible influence on him, because at that time, there was only one person with a badder reputation than mine, and that was Anita Pallenberg. It was like the Model and the Punk—Beauty and the Beast.

On my second date with Elvis, we went to see Nick Lowe play, and Elvis held my hand under the table—he didn't want anybody to see and thus blow his tough-guy act. After the show, we were invited to go to the studio where Toto was recording. Elvis was nice. He greeted everybody, and we all sat around listening. They were doing overdubs, which can be very repetitive. Then Elvis turned to me and said, "If I crawl out of here on my hands and knees, will you follow me? But you have to crawl." I guess he didn't want to insult anybody by walking out. He is courteous in his crazy way. He left first, and then Pam and I followed him. When we got to the door, a CBS Records executive was standing there. Elvis was so cute—you don't feel that kind of emotional purity too often in your life. We were in love.

We spent our first date together without consummating the relationship. It didn't matter if we were drunk; we just weren't going to fuck on the first night, which is not to say we weren't incredibly turned on. He had to leave the next day and fly to San Francisco.

After I had returned to New York, Elvis wrote me the first of many letters, and an invitation to find him at 48 Queen's Gate Terrace, London. The letter had been sent to L.A. Pam called me in New York and said, "Guess what I've got here!"

"What?" I asked.

"I've got a letter from—"

"Elvis?"

She said she'd pouch it. This was before FedEx.

"No. Open it and read it to me."

"Are you sure?"

"Yes, yes!"

This was the first letter he ever wrote to me. He'd written it from the Portobello Hotel. He said he'd gone there to spend the night in one of its coffin-shaped rooms, just so he could feel haunted by the shadows of my presence. That was poetic enough to stir the embers of passion in my burned heart. He wanted to know when and how we would next meet, and he said that when I was next in London I should drop by his flat (his address was enclosed), where he was quite obviously not living with his wife. He really knew how to pen a letter to a lady. For me, it was like getting a letter from T. S. Eliot.

It was the summer of 1978, the climax of the seventies, the greatest year of a truly great decade. From the beginning, he cast himself in the weaker role, claiming that I would not remember him. The seeds of some songs were clearly already sown—"Wednesday Week," for example, which was on the *Armed Forces* album.

Ironically, Elvis would become the one man I would never be able to get over. He would become the great love of my younger life, the center of it. And I would become his greatest muse.

By July, I had received two more letters and several postcards. He definitely wanted to know how to get in touch with me. He was separated from his wife, living in a flat in London with his keyboard player, Steve Nieve. He gave me the address and the phone number several times and started calling me periodically. I got the impression he was going back and forth with his wife. One time, he called me from Bermuda. He'd sneaked up to the hotel room to call. A postcard followed. He was trying to tell me that he was nuts about me. He called me on my birthday and sent me flowers and candy.

In another early letter, he said that when he first saw me sitting on a bar stool, the night the Runaways played the Whiskey, he thought he was in trouble again. He kept reviewing our meeting, repeating how much he wanted to see me. I realize now how similar it was to the first time I had met Todd—instant attraction. And to date, the most important relationship in my life had been the one with Todd. Suddenly, Todd and Steven and "the well of loneliness" on West Fifty-eighth Street seemed to fade into the past like old photographs. Something new and vivid was happening to me. I felt flushed with excitement all the time. Elvis said in one letter that he was fantasizing I would be forced by a band of masked men to board a plane to London!

Meanwhile I was miserable in Los Angeles—Elvis kept telling me that if God's burning fire didn't get me, the earthquake would— and he suggested that I fly to London and spend some time with him. London, that city of poets and butterfly rooms, which had never let me down, where I had always felt safe and protected and loved. What the hell was I doing in L.A.? In one of his phone calls, Elvis invited me to join him in London for his birthday on August 25.

I decided to go to London, where I planned to do a bunch of work, too, make some money, and come home. I never expected that I would end up staying there. At that point, I had never even made love with Elvis. After talking it over with my family, who encouraged me to pursue a relationship that I already thought might be *the one*, I posted myself to London like a mail-order bride.

By August 18, I was on the plane. All I could think about was that I had kissed him only once. I was going back to London again, to a flat I'd never seen, to a man who was married but separated, who I had never had sex with but who I was madly in love with, and who somehow fulfilled my Arthur Miller/Hugh Downs/Humphrey Bogart fantasy. Yet, ironically, I felt more compatible with Elvis than with any other man I had met in my life. There was some powerful chemistry between us.

Elvis's manager, Jake Riviera, wouldn't let him meet me at the airport because I was still "airport copy" for the press, so I arrived at Heathrow unattended. I was greeted by someone holding up a sign, then chauffered to Elvis's fourth-floor walk-up.

I'll never forget walking into his flat. There was a living room, a bedroom off the living room, and then a bedroom in the hall, which belonged to Steve Nieve and Farrah. There was a room with a tub, a separate room with a toilet, and a kitchen, which was at the end of the hall. It was the top flat at 48 Queen's Gate Terrace. Elvis and I stood there feeling awkward. I put my bags down. I had to unpack. We chatted while I unpacked. He didn't have a closet, so I had no choice but to find places to hang my clothes all around his room. Before I knew it, I felt that I had created a sculpture out of dresses, skirts, shoes, and blouses. The room was transformed from being bachelorlike and male to being very feminine. He had a loft bed. I had never slept on one before, so this was a new event for me. I didn't know what the hell a loft bed was. I was used to water beds.

After I had strategically placed all my garments around the room and made curtains out of skirts I didn't often wear, we went to dinner. We ate a gorgeous Italian meal, drank lots of wine, and, of course, fell more madly in love. When we got back to the flat, we were both so scared and so drunk, we fell asleep. After waking up the next morning, we made love. Personally, I had never experienced that kind of contact before. It was more grown-up and on a little bit higher level than sex with Todd had been. It was difficult for me to grasp this, and at that age, you tend to make comparisons. I was trying to differentiate in my mind all the different types of sex I'd had. With Todd, sex had been really comfortable, and I'd felt protected. With Steven, I knew we were obviously meant to breed—it was that animal noises like deer in the forest sex. With Elvis, I left my body. And it scared the hell out of me.

Afterward, I jumped up, took a shower, got dressed, and announced that I was going over to the Portobello Hotel to visit my friends. I think I freaked him out. I told him that when he got himself together, he could meet me over there.

I went to visit this one girl in particular. She was my best friend in London. I wanted to tell her I was seeing Elvis. I thought she was going to have a seizure. She didn't believe me. Elvis was the punk Bob Dylan, full of rage and mysteriousness. She said, "You fucking liar—he's not rich enough. Tell me it's Mick Jagger." Two seconds later, Elvis walked in. I thought she was going to choke. Then Elvis and I had a great breakfast.

Living at Elvis's in the fall of 1978 was fabulous, but it also presented dilemmas. By the time we met up in London to share three weeks of an unbridled and mutually satisfying passion, I had become his muse, his untouchable angel, and he had become my fantasy of the man I should run off with. It became impossible for us to stay away from each other. I can't say that I ricocheted from Rod to Elvis, because there was six months in between, but the relationship with Rod certainly affected the one with Elvis. I was poised for ridicule simply because I had just had this highly publicized relationship with Rod. In the British press, I was "Naughty Bebe," like some character in Victorian pornography. As it was, Elvis's camp immediately started spreading rumors about me and kept trying to set me up. I don't think anyone expected us to fall in love, but we did, and then the panic buttons started being pushed. His record company, his management, his agents, and his fans all thought he would become complacent and happy. Their cash cow might run dry! *Quelle horreur!*

Our relationship was like the meeting of two drama queens. Everything was a performance. Elvis was constantly falling onto his knees and yelling, "Tempt me! Tempt me! Make me sin!"

"I'm a fucked-up Catholic, too!" I would yell. "How am I going to make you sin when I'm trying to figure out how *not* to sin?"

We liked to make love with the blue TV light on because we thought it made our skin look beautiful. We'd turn the sound off and switch to a channel that wasn't broadcasting so we'd get the *Poltergeist* effect. Let me tell you: That man got at least seven good albums out of me! Maybe more. Think about it. Their cash cow wasn't about to dry up; he was about to go into outer space! Unfortunately, I'll never see any of the royalties.

Whatever, the beginning of our love affair was wonderful. I looked upon this time as an experiment to see if Elvis and I could have a relationship, and also as an opportunity to do some more modeling. I was always guaranteed work in London. Whenever I showed up at Models One, saying, "I'm back!" they'd scream, and I'd work the next day. I was also up for a big part in a movie at this time. They were going to film a Jacqueline Susann story about a young model who comes to London. The movie never got made, but Susann and I met. I wasn't on my Ron Wood schedule, and Elvis wasn't the kind of guy who slept all day. He got up and went to the studio to record and rehearse. He was a working boy, not a loller. Elvis didn't either encourage or discourage me to work. He would say things like "So then, when are you modeling?"

I always chose rock stars as boyfriends because I liked their temperaments—all the nervousness, unstableness, and uncertainty. It was dangerous, and fun. It made life interesting to wake up in the morning with somebody who was always in a different mood, but it certainly didn't represent much sanity or security.

I like unusual, one-of-a-kind people, those who stand out—for example, guys whose shoulders hunch; you don't know what they're going to do next. I can't stand muscles, and I don't like hairy guys. I like men who have femininity without being gay, because they often understand women really well. I love my "monkeymen." This might be vain, but I think most guys just can't handle the heat of being with me. I think women find it natural to dramatize. Men bitch about it, but then they'll lock themselves in the study, get inspired, and write a hit record. And after it hits number one, they'll still bitch at you. As far as I'm concerned, a woman's most important quality is her ability to inspire. I wanted to flirt with people's creativity and nourish it in whatever form of art they're involved.

Elvis weighed about ten-stone, which is about a hundred and forty-five pounds. He always wore suits, and his hair was longer then. He was just starting to get a little money. When he got his first credit card, he propped it up on the TV and we sat and stared at it. We tried to figure out what to do with it, and we decided to buy some jackets. So we went down to the King's Road and he bought us some flashy jackets.

In September, Liz Derringer came to London. Elvis was in the studio recording *Armed Forces*. We went to the studio to see him, and there was this lovely invitation sitting there for "Mr. Costello" to attend the party for *The Buddy Holly Story* that Paul McCartney was giving on September 8. Liz took a pen and put an *s* on the word *Mr.* And we went to the party. Liz was always thinkin'! By this time, I had gotten so much publicity in London that everybody knew that I was not Mrs. Elvis Costello; I was the other woman, the harlot. When I walked up with my little invitation, the doorman looked at me. Nobody knew what Mary Costello looked like, so I pawned Liz off as Mary! And then the guy wanted to know what the hell I was doing with Elvis's wife! I said, "My dear, please don't pry into things that are none of your business."

"For all you know, we could be having a threesome!" Liz chimed in in her weird imitation of a British accent. That, of course, ended up in the *Sun* the next day. I am forever grateful to Liz for that prank, because I got to see Keith Moon before he died. We sat down at a table with Linda and Paul McCartney and Annette, who was Keith's girlfriend. We hung around together and had a great time. Then Liz's friend, Denny Laine, an ex-member of the Moody Blues and now one of the guys in Paul's band, suggested a bunch of us repair to his house, which was half an hour outside London. Tagging along for the ride came Billy Idol, who was a bit dim, but a sweet kid with beautiful teeth. Upon arrival, I felt distinctly out of place, so I asked someone to call a taxi. Instead, my drink was spiked and I passed out. I think the others just wanted me to shut up. I woke up the next morning on the pool table with a blanket over me. Déjà vu. I immediately called Elvis, who was clearly irked, to say the least. "Where are you?" he cried. "I've been worried."

"I'm out in the country and I don't know what happened." I told him in a torrent. "But now I want to come home. . . ." He didn't believe a word. Can you blame him? With my reputation! Worse still, Keith Moon, with whom I had shared a champagne toast the previous evening, had died that same night of an accidental overdose of Antabuse. When I woke up, he was dead. He was always so nice. Whenever I saw him and Annette, they'd always give me a big hello and invite me to have some champagne with them. I cried a lot when he died.

The day after the party, Elvis went to work on his album at the studio. That night, friends carried his limp body home. As I helped him up into the loft bed, he hung his head over the side and vomited all over my shoes. Then he confessed how much he loved me, intercutting his declaration with asides. "I'll never be able to keep you in the style to which you're accustomed," he said. Between pukes, I was getting Shakespearean speeches. I cried and told him I loved him more than anybody and that none of those other boys meant anything to me.

The next day, he would barely speak to me. He was sure I had gone off and shagged Billy Idol. I tried to get Billy on the phone with him, but Billy was scared. He thought Elvis was gonna pop him one. In England, and with Elvis's crowd in particular, there was always way too much alcohol. But apart from the time he puked on my shoes, I didn't really hang out with a puking crowd in London as much I did in New York. The New York scene was much more grounded in drugs than the English equivalent. I hung out with all the punk rockers in London and they never even gave me that cheap English sulfate everybody was constantly snorting.

Things just kept happening in our lives, only now, instead of building positively, they began to destroy the delicate balance between us.

When Elvis was out of town touring, Chrissie Hynde and I would hang out together and do girlfriend things—like shopping at Harrods. Chrissie likes perfume, makeup, and nail polish as much as I do. She stood out because she looked like a biker chick, but she was soft and feminine, too, and a great girlfriend. She has always been very loyal to her women friends, which I respect and admire.

One night when Bob Gruen was in town. Bob, David Johansen, Chrissie, and I went out, and we brought Billy Idol because I felt sorry for him and I wanted to become friends. It was probably a big mistake to hang out with Billy Idol again, but it was not as if I ever did what I was told! We all went to a reggae club. In 1978, there was only one reggae club in England, and it was scary. There was not one white person in there. The Rastas were immediately friendly and sweet. "Hey d'ere, Chrissie mon! Hey you, Billy Idol. Hey, you pin-up queen." They fed us, and they told us the meat was monkey. Chrissie said, "That's bullshit; it's pigeon." It was really funny. Finally, we got led into a pitch-black room. The only things in it, apart from a hundred Rastas, were these huge speakers with the *boom boom boom* of the reggae beat. The only light in the room came from the tips of all the ganja cigarettes being passed around, so if you wanted to see anybody, you had to take a hit off a joint. The pot was like fairy pot—it was some sort of wonderful hallucinogenic ganja, pure marijuana rolled in joints the size of a baby's arm. That's why you could really illuminate somebody's face with one. We were dancing and listening to the music, which was very mellow and cool. This was when I really figured out that Billy Idol was a middle-class doctor's son, because he was terrified. He was reduced to tears. Chrissie and I were laughing our asses off because we could not believe how scared he was. We were both white girls, and *we* weren't scared. Billy was so terrified, he kept saying, "Hold me. Put me in the middle. Dance with me in the middle. I'm really nervous about this; I know I'm going to get my ass kicked." Chrissie and I spent an hour baby-sitting him, until finally Chrissie got fed up. She just turned to him and said, "Jesus Christ, Billy, don't you realize you're not going to die? The only person who's going to kill you is me if you don't fucking calm down."

Later in September, Todd came to town and wanted me to have a meeting with him about how long I was going to leave Liv in Maine. Todd and I got rip-roaring, shit-faced drunk. I am notorious for not being able to hold my liquor. I fell asleep in Todd's hotel room. Of course, Elvis didn't believe that for a second. I knew there was a lot of intrigue within his camp; I could no longer fight it. I was even accused of having sex with John Cooper Clark!

At the end of September, Elvis embarked on a six-week tour of Canada, Australia, and Japan. He couldn't take me, because British bands didn't allow women on the road in those days. Of course, they got up to absolute nonsense on the road. I'm sure it was horrifying.

So here I was, alone in London, with Mick and the boys only a call away. But I was determined to turn over a new leaf and be good. I did a lot of modeling work, but I couldn't help running around with all my friends some of the time. I became buddies with Steve Jones of the Sex Pistols. Rumors were flying around that I was having mad sex with all of them, of course. I was very good friends with Stevie, though. He was the funniest guy. He made me laugh. He could do impersonations of anybody.

The Sex Pistols had broken up earlier that year and Steve was having classic problems adjusting to having lost his band. It was a shame, because the Pistols made really good music. They had the same kind of impact that Nirvana did much later. It was basic rock 'n' roll, but there was a freshness in the delivery of the music. I can't understand a word Kurt Cobain sang, but it doesn't matter, because the music speaks volumes. I could understand every word Johnny Rotten sang. If you turned his voice off, the music sounded like updated Chuck Berry. What made it punk rock was Rotten's voice, and I think that's very important. The Pistols brought Chuck Berry up-to-date in 1976 just as the Stones brought Chuck Berry up-to-date in 1963.

I was also good friends with Helen, the Sex Pistols' dwarf mascot, whom I met at a photo shoot. She and I hit it off and she started taking me out to the clubs. Sometimes I would get really lonely while Elvis was on the road. My favorite memories are of Steve and Helen over at Helen's flat, this big gorgeous council flat the government paid for because she was a midget. We would go over there and she would make these huge meals. We would hang out and drink; they would smoke their hash and cigarettes. We'd watch movies and fool around and listen to music. Steve's roommate was the Pistols' drummer, Paul Cook. A couple of times the Clash's lead singer, Joe Strummer, came over to use their bathroom. There was a lot of traffic in and out of their place. Helen's house was a refuge. I loved staying there.

I was having a ball, even though I was anxious for Elvis to return. He was my boyfriend. I loved him. I was a little bad on occasion. I would make out once in a while with somebody, or I would dance with somebody, but basically I missed him. Meanwhile, I was getting beautiful love letters from him. When he was away, Elvis wrote letters like the ones Napoléon wrote to Josephine. We also engaged in several lengthy phone calls, which led to—for the first time in my life—phone sex. The overall tone of the letters and cards was one of great expectations, love, and desire. In one letter, he compared us to Tracy and Hepburn. He was already seeing this as a legendary romance.

When Elvis returned in November, we had an absolutely fabulous time. By then, we were openly, madly in love. He took away all my inhibitions. I was never much of a talker when I made love. I was quiet, even shy. My modesty and shyness always shocked people. Men expected me to be a little bit of a wildcat because of my reputation, but the only time I ever really acted wild was with Elvis. He would hold me down, and I would scream his name. He was the only man I had phone sex with, the only man I ever talked dirty to or exchanged those kinds of intimacies with.

About this time, his manager, Jake Riviera, and all of his people started to interfere. Nick Lowe said to me the same thing Joe Perry said about Steven Tyler. "If you hurt Elvis, if you do anything to hurt him, you're going to answer to me." Nick Lowe was Elvis's mentor and producer, a very important person in his life.

Elvis was the first man with whom I experienced both lust and a spiritual connection. Almost as soon as we slept together, I got pregnant! However, I always knew that I would never be the mother of his child—not that I didn't hope for it, not that I didn't dream of it, and not that I didn't expect someday to get married to him. I just had some instinctive knowledge that this love affair was doomed, even though I did everything I could to preserve it. This pregnancy ended in a miscarriage.

The turning point in my relationship with Elvis came when he really wanted me to stay in London with him for Christmas 1978. He wanted me to have Liv brought to us, but I went back to America and had Christmas in Maine with my family. Partially, this was because I had been separated from Liv when I went out to L.A. in the summer and then when I went to London that fall. I wanted to spend Christmas with her in the bosom of our family. I think that if I had stayed in London and created a Christmas with Elvis and my daughter, we would have gotten married. As it was, he spent Christmas with his son, Matthew, and soon to be ex-wife, Mary. I pushed him into a situation where he could depend on them more than on me. He was also getting the backlash from his camp, who took advantage of my departure to goad him: "See, told you, she's a wild child. She doesn't care about you. She's going back to New York to hang out with Ric Ocasek from the Cars. Nyaa, nyaa, we told you she was a rock 'n' roll slut."

Elvis came over in January 1979 to start his American tour. He met my family and stayed in Maine for ten days. Everybody loved him, and he was wonderful with Liv.

In January 1979, he flew me out to San Francisco for the first concert of his U.S. tour. That was when I got pregnant for the second time. I wasn't allowed to accompany him on the rest of the tour. While he was touring, the rumors about me and other men

Me and Elvis at Annie's in Maine–January
1979/BUELL PRIVATE COLLECTION

continued, which didn't help the situation. I don't think Elvis trusted me. I don't think we had a lot of well-wishers. I really didn't behave myself, because I thought it was completely innocent to go to dinner with Ric Ocasek or to hang out with this one or that one. None of them thought I was capable of commitment or fidelity. I, on the other hand, felt so deeply involved with Elvis by now, I fully intended to tell him I was pregnant. But then in mid-February, I had a second miscarriage. Meanwhile, Elvis was getting depressed about what was happening to our relationship because he was constantly on the road. Then in March, he had the notorious incident with Bonnie Bramlett, during which he made some extremely ill-advised remarks about black blues musicians that were intended to upset everybody, but blew up in his face, virtually destroying his career in the United States. By the time he got back to New York, where we were staying at the Mayflower Hotel, we had armed

bodyguards accompanying us everywhere, as he was receiving serious death threats.

Once again, I was exposed to that really high-powered, high-caliber degree of security and publicity. Photographers were jumping out of the bushes to get a picture of us crossing the road. Elvis was driven deeper into cocaine and alcohol and despair, and becoming more and more hostile toward me. He wasn't sharing his anger with me. Amazingly, I got pregnant by him for a third time, in New York in March. Uncertain myself by now about his feelings, I, too, decided not to reveal my emotions, so I didn't tell him what was happening to me.

Things started to fall apart. In retrospect, I think the pressure on Elvis was so great that he didn't know what to believe. By April 1979, he started flipping out. One minute, he'd be grabbing me and telling me he loved me, begging me never to leave him, and the next minute, he'd be saying, "Leave me! I don't deserve anything! I'm wretched. I'm horrible."

I think Elvis knew that he derived a lot of inspiration from not being happy—he's happier not being happy. He never thought that I would be faithful, because he never thought he could keep a girl like me. He was unable to cope with my persona. Yet I was hopelessly in love with him. I would've thrown it all away for him. Elvis and I would have single conversations that would range from horrible rows to phone sex. I broke all the rules for him. Our love was intense, adult love. But we were both too young to know exactly what to do. Plus, I was still a little insane from what I had gone through the year before.

I should have gone to a psychiatrist to work out my identity crisis and the lie I was forced to live: knowing that my daughter's father was this pirate named Steven Tyler but having to pretend it was the guru named Todd. At times, I felt like Mata Hari, yet at other times I felt like the women who were my heroes. I knew that Elvis was going to leave me and go back to his wife. His manager read him the riot act. It was very painful for both of us. We did not want to break up.

By April 1979 Elvis had sunk into an even deeper depression because of his confusion over me. When his manager and handlers filled his head with stories about me with other men, he crumbled. By Easter of 1979, we separated and I had a third miscarriage. I know that this miscarriage was a result of all the drama. Saying good-bye at the airport on Easter Sunday, we were both crying and hugging each other. We didn't want to be separated. We had to be pulled apart kicking and screaming at Kennedy Airport, because he was going to miss his plane.

After we were separated, I had a baby nervous breakdown. I'm from strong German stock, so I'm not capable of breaking down completely. I'm not the kind of person who is going to go off on a bender or do drugs. I just go inside and I don't come out of my apartment.

I never had as complete a muse-poet relationship as I had with Elvis Costello. For me, he was like a Romantic poet from the nineteenth century, a Byron or a Keats. Everything I did and said was incorporated into his music. After our relationship came to a halt in 1979, he recorded the *Get Happy!!* album; practically every song on it was influenced by the heartbreak Elvis was feeling. He kept a lot of his pain inside. He never thought he was good enough for me, and yet, he always had to act tough like Sinatra or Bogie. After I said that in print about him, he appeared on the cover of *Trust* in a Humphrey Bogart pose, a cigarette hanging out of his mouth. Everything I said, ate, everything I did, the cosmetics I used, every piece of clothing I wore with him he wrote about at one time or another. My fingernails, my tongue, my teeth, my eyelashes, my eyeballs— every documentable thing about my body and soul—he utilized in his art.

I adored this man. To me, he was Clark Gable, Humphrey Bogart, a man with an Irish temper and a penchant for drink. Stardom, cocaine and alcohol, and rock 'n' roll turned him into someone I didn't know anymore. I think he was afraid of his shadow, and so he went back to his wife. Easter Sunday 1979 became Black Sunday in my book, Bloody Sunday in my life. It would never, ever be over—*never.*

On the "Camp Lejeune" tour bus with Elvis during the 1979 USA tour/BUELL
PRIVATE COLLECTION

Elvis in bed with his shades/BEBE BUELL

I was really too young mentally to realize how much I loved him. It wasn't until well after he went back to England, back to his wife and his life there, that I realized this. After two years of not seeing him or talking to him, it hit me one day like a ton of bricks. I realized I had to start working on commitment. As I got older and everything started falling into place, I found I would much rather have married Elvis Costello than Mick Jagger any day.

After the breakup, I was inconsolable. My parents took me back to Maine. Too much had happened to me at once. They realized that I needed the protection of the family womb. I had been living in the apartment Todd and Patti had picked out. I had this small child, but my life seemed to have no direction. I'd been dumped by Rod Stewart, and I'd had this horrible situation with Elvis, who I'd thought was really going to be the love of my life. I was shattered that our relationship was over, and I just didn't think I could deal with New York City and living in the fast lane anymore. I needed sanctuary and security. I wasn't making wise decisions. Instead, I was acting frivolously, as people do when they're in pain and feeling desperate. I was weak and vulnerable. My mother and stepfather closed up the Fifty-eighth Street apartment and we left for Maine. I rented a cottage on Annie's property and devoted myself to motherhood. I had finally driven myself out of New York.

So there I was in May 1979, with Liv and Annie Noyes, my first cousin, who was raised as my sister. She had always been a sort of surrogate mother when I was a young girl; she took care of me when my mother was busy. She's ten years older than I. She was very helpful to me when I was raising Liv. I didn't want to leave Liv with nannies and baby-sitters. After I moved up to Maine, Annie always helped me when I would go down to New York. She was married and had a family of her own. She has a daughter and a son. They're both in their early thirties now, about ten years older than Liv. Annie used to live in Virginia, but when she married Teddy, she moved up to Maine.

In Maine, my life had structure. I had my own cottage. I never lived in someone else's place. It was a separate little house up on a hill, not attached to the main house. I was renting it for three hundred dollars a month. It was a beautiful little white wooden cottage with a front porch. You walked through the door into a big kitchen, which had a nice little table and a couple of windows. There was also a pretty good-sized living room, as well as two bedrooms and a bath, all on one floor. The family house down the hill was quite grand. A huge barn separated the main house from the cottage, so I had a lot of privacy. I suppose you would call it "a family compound." Ironically, I rented another orange car, like the one I had been driving when I first met Elvis in Los Angeles.

I didn't hear from Elvis for two weeks. I was extremely distraught. Then I got a letter, in which he professed his undying love for me. He wrote that nothing was working with Mary, that he couldn't get over or beyond loving me, and that he felt like a zombie. I responded, "Good-bye, but not for good. I know in my heart it's not for good." He didn't know what he was going to do; he said he had nothing to offer me, because he had to make his marriage work and be a good father to his son. And he told me to pay attention to "the clues." At that time, I didn't know what he was talking about. I later discovered that he meant I should pay attention to his records.

People ask me, "What songs were written about you?" My response to that is: It's not always so much a specific song as what kind of music was being made during the time we were together. And I can very proudly say that when I was involved with Elvis, he made some of the greatest records of his career. And the same is true with Todd: He made *Something/Anything?*; *A Wizard/A True Star*; and *The Hermit of Mink Hollow*—which are critically recognized as the best three albums of his career. You have to look not just at your influence as a girl who is the subject of a song like "Layla," say, but how your presence in that person's life affects all his work. And you might not always be the subject of a whole song so much as the inspiration of a line in the song. For example, the color of your eyes might be used in a song, and that might be the only mention of you. So it's really hard to pinpoint which songs are autobiographical unless the artist has stated this. Take, for example, two lines from my song "Normal Girl": "I like it in the car as I'm looking at the stars/ When I saw you in the bar, I knew you were a star." The first line is a reference to a particular time with Jack Nicholson; the second refers to a time with Elvis. Everybody knows Todd Rundgren's 1978 "Can We Still Be Friends" is about our breakup. And I think pretty much everybody acknowledges Elvis's "I Want You" is about me.

Elvis matured immensely as a songwriter on *Get Happy!!* In all his previous recordings, love was an emotion that entailed revenge, contempt, envy, and jealousy. For the first time in his career, he was exploring love as a pure emotion. It's a telling, if abstract, record, because it explores both his relationship with his wife and the one with me. It was definitely the clue that he wanted me to pay attention to.

You'd have to be an imbecile not to know what that record was about. It has "New Amsterdam," "Riot Act," and "High Fidelity" on it. Take the title "Riot Act": It's basically about being read the riot act, about your behavior, your actions, about what you're doing with your life. On the other hand, another song critics tend to think is about me, "Party Girl," isn't! "High Fidelity" is about a man struggling with his infidelity. People are trying to dismiss the girl as an ornament or a shabby doll, but he's pouring his heart out, saying, "But I love this person, this person meant something to me." New Amsterdam is another name for New York. So that song is about being in New York with me: It's about being entwined in my web and in my love and not feeling at peace with it.

CHAPTER 8

Almost Buell
1979–1983

I'm a normal girl
I like it on my back
When I'm lying in the sack
I'm a normal girl
Still shining like shellac
Stop giving me your flack
I'm a normal girl.
  "NORMAL GIRL," LYRICS BY BEBE BUELL

In August 1979, I met another rock 'n' roll singer, one who would soothe my soul and become my next boyfriend. The first time I ever saw Stiv Bators of the Dead Boys perform at CBGB, he was getting a blow job onstage from a member of the audience (America's number-one punk groupie, Damita X). After he got the blow job, he threw his belt over the steam pipe and "hung" himself. I thought, Wow, what is this shit? And I walked out. But I couldn't get Stiv out of my mind. I would see pictures of him and the Dead Boys doing disgusting things. Liz Derringer asked me, "Why do you think he's so cute?"

"I don't know. It's that weasel thing. I just love rats; I love weasels. I don't know why he's so cute. He just is, you know?"

"Ugh!" she replied. She just could not understand it.

I finally met Stiv at a party for Kiss upstairs at Max's. He was there with his fiancée, Cynthia, from the B Girls. Liz nudged me, "There's that guy. There's that weasel guy." I walked up to him; he had on a pink jacket with bright black stripes and he looked great. He was coiffed that night: Sometimes, he would grease his hair out

Me and Stiv Bators–1980, NYC–"The punk
Sonny and Cher"/MARCIA RESNICK

COUPLE OF THE YEAR
1. **Stiv Bators & Bebe Buell**
2. Cher & Gene Simmons
3. Rod & Alana Stewart
4. Mick & Bianca Jagger
5. Robert & Maureen Plant
6. Debbie Harry & Chris Stein
7. Linda Ronstadt & Jerry Brown
8. Nick Lowe & Carlene Carter
9. Sid Vicious & Nancy Spungen
10. Paul & Linda McCartney

1980 "Couple of the Year," Stiv and Bebe/*CREEM* MAGAZINE

and do a Brian Setzer, but he had a curl that night and he looked very cute. Since it was a Kiss party, we'd been drinking endless amounts of champagne. So I just walked up to Stiv and said, "I love you."

He looked at me and said, "You do?"

"Uh-huh," I said. "Liz and I love you."

"Well, how about if you just love me and not Liz?" he said. It was really funny. So he was standing there with his fiancée, Cynthia, who I thought was a little Goody Two-shoes, a little prissy boots, and, picking up one of the lines I had learned from Mick Jagger, I said, "Cynthia, I'm stealing him." And I took his hand and led him away.

I couldn't believe I did that. It's amazing what a few glasses of champagne will do. Turn you right into a little dog, but I kind of wish I hadn't done that. It was so mean. Anyway, Stiv broke up with Cynthia the next day, and I took him to Liz's, fed him, and gave him a bath.

Everybody thought we were much more serious than we were. We were really just extremely good friends, who loved taking the piss out of everybody. In the seventies, I was ringside for Iggy Pop, Alice Cooper, Todd Rundgren, David Bowie, then I dated the Bob Dylan of punk in the late seventies, and then I dated Stiv Bators. So I went from this bourgeois Steven Tyler/Todd Rundgren/Rod Stewart thing to the gutter—I went right downtown. And to tell the truth, I was happiest in the bowels of the punk-rock gutter, because that's who I was, too. That's what punk rock did for me—finally allowed me to admit who I was. It just made it easier for me to be me. It allowed me to have legitimacy as the person I was. It had been difficult for me to fit in with that bourgeois crowd I had been part of. Although Stiv was the epitome of punk rock—sharp, funny, and full of mischief—he went to Maine and stayed with Liv and me and had a great time. One of the things about Stiv that people didn't realize was that he was just a nice boy from the Midwest, who wanted to be Iggy Pop, although in some ways he was more agile than Iggy Pop. He was extremely bright and sweet, and on the domestic front, he was one of the tidiest and most fastidious people I'd ever met. He loved doing laundry, loved to vacuum. He was really, really meticulous about the way his jeans and T-shirts

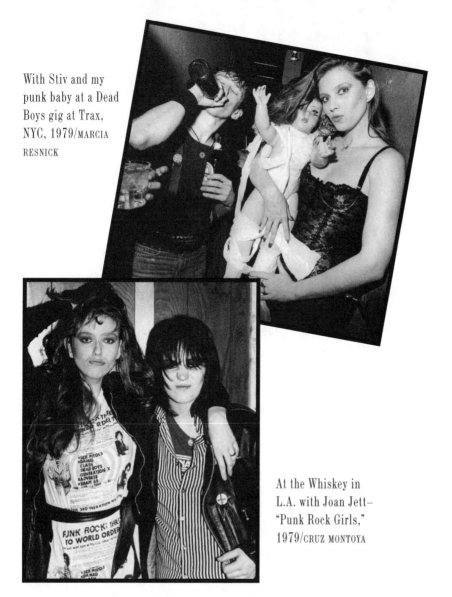

With Stiv and my punk baby at a Dead Boys gig at Trax, NYC, 1979/MARCIA RESNICK

At the Whiskey in L.A. with Joan Jett– "Punk Rock Girls," 1979/CRUZ MONTOYA

207

With Nico in NYC, 1979/BUELL PRIVATE COLLECTION

had to be washed and folded. Liv just adored him. Sex with Stiv was so wholesome—very high school, very Midwest, very endearing—it was hard to believe. He loved it when I wore big flannel nightgowns and thick socks; that turned him on.

I was out in L.A. with Stiv when there was a big party for Blondie at Fiorucci to celebrate a new record, *Eat to the Beat.* The band drove in on an army tank. In those days, the press officer followed people around the room and you would greet everyone. In the middle of the party, Debbie pulled out this huge bag of cocaine. "Debbie, you can't do that here," I told her. "There're lots of people around."

"Oh, don't worry," she said, "I'm shorter than everybody else here," and she surrounded herself with her crew and poured the cocaine onto her hand and snorted it.

"Where the hell did she get it?" I asked.

"Oh God," Stiv told me, "they give it to us."

I was thinking, isn't it interesting that record companies are actually giving the stars cocaine to keep them happy, to fuel them. Debbie was probably the most beautiful girl I have ever seen in my life, and I asked myself, how can she do this to herself? She was still so beautiful, though. Meeting Debbie wasn't like finding

Marianne Faithfull ravished on the floor of the Mudd Club, where I had to look through the layers of experience to find my beautiful Marianne, or when I had to discover Anita Pallenberg through the drug-induced bloat. Debbie was at the height of her beauty then, and evidently at the height of her cocaine use, too.

At that point, women in the rock 'n' roll world were considered to be the inspiration for the men, or the reason behind everything they did. People were always trying to blame me for any shift in the careers of my beau, just like everybody always blamed Yoko for John's decisions. When Todd went all spacey and cosmic, everybody blamed me for giving him acid. I was blamed for Rod Stewart looking like a rock 'n' roll boy again. When Stiv went solo, everybody thought he had turned pop and clean because of the domestic bliss I was bringing into his life. But this bliss was totally his idea.

It was the beginning of the eighties, nobody knew what was going to happen next, but the punk scene was still big. We hammed it up for the cameras and had a real good time. Stiv and I were photographed so often together, *Creem* magazine dubbed us the "Creem Couple" of 1980, and we fell neatly into that slot, becoming for eight months the punk Sonny and Cher. He thought it was a good way for me to release myself from the pain I was feeling. Everybody knew I loved Elvis, of course, and that was that. I would talk to Stiv about Elvis and tell him how my heart was breaking.

I loved Stiv—he was a great guy—but by the spring of 1980, he started doing a lot of coke and alcohol and began to change. He became violent—he would hurt himself and other people, as well as objects. But I was bigger than he was. I was a good four inches taller, and I outweighed him by about fifteen pounds, so he never fucked with me. He never struck me, but he often struck anybody who was around me. Sometimes, Stiv would get crazy. He'd bounce off the walls like a maniac, go insane. So I'd have to get him down on his stomach, put my knee into his back, and take his belt and tie it around his wrists. Then I'd sit on his legs until he calmed down. I likened it to epilepsy. That's what I used to say to him: "You had one of those fucking psycho epileptic fits last night."

In early 1980, we moved out of my cottage in the family compound and into an apartment at 34 Park Street in Portland, where we lived from 1980 to 1985. It was the bottom floor of a typical

Stiv snapped this picture of me coming out of the pool at the Tropicana Hotel in L.A., 1979/STIV BATORS

New England house. It had three bedrooms, a bathroom, a living room, a dining room, and a kitchen. We each had a bedroom; Liv's and my bedrooms were right next to each other, separated by a door. Actually, her bedroom and my bedroom were like one big bedroom that was separated by a door and a closet. At one point, it *had* been one bedroom, and then somebody had made it into two. We had a tiny guest bedroom. The house had a beautiful front yard with fruit trees. It was lovely

One of the strongest aspects of my character is that I am not

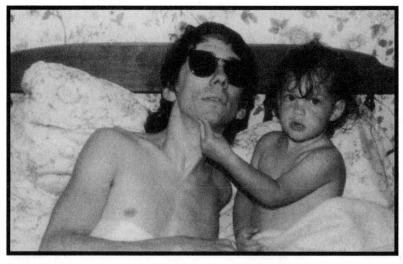

Stiv and Liv in my bed at my cottage in Maine, 1980–Liv adored Stiv/BEBE BUELL

given to sinking deeper into depression; I always have to be doing something. Every time my heart gets broken, it motivates me to do ten more projects. During the years when I'd had relationships with these special men, I'd been copping some licks. I started to do the things they always told me I could do. I decided to fulfill the dream I had had since 1972 and at last become a rock 'n' roll singer.

In 1980, before I even put together a band or performed live, I recorded and released an EP called *Covers Girl.* That record had my friend Ric Ocasek and the Cars playing on two tracks, and Rick Derringer and his band played on the other tracks, so it was me with two all-star bands. Working with Ric was wonderful, because he wanted to be a producer. I was one of his first guinea pigs. We recorded at the Cars' studio, Syncro Sound, in Boston. Ric admired me and respected me, and the way he treated me in the studio reflected this. "Hey, man, you're cool. Just do it," he'd say. "Just go up there and be yourself, be who you are. Just be the person I think is fabulous and it'll come across." Rick Derringer also respected me as a musical force. He thought I had a ton of talent. Unfortunately, people knew me as so-and-so's girlfriend or a model and a *Playboy* person. He said to me, "Bebe, if you had just formed a band when you first came to New York City, you'd be huge now."

As a result of that record, I wanted to put a band together and perform. By the time my romance with Stiv was flickering out, I had already started looking for musicians. I was hanging around with some of the local music people. One of my best friends was a girl named Beth Blood, who had a clothing store and was a bass player. She said to me, "My ex-boyfriend George is an amazing guitar player." She introduced me to him, and George Gordon did turn out to be this unbelievable guitarist. I had my guitar player, my bass player, and I had my sort of boyfriend, but he wasn't really my boyfriend, this guy Donny Crosby. He's this boy I kind of had a crush on up in Maine during that early eighties period. He played rhythm guitar. So I had George Gordon on guitar, Donny Crosby on rhythm, and Beth Blood on bass guitar. I guess you could say I had a kind of Spinal Tap thing with drummers. I finally found a drummer I was really happy with, this guy named John Rousseau. We called him "Rooster Rousseau," and that's when the B-Sides got to be their best. This was the original format. Later, Beth Blood was no longer the bass player. We dropped the rhythm guitar player, too, and brought another guy, Carl, into the band. So we had George Gordon on guitar, Carl on bass, and Rooster on drums. We became a three-piece power trio.

My first band, the B-Sides, 1981–(*left to right*) John Rousseau (drums), Carl Jordan (bass), me, George Gordon (guitar)/MARK HARRINGTON

While I was forming the band, I got up every morning at 6:30 and walked my daughter to St. Elizabeth's Day Care, then I went to rehearsal. Liv loved it. We have wonderful memories. Liv says one of her most beautiful memories is of the time when we lived on Park Street—we had these matching clothes, matching cowboy boots, matching nighties. I got the apartment when she was three. She went to preschool, which she loved, and then when she was five, she started kindergarten at the public school there. I would pick her up from day care at 3:00 P.M. and we'd go home and have playtime, a bath, then dinner. If I had rehearsals at night, which I sometimes did, Beth Blood would baby-sit; she lived right across the street from us. It was very convenient. Everything worked out great. If I had to go to New York for the weekend, Annie would take Liv.

In New York, I would stay with Liz and Rick. In 1981, when my EP came out, 85 percent of the record industry assumed that Ric Ocasek was having an affair with me, or, at the very least, that we were bonking in between tracks. Why else would he perform with me? Why else would he take a model into the recording studio? they asked, flabbergasted. Being a model turned out to be one very high wall I had to climb over to get any respect or recognition as a rock 'n' roll singer. That didn't bother me at the time, because I was determined to succeed and I just couldn't see any major obstacles ahead of me. Famous last words.

After I put together the B-Sides, I went back and forth from Maine to New York all the time. I would spend a week in Maine and a week in New York.

It was exhilarating performing with the B-sides. My first show

Kicking and jumping while performing with the B-Sides, 1981-1982/NORMAN BLAKE

was in 1980, on Halloween, at the downtown lounge in Portland, Maine. Ric Ocasek, Liz and Rick Derringer, and Paul Fishkin from Bearsville came from New York for that show. We did original material and some carefully chosen covers. We used to do the Tom Petty song "Wild One Forever." I did Iggy Pop's song "Funtime," and "Little Black Egg," all of which are on my EP. I also did "Hey Little Girl" by the Syndicate of Sound. The rest of the songs were original ones that I wrote with my band. I did covers because people always depended on me to find obscure and fabulous covers. The taste thing again.

The night scene in Portland was vibrant. There were a couple of great clubs—such as Geno's and the Tree Cafe—and all the national acts would come to play the Portland Civic Center. We had national acts in and out all the time. There was also the Senesta Hotel, which had a bar on the top floor that overlooked Portland. Everybody went there to hang out after the show. It was a very exciting time. I laughed when Seattle became such an important music mecca, because I thought Portland, Maine, had it over Seattle hands down.

The B-Sides lasted from 1980 to 1984. My first live New York performance was to a packed house at the Ritz in November 1980. I brought the house down and got a five-star review in *Melody Maker*. We started playing New York dates and doing short East Coast and Midwest tours. Joey Ramone was a big help. He would include me in his Christmas shows.

For the first time in my life, I felt like an independent woman. I was well liked by the toughest New York rock writers: Lester Bangs, John Holmstrom, Robert Christgau, Danny Goldberg, Ben Edwards, and Danny Fields. The smart people thought I was a pistol, that I was sharper than a tack. In one sentence, I could analyze something and tell you if it was cool or not. That was what I did—I gave great quote—and people thought that what I had to say about certain areas of the music industry was relevant and that my opinion mattered. In the early eighties, when I retreated to Portland to be a good mother, to get away from the craziness, and to pine for the lost love of Elvis, there was always somebody calling me from some record company or magazine to ask me my opinion. On one visit to New York, Liz told me that Pat Benatar's publicist wanted us to go down to the Bottom Line, watch her show, and give her our opinion about it. This was when Pat Benatar was going through her Pebbles Flintstone look—wearing her hair up and sporting spandex. We went down and watched her show. Her publicist wanted to know how we thought she should be dressed. "What are we, creative consultants?" I asked. "Shouldn't we be paid? Are you hiring us to be her stylist? Are you hiring us to make her cool?" I wanted to know why, if my opinion was so important, I wasn't getting paid. I was putting the B-Sides together, and I didn't feel like sharing my fashion tips or my look, because I was planning to use those things. That's when I started to get angry. I flashed back to the seventies, when I felt that I was used sexually and was just a fashion ornament for these guys, a press-getter. Once again, I felt hurt, tired, and used, and I couldn't understand why people thought it was so cool to hang out with me. Nobody took the time to explain it to me. But I saw that this was not going to make me a living. So I finally started to fight back. I not only formed a band; I started to ask questions.

In 1980, I started fooling around with Jack Nicholson, and that's what ended my relationship with Stiv. It hurt him, but I was trying to gain control of my life; I knew what I was doing. Stiv had gotten too crazy, and I wanted to hang out with Jack. Stiv thought I had really sold out. It was a very punk thing. I ended up going back to L.A. to hang out with Jack Nicholson's crowd, but my relationship with Jack actually started in New York, when I attended a party for the premiere of *The Shining*. We were in a club. I was sitting downstairs, and the top fashion designer of the year, Diane Von Furstenberg, struck up a conversation with me. Then, all of a sudden, she took me by the hand and led me upstairs to this private little attic at the top of the club. Inside, Zoli, who was temporarily my agent during one of many brief separations from Wilhelmina, was talking with Jack. Mick Jagger and Jerry Hall were also there. Diane took me straight over to Jack and deposited me in front of him, saying, "Jack, I think you might want to meet this girl."

JACK: Heeyyy!

BEBE: Hi! I'm Bebe.

JACK: Hey, Beeb! Thank you, Diane. Sooo, Beeb, what do you do? Let me guess. You're a model?

BEBE: Well, unfortunately, you're right.

JACK: Well, what do you mean by that, Beeb? [I realized that he had already picked me, then gotten Diane to introduce us. At this point, Mick and Jerry came over.]

ZOLI: Mick, you know Bebe, don't you?

MICK: Of course I do. She's the mother of one of my illegitimate daughters.

JERRY: Miiiick, that's not naahce! Don't say that!

BEBE: God, Mick, when are you going to stop teasing me like this?

MICK: Where did she get those lips? You tell me where she got those juuuicey lips. Because she didn't get those lips from Todd.

BEBE: Mick, stop it! You know that isn't true.

MICK: Oh, I know, darling. I'm just kidding.

BEBE: Well, stop doing that in public. You're embarrassing me in front of Zoli and Jack and everybody—announcing this in the middle of the fucking room!

MICK: Well, it's all right, darling. Why don't you come and sit with me and Jerry? You'll be all right. Just stay away from Jack. He's naughty. You have to be careful. . . . He's a womanizer!

BEBE: Well, what are you?

MICK: I am your friend, darling; you know that. And I hold your best interests at heart, and I don't want you going off with Jack.

BEBE: All right, but he's cute.

MICK: Darling, if you do run off with him, just know what he's all about. I know you—you're sensitive. I don't want you to get your little feelings hurt. [Finally, it was time to leave, and we all went to Jack's hotel room because he had the champagne.]

MICK: Come, darling, you're going with us! [I walked out on one side of Mick, with Jerry on the other. We dashed into a limo and were taken to the Pierre Hotel, where we went up to Jack's suite. When we got there, Jack started giving me all of this attention. Meanwhile, Mick and Jerry kept trying to distract me.]

JERRY: Do you know how to leg wrestle?

"I pledge allegiance to Mick," 1980/RICHARD CREAMER

BEBE: Yeah!

JERRY: *You do?* I've met a girl who can leg wrestle! I'm the champion leg wrestler. Do you think you could beat me?

BEBE: Yeah! [I had absolutely no idea what I was doing, but I was willing to give it a try. So we went back into Jack's bedroom and each put on a pair of Jack's very clean, very white men's briefs. Neither of us had been wearing any underwear, and when you leg wrestle, your dress ends up around your neck. We went back into the living room in Jack's underwear, got down on the floor, and started to wrestle. Jerry and I were going at it, and Jack and Mick were throwing money down. Naturally, Jerry definitely was the champion leg wrestler. She was six feet tall, to my five ten. She had length on me, and she'd obviously been leg wrestling since she could walk. We wrestled long enough that the men could start making bets; then she whopped my butt! Then a beautiful Australian actress named Rachel Ward arrived, and Jack immediately lost interest in me. He and Rachel disappeared into the bedroom and I was left with Mick and Jerry.]

MICK: See, what did I tell you? I predicted this, didn't I? Come with us. [We swept out of there and proceeded to go over to Mick's house to hang out. Of course, Mick suggested I sleep with them. Despite the gorgeous invitation, I refused.]

JERRY: Show us your titties! Come along—they're so beautiful!

The next morning, I woke up and we all had breakfast together. It was so cute. Then, in the middle of breakfast, the phone rang.

MICK: What do you mean? . . . No, I'm not going to let you. . . . No! Well, maybe dinner, but that's it! . . . All right, I'll let you speak to her. Bebe, Jack.

BEBE: Hi, Jack.

JACK: I know what I did last night was very rude and I want to make it up to you. [I didn't even have time to go home. I showered and Jerry gave me one of her dresses to wear—we're the same size. We went to dinner at a very posh Italian restaurant in the Village. We drank some great wine and the best champagne and ate delicious pasta. At one point, a girl came over to the table and started talking to Mick. Suddenly, Jerry hauled off and delivered a very efficient kick to one of her legs and the girl's legs buckled before she limped away. I was impressed.]

BEBE: How did you do that so discreetly?

JERRY: Lots of practice. When I notice they're disrespecting me, I let 'em have it, and I tell them to stay away from my man.

BEBE: Okaaayy! [She knew how to kick a chick with her high heels, man, and do it in a way Mick did not see. That girl knew she didn't stand a chance. I saw it flash across her face—I'm getting out of here!—and Jerry threw in a withering glare, all behind Mick's back. All of a sudden, that chick vanished! Meanwhile, Jack was being his most charming self, which is saying something. He was being darling to me, touching my back, staring into my eyes.]

JACK: Beeb, you're one hell of a good-looking girl. Damn! [Jack went to the men's room.]

MICK: Now, I'm telling you, Bebe, he's a playboy. If you insist on having sex with him, *I* insist you do it at our house. Then at least when he takes off, you'll have us to cry to. [We had this beautiful dinner and then we all glided back to Mick and Jerry's beautiful house in a limousine. I did spend that night with Jack at their house. The next day, Jack left early, but he kept sending me flowers every hour at Mick and Jerry's.]

JERRY: *Godamn! What did you do to him, Bebe?* Mick, this isn't like Jack, is it?

MICK: No, it's not. What the fuck did you do to him, Bebe?

BEBE: Nothing! We just had sex, very normal sex. There was no kink, no weirdness. It was just wholesome backseat sex.

MICK: Maybe that's it! But you've got to promise me you're not going to fall in love with him, because he'll break your heart.

BEBE: I'm not going to fall in love with him.

They wouldn't let me go home again that whole day. We went horseback riding in Central Park. Jerry had fifty pairs of jodhpurs and riding boots, so I was able to wear all her gear. Mick's a great rider, and so am I. Jerry and her sister Rosie came along, galloping through the park. That was fun. It also took on an eighteenth-century vibe when Mick would trot up next to me, stick his nose up in the air, and then gallop off. And I was thinking, Wait a minute! I've seen this before in *Barry Lyndon*!

After three days of round-the-clock entertainment, I said, "You guys, I've got to go home!" I'd been staying with Liz and Rick before this, so I went back down there. Liz kept me up all night because she wanted to hear everything.

Liz said, "I can't believe that you wouldn't sleep with them."

Jack ended up starting to like me. He called me all the time, and he even started calling my mom.

JACK: Hi! This is JACK! I just wanted you to know I think your daughter is fantastic. You did a good job, Mom!

MOM: Bebe! Jack Nicholson just called me. What's that about?

BEBE: Well, Mom, that's just Jack. He probably wants to make sure that I have a family and I'm not some street kid. [The phone calls persisted. At one point, I had both Jack and Warren Beatty calling me on the phone. I knew Warren well before I ever met him, because he would call my house all the time and talk to me in Maine. He knew Jack liked me, and I think it turned out Warren was from Virginia, too, so he would also call my mom. Now my Mom was getting phone calls from Warren Beatty and Jack Nicholson!]

MOM: Bebe! What's going on? They are both so charming.

In 1981, Jack flew me out to L.A. I stayed with my girlfriend Pam. Jack's house was on Mulholland and she lived just off Mulholland. He would drive over in the white Volkswagen he'd had since before he made it—it was his cover car—and hang out with me while Pam was at work. One time, I was down on my knees, doing my makeup in the bathroom, and Jack got down on his knees with me.

JACK: Well, Beeb, you know, you're growin' on me. I like you. What is it? I like ya.
BEBE: I like you, too. Mick tells me that you're gonna hurt me.
JACK: Well, I might, but you'll have a damn good time before I do! [Jack was just sweet to me. He'd call up and we'd have these funny conversations.]
JACK: Hi! This is Zeke. Is Beeb there? [He wanted me to call him Zeke.]
BEBE: Your voice is so Jack. You could call yourself Zeke the Greek, and everybody would still know it's Jack.
JACK: I know, Beeb, but I like Zeke. I want you to call me Zeke.
BEBE: Okay, I'll call you Zorba the Zeke.
JACK: No, just Zeke, Beeb! Just say Zeke.
BEBE: Okay. Zeke.
JACK: Thank you, Beeb.

Jack liked to sneak into theaters and see his own movies. One day, Jack and his agent, Sue Mengers, took me in a limousine to a theater in Westwood. We sat in the balcony to watch *The Shining*. I was blown away by the film.

JACK: So, Beeb, tell us what you think of the film. We'd like a female point of view.
BEBE: Well, you know . . . [I went into all my feelings about the film.]
SUE MENGERS: You know, she might be right for *Postman* . . . You're a beautiful girl. Have you ever thought about being an actress?
JACK: That Beeb, man, she's into the rock thing, Sue. She's a rock 'n' roll kind of girl. I don't think Hollywood and the Beeb would mix. [The person who starred opposite Jack in *The Postman Always Rings Twice* was Jessica Lange, another model. People always noticed something about me that made them realize I was a rock 'n' roll girl at heart. Jack was right: "Beeb's into the rock thing. Beeb

and Hollywood don't mix!" Jack knew that straight off, and he was right.]

SUE MENGERS: Well, you know, if you ever want to think about acting, Bebe . . .

One night, Jack came to visit in his Volkswagen so we could go driving around on Mulholland. We went parking and looked out at the lights. We came back from driving around and parked on this pavement area outside Pam's house. We were making out against the car; then we started to make love.

I'd never done it up against a car before, so I was having my first very cool sex-against-the-car-with-Jack-Nicholson lesson. He had my dress hiked up. It was very sexy and at the same time pretty much like high school demure. He didn't even have his pants off; he just had his fly down. So there we were, humping away, when Pam came roaring up the driveway on her way home from work. Simultaneously, Jack dropped his pants and her headlights shined on his bare butt. Pam copped a discreet peek, gave us two toots on her horn, and sped by.

BEBE: Just don't move.
JACK: But Beeb, my pants are hanging down around my knees!
BEBE: Well, just stay like that. Don't move. That way, maybe she won't know what we're doing.
JACK: Beeb, she's gonna know what we're doing—my butt was going fifty miles an hour here. [As he pulled his pants up and I smoothed my dress down, Pam returned and got out of her car.]
PAM: Hi! Sorry to disturb you two.
JACK: Oh heck, the Beeb and I were just having a conversation.
PAM: Yeah, you sure were.
BEBE: Pam, if you tell anybody, I'm gonna kill you!
PAM: Don't worry.
JACK: Beeb, I better go home. [He was crestfallen.] We just got caught!

Jack flew me out to L.A. a second time in 1981, but now Jack was different. He was staying at Warren Beatty's house, because he and Anjelica Huston, with whom he'd been involved in a deep, long-lasting relationship, were parting and having a bad breakup. As a result, Jack was going through one of his horrible depressions. He was eating too much and he was getting heavy. He was living at Warren's and a lot of women were coming in and out.

I was there with Jack, but he was so depressed he would cry all night; it was really bad. He was a mess, truly distraught. He loved Anjelica, but she went through periods of having had enough of him. They went through this a couple more times before they separated for good. Anyway, I was supposed to be out there to comfort Jack by being around him, although he was virtually inconsolable.

Warren, on the other hand, was really fun and upbeat. He didn't do drugs and his was good energy for Jack to be around. Warren played the piano. Actually, the first time Jack took me to Warren Beatty's house, Warren was sitting behind a piano. He looked up at me and said, "Jack tells me you like musicians."

"Well, isn't that interesting"—I laughed—"I would never have thought of you as a musician." Then he proceeded to play classical piano on such an accomplished level, I was mesmerized.

Warren would be up early in the morning, talking on the phone by the pool, eating his wheat germ, doing all his Warren stuff. I was up early, too, because I had a couple of modeling assignments, doing department store print ads through the Mary Webb Davis Agency, zipping around in a rental car Jack had thoughtfully gotten me.

On this visit, Jack and Warren were really trying to talk me out of being in the rock world, because I was getting seriously involved in my band, the B-Sides. "Beeb, you know, you're the kind of girl who could have her own sitcom," Jack told me. "You're funny!" They would impress upon me that I needed to grow up and get rid of the rock world. None of these men had married me, they pointed out. "Rock 'n' roll is so temporary," they said, worried that I would end up with nothing.

I tried to explain to them that it wasn't quite that simple, that this was who I was, in that I finally knew who I was, that I had formed a band and they should be happy for me. "But Beeb," Jack persisted, "ya know the thing is, you've got too much class to be in rock. I'm telling you, you're a classy piece of ass and that is just not going to be denied. You'd have to be a lot sleazier and a lot raunchier to be a rock girl. I just think you've got too much class. You need to get rid of these fucking sleazy guys! They're not good enough for you."

"I wanna introduce you to my friend Lou Adler," Warren chimed in.

"But he's a music person. . . ."

"No, no, no, he's a music person and a movie person and everything. You need somebody like that."

Meanwhile, Jack was saying, "Yeah, Mario would be good. . . ." And they started running off a list of all these men they thought I should see.

It was on one of these nights at Warren's house when I was once again allowed to become part of the boys' club, as I had been at the Wick. Warren, Jack, and I were sitting around, waiting for the girls to arrive, and Jack was saying, "So Beeb, tell me what you think of this one."

"All right, bring on the girls!"

The girls started arriving. I recognized a couple of them from TV shows. One of them was a girl from *The Nancy Drew Mysteries*. We were all sitting around the dining room table waiting for supper. The cook brought out this huge plate of ribs.

WARREN: Girls, dig in; dig in.
THE GIRLS: Oh no! We can't eat that! We don't eat meat!
WARREN: How about you, Jack?
JACK: Well, hell, I'll have one!
WARREN: Beeb, how about you—are you a vegetarian, too?
BEBE: Hell yeah, but I'm gonna eat one!
WARREN: I love you! This is why I love you!

We ate that whole goddamn platter of ribs, acting like the most disgusting people on earth. We had beer and everything. Warren even had the TV on, and we were watching some game like a bunch of rednecks. We were just like really on. Basically, we were putting on a show for the girls.

JACK: Warren, this is a movie.
WARREN: Yup, Jack, it is.

Meanwhile, the chicks were all bored out of their minds. Finally, two of them got up and started disrobing while walking toward the hot tub. I'll never forget Jack watching these girls out of the corner of his eye, and one eyebrow kept shooting up. Finally, he said,

JACK: Warren, I think all the chicks are in the hot tub.
WARREN: Yes, I think they are, Jack.
JACK: I think they know how to get our attention. [Turning to me] Excuse me, Beeb; I think it's time for me to make my exit.

He took off his clothes and jumped into that Jacuzzi. Warren and I, fully dressed, walked over to see how they were doing.

WARREN: So, Jack, should I get somebody to bring out a bunch of cocktails or something?
JACK: Yeah, Warren, that would be great.

That image of Jack sitting in the hot tub with six beautiful starlets all over him perfectly summed up the situation. I never had so much fun in my life, but I was also thinking, I bet he fucks every one of them and still comes back for seconds.

I went back into the house with Warren, who proceeded to play classical piano for me all night, until I ended up going to sleep. People like Warren Beatty and Mick Jagger, who could be around all the drug mayhem that characterized the 1970s, managed not to do drugs and yet still be the coolest guys in the room. That's one of the great things about them—they really do have their shit together. Even though I was in situations with Warren Beatty where drugs were being taken, I don't think I ever saw him take a drug. I know Gene Simmons of Kiss has never taken a drugs in his life, and he's certainly been in situations where drugs were being used. And I can pretty much guarantee that I've been with Mick Jagger when he was not taking drugs but everybody else in the room was.

Jack eventually came to bed. "Beeb, hey, Beeb," he whispered, "you sleepin'?" I was awake, but I didn't want him to know. There was no way I was going to have sex with him after he had had sex with six women, and I knew he had, so I just pretended to be asleep. I knew my relationship with Jack was going to change, and it did, becoming for the most part a platonic relationship thereafter. I wrote a song about this wonderful night, "Jacuzzi Jungle," and it goes like this:

I had to come here to find my way
To the place of never ending sunny days
Where the natives need a daily dip
In the Jacuzzi jungle

If only I could accept this trip
If I could enjoy the cleansing dip
Or a photographed love life on Sunset Strip
In the Jacuzzi jungle.

But I had been let into the boys' club once again. And I guess I might have made it in Hollywood, too, if I had been willing to do the Sharon Stone shuffle. I could have been represented by Sue Mengers, who was the biggest agent of the day. I could have had all the resources. But I wasn't even interested in checking it out. This is why a number of my friends have thought at one time or another that I have a self-destructive streak. They don't understand how I could ever turn down something so easily attainable. But the way I saw it was not self-destructive. I was just being true to myself. A lot of people saw this as me throwing away an opportunity to make a lot of money and have a successful career as an actress. But money has never been my motivating force.

I didn't stay with Jack, because I really didn't want to be riding around in somebody's Rolls-Royce, listening to eighties pop tunes. And I soon got fed up with trying to get Jack excited about the Mc5. My tastes were too raw for L.A. Ultimately, it was just not my idea of a good time. Whenever I tried to put on the records I liked, everybody suggested I was too adolescent, too immature, and freaky. And I kept asking myself, Why? Just because I like good music? Just because I'm trying to turn you on to good rock 'n' roll? I'm trying to get through to you, and you think I'm flaky?

When I got through with this second trip to L.A., I flew back to Maine and started playing with the B-Sides even more ferociously, but I still could not get Elvis off of my mind. I was both titillated

Promo shot for *Covers Girl*, 1981/RICHARD CREAMER

and inspired by what seemed to be numerous clues that led me to believe he still loved me.

In late 1981, Rhino put out my EP *Covers Girl*. At the end of the year, Robert Christgau picked it as one of his top ten records of the year in the *Village Voice*. That was even more fantastic than I had allowed myself to dream of. However, as far as I was concerned, the record's greatest tribute came from Elvis Costello, who released his album of covers, *Almost Blue*, shortly thereafter. I try not to exaggerate these concidences, but I couldn't escape the similarities between the two records. Mine came out first. In the cover photo, I'm tearing up a magazine cover. On his cover, there's also a big tear. All the songs on both records are about love—losing love, wanting love. And if you look at the word *Blue*, doesn't *Buell* jump out at you?

Around 1981 or 1982, Marcia Resnick was taking a lot of photographs of Johnny Thunders, and she was also taking photographs of me, so I started running into him a lot at her Canal Street loft. We renewed our friendship, and I think Johnny had a little crush on me then. He really reached out to me during that period, and if he hadn't been so scabby, I might've wanted to, but he scared me. Johnny was not a pretty sight—let's get real here. His hands were unbelievably disgusting. They were all plumped up like sausages, and they looked scabby and weird all the time. I don't like talking like that about somebody that I loved so much, but he just made me a little nervous. Sometimes you'd be talking to him and blood would just start to drip down his hand—not exactly somebody you'd wanna pounce on.

Back in Maine, in 1982 and 1983, I took acting lessons to keep from going crazy. This guy Billy B., who had trained with Stella Adler, had a workshop in Portland. He would organize what he called "fag fests." I fell into that crowd because I also thought it would help me to loosen up and to shed my fears as a performer. It did. Billy taught me movement; I learned how to touch a mike stand with conviction and finesse. We would do mime exercises, imitating a tree, a car, or a boat. We just played wonderful games and put together plays. I've always had my finger in that "fag pie" and always been part of their little dress-up games. One of my friends was also a hairdresser, so I would help him out at his hair salon, which was a blast.

I also had a brief affair with Richard Butler of the Psychedelic Furs. Good band, lousy relationship. I met him in Boston while I was performing with the B-Sides. We opened for them at the Channel. In the summer of 1981, I went out to Los Angeles for two weeks and hung out with them there. I was responsible for bringing Todd together with them. He produced their next record, *Forever Now*.

My friendship with Richard Butler was short-lived. He was an extreme and terrible alcoholic. It took me awhile to find out, because when you're first infatuated with a person, you don't see their faults. But when he came up to visit us in Maine for Easter, even Liv got handy at hiding his liquor bottles, and she was only five. When Todd produced them, they went up to Bearsville to work at Todd's studio, and they were living in the guest house. I joined Richard there. It was during that trip that I decided I didn't want to see him anymore, because he was drinking heavily and he was just really bad. He got so fucked up on cocaine and alcohol, he would find my most prized possessions, my diaries and love letters from Elvis, and start shredding them. When you say you love somebody and then you shred their most cherished possessions, that's not love; that's jealousy.

On the beach with Liv—summer 1981/BUELL
PRIVATE COLLECTION

Todd and I remained close. Karen Darvin, who was still his girlfriend, didn't try to ostracize me. She actually enjoyed the extended family. As a result of this, Todd and I worked together for a weekend in 1983, when he agreed to produce me. In the studio, he acted as he always did with me—like a dictator—but he was also sweet and soothing, and he kept encouraging me, telling me, "You can do a better vocal than that."

There were a couple of times when he yelled into my headphones, which was not a nice thing to do. When you've got your cans on, you don't want anybody yelling in your ear. He even made me cry, but later he told me he needed me to feel like that to get the effect of the vocal he wanted. I said, "Okay, Phil Spector."

Todd thinks musicians are toys and that he's always the soul of the music. We worked well together and got good results, but ultimately it was an upsetting experience for me, because after we'd finished working in the studio, we'd go back up to the house. One time, when everybody had gone to the city to shop, he made a sexual advance. We ended up having sex, but it was hard for me, because there was still that little girl in me that loved him. It was very manipulative and horrible. Especially because when Karen came home, he treated me like a doorstop. That was when I started to open my eyes to how Todd really operated. However, it wasn't until his current girlfriend, Michelle, came into the picture that relations again became truly difficult.

228

My seeing Richard apparently got Elvis's attention. There were a couple of people I fooled around with during that period. Brian Setzer of the Stray Cats became a friend, but we didn't really have a romantic relationship. He was another one who thought I was a great singer. We met on the road—we were both in Detroit at the same time doing shows—and I went to their Stray Cats show because my band had played the night before, that kind of thing. I met a lot of people during that time because I had a band. I hung out with Echo & the Bunnymen. They were my favorite band for a while; I thought they were just wonderful. I loved Squeeze. Sometimes I would hang out with Jools Holland, who also became a buddy. I knew that hanging out with Jools would get back to Elvis, because he was good friends with that crowd. From 1980 to 1983 until I got back together with Elvis again, I had a few silly, little frivolous, going nowhere relationships.

I hung out with the Cars. Ric Ocasek had produced me, and I was always going to Boston, where he lived then, to see him. I spent a lot of time in Portland, Boston, and New York in the early eighties. And I also made trips to L.A. because Jack Nicholson invited me. A lot of

Liv and her "daddy," Todd, in Woodstock at the house on Mink Hollow Rd., 1982/BEBE BUELL

the affairs I had or thought of having at that time were to get Elvis's attention. Anybody English, anybody I knew he would hear about, anybody that was on his record label could fit the bill. These were the games we played, and it was my intention to make him as absolutely, furiously jealous as I could—and believe me, I did.

CHAPTER 9

The Return of Elvis Costello 1982-1983

People would be so surprised
That you talk so sweet
They think you're nasty
And a creep
Such a bad, bad boy
But when we're all alone
And it's late at night
We talk in the dark
And it feels so right
   "BABY TALK," LYRICS BY BEBE BUELL

One day in the fall of 1981, my mother and I were driving around Washington, and Prince's "Little Red Corvette" came on the radio. When he sang the line "Bebe you're much too fast," my mother asked, "Aren't you upset about that?"

"No! I'm flattered. It's a beautiful song," I said.

"Well, no," she replied, "it's not really a beautiful song. It's about a girl who can't settle down; it's about a girl who can't stop running around. It's not a nice song."

"Well, Mom," I said, "it can't be about me. I don't know the man."

"Bebe, it's artistic license. He's taking the liberty of writing a song about you; it's your persona that he's writing about."

My mom summed that one up the best. People don't always write songs directly about people; they write songs inspired by people. At that point in my life, I had the reputation of being too fast, having way too many boyfriends, not being able to settle down, running around with pop stars. I don't know what made Prince write that song, but it certainly did open up a door for me to play with Elvis's head. Because everybody thought the song was about me. And I think Prince wanted to meet me. Pop stars of the day all wanted to meet me.

Anyway, this conversation gave me the idea of stirring up a rivalry between Prince and Elvis, which was easy to do with a man like Elvis. When Elvis wanted to get me back, or let me know that he loved me, or send me cruel messages, he did it in songs. Now, in an unexpected reversal of fortunes, I saw a way to infuriate him and make him jealous, using somebody else's song! I would allow him to believe the thoughts this song, and later others, conjured up.

In July 1982, Elvis put out the *Imperial Bedroom* album. That was the record that had people gossiping that perhaps he was still in love with me, because of a song called "Human Hands." I know that it made his wife suspicious, because I received a very nasty phone call from her. I was puzzled, but I handled her call with as much respect and dignity as I could muster. I just told her that none of those songs could be about me—after all, wasn't he married and in love with her?

She asked, "How could he miss me?—because the lyrics refer to missing a 'darling'—if he's *with* me?"

"Well, you'll have to ask him that," I said. "I'm terribly sorry." I never told Elvis about her call. I was afraid it would scare him off.

Then all of a sudden, Elvis started calling me again, and soon thereafter, the letters started arriving. He gave me an address where I could write him—some office. And of course I went a little over the top: I bombarded him with letters every day. I was so in love with him. I loved him so much that I completely lost control. Some people lose control with drugs. I lost control with love for Elvis Costello.

On August 12, I sent a telegram from Maine to his hotel in Columbus, Ohio. It read, "Dear E.C. Must speak to you. Apparent bad misunderstanding. Gone to my mom's to recover from cardiac arrest. Please call. Love Bebe." That flipped him out, because he thought I'd really had a heart attack. On August 18, I sent another one: "Dear E.C. Please call at 914-679-2528 as soon as you get this, no matter how late or early. Need to tell you an important love secret. Bebe."

I completely forgot that he was back with his wife and child. I acted as if he were mine alone.

I was writing Elvis my thoughts every single day. Then I got a six-page letter from him—sent on February 2, 1983—which brought me up short. When I got that long long letter in Maine, I was alone on Park Street, and I couldn't breathe. I hyperventilated. I laid it down on the table and walked around it a few times. I didn't just rip it open. I was preparing myself. I didn't know if he was going to tell me that he couldn't live without me, that he was madly in love with me and had to have me, or if he had written me a Dear Jane letter. Or a combination of both.

The letter was a masterpiece of concision, clarity, and, I think in retrospect, both honesty and intelligence. First, he told me to slow down, that he could not possibly absorb my daily emotional explosions, nor did he want his office staff to become suspicious. Second, he made it clear that he wished me well and thought well of me, but he reminded me that I was a mother, just as he was a father, and that the time we had with our children was short. He felt sure I would understand that his feelings for his son were similar to those I had expressed for Liv when I had wept over her picture in London back in the dulcet days of 1978. He wrapped it up by stating that, at the very most, all I could expect from him was a secret friendship based on occasional correspondence, and nothing like the avalanche of emotion I clearly wanted. He reminded me never to let anyone extinguish my spirit, pointing out that I possessed "It"—thus my fortune was in my head, not in my backside—and wished me success.

My immediate reaction was that he was confused, that he didn't really know what to do. But I still thought that because he had taken the time to write such a personal, compassionate letter, there must still be a lot of feelings there. So I immediately harbored fantasies that he actually was still in love with me but this was his way of putting me at arm's length. I thought he was just trying to be the good guy who was going to remain loyal to his son.

Whatever, as a result of this letter, I quit writing him, because I thought I had overstepped and that perhaps I was behaving a tad bit aggressively, a little bit too much like Adèle Hugo. The truth is, I was confused: One minute, I'd think that I was getting the old kiss-off; the next, I'd convince myself that I could read between the lines and that he wasn't completely kissing me off, that he was just trying to get the passion rolling again. I thought he wanted me to tempt him—his favorite thing is to be tempted—and that he was saying I'd better not get too close or he'd fall for me again. He'd created this situation where I had become the secret. So as I saw it, I was playing along, and I had backed off at his request.

I was on the road doing gigs in Philadelphia, Detroit, and other cities. There was a lot of pressure on me, a lot of talk about the band. *Covers Girl* had gotten a lot of good reviews and I had moved over twenty thousand units. Independent records were not as accepted in the mainstream as they are now. Jason Flom from Atlantic Records gave me development money to make a demo. One night I was out with Jason and his friend Zemsky. We were talking. He

234   Keith Richards at one of my shows at Trax in NYC, 1982/CHUCK PULIN

said, "You know, the number twenty-two has a lot of spiritual implications. A lot of people think the number eleven is a spiritual number, but once twenty-two comes into your life, you know something intense is going to happen." I was intrigued at the time, but didn't think about it again for a while. Little did I know what significance this number would have for me in the spring of 1984.

I didn't get in touch with Elvis again for about a month. Then all of a sudden, in March 1983, I got a call from him at my house in Maine. "Bebe, it's four A.M." and I'm like, "Yeah!" Then he said, "I told you to back off a little, but I didn't say to not get in touch with me completely! I haven't had one letter from you in the post. You're drawing more attention to yourself by writing nothing. Now the office is going, 'Where is she! She's gone off!' The first thing people think is that you've run off with somebody else."

"Well, I thought that we were just going to be friends. I'm doing what you asked me to do. You asked me not to go so nutty. And I'm sorry, darling, but I love you so deeply and passionately and I'm so thrilled to have you back in my life that I had to send you all those letters to let you know how much I adore you and love you and worship you."

"All right, all right, I understand, but you know we're treading into dangerous territory. If I see you again, I know that we'll be having an affair, and I can't, because if Mary finds out . . ."

"Well, darling, I don't understand how you can tell me that you would have to give up your career and give up your life and your work and everything. What do you mean by that?"

"Trust me, if you and I were to be an item, it would not go over very well with my camp—with my manager, with people. . . . This is not working."

"But why are you risking it all, then? Why do you want me back in your heart? Why do you need to speak to me at all? Why don't you just not talk to me?"

"Well, I don't know! I guess I can't live without you! All right, I've said it! I've said it! Good-bye!"

Oh my God, I thought.

There was no star 69 in those days; there was no way to call him back. I didn't even have an answering machine in 1983. I was just screaming to myself, thinking, What is he doing? He's mad! It was a really big step. And then I regained my composure. I knew he was mine. Whatever it was that I was igniting in him, it was fueling his art, his sense of danger, his mad love for me. I waited for days for another call, and I was climbing the walls. Of course, no call came. Then finally one night, he called again. That was his favorite thing to do—call me in the night—because he wanted to see if I was alone. I think he was recording at the time. He was making "Everyday I Write the Book."

When I answered the phone, he said, "I needed some time to think. I'm getting ready to come to America for the tour." *Punch the Clock* was coming out and his band, the Attractions, was getting ready for a major tour in August and September. Then he said, "I think we need to see each other. I think we need to see each other again."

I was really good at finding him. I was unbelievable at it. He used to call me Inspector Clouseau because I had a knack for finding him. There was this game we played—Hunt the Girl/Hunt the Boy. When I would meet him in hotel rooms, I would hide and he would have to find me. I think he was always really intrigued by my wit and intelligence and how I could pull things off. One time, he was rehearsing in Pennsylvania, and I called him up. I'd tracked him down at the rehearsal studio by calling his booking agent. I pretended I was looking for the road manager. Using one of my many accents, I told the booking agent that I had some important documents that needed to be sent over to him.

"Oh sure," he said, and gave me the number. So I called, asked for Elvis, and was told, "Oh, he's just arrived in the dining room for supper." So then I called the dining room and I asked for Mister Costello, I asked the maître d' to go over to Elvis's table and get him. He took the call, and he said, "Hello," completely nonplussed. I said, "Hello!"

"Oh my God! You've really outdone yourself this time! How did you do it?" he asked.

"I'm not telling you."

"This one's too good." That was when we decided that when he came to New York for a few days, we would see each other. We had discussed it. He was going to call me when he got to the city. I don't think he expected that I would find him in Pennsylvania, but that started off the cat and mouse game.

Elvis came back into my life during a fertile time for him. *Imperial Bedroom* was a critical smash—compared to the Beatles by reviewers. As always, he coded a lot of songs so I'd know that he was singing to me. When I went to the Picasso show at the Museum of Modern Art recently, I saw a lot of the paintings Picasso coded for his lovers Marie-Thérèse and Dora Maar. Elvis is the Picasso of his generation in that respect. We called each other Henry and Jane, because the second time around, our affair was meant to be a secret. His other nickname for me throughout the years was "Candy." Even in 1991, six years after we broke up for good, Elvis and Paul McCartney wrote a song together called "So like Candy." Maybe he was talking about a box of chocolates, but I don't think so.

Near the end of July, we met in his suite at the Parker Meridian Hotel in New York. I wrote in my diary, "I was going to visit him and when he opened the door the only light in the room was coming from the blue light of the TV." And when I got to the door of his room, not having seen him for three years, he had the TV light on. I thought, Oh my God, is this guy obvious or what? It was so beautiful and poetic, yet he was terrified to give me an ounce of encouragement, or to give me an ounce of his unrequited lust for me, which was oozing from every pore in his body.

The first thing you would tend to ask somebody in this kind of situation is, "Are you in love?" But the first thing Elvis asked was, "Why did Prince write 'Little Red Corvette' about you?"

"He didn't write that song about me."

"It has your name, Bebe; you're much too fast. I've listened to it on sophisticated equipment. I've turned all the instruments down. I've even listened to it on one of those horrible stereos where you can hear only one vocal. Bebe, I heard it."

"I'm telling you, it's like my mom said—it's about my persona."

He thought I was lying through my teeth, of course, and that I'd obviously had a mad affair with Prince. At this point, all these issues, from Todd to Bowie, came up. He was jealous of Prince because he came along out of nowhere, and he was a freak genius. He could play a lot of instruments and was the kind of artist who would never pay tribute to his influences. Prince's incredible success infuriated Todd Rundgrens and the people like that even more. Of course, Elvis Costello would never want to admit that he was inspired by such a new artist.

I finally confessed to him that I had never met Prince, but of course he didn't believe me, because it was my pattern over the years; I'd had all these luscious men in my life and pretended that I had never been with them, that I barely knew them.

But in this instance, I really didn't know Prince, and I was trying to convince Elvis that I really hadn't had an affair with Prince. But it was too late; it didn't work. I had already taunted him so much that he was sure I had had an affair with Prince. Elvis was very in tune with the media—a biography junkie, a media junkie—and he felt that I had this intriguing ability to get under the skin of musicians artistically. He knew I had gotten under Todd's skin, and now he felt I had gotten under Prince's.

He used to call Prince "a clown," "Kermit the Frog," "the Purple People Eater," "Matador Dick." He had all kinds of phrases for Prince, but I think it was just jealousy. Todd Rundgren and Prince also had their secret forms of competition, which neither one would ever admit to. This goes on in the music industry. And I've been involved in many of these artistic duels: I've been the subject of them, as well as the victim.

Elvis and I didn't make love that night. I played him my demo, and we talked about the future.

After we dealt with Prince, we discussed the drama that went around the release of the *Oui* interview that I did with Stephen Demorest in 1980. Everybody wanted to know me after that

interview. That was when *Oui* was owned by *Playboy*, and it had a lot of class and authority. So the interview was considered quite a coup; it was another shining moment. In fact, that interview gave birth to many things.

Elvis had been on the road with the Attractions in Holland at the time. And his wife happened to be with him. The entire trip to Amsterdam was spent keeping the magazine away from her, because the band and the crew knew about the interview and everyone was talking about it. Elvis had even seen it and thought it was really fantastic and charming. He was touched by the way he was depicted in it, but it was really a big drama, because he didn't want Mary to see it. He reiterated that to me when we saw each other again, telling me how dramatic and funny it was. Elvis pointed out to me that the red hue of the pages gave the impression that I was a redhead. My bush looked pretty red in that interview. In "Little Red Corvette," the car symbolized my pussy. Elvis said that writers get inspirations for songs from the hue of an interview. Songs can come out of watching a person walk by. Even if you've never met the person in your life, you can imagine an entire scenario with this person from one look. I said, "Really?"

"God, Bebe, you have no idea where songs come from."

"Well, I guess I'm good for a few of them."

"Don't be immodest."

"Well, I'm not being immodest, but the point is that it's not fair that I'm a walking song machine but I get nothing from it—no royalties, no security. Where's this going to leave me? Washed up on the beach, some tragic victim with no life, after I've spawned all these platinum records while you've bought your houses in the country and have your servants?"

"It leaves you a legend."

"Oh great, thanks. . . . It doesn't pay the rent."

"Who knows, maybe we'll all leave it to you when we die!"

"Yeah, right, as if I am going to outlive all of you. You're all going to kill me. I'll be the maniac muse. You're all driving me to death."

Elvis wanted more than to sleep with me. I think he wanted to love me and completely possess me, but unfortunately, he didn't think I was worthy of these feelings. He thought that I was a flirt, that I was having affairs I actually wasn't having. That had been an undercurrent in our relationship when we were together. And of course the people in his camp, from his manager to the members of his band, had always been prejudiced against me. They continually taunted him with stories about all these men I was supposedly sleeping with. The men I had been with were the most dashing kings of rock, considered the most beautiful rock stars, whereas Elvis looked upon himself as a fuddy-duddy, an awkward, unattractive man with flat feet and thick glasses. He just couldn't understand, believe, or accept that I loved him. Because of my insecurity, I thought the only way of getting him back was to make him jealous. I figured if I did that, he would fall on his knees again and whisk me off. I had no idea that you don't do that to an Irish Catholic—that's how you alienate them; that's how you drive them to the other end of the earth.

This reunion was filled with this exciting tension. At one point, he was sitting on the couch, and I jumped on him, straddled him, and wrapped my arms around him. He was protesting: "Now you know this is naughty. We're supposed to be friends. We're not supposed to be doing this."

"Oh, you don't want me to hug and kiss you?" I asked.

"Well, actually . . ."

"Well, why did you only leave the light of the TV on? Why did you want me to walk in here and see the blue light of the TV and nothing else?"

"Well, you know, I thought we looked better."

"This isn't mood lighting, Elvis; this is the way we used to make love."

"Don't say that."

"It is—it's the way we used to make love, Elvis. If you wanted mood lighting, there's an invention called scarves, which go over the lamps."

"Don't do this!"

"Come on, one kiss."

So we had one passionate, noble, and fabulous kiss. Then, of course, he had to be a drama queen. He leapt into the air and told me that I had to go home. Meanwhile, he had this huge erection. I could see it bulging against his leg. So I toyed with him.

"I've got to get my rest," he said. "I'm doing that recording session with Yoko tomorrow."

"I've got a dinner date with Robin Leach."

"Robin Leach!"

"I'm not drinking champagne in the jacuzzi with him. And he's interesting."

"He's a food addict!"

"Yeah, well, what are you!"

So then we had this big but cute fight. It was like a play fight, pads and paws. I could see his erection the whole time. It was ridiculous. I mean, all I had to do was touch him with my fingertips and he would get a hard on. And all he had to do was look at me in a certain way and I would have an orgasm. I had power over this man, but he had the same power over me. He could reduce my knees to Jell-O.

The next night, I went out to my dinner with Robin Leach and then we went to a party. I was timing a call to the studio where I knew Elvis was recording with Yoko. I called and asked for him and was told that he was just finishing up and he'd be leaving in thirty minutes. So I timed my escape. I made up some fib and told Robin I had to dash off. I zoomed over to the Parker Meridian and hid in the stairwell on Elvis's floor so I could just jump out and scare him. We were playing our games. I was in a beautiful blue dress. I could feel the tension in the air.

I was waiting for him to walk by, but he was walking so fast, it looked like he was running to get back quickly because he knew I was going to show up and pull one of my stunts. The second he closed the door, he threw it open and said, "I knew it was you! Where were you?"

"Not telling!"

That night, we kept ending up on the floor. It was funny. He would lie on his side on the floor and I would lie down next to him and we would talk. He was telling me about how incredible it was working on "Walking on Thin Ice" with Yoko, and how amazing she was. We talked about John Lennon and the Beatles. There was a lot of emotion. We were lying on our sides and staring at each other, and he finally looked at me and said, "I love you so much."

"Well, what about your wife?"

"I don't want to talk about that right now."

"Okay, it's a bit late; I don't think it would be a very good idea for me to leave the hotel at this hour. It's not very ladylike."

"You're right. It's not very ladylike at all."

"I think I'll sleep on the couch,"

"No, no, there's plenty of room for both of us."

"Okay, well, I'll sleep in my clothes."

"No, no, no, no. You don't need to sleep in your clothes." He took all his clothes off and got into bed. I was standing there in my dress and my stockings and everything, and he said, "Are you going to undress for me?"

The shy bug bit me real hard. "Noooo," I said. I crawled into the bed with all my clothes on, and he was naked. It was so sexy. Then he kissed me. I sat up and said, "Do you want to peel the tomato?" We stood on the bed and he undressed me; it was intense. He took my stockings off, and we made love.

I was happier than I have ever been, just to touch him again, just to feel him in my arms and actually be making love with him again. I'd thought at times that it would never happen again, but here we were. It was auspicious and beautiful beyond words.

The next morning, he was getting ready to hop on a plane to rush back to England. His poor wife, Mary, was having a medical procedure the next day. I remember him saying to me, "You naughty girl. How can you lure a married man to your bed when you know he's off to catch a plane to see his sick wife?"

"I can see you're really worried sick, aren't you?" I said.

"Well, I know that it's not serious."

"What if it is?"

"We already know that it isn't."

Then he went to take a shower. While he was gone, I decided to look through his papers. I wanted to see where his head was at. I found a notepad where he had been doodling, and there was a page that had my name written on it a thousand times, all different ways. That's when I saw Bebe-Blue, and I started to unravel the code. I couldn't believe it.

I'd noticed when he was packing that there was only one thing that he did not include—his little tour itinerary. "Elvis, you haven't packed your itinerary," I said.

"Aren't you supposed to find that while I'm in the bathroom and steal it and stick it in your purse?"

"Oh, okay! I get it," I said, stealing it, and putting it in my purse.

"I don't want to make it too hard for you to find me," he said. "I don't think we need to play hide the boy anymore."

"I'm meant to have this little booklet."

"Yes, darling, you're meant to have this little booklet, but I didn't see a thing. Did I?"

"No! No see nothing." And I just remember him kissing me and saying good-bye, and that was when he said, "Oh, oh, oh, just a minute, I've got something."

"What's that?"

"I got a little present for you."

"What?" And he reached into his pocket and dropped a string of cultured pearls into my hands. It was a beautiful necklace.

"Here, I got these; they reminded me of your teeth."

There's a song called "The Element Within Her" on *Punch the Clock*. In it, he's talking about the girl's eyes and he sings, "She's got two sapphires and a couple rows of pearls." So there you go.

CHAPTER 10

Across America with Elvis Costello 1983-1985

Mr. Never Forever
I have made you see
See the clockwork smile
Have a piece of me
Now there is only one thing
That gives us the right
And that is that we are.
Don't fight.
  "MR. NEVER FOREVER," LYRICS BY BEBE BUELL

In the summer and fall of 1983, the B-Sides were starting to become pretty popular. We felt we were going to make it, that we would be getting a record deal. Then when Elvis came back into my life, it was an insane time. Liv was six and just starting elementary school. At the time, I was on the road a lot, doing short regional tours with the B-Sides. With Elvis looming on the horizon again, I urgently felt the need to be able to travel at the drop of a hat. My mother suggested I let Liv live with her during the school year and attend the Congressional School in Virginia. Since it was located just outside of Washington, D.C., she would have the opportunity to mix with children of all races, colors, and creeds and have access to a sophisticated and structured life. My family encouraged me to let her go, and I agreed, although the thought of it made me ache. I missed her before she even left. In September 1983, Liv started attending the Congressional School and living with my mother and her husband, Liv's step-grandaddy, Les. She stayed with my mother from September 1983 until June 1984. She spent all school breaks, all holidays, with me.

My family was once again trying to help lessen my load so I could pursue my career. I was playing up a storm at Trax, CB's, Danceteria, the Ritz, and the Peppermint Lounge in New York. I was a full-time aspiring rock star. But as a result, I could not always make my own decisions about Liv. My mother made decisions for me; Todd made decisions for me. It sometimes seemed that everybody made decisions but me. Everyone was supportive; nobody wanted me to end up working in a supermarket in Portland. I was not a perfect parent, but I was not a negligent one. Every decision I made was based on what I thought was best for Liv, and if that meant going to my mom's and the Congressional School, or if that meant going out to Annie's when I had to go on the road for three weeks, that was a hell of a lot better than bringing in some stranger, as far as I was concerned. Back in pioneer days, families stuck together when they reared a child.

Liv never had any confusion about who I was. She knew I was Mommy. Grammy was Grammy, and Annie was Annie. Grammy, Annie, and Mommy. There has never been a conflict. And I don't think Liv ever felt neglected. I was a working single mother, and if people don't like what I did, they can kiss my ass. I'm a rock singer. I lived an entirely different life from that of most single mothers. I had been a star in the New York underground; I had been a *Playboy* centerfold. I was trying to do my best to be a mother and carry around the secret of her paternity—which was on my mind all the time—and make a living. It was a conflicted life. During these years, Liv never asked me about her daddy. As a matter of fact, she never questioned much of anything. I think she understood we were in a unique situation. We were two girls alone together, and in a different situation than the rest of her friends on the block.

My mother's husband, Les, and Annie's husband, Teddy, were Liv's father figures. On the average, I took Liv to visit Todd twice a year, three times at most. I would always go with her. Holidays have always been a big ritual in our family. For Christmas, we all congregated at Annie's. Liv has spent every Christmas of her life with me—most Easters, Halloweens, all that stuff was with Mommy. And if she couldn't be with me at my place on Halloween, I'd go to my mother's and be with her.

When he was back in America and on tour in August, Elvis complained that I was not making enough use of the tour itinerary book.

"Well, I thought that it would be appropriate, since we are making love again and you are married, that you dictate some of the way this goes." And then it became mad phone. Four- or five-hour marathon phone sex, talking about everything you could possibly imagine. This was when I wrote "Baby Talk," which goes: "Baby Talk/ In the middle of the night/ Baby Talk/ When you're holding me tight/ Baby talk/ Oh honey it's all right/ Cuz it feels too good to fight." I would call and leave messages. My code name was "Creampuff." (I guess it was a little obvious, but we were insane.)

A lot of our communication during the tour consisted of messages and poems. I spent the night with him on August 16 and wrote in lipstick on the bathroom mirror, "I love you!!!" Flying back to New York the next day, I wrote a poem, "Big Secret 8/17/83":

> *How can I keep it quiet?*
> *How can I play fair?*
> *It's a big secret*
> *One I didn't dare*
> *Don't tell*
> *A big secret*

One I'd better keep
To save us scandal
To stop the heat.

On the eighteenth, I wrote another poem:

In your gangster hat
And your movie star shades
You still looked like an angel
Hiding from the day
You say "I'm wearing my man's suit"
I say "It's a bit conspicuous"
But I must agree
It's still magnificent. . . .

And that night, Elvis told me he'd slept with another woman. On August 27, I wrote in my diary, "I finally spoke to E. tonight. I called and left a message and he called me back. We spoke for three hours. . . . Mary is not there and never was. He's been fooling around, but he says it doesn't mean anything. I believe him. We talked about me coming to see him, and he said, 'I give in.' We're talking about it being Atlanta—I hung up on him once because I was awfully jealous about 'Ms. Providence.' But sure enough, he called me right back and we talked for another half hour. I don't care what he says—I know he loves me. If he didn't, he wouldn't bother. He's gotten all mail except birthday package and birthday message I left in Chicago."

On September 1, I joined him in Atlanta. I checked in at the hotel under the name Jane Allen. Leaving the following morning was harder than any of the other times. I felt he was really opening up to me, that we were undeniably falling in love again. "Everything feels so perfect," I wrote. "I love him so much. Please dear God—let it be me." However, that was the last time I saw him on that tour, although we continued our mad phone calls and phone sex.

Meanwhile, Todd was giving me a hard time about Liv and money. Whenever he got mad at me, he would just stop paying for things. He could be cruel. This is a part of him that people don't understand. He can be a very vicious, dictatorial, pseudo-middle-

class tyrant! He completely tried to control me. And whenever he found out that I was back with Elvis or talking to Elvis, he would really get nasty and awful.

During September, I met with Jason Flom from Atlantic Records three times. On the seventeenth, we had lunch at Trader Vic's in the basement of the Plaza Hotel and he finally gave us a development deal, or so I thought, for me and the B-Sides. This was the first concrete support from the corporate record industry I had ever received. and it felt terrific. That afternoon, I met with Chris Butler, an ex-member of the band Waitresses, to work on a couple of songs.

On September 25, Elvis left and I went home to Maine. "Elvis would always say to me, 'You are pregnant with my album. Come on!' " I wrote in my final entry on this tour that I was torn between putting all my energy into getting a recording deal and wanting to fly to London to be with Elvis. I still love you, Elvis. I haven't forgotten. Not me. The flirting kind. (He wrote a song called "The Flirting Kind.") Thank you, darling, for all my beautiful songs.

I did not see Elvis again until he returned to the United States for a spring 1984 tour. In the interim, I was trying to pursue my rock career, but, as it turned out, Atlantic Records didn't see me fronting the B-Sides. They envisioned me dancing solo to the beat of a disco record! This became yet another big frustration. In the midst of all this confusion, I did another *Oui* magazine interview with pictures, hoping it would have the same kind of positive effect my 1980 interview did. I did it because I needed the money—a thousand dollars, which in 1983 was a lot. It was a group effort: Pierre La Roche, who was Bowie's makeup artist, did my makeup, Liz Derringer did the interview, and Marcia Resnick did some of the pictures. Unfortunately, unbeknownst to me, *Oui* had been bought by another company. It was no longer a *Playboy* publication. When the issue came out, it lacked all of the style of the previous one in its layout and design, and I came off looking uncomfortably like I was in the wrong place. We'd all tried to do something really great, but we fell flat on our collective face, with me taking the brunt of the bruises, of course. Worst of all, it really pissed Elvis off. He felt that it didn't have the same touch of class that the previous one had had and that it undercut the seriousness of my musical aspirations by drawing attention to aspects of myself that would not help me be taken seriously. Elvis was also upset because he felt that I had laid out too many blatant clues in the interview, suggesting he and I were still in love. He considered that a distinct mistake. I later discovered that he had been vexed that I had not used the interview money, which I had received while he was on tour, to join him for the week he spent in L.A. At the time, I thought his wife was going to be there. It reminded him of how I'd chosen to spend Christmas 1978 with my family instead of with him. If I had gone to L.A. it might have strengthened our relationship at a crucial juncture.

In April 1984, Elvis returned for another U.S. tour and I resumed flying to various parts of the country to meet him. On this tour,

Elvis was persistent about me joining him in Detroit for Easter. He kept saying, "We gotta be together. We gotta be together." Easter was the day we'd parted in 1979, so Easter was this special day for us. Easter 1984 fell on April 22. April was the fourth month and if you add 1984 it makes 22. I suddenly remembered what Jason Flom had said about the significance of that number. I chuckled quietly thinking, What's going on with this 22 stuff? This number seemed to be creeping up on me everywhere.

I got off the airplane in Detroit and got into a taxi. There was a white station wagon in front of the cab I was in. The car was going way too slowly, and my driver was getting agitated. Then I noticed that its license plate included the number 22. I checked into the hotel as Candy Bar, and the desk clerk gave me the key to suite 2202. By the time I got to the room, I was freaking out. I was trying to think of whom I could tell, but then I wondered, Are you supposed to tell anybody when you're having an experience that could be considered either insane or religious?

Elvis got back to the room and saw me crying, laughing, and leaping around, so thrilled was I to see him. The first thing we did was make mad love; we were just crazy to touch each other. We were nuts and he was a little drunk, because he had gone off to have drinks with the boys while I'd been sitting in the hotel room all night. He was on top of me and just as he came inside me, I threw my head back on the pillow and the digital clock next to the bed read 2:22 A.M. I felt something happen to me. Then we looked into each other's eyes and smiled. I was thinking, Why are we smiling? But on another level, I think we knew we had just created a child. We made love only once that night. We did not make love the next morning. We only made love that one time that weekend, and I will never forget it.

Elvis would have a different stance on what we should be every time I saw him. I was begging him for us to be together, and he would always respond, "I can't leave my son," not mentioning his wife.

"But isn't it better to be a father in a loving environment than a father who's fighting all the time?"

"Bebe, you know I'm an Irish Catholic. I was raised in a certain way. I have to make my marriage work, and you have to understand that if you want to be in my life, it has to be." Guilt and turmoil were consuming him. It seemed so Hepburn & Tracy.

He was making love with me, speaking to me on the phone, giving me gifts, paying a lot attention to me, but I was definitely the other woman. I think that if I had just been cool and allowed our love to take its course, in time his wife would have found out and he would have run off with me. He had a fantasy of our relationship taking some Shakespearean turn. I was impatient and American and persistent, and I wanted him to make up his mind and choose Mary or me. But he made it clear to me he wouldn't do that; he just wouldn't accept that. I couldn't understand how he could make love to me the way he did and say the things he said. I just couldn't comprehend how he could carry on this double life. I got to the point where I found it too hard. He would be sleeping, and I would lie there and cry and watch him sleep. Sometimes I would wake up and he would be crying, watching me sleep. It was just not working. He couldn't give me what I wanted; all he could do was tell me he loved me. Elvis is a very honest man, and he was obviously participating in something that he felt was wrong. But because of his love for me and his passion, he couldn't resist it.

Back in New York, I was staying with my girlfriend Melissa. I had to go into her tiny little tile bathroom for five hours to speak to Elvis on the phone because she had a big one-room studio and he would call me at 2:00 A.M. and we'd speak till 6:00 A.M. I had phone sex with him on the bathroom floor. I was completely off my rocker. I thought his heart and soul were mine, and I couldn't stand to live without him anymore. He would say the same thing to me: "I love you more than I can say. I can't tell you how much I love you. But everything is a waste of breath, because there's nothing I can do." He was still suspicious of me; he thought I was running around. He would hear stories about me with this pop star and that pop star.

This might have gone on much longer had I been willing to be his mistress, but I wanted to be his wife. I wanted us to be together once and for all, but I think he was afraid to throw Mary away and risk everything for me. I don't think he completely trusted that I was capable of what it takes. And maybe I wasn't.

If he had left his wife and son and gone off with me, the guilt and horror of it would have destroyed us. I think if I had just allowed him to dictate the pace of our return to each other, it might have worked out in my favor. But I was putting my foot on the gas, and he was putting his foot on the brake. He was going five gears in reverse and I was going five gears forward. Yet no matter how many fights we had, when we were alone behind closed doors, there was compatability and friendship and love that went beyond anything I've ever been able to find again. We ate together, watched TV, drank wine or champagne, laughed and told each other stories and jokes, chased each other, and took showers together. He would sit and watch me put my makeup on. "I've never seen a woman who wears powder," he said.

"Where have you been? Women wear powder."

"Well, I've never experienced anybody wearing powder."

"What does Mary wear?"

"A little blush, but I've never seen her wear powder."

"It's just a compact, darling," I said, dancing around the room. I loved telling him jokes or doing impersonations. I could make Elvis laugh so hard.

The last time I saw Elvis, he flew me to San Francisco—May 1984. I spent seven days living secretly with him at the luxurious Miyako Hotel. I was pregnant, but I didn't know it at the time. When I got to his room, he was waiting for me. We ran to each other.

I couldn't leave the room because we were afraid I'd be seen, so we ate all of our meals in the room. I was hidden from everyone. The night he played San Francisco, he left two tickets for me at the box office and he put me in the front row, seat 2b. The show was incredible. I sat there with my dear drag queen girlfriend, Ginger Coyote, who stood out like a sore thumb in the front row, while he proceeded to sing the entire concert to me. I'm sure his handlers must've thought that I was stalking him. Then I had to rush back to the Miyako before everyone returned there.

When he returned, he ran in and leapt on the bed, hugged me, and told me how beautiful I looked and how he'd wanted to attack me all through the show. We ordered this gorgeous meal, and then after we ate, we had mad sex. It was right out of *Tom Jones*. But we both knew when we made love in San Francisco that everything hung in the balance. There was something wrong with the way he was acting. I could just feel it.

We both had flights to L.A., but we had to go to the airport separately. My flight was an hour after his.

I had a photo shoot in L.A. for *Playboy* on May 25. It was called "The Girls of Rock and Roll." I was sitting there getting my makeup done. I felt nauseous, which made me realize that I was pregnant again. I was only one month pregnant, but I was starting to suspect something was up. My biggest fear was of having another little baby and no daddy.

In L.A., I was staying with my friend Jeffrey Conroy. Jeffrey and a friend were at a Lakers game, sitting in the same box as Jack Nicholson. They knew I was friends with Jack, so at halftime, Jeffrey turned to Jack and said, "We have something in common."

"What's that?"

"Guess who's staying at my house?"

"Who?"

"Bebe!"

"*The Beeb?* Oh my God. It's always fun to see the Beeb. What's she doing here?"

"Well, here's my number—she's at my house, if you'd like to call her."

"Oh hell yes!" said Jack. So he took the number, and sure enough, later that night, Jack called me and invited me over to his house. I told him the whole Elvis sob story and tried to tell him all about the mystical number 22. He said, "Well, Beeb, you know I've got my own connection to the number twenty-two. I was born on May twenty-second, so I've got a little twenty-two in my life, too." All he wanted to do was fuck me that night, and here I was pregnant, off in my cosmic world, trying to share it with him, but he was just humoring me. "Come on, Beeb, let's just have sex."

"I can't. I'm pregnant!"

"Yeah, but you're not sure you're pregnant!"

"Jack! When your period is two weeks late, you are pregnant!"

"I looovve pregnant women."

Jack was so sweet to me. I spent the night at his house and we did have sex, but I was still pining for Elvis.

Meanwhile, Elvis went on to Japan. After my stay in L.A., I flew back to Maine and wrote him a major letter, reiterating how beautiful our time in San Francisco had been and saying how much I loved him. It was poetic—all about how fated and star-crossed our love was. It was the most beautiful letter. I sent it to the usual British address he had given me. But ironically, this particular letter got rerouted directly to Elvis's home in Chiswick, because the postman knew Mary and Elvis, and when he saw that it was from America, he thought it might be important. Consequently, the first person to read this very private letter was Elvis's wife, Mary. I was sitting in my house in Portland, Maine, now two months pregnant. The phone rang. When I picked it up, I heard an English voice on the other end of the phone.

"Bebe?"

"Yes."

"This is Mary Costello."

I was totally in shock. "How did you get my phone number? Why do you want to speak to me?" I was terrified. The last thing I wanted to be called was a home-wrecker, but at this point, I knew I was pregnant, as well. I had not told Elvis, although I made some obscure reference to it in the letter without actually saying it.

"I knew he was seeing you again. I knew when I heard 'Human Hands' that he still loved you. I've had to carry this around with me; this thorn is the curse of my marriage. Who do you think you are?" It was terribly tragic and I felt just horrible. She said, "I can't believe he slept with you the night before he came to my bedside. God, please tell me you're not pregnant."

"I am pregnant," I said. Believe it or not, I told her before I told him. I cannot tell you why it happened this way, but it was very emotional. I was pregnant. I was scared. I was terrified. I was so in love with this man, and now I was really starting to believe that God wanted me to get pregnant because of the number 22, I was certain that I was on the right path—I didn't see the error of my ways, nor did I look upon myself as a woman committing adultery, as a sinner, or as the other woman. I considered myself the only woman meant to be with him. I even said to Mary, "How could you be so stupid? You've been living with him, and you can't tell from these songs that he's not writing about you?"

"Of course I can tell."

"Haven't you ever said anything to him? Hasn't there ever been fighting? Any remorse between the two of you?"

"Of course there is, this house is a perpetual, mad battleground; your name has not risen in this household with joy." Mary went on and on. She ran the gamut of emotions—she was even sisterly. She never once called me a slut or a whore. Not once. Although she was angry, she was never disrespectful. She was frustrated, almost fascinated—she couldn't believe it.

This went on for two hours; then she turned hysterical. "My brothers are Irish. I have money here in the safe in the house—I'll give you money to stay away from my husband. His soul cannot rest; you are haunting it. He speaks your name when he sleeps. I'm at the end of my rope." She started offering me money for an abortion, said she would pay me to get rid of the baby.

"Mary, where is Elvis?" I asked.

"He's in Japan." At this point she was just mad, I think; she had been calm at first, but now she sounded tough. I wouldn't have wanted to get into a big argument with her. She was kind of letting me know that these Irish brothers of hers would come and take care of me. At the same time, she was holding out some willingness to help me: Mary ended the conversation by saying, "Listen, if you need the money for an abortion, call me. I'll help you. Here's my phone number. But whatever you do, please don't have the baby."

Twenty minutes later, Elvis called me from Japan. Neither of us could understand how the letter got rerouted. I was trying to be diplomatic and yet hold on to what I thought was the only man I would ever love. Plus I was pregnant, vomiting. I told him I was pregnant, and he just freaked out. He said, "I see that we've got a very big obstacle here!

"How could you have been so stupid to have written that letter? How could you have done this? I can't believe this has happened."

"Maybe it was meant to happen. Obviously, I've written you hundreds of letters, and you've written me hundreds of letters. Why is this the one that got caught? Maybe this is all preordained—something's going on."

"But you don't understand. This cannot happen!"

"Well, do you want me to get an abortion?"

"Baby, I don't believe in abortion, but I will not help you with

255

the child. I will not be involved with this pregnancy. *I will not.* You did this on your own."

"*I* did? You've made love to me. How many times have I been pregnant since we met? Four. This is my fourth pregnancy with you and you're telling me . . ." I just went insane.

Then he got upset and started bawling, too, saying, "All right, all right, don't do anything. Just wait until I get back from Japan. Don't make any decisions. Don't do anything. I'm sorry, but don't do anything, just promise me." He was elated, but he was also frightened and angry. He said he couldn't think straight and he didn't want me to make any decisions that I would regret. "Okay. Okay. I won't do anything," I said, and then we hung up.

Ten minutes later, Mary called me and started terrifying me, telling me, "Elvis has bad genes and I have had deformed fetuses and I have had miscarriages with babies with seven heads."

On top of that, I was having morning sickness and losing my mind trying to figure how I was going to have another child out of wedlock, how I was going to handle having yet another secret in my life. My morning sickness was awful, very debilitating. All I did was puke from the second I woke up to the second I went to bed.

Once again, I was cast in the role of the evil home-wrecker, the other woman, the this, the that. Yet I was carrying the child of the man I loved more than anything in the world, more than life itself.

Elvis was faced with the implications of what this pregnancy would mean: an illegitimate birth, probably the dissolution of his marriage, a lot of money out of his pocket, and the support of another child, not to mention the pressure of his fans and handlers. My image of him at that time was that he was like one of those leaping dogs with his ears flying out.

Mary was threatening me. Plus, she continued to try to scare me to death by telling me more and more about Elvis's genetic problem, promising me that my baby was going to be deformed. I couldn't believe some of the things she said. But you have to remember that these people consumed a lot of alcohol. They were Irish. Mary would say a lot of awful stuff when she was drunk. But when she was sober, she could be very nice. I actually had compassion for her, even liked her. That was confusing me, too. I felt a certain bond with her because we were women. And I knew I had to get an abortion: I couldn't do this to myself again.

Neither Mary nor Elvis ever mentioned having spoken about the situation. I was just not coping well with any of this. I had just done some pictures for *Playboy* and had signed a contract for a development deal with Atlantic Records. I had a career at stake, as well.

At one point, I made up my mind to have this baby, with or without Elvis's support and love, and I believed he would come back to me.

That was my first instinct, and I should have listened to it. If I had gone ahead and done that, he would've stuck with me, I'm sure. But one day, I felt so awful in every way that I snapped. I called the doctor—I will never forget his name, because it was the weirdest name I had ever heard—Dr. Luck, who was German. *L-u-c-k.* I couldn't believe it. I was given some counseling about abortion, and then was asked, "Are you sure this is what you want to do?" I had twenty-four hours to make a definite decision. The next day, I went back and said, "Yes, I want to do it."

I was afraid of having a retarded child, given all Mary's warnings. I was suffering from morning sickness. And I was fighting to pay my rent. I did not have Todd's monthly money. My daughter was living with my mother. I wasn't getting any help. I was totally alone and terrified. This man I loved, by whom I was pregnant for the fourth time, said he wouldn't help me. There were all sorts of pressures: the fear of having a child out of wedlock shrouded in mystery and intrigue, I simply couldn't do that again, I didn't want it to be like one of the women who had Brian Jones's babies. I was a little bonkers at this point. I don't think that I understood anything clearly. I had no one to talk to. How could I tell anybody about all this? Plus, I was way out on a limb with paranoia and the magical twenty-two stuff.

I really want this to be told because I live with this terrible torment and carry it around. I think about it when I wake up and when I go to sleep, every day of my life. Because I did change my mind when I was lying on the table in the abortion clinic. I went in and lay down on the table and they didn't put me to sleep; they gave me a local anesthetic. They put me in a little gown. I was lying there with my feet up in the stirrups. It was horrible. They made me feel as comfortable as possible, but I wasn't aborting any child; I was aborting a child I wanted more than anything in the world, a child fathered by the man I loved more than anything in the world. And I felt this conception was preordained. (For three or four months before I became pregnant, I was repulsed by all meat. I became a vegetarian. Had I been purifying my body without even realizing it? I couldn't eat eggs; I was disgusted by the sight of meat or anything unhealthy or bad: It was almost as if I were preparing my temple for this child.) So you can see why I felt that being on the abortion table was going against nature. God desires us to love everything, and yet here I was with Dr. Luck. He told me, "You vill feel ein kleine pinch; it's a vacuum situation." They put it inside my cervix and turned on the machine. At that exact moment I cried out, "Stop! Stop! I can't do this. Stop!"

"I can't stop," he said. "It's too late."

I realized at that terrible moment that I had destroyed the most important, life-affirming thing in my life. I murdered it. I believe people have the right to choose. I don't believe anyone has the right to tell a woman to get an abortion or not to get an abortion, but I believe that for me at that time, I made the wrong decision.

Something inside me changed that day. I realized once the suction began and they vacuumed my uterus that the child was being ripped from my body—no muss, no fuss. I had felt a male spirit around me at all times, even before I became pregnant. He was obviously involved in the mystical 22; I firmly believed that. And that spirit said good-bye to me as it left my body. That night, I dreamed of a little boy who came to me and said, "It's okay." This person was real to me. I firmly believe that all pregnancies and all births have karmic connections for all of us. I know that that spirit has forgiven me, even though Elvis hasn't. Whoever that boy was is still with me, and I have never been able to forgive myself for what I did. It's just been horrible, because I look at the path I took to get this man, only to have had him throw it all away. Now I think of the words he wrote to me in a letter: "We've both done this to each other."

Elvis's songs came from the head games we played with each other, a mental chess—the way we communicated with each other through our art. And this was a time when nobody respected me for my art. People thought I was just a friend to the stars, a *Playboy* centerfold, a model, a groupie. The only man who had given me any respect for my gifts and my intellect—and he says it so well in "I Want You"—was the one man in my life, of all my lovers, anyone, who understood me, my talents, abilities, and gifts, my perceptions and intuitions. He was better than anything, and more than anything, he loved me.

I realize everything happens for a reason and that things are supposed to happen the way they happen. I look back on it now and realize I couldn't have had another child. Had I had another child out of wedlock with a pop star, I would never have been able to deal with the pressure when Liv's paternity became an issue. There would have been so much intrigue and controversy around her paternity and the mystery paternity of my son (I am sure it was a boy). I was at a crossroads and I chose the path of greater independence. And God has never let me forget I could've chosen my baby and maybe had my man.

In September 1984, I was living in Maine. I never wanted to go out with a man again. I did not even want to be in the rock 'n' roll world, though I was still with the B-Sides, and getting ready to form another band, the Gargoyles. I lost Elvis—I lost his friendship; I lost his love. It struck me that rock stars can be the chroniclers of great pain because they get so much love from their audiences. That's what keeps them going and enables them to write songs of the caliber of Elvis's "Human Hands" and "I Want You" and then sing them in front of millions of people without breaking down. When an artist who lives on his own—a painter or a writer, for example—suffers in a love affair, he doesn't have anyone to tell him he's great or applaud him; it's very different from the way it is for a performing artist.

Throughout this emotional roller-coaster ride that made me pine for the innocence of my earlier adventures, I continued to bring up Liv and play in the B-Sides. Liv had had a wonderful summer in Maine and was reluctant to return for her second year at the Congressional School. She didn't want to go back to my mother's—

she wanted to stay with me. She'd had a wonderful bohemian summer with her mother, free to run naked through the grass. We liked to go on cookouts and do other fun things. Liv was friends with all the kids on the block. She had a wonderful social life. When she was in school, she missed all that, and she missed me. When it was time for her to go back to my mother's for the second grade, she was not happy. She grabbed my leg and cried; she didn't want to leave. I didn't want her to leave, either, but my mother insisted, saying that it was the best thing for Liv, that my lifestyle and the way I was running back and forth between Maine and New York and going out on short regional tours with the band might not be the best thing for my daughter. She felt that during the first couple of years of her schooling, when Liv was learning the fundamentals, she needed some basic structure, which was the key word my mother used. Of course, I was not a believer in structure. I was a believer in organization, not structure, so there was a conflict. But you have to remember that I was a single mother, I had to make a living, which meant I had to work on the road. I played not only New York but also Philly, Detroit, and Chicago. I was trying to do the right thing by letting Liv go to a special school and spend time at my mother's.

Atlantic Records gave me some more money and I went into the studio and recorded a couple of tracks with the B-Sides, with Rick Derringer producing. I was very happy and excited for a couple of months and thought I was going to get a deal to make an album. But Jason Flom felt that if I was going to continue in the rock direction, my demo was too rough and he would have no way of getting the head man, Doug Morris, to fund me. Jason still thought I should go more into a dance-oriented mode. There was a girl named Stacy Q. who had a hit called "Two of Hearts" at that point and she had also been a model. They thought I could be marketed like that. Jason paired me off with two songwriters and tried to get something to come out of that, but I was just too defiant. These songwriters had had a couple of hits. We tried, we talked, but I wasn't into it, even though everybody else was.

I was hoping to get another independent deal, but it got very hard for people who were doing straight rock music in the early eighties because that whole romantic movement from England came over, and I was still doing really raw rock and roll—the wrong music at the wrong time.

The B-Sides had been together for four years. We had had many chances—we'd made demos and we had put out an independent product, but nothing had happened. We put a certain amount of time in; we got told the same thing over and over again. I also think my history and who I was presented a big obstacle. I think if I had never been a *Playboy* centerfold and had never dated a pop star, I probably would have had a recording contract. So we just decided to call it a day. People always said that I had a lot of talent and that I was a good singer; that was never in question. The problem was how to market me. Meanwhile, I had an opportunity to release some demos as a picture disc and I took it. I got paid three thousand dollars to put that record out.

I lied to Elvis and finally told him I'd had a miscarriage when he called me in Maine from London in the fall of 1984. He didn't believe me. Everything got horrible between us, and in one of my final conversations with him, I actually led him to believe that I was having an illicit communication with Prince. I was trying to continue to fuel his heart with jealousy. I was hoping that it would blow him off his ass, because after "Little Red Corvette," Prince was the hottest thing in the world. *Purple Rain* was out. There's this song on the *Purple Rain* album called "The Beautiful Ones." The word *baby* is repeated in the song, which is all about desire. Now Elvis made it very clear to me that in his songwriting, *baby* was a word he never used. He actually hated the cliché, but, after falling in love with me, he called me that quite often. He even went as far as to put out a duet with Nick Lowe of that old chestnut the Beatles covered on one of the earliest albums, "Baby It's You." The verse he chose to take in the duet was "Is it true what they say about you? You're never never ever going to be true." The French word *bébé* means "baby," and Elvis and I continued to use it when talking to each other.

I wrote Mary a letter and told her I had gotten an abortion. I think that triggered the song "I Want You." I believe that Elvis thought I had told Mary I had an abortion just to calm her down, but he thought I was going to be the martyr. In the meantime, his marriage had completely disintegrated and blown up to the point of

261

proceeds for a divorce. Elvis and Mary finally separated in 1985. That dropped the curtain on that marriage, and I think he had this fantasy that we would get back together again after I'd had his love child.

I shattered that fantasy in L.A. in September 1985. I was there to perform for a benefit for a girl named Michelle Meyer, who had cancer. I was going to get up with an all-star band, including Michael Des Barres and somebody from the Knack, and do a couple of songs. I heard Elvis was also in L.A., staying at the Mondrian. So I called him up on the phone. When I got him he said, "Bebe?"

"Darling," I began.

"Don't 'darling' me!"

"What do you want me to call you?"

"Where have you been? What are you doing? I haven't seen you in the press for a while. Did you have the baby?" I could feel the anticipation in his voice; he sounded excited to be talking to me.

"Oh, I've been around."

"Well, did you have the baby?" He said it like a child; I'll never forget it. I could see that he was curious. Obviously, he thought I had lied about miscarrying and that I had had our child. He could not comprehend me having an abortion, either, which is why he hadn't believed what I'd told Mary.

"No," I replied. And then my web of deception began. I lied through my teeth. I wanted to say whatever I could to hurt him. I think he'd had this romantic vision that I would prove my undying love for him by being a martyr and going off and having his child.

"What happened?" he asked.

"Well, I abused myself so much when I was pregnant because I was so unhappy and miserable, I drove myself to a miscarriage."

He hung up. I got into my rental car and raced into Hollywood from Santa Monica. It's a forty-five-minute drive, depending on the time of day and the amount of traffic, but I got there in about thirty minutes. I parked my car and walked on foot to the Mondrian Hotel. I was wearing pink jeans and a black leather jacket. I saw Elvis and Nick Lowe standing out front, waiting for their car to be brought up. They were going off to the studio to record "Baby It's You," I later found out. As soon as Elvis saw me coming, he put his dark glasses on and ran into the hotel. He was not going to face me.

That was the last time I ever saw him. I stood in the street. All I could feel was abject embarrassment and humiliation. I tried to call him again, and then I tried to write him. I got him on the phone one more time and said, "Please, please talk to me."

"I have nothing to say to you, you murderer!" He was livid. And that was it. He cut me off. I felt like all the wives of Henry VIII wrapped into one.

If I had gone off and had his child, I think we would be together today. If I had been the martyr and had the baby, I think I would have passed the test and I'd be his wife. We'd have six children, and I'd weigh two hundred pounds, right along with him. We'd be two fat, ridiculously happy maniacs in love.

To this day, I still cry over that abortion. If I had kept that child, I would have a teenage son now. I've had many regrets about that decision. Elvis didn't know what I was going through; he thought I was unobtainable, noncommittal, incapable of fidelity, a frivolous sort of "It Girl."

One day the following year, my girlfriend Pam called me on the phone at my apartment in Maine. She said, "Bebe, Elvis has done it this time."

"What do you mean?"

"Bebe, you have to get his new record, *Blood & Chocolate.*

"Really?"

"Bebe, remember the whole Prince thing?"

"Why?"

"Remember that song 'The Beautiful Ones?' wait till you hear the song 'I Want You'? It's got to be about you."

"No!"

"No shit!"

I ran down to my record store and got the record. When I looked at it, I burst into tears. Elvis used to tease me, because whenever I got my period, I made him go out and get me a Cadbury's chocolate bar. One time, he looked at me and he said, "Blood, chocolate." Not only did he make it the title of his album, but the song that was meant to push me over the edge was on this record. Coincidence maybe? It didn't feel like it.

"I Want You" appears to be a summary of his passion, his jealousy and his contempt for Prince, and his hatred and anger at me for having the abortion. The first time I heard it, the air went out of me and I fell to the floor, paralyzed. I could not move; I wept like an insane idiot at my apartment in Portland. Another song that reflected the situation was "I Hope You're Happy Now." Its venom was both obvious and cruel.

People don't do answer records anymore, but they used to be very big, and Elvis was very much into playing those kinds of mind games. And he wrote "I Want You" after he knew I had had an abortion. So he was letting me know very clearly at the end of the song that I'd killed our child. But he was also telling me that he loved me more than any other person on earth, and he knew that I had loved him equally, but because of the choices I'd made, it was over. He knew exactly what he was doing: He didn't just stick the knife in; he twisted it, too, spun it around. His writing was as pure as Kafka's. He might as well have been writing with needles on my flesh. He might as well have put the knife on the Ferris wheel in my heart, because it kept slicing.

It was also around this time that Elvis began seeing the young, elfish bass player from the Pogues, Cait O'Riordan. He went on to marry her the following year. They remain married today.

CHAPTER 11

Holding the Maine Line
1985-1990

Come on
Come on
I want U to dig it
I want U to feel it inside
Come on, come on
Come on & rock with us
Cuz honey we're all
Pink Inside
   "PINK INSIDE," LYRICS BY BEBE BUELL

In the fall of 1985, I picked up the broken pieces of my life and started to put them together once again, trying to make sense out of confusion, anger, and pain. The first thing I did was figure out a way to make some money. Todd was paying for Liv's private education, her clothes, and her upkeep, but he only gave me a tiny allowance. Based on the success of the B-Sides, I put together a second band, the Gargoyles. A year after my 1984 abortion trauma, I'd met a nice local guy, Charles Hall, who became the bass player in the band. Charles was dashing—tall, dark, and handsome. He

Singing with Brian Setzer in NYC, 1985/CHUCK
PULIN

was six foot one, skinny, and had black hair. He was also the best song-writer in town. Above all, he wasn't as jealous of my ongoing feelings for Elvis, as other boyfriends would have been. Charles was admirably supportive, sympathetic, and compassionate about the whole thing.

I always felt I was the leader of my band, but I also felt that everybody I played with was a friend. Charles and I were the Gar-goyles. It was our life: We ate, slept, drank, and lived the band. He left the Moguls to start the Gargoyles with me. And we recruited Steve Marshall and Todd Bricker. Steve was a guitar player in a band called Carol and the Charmers. And Todd was a local kid, who hap-pened to be a great drummer. Charles came from that "cave stomp" scene that loved the Cramps, a band we loved. I was also hanging out in that surfabilly scene—surfabilly is like the Cramps meet rockabilly. Critics called the Gargoyles "metalbilly," a hard rock and rockabilly mixture. I was inspired by Charles as a songwriter.

He was an incredible songwriter. He could just come up with these amazing licks on his bass right there in the living room, and I would immediately come up with the lyrics.

The Atlantic Records deal had not worked out because of changes in musical direction, so I decided to go all the way with a hard rock 'n' roll sound and have an even rawer band. I said, "Fuck the B-Sides! Now we have the Gargoyles! We're gonna make it scarier and nastier this time." I was doing the Gribo thing that's like Zodiac Mindwarp, or the Cult in England. Nobody in the United States was doing it, until Guns 'n' Roses came along. But of course, once again, I was doing something that was not accepted from a woman. Women were doing the big-hair bands, whereas I would

My band the Gargoyles, 1988–(*left to right*) Steve Marshall (guitar), Charles E. Hall (bass), Todd Bricker (drums)/MARK WEISS

wear leather caps, flamboyant vests with fake fur, short, loud dresses, over-the-knee buccaneer boots. It was spookier, more like the Cramps, a little dirtier and a little scarier. I had songs like "Gargoyle" and "Jacuzzi Jungle." I was not playing pop anymore; I was playing rock. And it really became my life.

I think the timing was a little better with the Gargoyles than it had been with the B-Sides. I had been working as a musician for five years, and people took me more seriously now. It was a gutsy thing to come back with this balls-to-the-wall, full-force, AC/DC, kick-ass band. And, of course, it had a cool name. Stephen King used to come and watch us play; he liked the whole mystique surrounding us. People used to say, "God, you should marry him, and then you could be Bebe King!" We hung out a little bit. One time he came down to see us play at the Tree Cafe. I saw him up against the bar, drinking a beer. I was so excited, I couldn't breathe. When they were in Portland, LA Guns came one time. The Cult came. One of my childhood idols, Alvin Lee of Ten Years After, came. I started to feel like a real musician.

I moved into a new apartment on High Street, and I was determined that I was not going to be sending Liv to Mom's anymore. She was growing up. She was so beautiful and fascinating and such a good little friend to me. She would tell me what songs she thought were good and what songs wouldn't work. Sometimes she would insist on going to rehearsal with me. That would upset my mother, but Liv loved it. She also loved being at my mother's, and being with Annie. My world was artistic, bohemian—running around the house barefoot, listening to Iggy Pop. At my mother's, life was about going to see *Cats* fifty times, having tea at the White House. With Annie in the country, life was comforting—good food, television, the fire, love, and family life. So Liv was getting the benefit of three worlds, and learning how to blend beautifully into any situation. I think that's why she's such a good actress.

In September, Liv, who was now eight, entered the third grade at the Breakwater, a private school in Portland. From 1985 until we moved back to New York in 1989, Liv and I were not separated except when I would go out of town for a gig. We also had three cats: Raheena, Little Man, and Seymour. I got them all up in Maine. Seymour was the rock star. I got Raheena from the Rescue League in 1984; Little Man also came from the Rescue League. He was the baby runt of the litter, but he grew up to be massive bruiser with big blue eyes. In some funny way, he was my soul mate. He was also a Cancer, like Liv and me, born in July. Seymour, our third cat, Liv found in a garbage heap.

I decided to try to be a normal person, which seemed to be the only choice. I didn't want to get pregnant again, so I got an IUD. I didn't want to be madly in love, either, so I picked a boyfriend whom I was very fond of and attracted to but whom I was never going to run off and marry. I wanted a musical partner. I wanted my own in-house Chris Stein, and that's what I got. Charles Hall was a pretty good all-around guy for me. He was my music partner and bass player, we wrote songs together, and we lived together. I felt that I had to step back from the crazy life I had led for the past twelve years. If I was going to be a musician, I couldn't keep drawing all this attention to myself as a friend of the stars. I had to get serious. Charles and I were a wonderful match sexually, very playful. We really had great sex. We dated for the next five years.

Since Todd was providing for Liv, we split the $600 rent three ways. Since Todd gave me money only for Liv's food and clothing, I had to come up with about $400 a month. I was making $300–$700 per gig. Everybody else in the band had jobs, and pretty much understood that this was my primary source of income, whereas my guitar player was a Domino's Pizza boy, my drummer was a bartender, and Charles also manned his parents' music store. My only jobs were rocking and Liv.

We were ready to fly pretty quickly, because Charles and I had worked on a couple of songs before we found the other people to play with us. I gave the Gargoyles a baptism by fire. After rehearsing for a few weeks, we started playing some local gigs. The response was good, so we started playing farther afield. Soon the Gargoyles had lots of gigs; we were playing every weekend. Liv went to my local shows and invited her little friends and schoolteachers. We also played New York regularly. Joey Ramone was putting us in shows.

My life consisted of Liv, the Gargoyles, and Charles. During the day, Liv was at school and I would work with the Gargoyles. At night, I would make her dinner and do homework with her, and then I would

Christmas in Maine–Liv, age 9, and Bebe, 1986/BUELL PRIVATE COLLECTION

go off and rehearse. I literally lived one block from my rehearsal space. If I had to do a three-hour rehearsal from seven to ten, Liv would go over there, hang out, and do her homework on the floor.

My cousin Annie didn't live far away from us. I had numerous baby-sitters. We lived in a really nice apartment and I had lots of friends. My next-door neighbor had a little kid, Jeffrey, who was one of Liv's best friends. They were the ones who found Seymour in the garbage.

I had a nice relationship with Charles, but he was a drinker, so that did bring a lot of madness into our relationship at times. He was not as bad as Richard Butler. Charles would go for days without drinking, but when he drank, he tended to get macabre, withdrawn. I had a Santiago painting that my daughter now has which is worth a lot of money. One night, he got drunk and he threw a goddamn cheeseburger at it. The next day, he didn't remember doing it.

The years 1985–1989, when Liv was ages 8 to 12, were four of the happiest ones in my life. The best part was having Liv with me full-time and becoming a good mother. In the second half of the eighties, our place was a big, happy, noisy place, full of rock 'n' roll music and children. I was always cooking big meals. I really blossomed as a productive, involved mother, and Liv was definitely not lacking any kind of stimulation, scholastically, artistically, or emotionally. During this period, I gave her all my attention. I encouraged her interest in art and music, and I encouraged her to make friends and get involved in outside activities. I fostered spiritual growth and beauty.

This was a different type of life than I had ever had before. Because apart from being a rocker, I was living an ordinary life. There was a modeling school in Portland, and I worked there as an instructor for a little while, teaching the girls how to walk and talk and put makeup on. A friend sometimes asked me if I wanted to work at his hair salon, and he would give me fifty dollars. I helped my friend Billy with some of his productions. He sat me down and said, "You have remarkable talent, so don't waste it." Here was yet one more person telling me to get away from rock and do stage comedy. Everybody thought I was a modern-day Carole Lombard and comedy was what I should be concentrating on. Billy wanted me to act in Oscar Wilde's *The Importance of Being Earnest*. I was having an acting career thrown at me, but, of course, I chose rock again!

I have lived my life as if it were a poem, letting one perception follow immediately upon another, without questioning why. I never know what is going to happen in the next stanza until I come to the end of the preceding one. As I look back at my life in 1986, I feel that I was blessed to have been able to compress so much adventure into such a short period of time. I cannot help thinking that the Portland period was the first time in my life when I was in control. Finally, I was the star of my life. I was also writing and directing the movie, and it felt very good.

It had always been on my mind that I was going to tell Liv who her real father was one day, but I had no idea when or how. When she was sixteen? Eighteen? The decision was partially taken out of my hands when Steven Tyler entered my life again at the end of 1986. He had just gotten out of a drug rehab clinic. Liv first met him, somewhat auspiciously, I thought, backstage at a Todd Rundgren concert in December 1986. Liv, Charles, and I drove down to see "Daddy" play the Paradise Club in Boston. He had little gifts for Liv and we had a nice reunion.

Todd Rundgren
Boston
1986
12/14
two week
Wonder Tour

Backstage, out of the corner of my eye, I saw Steven and his soon-to-be wife, Teresa, come in to say hello. They were looking so much better than usual; I almost couldn't believe how sober they looked.

Steven's eyes shot to Liv, who was nine then. She took one look at him, and I realized that somehow she just *knew*. She had an immediate attachment to Steven. Todd had given her a Casio sampler, but it was Steven who spent most of his time teaching her how to play Aerosmith songs on it. When they parted, there was no mistaking the tears in Steven's eyes. It was a big turning point. That was when Todd and I gave each other a look that said we knew it was just a matter of time. That was when he started to weave his web of Toddness around us.

After this meeting, Liv wrote in her diary: "I don't know why but I think I feel like Steven is my daddy." She had an immediate sixth sense about him before she had the courage to share it with me. And she didn't show me that page in her little diary until a couple of years later.

In the 1980s, Todd and Michelle had moved to a beautiful big house in Sausalito, just over the Golden Gate Bridge from San Francisco, in Marin County. He kept Karen, the mother of his sons Rex and Randy, in a house next door. He is the only man I've ever

The night Liv met Steven Tyler for the first time—December 14, 1986—Boston, Massachusetts, at a Todd Rundgren show/BUELL
PRIVATE COLLECTION

met who lives with more than one woman and makes it work. I swear that if Todd could live with a harem, he would. Now he began a campaign to make me look like the less attractive of the two parents in Liv's eyes. Whenever she saw Todd, she would be showered with gifts, treats, festivities, and fun. I was a struggling mother. I lived in Maine; I didn't have a house up in the country in Woodstock and a beautiful home in California, or American Express cards to go out and eat sushi. Todd did. And his girlfriend Michelle did not embrace me and accept me the way Karen had. I felt Michelle was jealous of me and felt threatened. Soon, Todd started to insinuate that we should all move out to California so we could live closer to one another.

Between 1986 and 1988, Aerosmith made one of the most extraordinary comebacks of all time. After self-destructing on drugs to the point that they'd lost everything, including their audience, they had reformed and were now drug-free. They wrote some great new songs and put together an exciting new stage act. They had a hit album. They had just signed an extremely lucrative long-term record contract. And Steven Tyler became once again one of the richest and most attractive men in rock 'n' roll.

In August 1988, Steven invited us to a big outdoor concert before a huge audience at Great Woods in Massachusetts. Charles, Liv, and I drove down. We were given the rock royalty treatment. The security people gave us laminated passes to all areas and escorted us to Steven's dressing room. The only other people in the room were his girlfriend, Teresa, who was pregnant with their daughter, Chelsea, and Steven's nine-year-old daughter, Mia, with Cyrinda Foxe, from whom he had only just obtained a divorce. The tension was electric. The way Teresa saw it, I was a threat. Just as Aerosmith was hitting the top again, here I was, resurfacing with a child she did not want to believe was Steven's. Steven had tears in his eyes when he saw Liv and he was barely able to stop his face from turning into a puddle. I was having trouble not freaking out as I laid eyes on Mia for the first time. She was wearing exactly the same outfit as Liv—black stretch pants and an Aerosmith T-shirt. They both wore braces and had gotten their hair permed to go to the show. They looked like bookends.

Steven took Liv around and introduced her to everybody, in-

cluding Mia, whom she was meeting for the first time. Liv and Mia immediately clicked in the thrilling atmosphere backstage, where Guns 'n' Roses were preparing to open. The girls rushed off in search of the Gunners' dressing rooms. When Steven finally brought Liv back to me so he could go and prepare for his performance, Liv said, "Mommy, why does Steven cry every time we meet?"

A couple of hours later, as Liv and I watched the show from the VIP seats in a roped-off area near the front of the stage, we both spotted Mia standing backstage, watching her father perform. From that distance, seeing her in silhouette, there was something eerie about her resemblance to Liv. Instantly, we both realized that she could have been Liv's twin. That's when I think it really hit Liv. She had been looking at Steven's legs in the dressing room and on-stage, and she had decided that their legs were similarly shaped. Liv watched the show with increasing fascination. Two or three numbers later, in the middle of a great rendition of Aerosmith's signature song, "Dream On," Liv said, "Mom, that's my father, isn't it?"

"Yes," I said immediately, nodding, smiling, and crying. The rhythm of the moment just felt undeniable; it was such an electric second, and I did not see how lying would have been beneficial to any of us at that point. During the remainder of the concert, Liv and I went off and sat on a bench underneath a tree near a hot dog stand, and we had some talking time. The first thing she said to me was, "Oh my God, Mom, Christmas! Can you imagine?" She was thinking about Todd and his family, my family, and now Steven's family. She was just thrilled!

As the show was coming to an end, we went backstage. In the dressing room, I whispered to Steven, "She knows." He gave me a long, penetrating look and murmured, "Holy shit!" Then he turned to Liv and embraced her. We ended up in a three-way hug, with Steven facing me and Liv hugging him from behind. I call it my "Steven sandwich."

On the long drive back to Maine, I told Liv why Todd had been her daddy for her first eleven years and why Steven hadn't been. I explained to her that I felt she had been fortunate never to have known her father as a drug addict. She never experienced the horrors, unlike her poor little sister, Mia. What I could not have

known that night was that the last few magic hours were only the first steps in the sometimes-torturous three-year passage that would ensue before Liv could assume her rightful name and place. They would be among the greatest and hardest years of my life.

I had always worried about how the revelation about Steven being her father was going to hurt Liv or screw up her head. I soon discovered, however, that my major problem was not going to be Liv, but Todd. In a sense, given the situation, Todd was the most vulnerable person involved in all this. We also had his parents and his children, Liv's stepbrothers, to think about. There was a lot at stake.

At first, Steven, Liv, and I decided not to say anything to Todd. But Todd heard about Liv seeing Steven, and he sensed that the transition had begun without him. He quickly retaliated, becoming vindictive and extremely nonsympathetic to me. In fact, when he discovered that Steven knew he was Liv's father and he saw that things were beginning to take a different turn without him, Todd became scary.

Todd had an extraordinarily empowering effect upon women, akin to that of a cult leader over his flock. He still had a hypnotic hold over me. Now he started seriously trying to persuade me to move out to San Francisco with Liv. He promised to set us up in yet a third house, buy me a car, and send Liv to a private school out there.

I smelled a rat right away. First of all, I did not believe Todd could afford to run a third house. In reality, I would have been stashed in a small apartment in San Francisco, while he lorded it over all of us in the big house on the hill. The big dinners charged on his American Express card, the big-screen TV, the dogs, and Liv's stepbrothers might have lured Liv, enticing her to be where it was more homey. I wasn't going to let that happen. Plus, I didn't want to be part of Todd's harem. I knew what that would be like, because over the years, when he and I were no longer a couple and he was with Karen and then Michelle, he continually tried to have sex with me whenever I visited. Michelle completely destroyed whatever welcome mat had previously been laid out.

It felt like Todd was trying to take Liv away from me not because he thought I was a bad mother but because he did not want anyone to find out the truth. I think he knew I was allowing Liv to be around her real father. This infuriated Todd, and he was attempting to slip Liv away from my mooring. The thought of this threat alone was enough to reduce me to a basket case.

Steven kept saying he wanted to take over paying Liv's support, but Todd's name was on her birth certificate, and it became obvious that this was going to be a more complicated transition than we had hoped for.

Todd felt that I instigated the reunion, I caused Liv to figure out that Steven was her father by allowing her to be in situations where she could look at him and look at her half sister and put two and two together. My daughter is bright and astute, and blood is thicker than water. When two deer meet in the forest, they know they're deer. And they smell each other and they know that they're from the same species. It's the same way with people who find each other after years. The connection between Liv and Steven was undeniable. The thing that really infuriated me was that Todd felt that an eleven-year-old could not possibly have figured that out for herself. He assumed I would have had to have planted the thought in her mind. I was hurt, and so was Liv. She was confused that he didn't think more of her intelligence. Todd said, "Oh my God, Bebe, she's only a little girl; he's a big glamorous pop star! She would be just as happy if it was a guy from Guns 'n' Roses or Mötley Crüe!" I was so angry, I almost smacked him.

"Please, give me a fucking break!" I said. "What's happening here between Liv and Steven is a little bit more special than that. And I'm sorry that you're hurt, but didn't you realize that this was inevitable? Didn't you know that eventually the truth would come out? Why can't you find it within yourself to be happy for this child—and to be happy that her father has now achieved sobriety—and let go of your anger? Plus, it's going to cost you less money now. Let the guy who can afford to pay for it do that."

This nonsense went on for three years, during which time I was endlessly manipulated by both Steven and Todd. On the one hand, I was frightened that without Todd's input, I would not be able to send Liv to private school or do all the things I wanted to do for her. On the other hand, I was frightened that if I started any legal action in the form of a paternity suit against Steven, we'd have a mess on our hands. The way everybody behaved after this moment was the true test of all of us.

In 1989, when Liv was almost twelve, we moved back to New York. She just said to me, "Mom, if we don't get out of Maine now, you're going to crack up, and I'll lose my chance to experience the rest of the world."

Liv, Annie, and me at Annie's twenty-fifth wedding anniversary in Portland, Maine, 1990/BUELL PRIVATE COLLECTION

I had maintained my primary residence in Portland for nine years now, and it was obvious that the times I felt best were when I was going to New York to play a gig. In the late eighties, the Gargoyles were getting a lot of attention. One of the reasons that prompted me to return to New York in 1989 was a big billing that Joey Ramone put me on at the Ritz. He also had me open for the Ramones periodically. It was because of the attention I was get-

With Joey Ramone at a Gargoyles gig where we opened for the Ramones in NYC, 1989/MARCIA RESNICK

ting in these larger-scale venues that the Gargoyles started getting hot. There was continuing interest from record companies, so it was a very exciting time for me. I credit Joey for helping to legitimize me in the New York rock community after I had been stuck up in Maine for so long. I love Joey.

I think Liv saw that I was starting to come into my own again; plus, she enjoyed her visits to New York, with pit stops at the best toy store in America, F. A. O. Schwarz. So we decided to move. I went to Annie and said, "Annie, I know it's been a long time since I've asked this kind of favor, but I'm gonna ask you to let Liv stay here for a couple of months while I set things up for us in New York. We're moving back." Once again, my family stood behind me.

Charles and I went down to New York first to set up an apartment and get everything together. Liv came down, too, but she was still staying with Annie in Maine until we got everything set up. We didn't move right into our own place. We stayed with friends in the same building we ended up getting an apartment in. It was at 320 East Twenty-second Street, between First and Second Avenue.

On the night we left Portland, we had everything packed, but we had only two of our cats. We could not find Seymour. "We're going to have to leave without him," Charles said. He was going to drive the van back to Portland after he dropped me off in New York, so for him, time was of the essence. Everybody was crying. Little Man and Raheena were safely in the van.

"Let me just check the basement one more time. I can't leave without Seymour," I said, almost in tears. I went down and, sure enough, he was sitting on top of a heap in the basement, glaring at me. "Seymour, either you come now or you're gonna stay here!" He leapt into my arms, literally, because I think he was afraid we were going to leave him. He probably thought we didn't love him anymore. He'd seen us packing, and you know how cats are about their house getting changed—very uptight about that.

When they saw Seymour and me coming back toward the van, Little Man and Raheena got all excited and happy. When Seymour got into the van, they ran right over and started to smell him. They began to purr, having their own little conversation: Where have you been all day, you drama queen? Caused a lot of bullshit around here!

Anyway, I was thrilled, I was crying with joy because I had all my babies in the car with me, and here we were, going back to New York City.

My romance with Charles was on the wane, but for a while we stayed together for domestic and commercial reasons. The band was the focus of our lives. From the summer of 1989 through the summer of 1990, we spent all our time rehearsing, writing, getting to know people again, going to see Hilly at CBGB, meeting club owners, going over to the Continental and getting gigs. This was the closest I came to real success with the Gargoyles.

The band was becoming so popular, there was true label interest in the band, not just fuddy-duddy interest. We were opening for the Ramones frequently and we were a good draw. The owner of CBGB, Hilly, used to say, "The Gargoyles, bring 'em in." Other musicians liked the Gargoyles, which was another cool thing. I had really worked hard and I think people were starting to give me a break. To be back in New York City, to have my own apartment, and to be in a hot band—all were a dream come true.

If I had had a manager and an attorney, I think the Gargoyles would have secured a deal, but I still didn't have all those ingredients in my pie yet. And right when I met the attorney Michael Guido and everything started to come together in some way was when the whole paternity issue went public and blew up in my face. I think that if I had put another six to eight months into the Gargoyles, we would have gotten an album deal.

I also had to find the right school for Liv, because she had the same thing her father and I had—attention deficit disorder (ADD). When you have that affliction, you're just a ball of fire—sitting down in one spot for ten minutes is more than one can bear. So I wanted to look around at schools that specialized in students with ADD and would be able to accommodate a hyperactive artistic child. I found York Prep, located at Sixty-eighth and Lexington, near Hunter College. It had a lot of kids with ADD, and the teachers in their system were equipped to handle them.

Six months after moving to the city, I got a downstairs apartment on Twenty-second street, and Liv joined us. I'll never forget the day she arrived with all her boxes. She started attending York

Prep, a comfortable fifteen-minute subway ride straight up the East Side. I couldn't go out much because I had my child living with me, but she was also getting to an age where I could leave her alone for a couple of hours if I wanted to go to a show, or she could have a girlfriend come in and spend the night. I joke that drag queens helped me raise Liv, but it's actually true, because they were the only people I trusted her with. I was very, very secure about leaving her with Miss Guy or Michael Schmidt. Those queens protected her with ferociousness. I'd have one of the drag queens come over and they would make popcorn and watch a movie. Liv loved it. She would end up with false eyelashes and a ton of new clothes.

Charles knew all about the paternity issue before it actually became public. He felt the pressure of having to be my psychiatrist during the whole thing, listening to me going on about what I was going to do about Steven and Todd. Trying to keep a band together, dealing with a romance that was falling apart, and raising Liv took their toll on me, as well. About six months after Liv moved back, I threw Charles out. Our romance was over. We were basically just in the band together, which was often very stressful. There wasn't a lot of compassion between us, and I was jealous when he started screwing around with other girls. That was the end of the Gargoyles. It was terribly hard for me to give up that dream again, especially when I felt so close to success, but I had no choice.

By the fall of 1990, I could not focus my energy on anything but Liv, Steven, Todd, and the paternity issue. Now I picked up the mantle of supermom, dedicating all the time it would take to shepherd my daughter through the difficult tribulations of shedding one father and gaining another, if richer, one. Todd and Liv had a good relationship when they were together. In the second half of 1990, even this level of involvement broke down when he started making his monthly payments later and later, and sometimes not at all. I was working three part-time jobs, and we were still barely scraping by. I worked in a health-food store, an antique shop, and did some rock 'n' roll consulting work.

Some of my financial problems were awful, but Liv was divine. She would hold me and love me, stroking me, talking to me, and rubbing my feet. She's a remarkable girl, and that's why I've always said that she has an old soul and we were buddies for thousands of years, because basically she walked me through it. She certainly coped better than I did. At one juncture, I had not paid my rent for three months and the marshal posted an eviction notice on my door. At that point, I broke down and called Todd, screaming and crying. "I can't pay my rent. Charles has moved out; I'm here alone with Liv!" I told him, explaining how bad things were. He came through and paid the three months back rent, but he was still insisting that everything would be a lot easier if only I would agree to move to San Francisco. Apart from seeing through this ploy for what it was, I was sensitive about having my daughter's upbringing controlled by somebody else. In the eighties, when my mother had insisted Liv spend two years at the Congressional School, I had felt as if I was losing control of her. I told Liv how I felt, and when Todd gave an ultimatum, saying she had to move to San Francisco or he would withhold financial support, Liv chose to stay with me. Choosing between us was not an option.

At this point, I started to panic. I called Steven and explained to him what was going on. I said, "Steven, we've gotta do something about this support. We've gotta make up our minds, because I know what's going on here. I need to be in a position where I can take care of her, and I don't want to be dependent on Todd anymore."

"We can sort it out," he said. "Don't worry. I'll start paying for her school." He did start paying for her private school even before he began giving me child-support payments. I also told him that I was not going to let Liv go to San Francisco and that I wasn't going to go, either, as I didn't want to live there. And I asked him to talk to Todd. "Okay, it's time," Steven said. "I'll do it." So he called Todd.

Todd was very mean to him. He told Steven that he did not deserve parental privileges. He thought it was a privilege to be a parent and he felt Steven didn't deserve the privilege. Todd felt it didn't matter who was her biological father. Steven was an absentee father. Steven retorted, "Well, you know, you haven't exactly been there, either. I mean, just because you give somebody some money and see them twice a year doesn't make you a father." My answer to that was that whatever Todd did, it provided Liv with some sort of security. And she says to this day that there is nothing like a Todd hug.

I wanted to make as harmonious a transition as possible, but of course it didn't go totally smoothly, because Todd was not going to hide his egotistical feelings. There was no way Todd would put Liv first; he put himself first. He should have been happy for Liv and he should have offered to be a parent along with Steven and me. Steven suggested that to him. "Why can't we both be her father?" he said. "I'm not trying to come in and take your place, Todd. I don't want to take your place, but I am her father and I would like you to let me be her father. I'm sorry for the years I missed. I missed a lot when I was a drug addict."

"Fuck you, asshole!" Todd replied.

Todd wouldn't even give Steven the time of day. As soon as he got off the phone with Steven, he went into assault mode. First, he called my mother, telling her, "Dorothea, Steven Tyler has reared his ugly head." Fortunately, my mother saw through his plan to get Liv to San Francisco, which she had always been against anyway, fearing that Liv would turn into a hippie!

Steven called me and told me that he had made zero headway with Todd and that we were going to have to pursue a legal route. He told me to get a lawyer and that he would pay for it. On the advice of one of my lifesaving queens, I hired Raoul Felder.

Felder was considered the number-one divorce attorney in the world. I asked him to negotiate a settlement between Steven Tyler and me for paternity. Felder told me that the first thing one needed was a blood test to establish legal paternity. We had to prove that Liv was Steven Tyler's child. Not only did it have to be established for Todd's benefit, but Teresa, Steven's girlfriend at the time, and now wife, wasn't sure, or she was pretending not to be sure, of Liv's paternity. So she also needed to be convinced legally. In order for it to be done legally Steven was served and asked to report for a blood test. I was also asked to take a blood test, as was Liv. The results confirmed that Steven was Liv's father. The state of New York then required him to pay child support.

Felder laid out my legal options, pointing out that Liv was entitled to one-third of Steven's income, dating back to her birth. If I

Mother and daughter, 1991/BOB GRUEN

had gone after that kind of money, not only would I have made Liv an instant millionaire; I would also have secured my financial well-being for the rest of my life. The downside was that during the suit, which Steven would undoubtedly have fought, I would have had zero resources. And such a case could easily have stretched out over years. On the other hand, I could take the amicable path and simply negotiate a reasonable support-payment schedule until she was eighteen. In the interest of getting on with our lives and maintaining Liv at her private school, as well as wanting an amicable relationship with Steven and his family, I chose the second route. Consequently, Steven had to pay child support only for four years.

We asked for ten thousand dollars a month and settled on five thousand. On top of that sixty thousand dollars per year for four years, Steven paid her school fees—fourteen thousand per year—and her medical insurance. He also immediately gave me a lump sum of twelve thousand dollars so we could move into a better apartment with a doorman and security. (This from a man worth an estimated $50 million.)

One of the things you're supposed to do in these negotiations is at least make sure that you're protected for the future. I walked away with nothing for myself. I decided that my ongoing relationship with Steven was more important, for both Liv and myself. I did not want to be ostracized and booted from the Aerosmith camp. I had already been booted from Todd's camp and I don't think I could have coped with another loss.

Steven and I had a good relationship after the settlement. We would go to shows; we would have extended family gatherings. Sometimes when he came to pick Liv up, we would have fifteen minutes or so together at the apartment, but Teresa never left Steven alone with me. She relaxed when I got married in 1992 and became more open in her correspondence. She sent me Mother's Day and Christmas cards and even little Christmas presents. Teresa and I bonded to some extent because we both thought that Cyrinda's behavior toward me and the rest of us was deplorable. We never felt that Cyrinda gave Mia very good feedback. I mean, the worst thing you can do is tell a child that their parent is a creep. You cannot do that, because it destroys the child's self-image. Her father is still a part of her. There was constant warfare going on between Cyrinda and Steven, but that was not the case with Steven and me. It was very important to me that there be no tension between us.

Todd was furious. I think Liv handled it with a lot of dignity, and I respected her for that. She always had a great deal of respect for the sensitivity of the issue. As a matter of fact, when I was flipping out in 1991, it was Liv who said, "It's okay, this stuff happens to people all over the world, and the only reason that people are paying at-

"Flower Girl," 1991, NYC/BOB GRUEN

tention is because you and Daddy are famous." I also think she handled it that way because of how she was raised, and because of the energy around her. I did not look upon change as something to fear or something bad; I taught her to look upon everything as something that happened for a reason, so I think she carried that with her. I believe that she gets much of her spirit, her work ethic, and her resilient ability to adapt from me, as I have always tried to have an optimistic viewpoint.

CHAPTER 12

Liv Takes Center Stage
1991-1996

Shine little star
It's easy to shine so brite
Cuz U are
The sweetest star of all
  "BRIGHTEST STAR," LYRICS BY BEBE BUELL

I had to take the spotlight off myself during these really important years for Liv, when she was forming a self-image. It was hard, because, like her father and most singers, I have an ego the size of Asia. But I have never had a problem giving too much love, even at the risk of losing my identity. This is an important part of my story: Even though I have an artistic temperament, I would put that on the back burner for somebody I love.

One morning when Liv was thirteen, she came into the living room for breakfast, and I noticed in a flash that she had transformed overnight into the most beautiful child I had ever seen. "Oh my God!" I whispered. "She's beautiful!" She had been five nine for months, but now she had gone from being an awkward twelve-

Liv's first magazine cover–1980– we couldn't get her to remove the mask/MARCIA RESNICK

Outtake from the *Soho News* cover shoot/MARCIA RESNICK

year-old with braces to a swan. It was as if by finally possessing her own name— Liv Tyler—she had become a flowering rose.

The public's discovery that Steven was Liv's father was auspicious, and she handled it beautifully. But the media immediately began to haunt her. Suddenly, everybody wanted to know about Liv Tyler. She became—like her mother before her—the toast of New York without blinking an eye.

With Liv at a Peter Max art opening–her short time as a model in NYC, 1992/CHUCK PULIN

The press began to write about everything she did—from what school she went to, to where she spent her Saturday nights at the movies. We were still living on Twenty-second Street. The building didn't have a doorman, and there was a brothel above us. A lot of johns would knock on our door at 5:00 A.M. Now there were also packs of photographers lurking outside.

For the previous two years, Liv and I had regularly walked past a magnificent apartment building called the Rutherford, a few blocks away on Eighteenth Street and Second Avenue. We would peer up through its windows into these awesomely grand-looking apartments. Liv always said, "God, Mom, I wish we could live there!"

"Well, darling, we can't afford it!" I always responded.

When Steven's twelve-thousand-dollar check arrived, I went straight over to the Rutherford and rented us the penthouse duplex for $2,500 per month. When Liv came home from school that day, I coyly asked her, "Wanna go see where our new apartment is?"

"Yeah! Where is it?"

"It's a surprise!" I said, adding as we walked out the front door, "It's within walking distance."

"Mom! Don't tell me!"

"Yup, and we got the top!"

"We're on the top?"

"Yes! We're going to be the princesses on the top of the Rutherford!"

"Oh my God!" she screamed, leaping into the air. "I can't wait to fix my room up!" The delight and happiness in her face made it one of life's great moments. The building had big Gothic columns outside. It was right across the street from the Hospital for Joint Diseases, which always made me laugh as I gazed out the window and lit my six o'clock cigarette.

This was a quiet time on the boyfriend front for me. I didn't think I could give Liv the full attention she required if I was also going to be involved in the complexities of a romantic relationship. The two did not appear to be compatible. I was still hanging around with Ric Ocasek so much, people continued to believe we were having an affair. But Ric had been a close friend for fifteen years, and he re-

A MODEL'S HELP NETS LIV A COVER

Even supermodels — New York's top growth industry — are taking second jobs these days. Paulina Porizkova is promoting Liv Tyler, 15, the daughter of Aerosmith's Steve Tyler and former model Bebe Buell. Paulina snapped shots of Liv (including this one with her mom) and shopped them around town. It paid off. Liv's got the cover of next month's "Seventeen." Liv also read for the new Arnold Schwarzenegger flick.

Paulina's photo of me and Liv/*DAILY NEWS*

mains to this day one of my oldest friends. He was married to Paulina Porizkova, a great beauty and a successful model—she was the Estée Lauder girl at the time, one of the top accounts among the supermodels.

Paulina was also a good photographer. One day, she told me she wanted to photograph Liv. And, in an uncanny reenactment of my 1974 *Playboy* experience—with Paulina Porizkova in the Lynn Goldsmith role—she took a series of pictures that would unlock the doors to another world for Liv.

Paulina's pictures turned out to be astonishing. Liv looked like she had popped out of Sophia Loren's womb ready-made. She sparkled like an Italian princess. Paulina asked me to let her take the pictures to the fashion magazines. The response was overwhelming. But for the record, neither Liv nor I ever wanted her to be a model. I never cared if she was or wasn't. It was Paulina who really pushed this modeling thing, and I began to think that she wanted a lot of the attention for herself. Although I appreciated what Paulina did, I didn't always agree with the direction she felt Liv should go in. This inevitably put a strain on our relationship, partly because of my sensitivity about other people making decisions about Liv's future. I resented Paulina feeling that she could take the reins of my child's destiny. My priorities were Liv's education, her sanity, her security, not whether she appeared on the cover of *Vogue*.

Interview magazine, which was and is one of the most influential magazines in the world, immediately did a spread on Liv with a photo by Paulina. "Mom, what do I say?" Liv asked. "I've never done an interview before."

"Right up front, tell them that you want to be an actress," I responded. "Don't paint yourself into the model corner. It's a very hard corner to get out of. Make it clear, right away, that you want to be an actress. Trust me, honey. I don't know how I know this, but I have some kind of intuition that you're going be an actress, and it's good to start preparing for it now."

"Well, I want to be a marine biologist!"

"Great! Go to college! Study to be a marine biologist. There's no reason you couldn't do both, but being an actress is better than being a model. Leave yourself open to sensible choices."

"Okay," she replied.

When they called her up to do her first interview, she said, "I

With Liv in the Amazon shooting a commercial for Bongo Jeans in 1992. Two months later she would star in her first film, *Silent Fall*/BUELL PRIVATE COLLECTION

don't wanna be a model. I wanna be an actress. Modeling is too skeezy!" But modeling is a good first step.

Yes! I thought.

That was when the bidding war began.

When I saw that this was going to be huge and that my daughter was all of a sudden going to become this sought-after model, I knew I had to protect her, so I decided to be the person in charge of taking care of her professionally. I knew I was qualified, and that I was going to be the only one who would love and protect her. I also knew that I would make decisions based on her feelings and not on somebody else's. That was when I told myself, Okay! The first thing you need to do is get this child an agent.

Every agency in New York City wanted her. She finally signed with a new agency, Spectrum. We went with them because they represented Niki Taylor, another young girl who was doing well. I wanted Liv to be associated with an agency that knew how to take care of young girls. I also liked the people there. When I went in to meet with them, I talked with Stewart Ross, who became one of my best friends. (He and I were born on the same day, two minutes apart, so I thought there was a connection there.) I also acquired an attorney for Liv, George Stein.

We negotiated a fifty-thousand-dollar advance with Spectrum. In those days, that was unheard of. They wanted her so badly that, instead of risking losing her to Ford or Elite, they agreed to this advance. And believe me, we needed the money. We needed furniture and a fax machine. Just because Steven Tyler was giving Liv five thousand a month didn't mean we were set. We had enough to move into our wonderful apartment, but we were sitting in this gorgeous huge space with nothing in it. We didn't even have a couch!

It's not cheap to start up a career. You've got to be groomed when you go for appointments. We joined her up at the gym. We got her hair done; we got her facials; we wanted her to be dressed beautifully. Mind you, she was always a girl who never wanted anything, because I come from a very nice family. My mother and our extended relatives had always been generous, so it wasn't a question of being able to buy a new wardrobe so much as the quality of the wardrobe. We went from shopping at Bloomingdale's to shopping at Prada.

If the people at Spectrum had spent five minutes checking out my career, they might have thought twice about signing Liv. They were not thrilled when I turned down a lot of jobs for her. In fact, I turned down some jobs that made them think I was insane. I didn't want Liv to get too famous as a model, and I did not want her to become a supermodel, which she was as much a candidate for as I had been. I wanted her to stay her age. She worked for magazines with a young readership, like *Seventeen* and *YM*. I made sure that nobody was going to make my daughter grow up too fast, that nobody was going to meddle in our lives, and that nobody was going to control me, or her. If Liv didn't want to go on an appointment, she would lie to me: "Mom, I have to stay after school; I have detention." I would laugh when I hung up the phone, because I knew that she was lying.

"Okay!" I mean, I would cover for her with a smile on my face. I didn't care. I secretly never wanted her to be a model.

I am proud of my daughter, proud of how I brought her up and of our relationship. And I'm proud of the work we collaborated on in the 1990s, but I am not one of those mothers who sacrifice everything for their child. I don't believe in that. I think it's bad for the child. It was much better for Liv to have a happy Bebe than a sad, lonely Bebe.

In October 1991, after going for a year without male companionship, I met a guitar player named Coyote Shivers. We met at a CBGB Gallery party for Bob Gruen's birthday. They had on display a punk rock photo exhibit organized by Stephanie Chernikowski. All kinds of cool people were included in it. I went to the party with Liv and Debbie Harry. The moment I saw him, I was standing under a photo of the Dead Boys. At first, Coyote reminded me of Stiv Bators. He was tall and handsome, with a traditional rock and roll face—in the Keith Richards/Ron Wood mold. Then it turned out he was a Libra, like Stiv, and I was picking up all these Stiv vibes. At the time, I was one of the walking wounded emotionally. I would never have looked at this guy twice if I had not been so vulnerable. I think attractions come largely from the way you're feeling about yourself and what's going on within you. Most of the time, I'd dated slightly older men. Now here was this younger guy who seemed to fit my ideal, but it was an immature move to go for someone who had no job and no life. He was twenty-five and I had turned thirty-seven in July. I was still pretty beaten up from the loss of Todd and the trauma of everything that had happened.

I had not had sex in over a year. Since Charles and I had broken up, I had had a brief flirtation with a guy named Gary Sunshine, who rejected me mercilessly. But rejection is God's protection. I've been rejected as much as I've been accepted; rejection comes with the territory. I mean rejected in terms of not having things the way I wanted. My relationship with Todd was never the way I wanted it, my relationship with Steven was never the way I wanted it, and my relationship with my father wasn't the way I wanted it. I had experienced much male rejection in my life. The only thing I was certain about was that I could lure any man I wanted into my bed. But I could not lure any man I wanted into a stable relationship.

My relationships with men were always turbulent, even when they went on for years. These guys liked turbulence; it was part of their music. I don't, but my life has been based on so much turbulence, I obviously responded to it on some level. The best thing I could say about myself at this point was that I had been through so much and kept so many secrets, but I was still not jaded. Elvis had written me a letter once in which he told me not to let anyone extinguish my spirit, that I was truly one of the most original people he had ever met. I held on to that thought, even though I still didn't know who I was and, romantically speaking, felt like a Ping-Pong ball.

The meeting with Coyote was as pivotal in my life as meeting Todd. I didn't start going out with him right away. After we met, we pursued each other in an indirect, funny way. He called me and said, "Do you want to take me out for coffee?"

"Call me when you can take me out to dinner," I replied. A couple of months later, in January 1992, he did. We went to the Sidewalk Café, which has very cheap and very good food.

When I started seeing Coyote, Liv was fourteen and just starting to model, and I was managing her career. I was starting a new chapter in my life, but at the same time, I was feeling so liberated that I wasn't sure if I really wanted to be in love again. On Valentine's Day in 1992, he whipped out a bunch of roses from underneath his long vampirelike leather coat, and I just melted. Coyote was like an angel to me when I really needed to be loved and understood. By March, he had moved into the Rutherford. I called Coyote my "Combo Man" because he seemed at the time to be a combination of all the good things I've known in men. Not only was he a combination physically of every man I'd ever loved and then some, but he also appeared to understand me completely. I knew then that I had finally met my lover and my husband in one man. But meeting Coyote also rammed home the realization that Elvis Costello would always remain my unrequited love.

"I am going to get married," I told Liv.

"Are you sure, Mom? Is he the right person? Do you really love him all that much?"

That's when I told her that deep down I really loved Elvis but that I had to have happiness and that, on a practical level, I loved Coyote. At the same time, I impressed upon her that I would never love anyone like I loved Elvis and her father. I said those two men were the most important people in my life after her but that I could never expect to love like that again. Meanwhile, I needed companionship, love, and support. God knows what kind of mixed signals this convoluted scenario sent Liv, but she said she understood.

My wedding day—at the reception with Leee Black Childers and Debbie Harry/BUELL PRIVATE COLLECTION

So on June 30, 1992, at the grand age of thirty-seven, I, Bebe Buell, now in my fourth incarnation as a manager, career strategist, and publicist, married this twenty-six-year-old unknown singer-song-writer and rock 'n' roll guitar player, Coyote Shivers. Because Paulina and Ric lived in the fashionable Gramercy Park neighborhood, they had a key to the otherworldly, rather English-looking private park, so I was married there. It was a guerrilla wedding, because we didn't have official permission to use the park. We got Paulina's secretary, who was pregnant, to be our lookout and bodyguard, figuring, Who would interfere with a pregnant person?

The ceremony was conducted in front of a monument to the great American writer Longfellow. I wore a white dress made by Ulla Kivimaki, who is now an established designer. When I first lived in London, Ulla was my Finnish roommate. She made my six-thousand-dollar wedding dress for fifteen hundred dollars. My old nemesis, Todd's ex–road manager, Susan Lee (now Hoffman), with whom I had become friendly again at the end of the 1980s, generously paid for the dress as my wedding gift. I went in the side gate and walked up the pebbly path. My guests stood in a group around the monument. A female preacher read from *The Prophet*. Coyote and I recited an "Exchanging of the Roses." Liv wore a beautiful sparkling orange-gold gown. We had a reception up the road at Mareno, an Italian restaurant on Seventeenth Street and Irving Place.

With Liv on my wedding day, June 30, 1992/BUELL PRIVATE COLLECTION

I'm not sure how my marrying Coyote worked out for Liv. The three of us shared our big comfortable apartment in the Rutherford until 1996. She never complained. He was more like a friend to her than a stepparent. He was only twelve years older than she was. She turned fifteen on July 1, the day after the wedding.

Later that year, Liv and I were in the jungles of South America, where she was shooting a Bongo Jeans commercial. One night in the middle of the jungle, when we had not seen hot water for two weeks and were being pursued by the flying rats they called mosquitoes, Liv made a big decision: "When we get back to New York," she told me, "I am going to start switching from being a model to being an actress."

David Croland knew a man who wrote a column called "Style and Substance" in the *New York Times* about new people on the scene. He did a profile of Liv, focusing on how she was a high school student and model and the daughter of Steven Tyler of Aerosmith and Bebe Buell. The article said she wanted to be an actress. It was accompanied by a striking head shot by David. Liv looked like a young Audrey Hepburn, otherworldly, proud, and confident. Her confidence made you wonder where one so young got that strength.

An agent named Scott Landis at Innovative Artists saw the piece and called me up. "I want to meet Liv," he said. "I think she's got one of the most powerful looks I've ever seen in my life."

"What do you want to meet her for?"

"I want to represent her as an actress."

"Okay. We'll come meetcha."

When we met Scott, I instantly felt a connection, and I signed Liv up with Innovative Artists. Scott called me the next day and said that he didn't know why but he was sure Liv was going to be a star, that she just had a certain quality. Shortly after that, he called and announced, "I have an audition for Liv. It's a movie called *Silent Fall*."

I read the script. The film was a psychological thriller, and Liv would have a chance to play a multifaceted role. It was a challenging first role for a young girl. She was sixteen but would play a nineteen-year-old, which intrigued me because I'd always thought Liv was a little more poised and dignified than most girls her age. The women in my family have this way of carrying ourselves. She was like I was at her age. I decided that the role in *Silent Fall* was definitely a good one, and when I heard the film was going to be directed by Bruce Beresford, whom I adored for his Oscar-winning movie, *Driving Miss Daisy*, I was delighted. Richard Dreyfuss was starring.

Liv went for the audition with two top casting people, Joseph Middleton and Sherry Rhodes. The next thing I knew, we were on a train going to Baltimore to meet the director for the final audition. They wanted her to be girlish and show up for the audition in a flower-print dress. Instead, I suggested she wear a pair of cutoff jeans and a T-shirt. I wanted them to see those legs. Nobody's got legs like my kid. When she walked into the audition, they said to her, "Doesn't your mother know how to dress you?"

"Yeah, she does," Liv replied confidently. Because of that stance, she stood out. It was a two-hour screen test. They would see five other girls before making the final decision. She was going to be meeting the producer, the director—the whole nine yards.

When Liv auditioned, I didn't breathe down her neck. Rather than sitting in the room like a panting parent, I stayed at the hotel. I had a car take her and bring her back to me.

"Mommy, your idea to wear the cutoffs really worked!" she told me when she returned to our hotel. "They were so pissed off, but boy, they noticed me!" And then she said to me, "Mom, can I ask you something?"

"Sure, honey. What?"

"What does *emancipation* mean?"

"What do you mean, darling?"

"Well, Mom, they asked me if I would be willing to emancipate from you."

This meant she was asked legally to separate herself from her parents and become a legal adult. Producers try to get young kids to emancipate so that they won't be governed by the Screen Actors Guild rules that are set down for children. Therefore, they work longer hours, and they are not obliged to have a tutor on the set. They'd had the nerve to do this behind my back. One thing I've learned with children is that you don't go nuts. You don't scare them. I wanted to see how she'd responded.

"Who said that? Darling, how did you handle this?"

"Well, I told them that I loved my mother and that I didn't wanna emancipate. I told them absolutely not, that I'm too young."

"Well, honey, I—"

"Mom, you don't have to worry, because I don't want to emancipate. I want to finish school, and I don't want to leave you. I'm too young; I'm only sixteen and I want to stay with my family; I'm not ready to be on my own."

I burst into tears and we held each other. Then I said, "Honey, I know you're gonna get this part."

"How do you know, Mom?"

"Look what room we're in."

"What room are we in?"

"Go look at the door."

The room number was 2222.

The next day, Sherry Rhodes called and said, "She got the part. We're so happy. We were pushing for her."

She had the female lead. The lead lead. The movie revolved around her and her autistic brother. We went back to New York on the train, squealing all the way. Liv said, "Mom, no more modeling, right?"

"Noooo, no more modeling!" In fact, I let her do a couple of modeling jobs, but we were happy that these were going to be kept to a minimum. She did a big Pantene hair commercial because it was for a lot of money. Despite trying to play down the modeling, Liv was one of the modeling industry's top teenage cover girls in 1992.

Now I was faced with another decision: whether to become Liv's manager on a full-time basis. I could see that everybody was going to try to control my child's life, and just the thought of it pissed me off. It was time for me to exercise full control, and I put my foot down. Personally, I had no desire to be anything but a great mother, but under the circumstances, I felt it was my duty to become Liv's manager, publicist, adviser, companion, and best friend. I had said good-bye to my rock 'n' roll career. At the time, I didn't really know how mightily mad and frustrated I was about that. All I knew was that I was not going to let my child have an identity crisis like I had had, and I was not going to allow her not to love herself like I had. I saw the possibilities of both such things coming like a freight train. Little girls who don't have fathers can get very screwed up. And in Liv, I saw the potential for a very severe identity crisis. My path now lay in shepherding Liv through her career until she was old enough to take care of herself.

From 1991, when she was fourteen, through 1996, when she was nineteen, I orchestrated her acting career. Liv knows that, as does everyone else; it's not a secret. I handled the management and the publicity. However, my daughter has always been independent and forceful when it comes to her career. I never put pressure on her about acting.

After *Silent Fall*, she went on to make *Heavy, Empire Records, Stealing Beauty, That Thing You Do, Inventing the Abbotts, Armageddon, Cookie's Fortune,* and *Onegin.* All these films were projects I encouraged her to participate in. I also tried to handpick people along the way—talent agents, publicists, lawyers—those I thought would be the best ones for her to work with.

As her manager, I made 10 percent of her earnings. I wasn't paid anything as her publicist. I didn't reimburse myself for business expenses, and I didn't charge her for offices. I just took a straight 10 percent and ran my business and our lives with that money and Steven's child support.

From the outset, Liv's money was well looked after. We had an IRA for her; we had savings accounts. I didn't think I had the right to invest her money. I didn't want to put it into stocks. I didn't want to do anything unsafe with it. We put it into a money market account that earned interest, and of course we had expenses. It's not cheap to be a movie star. She did not leave my tutelage broke, like a lot of child actors do, suffering from the Shirley Temple syndrome. When my daughter left my nest, she was not only positioned as a major film star; she was a very wealthy young woman. Her money was neither improperly used nor squandered.

By law 10 percent of the money has to be put aside for the child. Liv and I were a team. We weren't overextravagant; we did not run around in limousines. In fact, Liv still took the subway to York Prep, even when she was a senior. And we kept our lifestyle sane. I was thrifty. Everybody was impressed by my honesty and the way I handled things. Liv was permitted to spend her money pretty freely, but there were limits. She was allowed to spend her own money on clothes, but she didn't have credit cards—she wasn't allowed to go out and be a complete nut or anything. I wanted her to learn how to take care of her money. Actually, she was sensible, and when I would make a nice 10 percent commission, I would do something special, like take us on a vacation.

It was important for me to keep Liv balanced. I made her do her homework. If she was out late, she got in trouble with me. She was not allowed to be a spoiled brat. Some of my generation's children treat their parents like servants. That was not permitted in my household. Luckily, she didn't want to treat me like a servant. She admired me, respected me, and appreciated me for what I had done for her. A greedy mother, on the other hand, could just have pushed the modeling and turned her into a cash cow.

Silent Fall was filmed in Baltimore. We went down there for three months, staying in a two-bedroom suite in a hotel. Sometimes, Liv would have to get up at 5:00 A.M. to go to the set. She was in a hurry all the time and everything was a mess. I tried to establish a home environment there, cooking, stocking the refrigerator, keeping the place looking homey, making sure her clothes were clean and everything was calm. I usually made an appearance on the set every day to be certain her tutor was getting her schoolwork done. That was important to me. I would sometimes go back to New York for a couple of days, but she always had a tutor and supervision. And I trusted her. The director, Bruce Beresford, being a father, also kept an eye on her. And my mother lived twenty minutes from Baltimore, so she would make it her business to pop in there regularly, too.

I was more involved creatively in Liv's second film, *Heavy*, directed by Jim Mangold. When I read the script, he had nobody attached. His dream was to get Shelley Winters, and he got her. I had several ideas. I told him I thought Debbie Harry should play the waitress and that Evan Dando would be perfect for the part of the slothful, musically inclined local boy who dated Liv's character. I also thought Thurston Moore would be perfect for the score, which he proved to be. So I helped bring those three talents into that movie. *Heavy* was filmed in a small town on the border of New York and Pennsylvania. I went with Liv upstate. We had a hotel room with adjoining rooms. I was supplied with a rental car, so I drove back and forth to the set all the time; I was very much a part of the movie, and it was like working with a family. I was allowed to spread my artistic wings, and Jim respected me and listened to me.

When Liv got the part, in *Heavy*, friends and acquaintances suddenly realized that while she had extraordinary talent, I had good ideas about how to guide her career. That was when people started to think, Bebe's definitely got a

"Sisters," Liv and Mia, 1997–NYC/BEBE BUELL

gift for spotting talent, knowing how to do things. I was getting suggestions from people who said, "Maybe you should be a casting director." Others thought that maybe I should become a manager within a large company. People had all kinds of ideas, and it was exciting. I soon realized, however, that it was a full-time job taking care of Liv—making sure she got an education, that she didn't get into any trouble, and that the projects she chose were good ones. I would not really have had the time to do anything else.

Heavy was a close set for me and I really enjoyed it. Debbie and Liv bonded on that movie. They were both born on the same day, July 1, and they have a lot in common. I also got my first screen credit as a creative consultant on *Heavy*. I was over the moon.

As much as I loved being Liv's manager, there was a lot of stress involved with the job. I was married, orchestrating two careers— my husband's, as he was an aspiring rock star, and my daughter's. And for a short but wonderful time, I also managed Debbie Harry's film career, trying to organize a second career for her as an actress. And that year, my marriage started to suffer. My husband felt I wasn't giving him the attention he needed, that I was giving all the attention to Liv. But the fact was that the public's interest in Liv was so much greater than the interest in him.

Rock music had always been and continued to be a life force for me. I couldn't get up in the morning without rock 'n' roll.

Throughout my years as a manager, the first thing I did when I woke up, before coffee, was listen to rock 'n' roll. It was part of who I was. I had temporarily given up my aspirations to be a rock star, but I could never have gotten divorced from rock 'n' roll. It was more important to me than just about anything except Liv. And Liv absolutely shared my enthusiasm. She loved Ella Fitzgerald and the Beatles. The Beatles and the Stones have had a consistent effect on people for the last thirty-five years. I talk to kids now who are in their early twenties and they tell me that the first time they hear *Sticky Fingers* or *Let It Bleed*, they can't believe it; they are just blown away! Or when they hear Hendrix on *Are You Experienced?* for the first time, they cannot grasp that this huge mountain of sound coming out of the speakers was actually made on a four-track.

Our daily routine at the Rutherford consisted of me working at orchestrating Liv's career (I also cooked beautiful dinners every night), Liv working and going to school, and Coyote doing nothing.

Coyote was supposed to be creating, writing songs, rehearsing. I was pushing him, nurturing him as I had with so many men in my life. And I was confident that I could make his career work. But I think it was a problem for Coyote to be put immediately into a position of comfort, wealth, and security. Plus, he was Canadian, and by marrying me, he got a green card. I also think that because of my past and my track record with respect to the men I had dated, he had this impossible desire to compete and to be as fascinating as they were. Meanwhile, he had never expressed any desire to have his own band or be a front person. I had no idea he had written any songs, or whether he could sing. As far as I was concerned, he just played guitar. This other Coyote Shivers emerged after we had been together for a while. I remember the first time he ever played me a song he had written. I had been married to him for about a year. He came back from Canada after a visit and played me one of his songs. I was shocked, to say the least. He was clever, and he seemed to have some talent and a certain savvy. I thought, this is interesting. But I never saw that drive in him. He seemed not to take his own talent seriously.

I pretended that something was happening with Coyote that overpowered and overshadowed what had happened with Elvis. I realize in retrospect that it did, but only inasmuch as I actually married him and spent seven years with him. In that sense, there was a shared intimacy that went beyond the unrequited love for Elvis. But Coyote was constantly suspicious. So one day, I told him the truth. "I still care for Elvis, and I am carrying an immense torch and I am still hurting," I admitted. "I tried to pretend I still love Steven, that I love you, that I love everyone but Elvis. But the truth is, I always loved Elvis and I will have no peace and no rest until he forgives me for what I did."

"Well, I am with ya," said Coyote, much to his credit. "I think ya need ta talk to him, you know. I think you need to find him."

He did encourage me to have a conversation with Elvis, not to go after him, but at least to sit down and have a tête-à-tête. He felt it would really help me, and release me. Elvis had gotten really fat and overweight since I had last seen him, so I think what Coyote was really hoping was that if I saw him now, I would be cured—that maybe the schoolgirl love I had for him would collapse underneath his bloated hugeness. I think Coyote thought that I was just hanging on to a memory, and of course he was correct, I was, but the real question is, Why? One of the reasons why I was hanging on to the memories was because Coyote was not a mature man; I was married to a child.

One day in 1993, a publicist friend of mine called to let me know that Elvis was at the Michelangelo hotel in New York by himself and suggested that maybe this would be a good place for me to try to contact him. I started to write Elvis another letter, once again pleading with him to speak to me so we could make amends and let go of past pain. I begged him to save me from the pain because I couldn't take it anymore. It was like feeling responsible for a car accident, or for somebody drowning. I was suffering from having chosen to have the abortion, and I felt like I had ruined his life and caused his marriage to break up, although he had also entered into a new marriage and seemed to have found a lot of happiness. So I couldn't understand why he would not want me to be released from my agony. Naturally, I received no response. It just threw me into another fit, but now I understand why he couldn't respond: He cannot see me again because of all the past baggage. Too much has happened and he is married again. I just wish we could be friends. It

seems so sad.

Meanwhile, back in the business world, I was getting a reputation around New York for being quite a negotiator, a powerful management force. Nobody fucked with my daughter, I'll tell you that right now. Nobody fucked with anybody I worked with. I had an instinct, but I also had watched the greatest managers—from Peter Grant to Albert Grossman—and I knew how to intimidate at the negotiating table. If I had really wanted to develop a career in management, I could have merged with a company or begun my own management company and gone on to become a powerful woman. The problem was that I lost my passion for it when I did not love my client. I was driven by love, not power. I love Debbie Harry like a sister, so working for her was for love, too. And I loved Coyote as a husband. But when it came to doing it for people whom I didn't love, it became tedious—I am not a baby-sitter. I had been extremely frustrated by having to hang up my rock skates, so now I had zero tolerance for tantrums or any kind of artistic bullshit. I knew, therefore, that my days as a manager were going to be limited. Plus, I didn't really look upon myself as Coyote's manager, because I had no desire to manage a rock performer, and eventually we brought somebody else in to manage him.

Liv was now seventeen. Her next movie, *Empire Records*, was another film that I was closely involved in. Coyote was also in it. The filming was to be in Wilmington, North Carolina. We went down there and rented two town houses right next to each other on Wrightsville Beach. Coyote stayed in one and Liv in the other. I was able to return to New York more often because Coyote was there to supervise Liv and her tutor. My mother joined us for Thanksgiving and we cooked a big meal. Once again, I got very close to everybody involved in the movie. It was a lot of fun.

I actually helped get Coyote into a couple of movies. He had a song called "Sugarhigh" on the soundtrack of *Empire Records*. He was also in *Johnny Mnemonic*. He put out an independent CD in 1995. But my husband had an inability to understand the work ethic. I was constantly making excuses for him, lying to people and trying to make them think he was busy as a bee. In reality, all my husband did was sleep until the late afternoon, wake up, and sit in the corner smoking cigarettes, drinking coffee, and staring out the window.

On Friday night, he might motivate himself enough to schlepp out to dinner with me, but the only thing he showed any real enthusiasm for was the fabulous party Michael Schmidt threw every Friday night at Don Hill's called Squeezebox. Squeezebox was and is a wonderful platform for artists of all kinds to try out their acts before a sharp but appreciative downtown audience. Those drag queens like Mistress Formika and Lily of the Valley and Sherry Vine can really sing and put on a show. So when they invite you into their camp, you know you're doing something astonishing. During these years, it was the only place in New York I knew of that upheld some of the spirit of fabulousness and belief in ourselves that had been the soul of Max's Kansas City back in the seventies. Otherwise, Coyote was only good at doing nothing. Occasionally, we'd go to the movies, although it was like pulling teeth out of a wild animal to get Coyote to go. The bottom line was that he just liked to be on his own. He was writing songs, and he did turn out to be a clever songwriter. I have to hand it to him: He was by no means an untalented guy, but he was not a motivated one. And I had grown up being close to some of the most motivated men in the world. Even Charles Hall had motivation in his belly. The only motivation my husband had was the motivation that I gave him. And it became painful to watch as I started to feel increasingly vulnerable.

Even though I had child support, I knew it was going to last only until 1996. I had a great job managing Liv and made $200,000 over the four years I did so, but I knew that was probably going to end around the same time the child support did. There comes a certain point at which a mother and a daughter cannot work together anymore. I had the common sense to know that I would have to let go. So I knew I wasn't going to be doing that job forever. And the part of me that wanted to get back to my rock and roll roots didn't want to do it forever anyway. The truth was, I really had no desire to be a powerful Sue Mengers-type agent. I just wanted to rock. And if I had to rock vicariously through my lazy husband, I was going to do that.

While my relationship with Coyote started to go into a long spiral, Elvis was still doing all kinds of things to antagonize me. When I was working with Debbie Harry, for instance, they began to perform together on occasion with The Jazz Passengers. Then when I tried to attend one of their concerts, he refused to allow me backstage! He even had bodyguards to keep me at bay. He would continue to torture me, much like Beethoven tortured the woman whom he loved until his death, and whom he would never admit he loved until he was on his deathbed.

As my relationship with Coyote began to fracture, cracks also started appearing in my relationship with Liv. One of the problems grew out of the fact that every time a major profile of Liv appeared in a magazine, at least a third of the article, if not more, focused on her parents! Aerosmith continued to be an extraordinarily successful band and Steven was a magnet for publicity. Our unorthodox union was like money in the bank of the publicity mill. So I think Liv was feeling not only that I controlled everything in her career but also that I overshadowed her. The fact that I was driving the bus put an odd spin on the situation. She wasn't saying it, but she wanted to make a break from me. Simultaneously, I think everybody around me was getting a little jealous of my position, because I was the conductor of this supersuccessful and increasingly famous person.

I was in a difficult and isolated position once again. Liv's career and fame had developed so fast, it was hard to digest. I was the only person who really knew what was going on at all the different levels, and in the heat of the fast-moving days, weeks, and months that flew by in a flurry of activity, I wasn't able to stop what I was doing to explain my every move. I understand now that everybody who had given me such an enormous amount of help bringing Liv up felt it wasn't fair that I should suddenly not take into account their input, but at the time, I didn't see it that way. I just expected them to trust that I knew what was best for her. After all, this was my territory; I had been in the entertainment industry for twenty years. The irony was that I knew how fame of the magnitude Liv was experiencing and the speed with which it came could drive people nuts, but I didn't realize that it was driving me crazy, too.

At the time, I was sure that I knew what I was doing, and the results support that belief. On the other hand, I also know that in the pressure-cooker atmosphere I was living in twenty-four hours a day, I was at times unbearably rude. I came across like a monster. One reason I didn't want to remain in the business was specifically because I knew that agents and managers are by definition monsters. They have to be. It's a cutthroat scene. If you don't win, your client loses. I wasn't always very nice to my mother when she called on the phone. I'd snap, "Mom, I can't talk with you now. I'm on the phone with *Time* magazine! Good-bye!" *Slam!* When Liv would come home from school, she'd say, "Mom, I don't know . . . I—" But I'd snap at her, too. "Honey, you know what, we'll talk about that later!" *Wham!* Sometimes, I was downright horrible. "Mother! Mind your own business and stop telling me how to run Liv's career! I know what the hell I'm doing!" *Slam!* All I can say is, you had to have been there. You get caught up in the wave of a business where everybody is putting everybody else down and people are constantly threatening to kill one another. Millions of dollars are at stake on a daily basis. It's not a world I'd ever want to get involved in again.

I love my family, but I couldn't include them in every decision. Although I can see things from their viewpoint: Okay, I moved back to New York, Liv became a star, and they were just left out. So I can definitely understand how anybody I hurt felt, but it took three years of therapy and reflection to get to this point. The job had become too huge and my time for people had become too short. But I couldn't see that while I was in the thick of it. That's why those people who are successful managers are tough. You really have to like being tough to have this kind of job. It wasn't an easy job for me, because being a bitch who regularly curses at people all day long is simply not in my nature.

Liv made her next movie right after she graduated from high school. *Stealing Beauty* was the most important movie of her career thus far. It was directed by the Oscar-winning director of *The Last Emperor*, the great Bernardo Bertolucci. It was filmed in Tuscany in the summer of 1995. She graduated from high school and left for Italy a week later. She wasn't yet quite eighteen, so I was still traveling with her, though I would go back and forth from Italy to the United States. I would scope out the situation and if I felt that she was in good hands and that things were running smoothly, I'd feel free to leave. I trusted Liv; she was not a baby. She was about to have her eighteenth birthday, so I had to respect that she was growing up. I didn't want to breathe down her neck, but I spent quite a

My mom, Steven, and Liv at her graduation party, 1995/BUELL
PRIVATE COLLECTION

Me and Steven at Liv's graduation party at the Ritz-Carlton Hotel, NYC/BUELL
PRIVATE COLLECTION

bit of the summer with her there, and it was a wonderful experience. Coyote even came over a couple of times. I also had Annie and my mother fly to Italy. They paid for their own tickets, but I helped get them over there, put them in a hotel, and had them on the set and at the premiere. Annie, my mom, and I were all on the set when Liv did the scene where she exposed her left breast.

I loved Bertolucci. He sees things quite from the male point of view, which is probably why I always got along with him. He was a charming man. He always introduced me as the other B.B., which was sweet. The producer, Jeremy Thomas, had also produced the documentary about the Sex Pistols, *The Great Rock 'n' Roll Swindle*, back in the seventies. He had an enormous amount of respect for me, and they made a point of including me in the promotion of the film. They wanted me to work closely with Mark Urman, who was the publicist. I became good friends with Valerie Van Galder from Fox Searchlight, the company that produced the film.

I'll never forget the first time I met Bernardo. After we had all gone out to dinner one infamous night, he was talking about my past, and he asked me, "So, when you were a crazy young girl, what was it like to cast all those penises?" I almost had a stroke. He thought I was Cynthia Plastercaster—the Chicago-based woman who, as a teenager, made plaster casts of the erect penises of as many rock stars as she could. Today, these sculptures are seen as works of art. It brought home to me how powerfully the term *groupie* lumps every girl who ever went out with a rock star into one big cauldron. It covers any female associated with a rock star unless she's got a guitar strapped on like Chrissie Hynde, who's dated more rock stars than all of us, or Courtney Love, who's dated more rock stars than Chrissie Hynde. These girls don't get tagged because they've got their penises on! They're fighting back with their instruments, which gives them some validity in the public's eye.

I sat Bernardo down over a nice bottle of Chianti and some pasta and explained the whole thing to him. I told him who Cynthia Plastercaster was, how the groupie phenomenon arose, where it came from, how it originated in Los Angeles where it was invented by the GTOs and Frank Zappa. I said I couldn't have possibly been casting anybody, because I was in high school at the time. Bernardo was enthralled. He and his producer, Jeremy Thomas, both loved it. They lingered over my every word, fascinated!

Soon, everyone wanted to hear my story, from Sinead Cusack to Jeremy Irons. Everybody was *fascinated* with my tales. After that, everyone loved it when I returned to Italy. When you're over in the middle of Tuscany, trust me, there isn't a whole lot to do. Your life centers around wine, dinner, and telling stories. They'd say, "Oh my God, she's coming back. Yes!" I had great tales, and I would make tea and we'd sit around and talk. They wanted to know everything. They loved hearing the story about me and Steven, and Liv, and stories of living with Todd, meeting Mick, and running around modeling. They just hung on every word. One of their favorites was the story about the raccoon flying first-class; that always made everybody laugh. Plus, Bernardo and I had a couple of friends in common, like Jack Nicholson. We could be there all night telling stories about Jack and laughing.

I adored Bernardo, and he grew to respect me and to appreciate my judgment and opinion. The first time he invited me to look through the lens at a shot he had just set up—of a gorgeous panoramic view of the Tuscan hillside—I experienced the thrill of feeling that I was a part of a marvelously creative experience.

Annie, Bebe, Mom, and Liv in Venice, Italy, summer of 1995/BUELL PRIVATE COLLECTION

Me, Liv, and Bernardo Bertolucci, who directed Liv in *Stealing Beauty*, walking the Palais Steps–Cannes Film Festival, 1996/BUELL PRIVATE COLLECTION

CHAPTER 13

Stolen Beauty
1996

I was strolling by the seashore
I was walking in the sand
When up jumped something
That went for my hand
I looked down
I had lost my leg
The next thing I knew I was losing my head
Shark bite . . .
    "SHARK BITE," LYRICS BY BEBE BUELL

Liv's career took another quantum leap in 1996 when she signed on to
star in two movies, *That Thing You Do*, which was Tom Hanks's direc-
torial debut, and *Inventing the Abbotts*. They were to be filmed back-to-
back in L.A. over a period of six months in 1996. My mother urged me
to rent a house in Hollywood and move out there for the duration, but
Liv was eighteen now, and she neither wanted nor needed me breathing down her neck twenty-four hours a day, every day. At the same
time, I didn't want to stick her in a hotel with no supervision for such
a long time in a place like L.A., which can really play tricks on you.

Since 1992, Susan Hoffman and her husband, Peter, had gradually become closer and closer friends of mine. By now, they were both up to their armpits in the movie business. Susan had produced a string of films by Barbet Schroeder. Peter was an attorney and financial consultant who specialized in putting together film financing. They had a lot of money, and since my wedding in 1992, they had gone out of their way to be generous. In fact, we had renewed our friendship before we even knew that Liv was entering the movie business. It seemed like a coincidence, although, in retrospect, it appears to have been fate, too. There are karmic intertwinings here that have yet to be fully digested. We are all Cancers— Susan, Todd, Liv, me. If you're into astrology at all, you'll know it's pretty rare to find so many people with the same birth sign who are closely associated.

Peter had handled contracts on four of Liv's films, among other things, and refused to be paid. He saved Liv thousands and thousands of dollars in legal fees. In the winter of 1995, we had all gone on a vacation to Saint Bart's together for two weeks: Coyote and Liv, Susan and Peter, and Peter's two daughters by his first marriage. It was a big family affair. Every time they came to New York, they would take us out to dinner. We were making frequent trips to L.A. because of Liv's work. Whenever we went there, we stayed with Susan and Peter. There was a lot of back-and-forth, lots of phone conversations. Above all, Liv was impressed by Susan and enjoyed what had, in the last year, become their long, nurturing heart-to-heart talks. In retrospect, I wonder why I did not see the parallels between the way she had seduced me into thinking she was my friend in the seventies, but at the time, I could not see anything wrong with this picture.

When the Hoffmans insisted Liv stay with them in their luxurious mansion in the Hollywood Hills for the six months of filming, it seemed like the perfect solution. I didn't realize that, according to the rules of Hollywood, I was essentially handing them my daughter on a golden plate.

In early 1996, it appeared that Liv was becoming increasingly influenced by the Hoffmans, partially because in my absence Susan took the liberty of sharing intimate secrets about our past friendship as it centered around Todd before Liv was born. Naturally, Liv ate this up with the fascination that a child feels about the emotional theatrics of her parents. In return, she shared with Susan her growing uneasiness about my control over her career. She expressed her dismay about how much of the press attention she received focused on me and Steven, and elaborated on the standard teenage daughter's feeling that I had become an overbearing presence in her life. Of course, when Liv explained her anger over these issues, Susan, as an adult, should have called and told me that Liv was experiencing a lot of anxieties about all this. Then we could have discussed it and solved the problem. Instead, in my eyes, Susan grabbed the opportunity to alienate me.

The combination of teen angst and the classic mother-daughter struggle for control was magnified a thousand times by Liv's wealth and fame. She had tons of money, she had complete freedom to come and go as she pleased, she had a car in L.A., and she had her own apartment at this point next to mine at the Rutherford. So on one level, I don't know what she was rebelling against, but I don't think mothers ever really know what their daughters are rebelling against. When girls hit eighteen or nineteen, they just want out. It doesn't matter if you're the coolest, most lenient parent on earth; there is a certain battle of the wills that occurs between mothers and daughters. As far as Steven's and my presence overshadowing Liv's in magazine profiles, or, in my case, on some movie sets, is concerned, I now can see how she had a right to complain. But it was not an easy situation for me to deal with, either. The paternity story, which was the one that involved Liv the most, was *our* story. In the process of writing this book, however, I started to unravel my various deficiencies. I guess I simply didn't notice that it was bothering her.

It was obviously not easy to be a young girl who became successful so rapidly and have parents like Steven Tyler and Bebe Buell. I mean, we're not demure creatures. When we walk into a room, it's Kaboom! We're here! I've been known to upstage Mick Jagger. And it has nothing to do with trying to compete or steal the spotlight from anybody. That's not where a consciousness like mine lies. I'm just being me. But maybe my wearing the hat as the manager and the publicist and the mother, and on top of that being Bebe Buell, was a bit too much for Liv to handle. I can see that the Bebe Buellness of who I am was sometimes embarrassing for her as well because of my past and my reputation. "Oh, wasn't your mother a *Playboy* centerfold?" And here I was, wheeling and dealing and doing big contracts with film studios. It's understandable that somebody could think, What is wrong with this picture?

It's not hard to make a young girl feel uncomfortable. I was obviously not doing it to be vicious. I was not in competition with Liv, and I was not trying to get any glory out of my child's success. Glory meant nothing to me. I sympathized completely with Liv. Liv is a lot quieter than I am, much more soft-spoken. She is a lot shyer.

I thought she understood, but I see now that I had set her up as the Buddha and the know-it-all when she was four, so I overestimated what she could retain and tolerate. I now see how Liv was suffering, how she desperately needed to be acknowledged for her own accomplishments. She had had enough of Mom and Dad being the focal point of her interviews. I only wish I had seen that clearly then. I would have explained to her that the story of her paternity was an irresistible one and that she hadn't lived enough of a life yet: "Go out and save the whales or go to Yale and then they're gonna have something else to write about."

At the time, she asked me, "Mom, why is it that all my articles are more about you and Dad and they're never about me?"

"Well, honey, that's because . . . I guess it's an interesting story."

"I don't want you to talk to the press anymore. Susan doesn't feel you should be speaking to the press," Liv told me.

With Susan Hoffman in Cannes, 1996/BUELL PRIVATE COLLECTION

Liv, Steven, and Bebe at the L.A. premiere of *Stealing Beauty*, June 1996/CARL SAYTOR

Me and my former husband, Coyote Shivers, with Steven and Teresa at the NYC premiere of *Stealing Beauty*/BUELL PRIVATE COLLECTION

"Well, honey, I'm the one who coordinates the articles. If somebody wants to ask a question, I could say, 'No comment,' but they're gonna dig up what they're gonna dig up anyway. Isn't it just better for us to be honest with them and tell them what they want to know? They'll get tired of all this soon. Don't worry."

I must admit that I had become dependent on being Liv's manager; it had taken on too much importance. It was my job, but it had also become my life. I realize now that it's not appropriate for a parent to depend on a child to that extent. I think that parents have to be the ones on whom the child can depend. I was the one whom Liv could depend on for business, but I was so busy that I had forgotten that I had to be her mother, too. When she came home from school, I would be sitting at my desk, making deals. She would want a hug or help with her homework, but I didn't have time, although I always found time to spend with Liv in the evening. Most of the time, however, I was too busy trying to fight off all the vultures who were attempting to control a piece of her. Furthermore, I was not as capable a manager as I liked to think I was. You have to have a cutthroat personality to manage a major star. You need to be able to tell people off on a daily basis. And I'm just not good at that. My advice for any parents who find themselves in this dilemma is, bring in a partner. Do not do it all by yourself, because there will come a day when you'll be asked not to do it anymore. You'll have to learn that your child has left, and that you have to either continue this line of work with a new client or move on.

I was never a strict disciplinarian, but I had to hold the reins in order to guide both Liv and Coyote. In 1996, the reins snapped.

Shortly after we returned to the United States from the Cannes Film Festival, I flew out to L.A. to celebrate Liv's nineteenth birthday. She had just signed a huge contract with Lux, which I had coordinated with International Management Group, for a million dollars. After her birthday, we were scheduled to fly to Tokyo together to do the Lux press campaign. I had never been to Japan, so I was excited about the trip. However, the next four days turned all my plans upside down.

On July 1, I arrived in Los Angeles and checked into a hotel. On every previous visit to L.A. over the past four years, Liv and I had stayed with the Hoffmans, but on this occasion, I had not been invited to stay at their house. Under the circumstances, I thought that was particularly odd. The fact that it was my daughter's birthday but I had not been involved in any of the preparations made me feel even more ostracized. I asked Susan if I could help pick out the cake and have some say in planning the party, but I was told that everything had been taken care of.

The next day, after the brunch, Liv and I went shopping together. At this point, I was still planning to go to Japan.

On July 3, I sat in my hotel, while my daughter was at the mansion with the pool up on the hill above Sunset. I sat there thinking,
What is wrong with this picture? Unfortunately, right smack in the
middle of this difficult time, one of the worst examples of the press
paying as much, if not more, attention to me than Liv came out
when Roger Friedman's cover story on Liv was published in the influential magazine *Manhattan File*'s June issue. This was the article
that pushed Liv over the edge, because Roger really overdid my
part in the interview. It's all in the past now and Liv and Roger are
good friends. At the time, I was too close to it to see that it might be
viewed negatively by Liv; I just thought he was being nice.

Finally, I went over to Susan's to see Liv. As soon as I walked in,
Liv told me that she wanted to speak with me. As I followed her out
to the pool house, I didn't have a good feeling in my stomach. We
sat at opposite ends of a couch. She started speaking very softly and
sweetly. "Mommy, I love you very much. You've done an incredible
job for me. I wouldn't have any of this if it weren't for you. You've
been just wonderful, but I feel that your being my manager is coming between us as a mother and a daughter. I don't feel that you
have the time really to be my friend anymore. I miss you as my
mother. I feel that this job has gotten to be way too much for one
person to handle. I think I should have a publicist. It's probably
been hard for you because you've had to talk to all these people and
arrange all the interviews, so they sneak their little interviews in
with you. Mom, I don't completely blame you that the media has
jumped on you and Dad so hard—I understand that this is an interesting story—but there's gonna have to be a time when we force
them to stop writing about it."

I told her that I felt that was fine but that there should be a transition period. That way, we could ease into this change so as not to
cause any trauma. Liv had already been handling her own money. I
hired a business manager when she was eighteen, the same one she
still has to this day.

"No," Liv responded, "I don't want a transition period. I want
you to stop being my manager now."

If I hadn't felt so beaten down and threatened by Susan at that point, I probably would have handled it just fine, but I was just so lost, and everything had happened so fast, just as I had feared. In six weeks, I had gone from being "Bellisima!" on the Palais steps in Cannes to being discarded and pushed out of the game.

At first, every emotion imaginable ran through me. I felt a great sense of relief, but also a tremendous sense of fear for Liv. I was terrified that people would take advantage of her. I was upset. It was like breaking up with a boyfriend.

Then Liv said, "Mommy, I think I even want to keep you involved in my career on some level. Maybe we can work something out. Maybe you can do a little light press, even though that seems to be the problem. But you're so good at it, so maybe there'll be some way that we can work together a little more. But I don't think it's good for me for you to be my manager. Not because you're not doing a good job, but because you're my mother, and you and Dad have real rock and roll reputations."

"Okay, honey, when we get back from Japan, we can start putting everything into motion. I hope you'll let me help you choose a good publicist," I replied.

"Well, you know, Mom, I don't want you to go to Japan with me."

That was a real slap in the face. I hadn't seen that coming at all. "You're kidding!" I said. "I put this whole deal together! I did this for you! How can I not be there?"

"Well, I don't want you to come," she insisted. "I would much rather Scott Landis come."

"Oh! So now they're gonna do the job I started! They're going to finish the job for me! Scott Landis had nothing to do with this deal. I can't even go out with dignity; I can't even go out with my head held high." I started crying.

Liv kept saying "Mom, I'm sorry, but I really think this is best for both of us."

I went back to my hotel room and called Coyote in New York. "You know what?" he said. "Just get on a plane and come home. Walk away."

As I flew back across the country on the red-eye on July 4, I kept hearing Liv's voice in my head: "This is for the best. This is better for us. Don't worry; don't worry."

Coyote and I had planned a trip to Saint Bart's from July 10 through July 18 to celebrate my birthday. While I was there the story broke in the *New York Post:* TYLER FIRES MAMA FLACK. Reducing me to a publicist when I was not only the manager but also the catalyst of Liv's entire career completely devastated me. And in my opinion, that ruined my reputation.

My management career took a sharp nosedive. If I had wanted to continue it, I would have had to have joined another agency and started as a junior agent. There were a lot of people who sided with me. Every magazine I had ever worked with, and anybody who had ever worked with me in a business capacity in conjunction with Liv, knew that I was fiercely protective and a smart deal maker, and that I loved my daughter immensely. They knew that I had not stolen her money and was not a lavish spender. I hadn't opened offices on Park Avenue. I'd tried to cut corners and do things economically. In fact, that became my downfall. I'd chosen Peter Hoffman as a lawyer, trying to save Liv many thousands of dollars in legal fees. I had just refused to believe the cliché Hollywood stories. My biggest downfall came because I was too trusting. I will never trust like that again. It's a pity, but I am no longer innocent. I am a much tougher person now.

While Coyote and I were in Saint Bart's, Liv had all of her things removed from the Rutherford. I had gotten the apartment next door so she could have her own space, but we still lived together, as the two apartments were connected. When I got back home, I went over to check on her place, because we had been gone for ten days. I walked in and discovered it was empty.

Liv didn't have to move one thing, because she was on a movie set in L.A. Annie and her friend Lyndall went down and packed up the entire apartment, and Scott Landis, Liv's agent, moved the stuff out and put it in storage. I felt that somebody had taken a chain saw to my legs. I was cut to the bone. I think everybody had been afraid I would freak out and not let Liv move out of the apartment, but the lease was going to be up in three months anyway, and we had discussed her moving out and getting her own place. Everybody was overreacting, as usual, and acting like a bunch of chickens with their heads cut off, me included. I felt an indescribable rage against anybody who'd participated in that move. I was unable to take this out on Liv, because I understood why she had done it. She was nineteen, and she'd had such a huge, sudden success, and everybody wanted a piece of her. I couldn't blame her or be angry with her. I felt compassion and love for her and I missed her.

Liv and I tried to have a couple of phone conversations, but during one of the conversations, Coyote got on the phone with her and really lost it. He was saying, "You better not do anything to hurt your mother! This is ridiculous. I can't believe you're with these disgusting fucking people! How could you do this, Liv? How could you come in this house when we were away and move your things out? I had never heard him scream like that. He was just so angry, and in his eyes he was trying to protect me. We were both confused.

He screamed at her horribly and it was awful. The conversation with Coyote was a very traumatizing moment for Liv. After that, she decided not to talk to me, and we didn't speak for the next five months.

I don't blame anyone for this—it was a very emotional time and the Hoffmans should not have been involved. They betrayed my trust as adults, and Susan seemed to enjoy my pain. It was the same old wound from the Todd days opening again. It seemed to me—and to many others—that this was her revenge. But revenge is not always sweet, and blood is thicker than water.

CHAPTER 14

Breaking the Silence
1996-1998

The message here is clear
Sad but it's true
Never let the sharks
Take advantage of you
I looked down
I had lost my leg
The next thing I knew I was losing my head
Shark bite . . .
   "SHARK BITE," LYRICS BY BEBE BUELL

Back home in New York, I took stock and did some deep soul-searching. Shifting through the embers of my crashed and burning career, I kept coming back to the fact that what I really did best was rock and roll. My heart beats to the pulse of rock and roll, and I realized I had to go back there. I had to find that place in me that becomes happy through music.

   I have no regrets about what I went through with Liv. If she had not been a big movie star, the split would have been a lot easier. It would have been what every mother and daughter go through. A few fuck yous and "I'm going to college. Fuck you!" You know, "Yes, I'll date him if I want to; Mom, don't tell me what to do. I hate you!" The usual bullshit! But when you're on the cover of ten magazines in one month and you're the biggest teenage star in the world, which Liv was in 1996, it's not so simple. She was only nineteen. Jesus, I'm surprised she handled it as well as she did.

Luckily, I had saved some money, I had enough to pay my rent at the Rutherford for another year and rethink my future. I was forty-two. I still had Coyote. We continued living together at the Rutherford, sans Liv, and I devoted my time from the fall of 1996 to the fall of 1997 to making my husband a rock star. By the end of 1996, I had come to understand that my problems with Susan had caused a lot of the miscommunication between Liv and me. Everything was being repaired as far as that was concerned and I was slowly rebuilding my relationship with Liv again. I wasn't working for her anymore, but she still asked me what I thought. She still to this day has never replaced me with another manager. So that in itself, was a tribute to the wonderful job I had done for her.

It took the rest of the family a little longer, but by Christmas we were all okay. This left me free to devote my life to trying to make my husband famous.

I went to countless meetings with record executives, I booked his gigs, and I worked the phones, trying to light a fire under his ass. Unfortunately, there's more to being a rock star than being cute and having some talent. He has some talent, he's great-looking, and he's good live, but he lacks the thing you have to have in

With Michael Schmidt at the MTV Video Awards, 1996/BOB GRUEN spades to be successful, and that's motivation. You cannot sleep every day until 3:00 P.M. You have to go around and see people; you need to hustle on the phone. You cannot lock yourself away and expect miracles to happen. Even if you hire a manager—which we did, Nick Moyle—you still have to have a certain persistence and a presence, which Coyote didn't have. Coyote was a laid-back guy from Canada.

I had called him my "Combo Man"; now I called him "Mr. Passive-Aggressive." He was one of those people who gave the impression of being very laid-back, but he never felt that I loved him, because he felt that I still loved Elvis.

In the spring of 1997, Sky News TV flew me over to London to do an interview for them and appear on a talk show on an Irish station in Dublin. I got a first-class round-trip ticket on Virgin Airlines. Every time in the past when I had gotten stuck in a rut, going to London seemed to jump-start things again. This time would be different.

I had never been to Dublin, from whence my once true love hailed. I was booked into a hotel owned by U2, which I found doubly ironic. By the time I got there, Elvis was back in my consciousness to such a degree, I was feeling haunted. I had been dreaming about him so much that I'd stopped letting my husband touch me. I became sexually unapproachable, despondent, bordering on desperate.

Mat Snow, who was a good friend and the editor of the best rock magazine in the UK, *Mojo*, took me to dinner in Holland Park, a neighborhood where Elvis also kept an apartment. He let me unburden my heart. I talked to Mat about my love for Elvis, pouring out my pain, the story of my bad marriage, and this terrible predicament I had gotten myself into. Mat's response was, "Well, why don't we do an interview and tell your story? Maybe if Elvis knows the truth, you could be friends." I had used the interview form in the past with mixed success. Desperate times called for desperate measures. So we did the *Mojo* interview. In it, I attempted to make sense of my position as Elvis Costello's muse, and I tried to make it clear that I still carried a giant—emotional and artistic—torch for him. Unfortunately, because of the realities of magazine publishing, the story wasn't given the kind of space it needed to

"Blond on Blond" with my soul sister, Debbie Harry–NYC, 1997/LEEE.BLACK CHILDERS

plumb the depths of such a complex topic. Instead, it highlighted the juicy bits, resulting in a skewed love letter that badly misfired.

When it was published in October 1997, the interview turned my life upside down. It was intended as a peace offering to both my husband and Elvis, and a way of exorcising Elvis from my life. It ended up having the opposite effect. I didn't get any response from Elvis and I lost my husband.

Coyote was heartbroken. He felt embarrassed, hurt, and ridiculed beyond repair. He saw himself in the public's eye as a cuckolded chump. He had delusions that all of our friends on the New York rock scene were laughing at him. He reminded me of the way Todd had reacted when the paternity story came out. Coyote was a broken man. He started going through my papers, taking documents that I had been carefully saving for years, tearing pages out of my diary. I'm not saying I was right, but the way he chose to handle it was puerile.

While I was fighting a losing battle on that front, I realized we couldn't afford to live in the duplex at the Rutherford anymore. The rent had now climbed to $3,900 a month. The time had come to pare down our lives and get back to work. I could not coast off the money I had saved, nor could I fool myself about managing Coyote's career anymore. It was not happening.

Near the end of 1997, I found the delightful little apartment I am living in today. It's not as grand as the one in the Rutherford, but it's equally charming and inspiring. It has a terrace overlooking Eighth Street and Fifth Avenue, which is a perfect place to write rock

Guest DJ with Jayne County, 1997/BUELL PRIVATE COLLECTION

songs. All I have to do is look down on the human intercourse below.

In December 1997, I banished Coyote to Canada for a couple of months. I had no breathing room, no time to think, because I was obviously the only focal point of his life. I told him to get out of my hair while I packed up the apartment. I couldn't stand it anymore. I was so disgusted with him because of his increasingly destruct-

My dear confidant and friend, Ginger Coyote, 1997/BUELL PRIVATE COLLECTION

ive behavior. I went up to Maine to be with my family for Christmas. I sure as hell didn't want to spent Christmas with Coyote. I didn't even show him the new apartment until I had already signed the lease.

I had about fifteen thousand dollars. It was going to cost me at least eight grand to make the move. I was working on a severely limited budget. In the spring of 1998, I moved to my new apartment, which was, I felt, better suited to a single person. After much in-depth soul-searching, I decided to focus on the dreams and visions I had for myself, rather than focusing on others, as I had been doing since 1972. This was to be my launching pad.

In April 1998, the day the movers were coming, Coyote returned. He wasn't much of a muscle man and he detested moving. My best memory of his coming back from Canada was telling him two months later, "You know, you have to leave. I think you should go to L.A." The way I saw it, I thought I could do a John and Yoko. "You've got to go to L.A. and find yourself," I told him. "And L.A. is probably the best place for you to go. They'll probably love you musically out there. [Notice that I said *probably* twice; I wasn't as sure of my forecasts as Yoko.] Maybe the separation will do us both good." He drove out there with his friend Georgie Seville, leaving me in New York, alone at last. I felt like I had lost everything.

After Coyote split, things really got bad. And then I discovered there were two biographies about Elvis in the works. One was by Brian Hinton, the other by Tony Clayton Lee, and I became paranoid about how I would be depicted in them. How would my part be interpreted? When I found out that Brian Hinton wanted to talk to me for his book, there was a part of me that was afraid, as I didn't want to jinx anything. Brian's number had been given to me, along with a note: "Please call Brian Hinton." I was looking at it one day, and I thought, Fuck it, I'm going to call him and see what's up. When he started to tell me what he had pieced together, I got chills. I was freaking out because he knew a couple of things even I didn't know, and I was trying to digest the fact that others knew of this relationship and all the nutty back-and-forth nonsense. Hinton said, "I've done a lot of research for this book, Bebe, and you'd be very surprised at some of the great minds that make a living out of dissecting clues, rock 'n' roll undertones and messages, and I have completely unraveled the mystery of you and Elvis." I said, "Tell me some of the things you know about." And he started listing them, and I thought, Oh my God! He said, "Are you gonna deny any of this?" The real burden of being a muse is that nobody's allowed to know about you, unless you're a celebrated muse, like Gala was for Salvador Dalí, or Linda McCartney for Paul. But when you're the mistress, the secret muse, a guy will let you be committed to an insane asylum before he will let the secret get out. Elvis's clues are so blatant, you have to be almost an idiot not to figure them out: When the *Best of Elvis Costello* came out in 1994, "I Want You" was the twenty-second and last song. Gee, I wonder if he did that on purpose. The combination of the number 22 and the "I Want You" is unbelievable. "Mighty like a Rose" had appeared along with "So like Candy" in 1991. Then *All of This Useless Beauty* came out in 1995.

I was frightened by the effect that the *Mojo* article was going to have on my standing in these books. In a feeble attempt to pacify my husband, and to get Elvis to forgive me for everything once and for all, I wrote a letter to *Mojo*. It was slated to be published exactly one year after my 1997 interview: In it, I pretty much apologized to everyone for my feelings. I wasn't saying that what I'd said earlier was untrue; I was saying they were feelings, not the truth as I knew it now. Then I proceeded to call my husband the love of my life in the letter, hoping to try to take away some of the hurt I had caused him.

I was lost in my memories of Elvis, largely because I felt so unsafe in my marriage. It offered no security of any kind, financial or personal. After being married to Coyote for two years, I had started thinking, oh my God, I jumped into this too quickly. But I stayed married to him for seven years. It was a long time. The nineties were Coyote's. I met him in 1991, married him in 1992, and divorced him in 1999.

Coyote went back and forth between L.A. and New York several times between January and June of 1998. I was still trying to work things out with him; I didn't want to be alone. But when my husband was at home that summer, he went through my personal papers. I had gone away for a few days with Annie and my mother to Mississippi to visit Liv on the set of *Cookie's Fortune*. Coyote was still seething from the original *Mojo* article. I found out that on May 1, he had met a girl whom he liked. By the time he came home to me in June, he was looking for a way to get out of our dead marriage. When he found my personal writings about Elvis, he photocopied everything. When he got back to Los Angeles, he started faxing them to me, to let me know that he had them. On top of the emotional turmoil and trauma that I had gone through with the loss of my career, my child, and my dignity, once again feeling that my work was not appreciated, this further exacerbated my fears. It all became too much for me to handle.

In the summer and fall of 1998, I had a small nervous breakdown. I developed psychosomatic illnesses; I thought I was dying of cancer, when actually, I was dying of my life. I began to be frightened of everything. I couldn't overcome the feeling that nothing I did worked. Elvis never called me to say he forgave me for everything and hoped I'd have a nice life. I hadn't made any kind of peace with Elvis. My marriage ended—my husband cheated on me and ran off with another woman. There was not going to be any John and Yoko: There wasn't going to be any forgiveness; there wasn't going to be any turning back. When I lost my husband, I pretty much concluded that I had lost everything. From June to September of 1998, I lost my mind. My problems with Liv were probably a part of what pushed me over the edge, but it was Coyote's betrayal that finally broke me.

I am not the kind of person who flings herself off a roof or takes heroin. I just withdrew into my inner world of madness. I was sure God was punishing me for everything. Every fear I had ever had in my life combined into a giant tidal wave that rose up and threatened to engulf me.

I told David Croland and my daughter that I was dying. I actually told them that I had leukemia, because I was sure that I did. I thought I was such a bad person and had hurt so many people that the blood running through my veins had to be contaminated. When I told Liz Derringer I had leukemia, I even named it. I didn't just have leukemia; I had "exotic leukemia." I told people it came from the Himalayas. I convinced myself, but I don't think Liv really believed me. She knew I'd really lost it this time.

Finally, my mother, bless her heart, walked me through it, mostly over the phone and on occasional short visits. Roger Friedman was also a major supporter. Several other close friends like Liz Derringer assured me that they were still there, that they still loved me, but if it hadn't been for my mother and Roger, I don't know how I would have made it.

I just lay on the couch all the time. Eating was not agreeable; socializing was out of the question. I talked to my dog. I mean, I actually believed I had some conversations with my dog. I also spoke with Little Man, the surviving cat, who finally died in the spring of 2000. "Little Man, what should I do today?" I'd say to get the ball rolling. "What disease am I dying of today?" Borderline personality disorder is what you get from years of rejection, trauma, and pain. I also had *trichomaniaolia*; I would pull my hair out until I had big bald spots. I was self-mutilating; I was trying to pull my head off.

Coyote's final crowning visit to the apartment was in August, right in the thick of it. He came back because he had gigs I had set up for him. I was so completely out of my mind that I wanted him to stay with me. I was hoping there could be some kind of reconciliation, but I finally admitted during this final visit, when he came in the door with a hickey on his neck and he had removed his wedding ring, that it was over. Hickeys, photos of a girl I found in the pocket of his jacket, sleeping fully clothed on the couch—these were signs. That was during one of my psychosomatic episodes. He stayed for only three days, but it was so awful that he finally left to stay with his friend Georgie. When he left, I knew that was it. Later, I wrote a song about him called "Voodoo Doll." "I want a sure-fire way/ To get you creep/ You can talk all you want/ But watch your feet/ I've got my pin in ten inches deep . . . "

I really teetered on the brink of madness. I always thought I was way too German to crack up, but finally I saw that even Germans can crack. However much I dreamed or fantasized about it, I realized that Elvis wasn't going to rescue me, that I wasn't going to have a fairy-tale life with a happy ending. I knew I wasn't going to be with the father of my child, and I knew that Coyote wasn't going to come back into my life, and that it was all for the best. My daughter was not going to respect me if I didn't get my shit together. My mother was there for me, as she always had been, and I knew that parental love meant she would support me. But I also knew it was up to me to get my life back on track.

Roger tried to convince me that I wasn't crazy and that everything had just come to the point where my emotions were manifesting themselves in physical symptoms. My mother begged me to go to a psychiatrist, and Liv offered to pay for it. My spark plugs were worn out, and my ball bearings needed replacing. It was embarrassing for me to admit I needed a shrink, but I finally went to a woman, Dr. Donna Lewinter, who saved my life.

When she met me, I was a miserable, overweight, confused, ridiculed woman who saw no hope for the future at all. She somehow convinced me that I wasn't certifiably crazy and I didn't need to be taken to a loony bin. She also convinced me I wasn't dying of any exotic diseases.

Dr. Lewinter put me on an antidepressant called Zoloft. I took awhile to adjust to the medication. For the first few days, I slept the whole time; my body was adjusting. Then one day, I felt the spark plugs in my brain tweaking, static sparks connecting up, and I realized right then and there that we really are nothing but walking electricity.

When the Zoloft started to kick in, I had a newfound burst of creative energy and love of myself. I thought, Jesus Christ, why didn't somebody put me on a fucking drug thirty years ago!? The women in my family are just way too proud to admit weakness. God forbid that we should ever deal with reality. I didn't know I was depressed, since I had a wonderful way of masking it. I would love people to pieces, sublimating my depression by helping others. I wore an Yves St. Laurent cloak over my depression, but trauma after trauma made it manifest itself. Zoloft also curbs obsessive-compulsive disorders and any kinds of cravings. I felt ill if I drank alcohol, so I couldn't drink anymore. I was never a big drinker, but now I couldn't even have a cabernet socially. Even pot didn't agree with me.

Liv and I started to talk about everything that had happened. We were both going to therapists. My advice and opinions became important to Liv again. I was prouder of Liv than anything or anybody in my life. Her success helped make me feel better about myself. I knew I had done a good job. And as we became friends again and started to talk things out, she told me she understood how what had happened would have enraged and hurt me. And she sympathized with me about how I must have felt at that time. But she wanted me to understand how *she* felt at the time, that she wanted her freedom. She said, "I didn't want to hurt you, Mommy. I know how much this job meant to you and I know how hard you worked, but I wanted my independence."

The combination of having so much love from my daughter and from my mother when I had hit the bottom meant everything to me. I did not want to disappoint them; I wanted to show them that I was worth a lot. I think they understood that. Although pretending to be ill was cruel and selfish, it was also a loud cry for love. I wanted to be loved and protected; I wanted to be taken care of so badly that I thought the only way I could get the attention and love I needed was to fake my own sickness, like faking one's own death.

All of a sudden, my confidence shot through the roof. I began to become obsessed by my art. I started singing again, jumping up onstage every chance I got. Finally, all my drag queens were saying, "Beeb! It's time to come back; we're here!" My queens took me back. Their influences and perceptions were always the sharpest.

Before I knew it, the Squeezebox Band was my band, and my divorce proceedings had begun. I felt like another person. I called everybody and apologized for telling them I was dying.

In the fall of 1998, Liv and I were seeing each other regularly when she was in town. Joaquin Phoenix was around, but they didn't live together. She had her own apartment on Ninth Street and he had an apartment in TriBeCa. She regularly went down to his father's compound in Costa Rica and to Florida to visit his family. Our relationship continued on the upswing. We would have supper together.

I will never forget my relationship with Liv building again, and how joyful I felt when we would go to dinner together. She got her own lawyer, who is one of the best in Hollywood. She still has the agent I originally hired for her, Scott Landis, and he's become a major force in Hollywood moving to CAA, with Liv. She also still has the business manager I hired for her. That makes me feel safe, because I know that she's got good people around her. I think that when it came down to real hard-core economics and sensible thinking, Liv always turned to me. She's got wonderful publicity people. She's in a wonderful blue-chip situation, which is rare for an actress in her early twenties.

Liv broke up with Joaquin at the end of 1998. Since then, she's been with an English musician named Royston Langdon. I adore him. Royston and his brother Antony are in the band Spacehog. They're signed with Danny Goldberg's label, Artemis. Royston appreciates and knows who I am. I'm glad that Liv's with him. I love the fact that she's involved with musicians. I'd rather she be with a musician than with an actor. I don't have anything against actors, but we're music people—that's our lineage. Liv might be a movie star, but she has a rock and roll pedigree. She is "rock royalty," as Stella McCartney calls it. Rock people stick together. I can go to some expensive party uptown at the Russian Tea Room, but there's a safety that I feel when I'm in the bowels of the Lower East Side.

At a movie premiere with Liv, 1998/JIM SPELLMAN

I'm much more comfortable pressed to the front of the stage at CBGB, watching some sweaty band. I'll always have that kind of spirit. Liv is pure rock 'n' roll, and she's come to terms with that. I love the person that she's become.

I don't regret that Liv and I went through what we did. We learned about betrayal, success, and how crazy and nutty people can get around that kind of fame and success. All of those losses were lessons for me. I was meant to go through them. I needed to learn to shed my desire to help and groom others and make myself the number-one priority.

Me, Mom, and Liv on Christmas 1998, in Maine—showing off our new jewelry/BUELL PRIVATE

CHAPTER 15

Normal Girl
1998-2000

Everyone knows I'm the one
I'm the girl from the Sun
I'm not from the moon
I shoot stars from my womb
I live in N.Y.C.
I'm a very, very lucky one
I'm born to be in N.Y.C.
I get to have a lot more fun . . .
   "NORMAL GIRL," LYRICS BY BEBE BUELL

In the winter of 1998, I began my comeback as a rock 'n' roll singer in earnest. For once in my life, I loved *me*, and for the first time, I realized that nobody was going to do it for me but me. Nobody, not even my own child, was going to save me. I had gone through the proverbial self-destructive moment. It didn't manifest itself the way it did with my heroines, Marianne and Anita. I did not become physically ravaged; didn't become a drug addict; I didn't become a mere shadow of myself; I didn't hibernate. I didn't move to the Antarctic; I didn't go off and marry the woodcutter for the simple

With my childhood idol, Marianne Faithfull/AL RENDON–PERMISSION
VIA LYNN GOLDSMITH

life in Connecticut. I didn't, finally, put on that tight dress and go
land my millionaire. Most of my girlfriends were saying, "Bebe,
you can have any man in the world!" But money's never been my
driving force, ever! I finally concentrated on my artistic goals and I
got my body in shape. I lost thirty pounds in eight weeks, which
was no mean feat. That achievement gave me a terrific belief in my
ability to do anything I set my mind to.

By taking my time and working carefully, I put together the
Bebe Buell Band, and we started rehearsing hard. When I resur-
rected my career and decided to crawl back onstage again, it was at
Squeezebox, so once again my fags were there. I am the only
woman who has ever played Homocore, Dean Johnson's fag party
at CBGB. In 1999, I was the queen of Homocore. I was the only
woman, and I headlined! Everything started falling into place, and
the songs started to pour out of me. I'd be walking down Broadway
and two songs would come into my head. I'd run to the phone and
sing them to my answering machine so I wouldn't forget them.
Songs come from a place I have never been able to discover completely. I don't think you can sit down and consciously write a song.
I find that the best songs I've written were just bestowed upon me,
coming from someplace that I do not know. I don't think a great
song has to come from a God-given talent. A great song is given to

you as a gift. "Normal Girl" was the song I had to write to explain to people who I was. It's my autobiography in a song.

At forty-five, I was beginning to find myself, discovering who I was. I think that I have always been an instrument, I have always been a vehicle for channeling art. I am one of those people who generate art, inspire it, and I love that. If you want to be someone, maybe all you have to do is visualize it. Now I see myself as a powerful woman-man who can perform and who can channel all her favorite people, dead and alive.

I suddenly felt like a warrior. I started watching TV shows about strong women, like Xena: Warrior Princess. Hillary Clinton became attractive to me. I started to want to run into Fran Lebowitz and Lisa Robinson again. I just felt there was nothing that could stop me. I spent New Year's Eve of 1998 in the balcony of the Bowery Ballroom with Annie Leibovitz, Anita Pallenberg, and Susan Sontag, watching Patti Smith.

At the beginning of 1999, I was performing again, and getting interest from major record companies. I'd gotten my body back; my family had forgiven me for being a psychosomatic disaster; my daughter loved me. I was getting a divorce. I was even bonking this adorable Bam Bam, an appropriate name, because that's what he

With Lou Reed at Mick Rock's VH1 photo party in NYC, 1999/MICK ROCK

was, a bam bam, nothing more. It was my first real fling. I was even thinking I might get rid of him because I didn't want any man in my life.

All my creative energy went into developing a sense of self. I was almost afraid to have sex, for fear that I would not be as good on-stage as I was. A lot of people were commenting on this powerful aura of electric energy that I emanated.

I didn't want a man; all I really loved was my family, myself, and animals. I became a vegetarian again.

I finally let myself be me. I just became Bebe. I no longer needed to find my validity in others. I didn't give a flying fuck what any-body thought of me. It was an attitude that served me well when I went up onstage and rocked.

In October 1999, Coyote and I were finally divorced. He moved to L.A. and has stayed out of my life. He has since remarried, but he still carries a lot of overboard anger, even today.

As for Elvis, when the Burt Bacharach/Elvis Costello collabora-tion, *Painted from Memory*, came out there was an article about it in *Details*, which said, "And the lyrics, most of them dealing with lost love, broken relationships, happy days long gone, or missed oppor-tunities, dwell almost gleefully in the past." (In "My Thief," there is a man who would rather have haunting dreams than no dreams at all.) It went on to say, "The lyrics stand among Costello's best. They are all so focused, in this case on a mood very much like that in 'God Give Me Strength,' which appears here as the album's closer. 'It's a sad song which didn't have a heated frame of mind,' Costello said of that track, poignantly pinpointing it perfectly, 'Where you halfway enjoy being sad and halfway use it to go to some other place.' " I rest my case.

It's scary what Elvis does. He writes these lyrics because he knows I will see them, but he also knows that if I try to express this to people, they will think I am nuts. He wants people to think I'm crazy; it delights him. *But deep down he knows the truth.*

I have no regrets that the *Mojo* interview ended my marriage. I should never have married Coyote; I had no business marrying someone I barely knew. But when I put myself into these situations, I somehow get myself out of them. I have managed to turn the pain into energy. And as I have been writing this book, I've been discovering many things. I realize that I'm in the zone. I am undergoing a spiritual awakening, a rebirth as a woman. For the first time in my life, I am free. I am stuck 100 percent with me, and something is happening to me both spiritually, and professionally as a woman. I'd decided I wasn't going to let age or experiences stop me from being who I am. When I least expected it, I met a wonderful man, Jim Wallerstein.

When I broke up with Coyote, I rented a car, took the mattress I slept on with him, put it in the trunk, and drove out to New Jersey with my crazy friend Liz from Colorado. We were pretending we were Mafia wives looking for a place to burn the evidence. We had lighter fluid, the whole nine yards. So Liz said, "Let's go to

I still love top hats—Bebe today, 2000/DAVID CROLAND

Hackensack; I know my way around Hackensack." Liz knew her way around because she had lived in Hackensack as a young girl. So we drove to Hackensack. It was so much fun. We went to this open lot, where you could imagine many murders having occurred. We burned the mattress I slept on with Coyote, and it was great.

I told Jim Wallerstein this on our third or fourth date. He was

With my sweetheart Jim Wallerstein–
March 2000, NYC/DAVID CROLAND

Me and Jim with one of my oldest and
dearest friends, Bob Gruen, at his
opening/BOB GRUEN

born in Hackensack, the town in which I burned my marital bed. I think that is just fabulous. I wrote a song about Jim before I even met him called "Cosmic Kiss": "Wrap me up in your cosmic kiss/ I've always wanted to feel like this./ Cover me in your warm, soft fire/ Speak to me with your cross-fire choir." Everything about my life is starting to jell. It's a wonderful moment for me as a human being, and I feel fortunate to be able to share it.

And my mother, God, I just love her so much! I have a great deal of respect for her, and now I realize how much she loves me and that I didn't appreciate this love for a long time. My mom, my daughter, and I are this dynamic trio. Liv lives in New York, but she travels constantly. When she's here, we go to dinner or to a play. She'll invite me to a screening or to an event with her and we'll go on a little date. We're great friends. It's a wonderful relationship. It's really fun to hang out with her now, without the pressure of being the person who calls the shots: no, leave her alone, step back, no pictures. It's kind of fun just being the mom and watching her blossom. It's really exciting, and I'm loving it.

Another thing that I love is that the younger generation accepts me for who I am and what I've done; perhaps they understand me better than my peers. I love the fact that when I go to a club now, some twenty-two-year-old model will come running up to me saying, "Are you Bebe Buell? Oh my God, I loved you when I was twelve!" It never ceases to amaze me. I sign more autographs now than I did when I was a top model. I'm always appreciative and grateful for people's attention and the fact that they notice what I did.

It's like they say: If you do anything long enough, you begin to gain respect. For me now to have the respect of my peers, who used to call me names because I had a pop-star fetish, is something to relish. People come up to me now and say, "You deserve whatever you're getting. You're a wonderful mother. We hope that you have all the success in the world." That kind of thing proves to me that I had all my priorities straight.

Although I've had lots of ups and downs and twists and turns in my life, I am proud of everything I have done. I am proud of having brought to all of my relationships a positive, encouraging, collaborative energy that has been a source of inspiration for others. I'm

341

proud of having come through twenty-eight years on the rock beat with a rebel heart, without having at any time come even close to being an alcoholic or a drug addict. As far as I know, that alone is a fairly unique achievement.

I finally came full circle in my life, after I'd gone through all the horror. I got my head together. I no longer needed the antidepressants; they'd done their job. I saw my shrink once every three months, instead of once a week. I was at a point where I was empowered, and I felt strong.

On July 14, 2000, I played a birthday concert at Don Hill's, which was the best experience of my performing career thus far. Don's is a small club in downtown Manhattan, and I'd played there many times. It holds a couple of hundred people, tops. Normally, I'd hang out in the club before a show because it feels like an extension of my living room. I'd talk with people. But this night was special. I went early and stayed in my dressing room, getting ready to

Getting ready to rock—the dressing room at Don Hill's before the show, 2000/BOB GRUEN

With my old mate, "Keef", 2001/LIV TYLER

go on. I could feel the club filling up. I was nervous, but in a way, you want to be nervous when you perform.

I had to walk from my dressing room through the audience to reach the stage. As soon as I came out and saw the crowd, I got this wonderful feeling I always get when I know people are there because they've heard that I'm good: "This chick can rock! This girl can really put on a show!" When people saw me coming, the crowd parted to let me through. I felt their energy. People were yelling, "Yeeeeaaaaah!" I was walking through a corridor of positive energy. People were patting me on the back, and all around me, I heard them saying, "Happy Birthday, Bebe!" Wow! I thought. These people are really giving me support.

My band was already onstage. They started playing our opening song, "Cool." There are no stairs at Don Hill's, so I had to roll onto the stage. Then I just stood there and looked at the audience, inviting them to let me know they were happy that I was there, and they did! They all ran to the front of the stage like a wave; it was mind-blowing. They were pressed up against it, girls and boys and young kids and superstars. I looked into their faces, and I saw Joaquin Phoenix! I also saw my daughter, Casey Affleck, and Carey Hamilton. I was thinking, Oh my God, everyone is really embracing me. I like the youthfulness of my audience; they dig what I do. I'm not playing for a bunch of blues connoisseurs; I'm playing for kids, and they love it.

It's a little nerve-racking when you first go up onstage. As I started singing "Cool," I was feeling that first rush of adrenaline. It was so intense, it hurt a little at first, but then it felt like a million bucks. As soon as I'm onstage, all fears and inhibitions are erased; I become another person—the mother of rock 'n' roll—but I feel like Iggy Pop. I feel strong; I feel like I own that stage. And it just gets better as the show goes on.

I did a whole set of my own songs, plus two covers, "Baby Baby," an old Vibrators hit from the seventies, and Motörhead's "I'll Be Your Sister." Normally, I leave the stage at the end of the show and wait to be called back, but this night, I just said, "Do I really have to leave to do an encore?" Because I didn't want to leave that stage. So I didn't leave; I did "Get Some" and "We Call It Rock."

After the show, I went straight down to the dressing room. Before I knew it, the place was crawling with people. Someone brought me a bottle of champagne. Liv was saying, "Mommy! It was the best show you've ever done! Oh my God! You were amazing!"

"Honey, you say that every time I play."

"But it's the truth! Each show gets better. Every time I see you, it gets better and better." To hear that always makes me feel a good feeling, because I know I'm growing as a performer. I don't think any entertainer ever feels satisfied; you always think you could do better. So when people tell you, "It's the best show you've ever done!" you think, Okay, at least there's growth. That's very important to me.

I was more surprised to hear Jimmy Page was at the show than anybody else. He was in town with the Black Crowes, and I guess he was curious. I think anybody from my past is curious to see me play. Michael Stipe also came to the show, and he told me how surprised he was, how refreshing it was, and how happy he was that I was good. Steven Tyler has seen me perform, and he calls me the Ayatollette of Rock 'n' Roll, whatever that is. I've had people from bands come to see me. I hear sometimes about people who have been at a show, but I don't know because they leave before I come offstage, or they leave while I'm in the dressing room. Not everybody who comes to see me comes back and says hello. When Danny Fields came to see me for the first time, he got on the ground and kissed my feet. He was so cute. He might have had a few, but he got down on the floor and literally kissed my shiny leather boots. It was utterly charming.

I kept wanting to go back upstairs, where there was more air. It was July, and it was close down there, but people just love to squeeze into a space that's too small. Andy Warhol was right when he said, "Always throw a party in a room that's too small, because it will look like it's more crowded." I always think of Andy in those kinds of situations, because everything he ever said always turns out to make perfect sense eventually. Finally, after we hung out downstairs for a long time, we went upstairs. A lot of people had left, so we had the club to ourselves. Bob Gruen stayed, as did all the kids. And there were people like David Croland and Liz Derringer, people who have known me since the beginning. It was fun. Liv gave me a birthday cake and sang "Happy Birthday." It was a complete shock to have Joaquin there. Despite the fact that he was my daughter's boyfriend for three years, he and I never really did get close; there was always tension between us. So to have everything come full circle, to have him at my show, giving me support and expressing satisfaction about the performance, really touched me. He gave me a hug and said, "You were amazing!"

I hear that kind of thing a lot. The other thing I frequently hear is "I have a newfound respect for you now. I had no idea." Why should anybody be shocked that I'm a competent performer? I've seen the greatest performers in the world onstage, and I've watched the greatest managers in the world do business; I've watched successes and downfalls. I've sucked it all in like a human sponge. Why should it shock anyone that being onstage would be second nature to me? Also, why don't people remember that I started performing in 1980? I've been onstage for twenty years, and I'm a veteran.

I've had my supporters: Joey Ramone thought I was great ten years ago, and Rick Derringer thought I was great twenty years ago. So did Ric Ocasek, and Todd, but there was always an undertone that maybe people thought I was great because they had a crush on me, or perhaps they were coming to see me because I had dated them. Sometimes I felt like the Marion Davies of rock 'n' roll.

When I go up onstage now, I feel like I own that stage, and it's definitely a very good feeling to have people come back and tell me I look like I own it. But the twenty-year-old who's in the front row, going mad over me, who thinks I'm twenty-eight, doesn't realize he was born the same year I stepped onstage. Some of the younger people who come to see me now say, "Wow! She's the best-kept secret." I want to tell them, "No, honey, I was doing this before you were born."

Rock 'n' roll keeps you young. I don't think you're ever too old to rock. In fact, I don't think you're ever too old to do anything. We need to get rid of that kind of age barrier. If I can accomplish becoming a full-fledged rock star, not just a cult figure—"Cult Mommy," as Liv calls me—and garner success in my forties, I think it would be a victory not only for me but for women everywhere. Society would have to stop putting boundaries on talent.

In August, I went up to Portland, Maine, to give my first show there in eleven years. My last performance in Portland was in 1989, with the Gargoyles, right before I moved back to New York. So this was a return to my hometown. My mother and the rest of my family were going to be there, along with lots of other people. It was an event for Portland, and it was a greater homecoming than I could possibly have imagined. Portland is a wonderful, sophisticated little city. It's got everything—drag queens, crack, museums. I sold out the show, and it was a triumphant return for me, a total rush.

Every time I've returned to Maine during the past six years, I've had a dream that I would own a house there, so I go and look at houses. Our family real estate agent, Karen Wright, who's gotten everybody in my family their houses, would take me around and humor me, showing me houses I could never afford. But finally on this August visit, my luck turned. I heard about a little cul-de-sac, where all of the houses were beautiful little new Victorian-style ones. This seemed too good to be true, because I wanted a house that didn't need 500,000 dollars worth of work, but at the same time I wanted it to look like an old house—in fact, a Victorian house. And now, with the same kind of magic that has made writing this book such an adventure, there was one for sale. It had everything from a hot tub to a two-car garage—even a place for a basketball hoop. I couldn't have dreamed up anything better myself. It was exactly what I wanted.

It was an off-white two-story house with a blue metal roof and wraparound porches on both levels and was situated on half an acre of land at the top of a small hill. You walked in the door and entered a grand cathedral-ceiling living room with a fireplace. There was a guest room and a hot tub off to the right and a kitchen that was large enough to hang out and talk to your friends in while cooking. The area was all open, like a loft. The basement was another dream come true, because I wanted to build a recording studio. On the second floor, there was a spacious landing, another small guest room, and then the huge master bedroom, which also had a fireplace and cathedral ceilings, as well as a big round window that looked very Victorian. There was even a lot next door, which I imagined building a pool on someday.

My mother, my cousin Annie, our real estate agent, and Jim were with me when I looked at it. When everyone got back in the car, I started to cry. It was my dream house, and I was thinking, Why can't this be a year later, when I'd have enough money to buy it?

I knew this was my house and that I was going to get it, but I wasn't sure how. When I got back to New York, I went over to Bob Gruen's to get his opinion. I was fretting away, trying to figure out how I was going to buy this house. Bob was enthusiastic. "Sounds great. I hope you get it," he said. "We'll come visit."

"You don't understand, Bob!" I said. "I designed this house in a dream, and God went and built it. Then he just tapped me on my shoulder and said, 'Oh, Bebe, the house is ready.'"

I called my apartment from Bob's place to check my messages. Liv had called, saying, "Hi, Mommy, I'm back! I've got something for you that I got in Morocco."

I immediately called her and said, "I'm right around the corner at Bob's."

"Come over," Liv said. So I went over. She took one look at me and said, "What's wrong with you?"

"Oh, well, I found this house, but . . ." I proceeded to tell her all about the house—we talked about the pros and cons.

Anyway, she thought about it and I think it made sense to her. I also think it gave her a lot of joy that her whole family would be in one place, because my mother was moving to Maine, too, and Annie was already there. I adored the place, so she'd have us all together. Plus her dad lives only an hour and a half away in Massachusetts. The timing was perfect. I figured I was going to be so busy for the next few years, I was going to need this place to unwind myself. It would be a great getaway for Liv, too.

Liv consulted with her business manager, and he talked with me and the real estate agent, and then the real estate agent spoke to the owner. It was a private sale, as the house wasn't on the market; that's another reason I think the timing was so synchronistic.

In the winter of 2001, the sale went through. I now own my dream house, thanks to my darling daughter and her unusual generosity and sweetness. What a wonderful thing for her to do for me. The way my life has come together has given me a new confidence. I've always had great posture because of my mother. Some models have horrible posture, but I don't. My manners have always been impeccable, my carriage always grand, but I used to walk like a girl who was scared. Now I'm fulfilled. I've got the strut. I feel like Iggy Pop, man. I strut; I walk like a lizard now. I'm in the zone. Anything is possible.

EPILOGUE

'How I Became Bebe Buell'

I was born on Bastille Day, July 14, 1953. My father wasn't home at the time, and my mother didn't want to give me a name until he got back, so all the nurses called me Baby Buell, and that just stuck. My formal name is Beverle Lorence Buell. My father wanted to name me Courtney—isn't that scary—but my mother became attached to the name Bebe.

My father left us and my parents were divorced when I was two. My mother did not remarry until I was eleven, so I grew up depending exclusively on girls for loyalty and friendship. My mom became a role model for independent women. I got my strength from my mother's side of the family. My grandmother was a strong German woman who took no shit from anyone. My mother didn't, either. It meant that I had an open mind about women's abilities. My mother came from a very large family and I had a lot of cousins. My mother's sister died and my mother adopted her daughter, Ann, when she was an infant. My cousin's ten years older than I am. She was raised for her first ten years by my grandparents; then my

The only photo of me with my mom and dad. They were divorced in 1955. My fifth birthday in Virginia Beach, Virginia, 1958/BUELL
PRIVATE COLLECTION

Me, age 4, and Mom at Virginia Beach, Virginia, 1957/BUELL
PRIVATE COLLECTION

mother took her in. Mom always made sure that Annie and I had the best clothes. We always lived in nice places and had a Plymouth station wagon or a Cadillac. My mother decorated everything gorgeously. I considered my mother a very beautiful woman. To me, she looked like Marilyn Monroe. She was blond, gorgeous physically. She modeled, and she worked in a fashionable woman's shop, Rose Hall. She dabbled in operating a charm school in Houston, Texas, before I was born.

In his forties, my father went on to get his Ph.D. in psychology and teach at the university in Tallahassee. He was considered highly intelligent and gifted. He was certainly in a position to contribute more than the one hundred dollars a month he paid my mother for child support, and to take more of an initiative to see me.

I have really weird, vague memories of my father darting in and out and always looking dashing in his military uniform. He was a commander in the navy, a pilot, a war hero. He was born in Iowa. He was a handsome devil—a lady-killer. I inherited his eyes. He smelled like newness. He had that school-supply smell. Maybe that's why I didn't like school. But he really didn't mean much to me because he wasn't in my life for very long. And when I did see him, it was always painful, never pleasurable. I always had the feeling that he would be leaving soon. And I didn't like the energy between him and my mother. It defined the way I looked at men for the rest of my life. I always looked for the dominating, dashing man in a uniform who was always saying good-bye and rushing off. That made me angry as a child. I felt that *I* wanted to be free to go away, to fly a plane. I have absolutely no problem with not having had my father in my life.

A tragedy happened to me in 1957, when I was four. I had a tonsillectomy, which was performed by a drunken doctor. His knife slipped, which caused me to bleed profusely. My throat was badly lacerated, which may account for my R&B voice. I was in a military hospital, so the doctor was protected from lawsuits. I had packing in my nose and a pad underneath me, because I was bleeding both externally and internally. I was given blood transfusions. According to my father, I almost died. He came to see me in the hospital. I have a powerful memory of my father visiting me. There were welts all over my arm from the transfusions, and I was crying. My father panicked. He removed the IV needle from my arm and took me in his arms. I was screaming, and he was screaming at the nurse that they had overtransfused me.

Between the ages of five and eight, I went through an impish phase, where I looked exactly like Mia Farrow. My mother had my hair cut short, and I was a lean, sun-kissed cherub. I suddenly had an effect on men, which perplexed me.

I visited my grandparents in North Carolina, where my cousin Annie lived. She had her walls covered with 45 sleeves of Elvis Presley. Even though he was a German farmer, my grandfather Curtis was one of the coolest guys. He had the bluest eyes and an amazing head of hair, like a whip. He would put grease in it every day to make it gorgeous, and he could play the banjo. So very early on, I was drawn to people who were artistic, had great hair, and could play a stringed instrument.

My mother really did her best to make my life colorful. She had bohemian friends. She knew decorators, people who did Broadway shows. She was the only person in the neighborhood who tolerated gays. She had friends in New York City. My mother's friends Poppy and Tilly had a book at their house with a photograph of Oscar Wilde. It was that famous one of him when he first came to America—standing in a blue velvet room like Napoléon, wearing a magnificently ruffled shirt. His long black hair was parted in the middle, the way John Lennon wore his in 1970. At age eight, I thought, Okay! That's the guy for me! I had a similar reaction when I saw pictures of Liszt or Chopin. Their essence sparked the same thing in me that was sparked by Brian Jones. I latched right onto anything English.

Like Liv and me twenty years later, my mother and I were "different." Mom had the coolest clothes. A marble table was the only thing that sat in our sixties living room. And we had an orange carpet and fashionable drapes! My mother had a flair for fashion and for life! I always had a beautiful bedroom. My mother was so offbeat and interesting. Once, she picked me up from school and said, "Oh, I have a beautiful present for you. You'll just die!" She'd created a headboard for my bed out of an abandoned Victorian fence. She decided to have it painted purple, then stuck it on the back of my bed. Soon I had a feeling that I was different from the other kids—people treated me differently. I was more provocative than attractive. I had a big presence even when I was a kid. I wanted to be both loved and heard.

At ten, I discovered my first role model, the British actress Hayley Mills, who appeared in *The Parent Trap*. I was a sucker for this movie about twin girls, one English and one American, trying to get their parents back together. I fell madly in love with her when she sang that song "Let's Get Together." It was the first time I saw a girl who looked like me play the guitar, and it killed me. I wanted to be like her. People thought I looked like her because of my blond hair and blue eyes. But what attracted me most were her bangs, her singing, and the way she licked her lips. By the time I left the theater, I'd licked my lips so much, I got a chapped ring around my mouth.

I first heard of the Beatles when I was in fifth grade at a Catholic school in Virginia. One of the girls in my class had an older brother who came to our school one day with English magazines featuring pictures of the Beatles. In the next month or two, all the American teen magazines followed suit. We saw the pictures before we heard the music. I was totally into George and his girlfriend, Patti Boyd. I thought she was everything a girl should be. I loved everything about her when she appeared in *A Hard Day's Night*. I followed their girlfriends as closely as I followed my favorite pop stars—how they dressed, what they looked like, and how they met these rock stars. The whole scenario was very important to me. It was the hair and the vibe: I was used to the Elvis Presley greaser thing as being attractive, and when the Beatles came along, they seemed fresher, more rebellious. They were dressed in suits—I thought they were very stylish, but I really wanted them to take their jackets off so I could see what was underneath. When "I Want to Hold Your Hand" was released, everybody in the school went nuts. We weren't really listening to rock music at that time. We listened to a very tame kind of pop music, or the black music that was coming out of Detroit and Roy Orbison. I had some friends who became entirely obsessed with the Beatles. Even though they were singing about holding hands, there was something very sexy about it. I listened to the Dave Clark Five right along with the Beatles. They were very fun; their sound was a little edgy.

When we lived in Virginia Beach, Annie was seventeen and in high school! She let me go out with her and she would make me duck in the backseat when we went to the movies. I did all that *American Graffiti* stuff. I got to play all the games when we drove around the drive-in. I would be the one to get out of the car and fetch the guy, then take him back to talk to my cousin. I got to be a little sister, which was really wonderful.

"Water ballet": being held above Charles "Tommy" Cayce, the grandson of psychic Edgar Cayce and my swimming instructor in Virginia Beach, 1960/BUELL
PRIVATE COLLECTION

The first experiences I had going to shows were when my cousin would take me to multiple-billed rock shows. We saw Sonny and Cher, Herman's Hermits, and Gerry and the Pacemakers on one bill. It was the excitement of the participation and everyone's abandon that I really loved about rock and roll. It oozed sex. It absolutely molded my desires of what I wanted in a mate. It wasn't Elvis Presley who did that for me. I think he looked cool, but I thought he had the same hair as my grandfather—a pompadour. Now when I look at Elvis, I think he oozes sexuality, but almost in a wholesome way.

I went to an all-girl Catholic boarding school, which was very strict. In the sixth grade, I got a transistor radio. But we weren't allowed to listen to radios except at recess, so we used to listen to them under our pillows at night. I remember the first time I heard songs like "Valerie" by the Monkees. At that age, you start experimenting with all kinds of things, such as masturbating. My first sexual excitement came from listening to my transistor radio in my bed. And I felt the same thing on horses, of course. We all got off on horses when we were twelve. Riding and swimming were my favorite sports.

When I was twelve, I really loved the Animals. The Rolling Stones sang about sex, but the Animals sang about rebellion, about getting out of a town and "It's My Life"—all the things that you could relate to if you were living in a small town. Eric Burdon represented something a little bit taboo. The first record that my mother actually confiscated and wouldn't let me listen to was my Animals record, because I would march around the house singing at the top of my lungs "We Gotta Get out of this Place" and "It's My Life." My mom thought I was a little young to have that kind of attitude.

There was a stupid dance that Freddie & the Dreamers did, and everybody at school was doing it. Annie knew about all the dances, like the Dirty Dog. She taught me the Dirty Dog, and I taught the other girls in school how to do it. I went to school one day and said, "No, no, no, that is not how we dance. Let me show you how to do this dance called the Dirty Dog." There I was, grinding my brains out, and the nuns came along and sent me home. They told my mother I was making vulgar gestures at the other students. I got sent home for making "obscene gestures." I was lucky because Annie knew a lot about music. She told me the Dirty Dog was derived from black music, and that the Stones and the Animals derived their dance steps, sliding across the floor and all that, from James Brown and Little Richard.

I remember the first time I saw a real rock 'n' roll bulge. It was on Mick Jagger at my first big rock 'n' roll concert, the Stones at the Virginia Beach Civic Center, when I was about twelve. I had my little Marianne Faithfull haircut and was ready to go. And my mom let me wear lipstick, so it was a big night for me. Mick was wearing white trousers, so the bulge was just ridiculously prominent. From then on, whenever I saw a picture of a cool rock 'n' roll guy, if he didn't have a bulge in his pants, I would think, Something's wrong. A bulge was style; it was sexy. It was a statement. I had my Instamatic camera with me, but she forbade me to go to the front, where there was a whole line of policemen. But as soon as she went to the bathroom, boy, I charged. And it looked real funny, because nobody was charging. I remember Mick Jagger looking out into the audience and saying, "You really are a quiet lot." Nobody was screaming. But I ran up, knelt down, picked up my camera, and went *clicko*. I have pictures of Brian Jones. To the Stones, it was wonderful that somebody was moving. Finally, this cop came over and grabbed my arm, and it was real intense, because he did not move from his position against the stage. He was macho! He tried to move me, and I said, "No way." Keith came over to the edge of the stage and took his foot and pushed the cop lightly with it. He said, "Leave her alone. She's just a little girl." And they let me stay there. It took five fucking minutes for the whole place to be up and screaming, "Yeah, if she gets to do it, so do we!"

When I was little and playing rock star in front of my mirror, using my hairbrush for a microphone, I would put on a pair of tight pants and stuff a sock in there and pretend I was Mick Jagger. I really wanted to be a boy. I liked that look, and I liked what it represented.

One Halloween at boarding school, I dressed up as a witch, but underneath I had on another costume, which made me look like Mick Jagger. When the nuns turned around, I pulled up my witch costume for my classmates. The nuns turned back and I dropped the skirt. Finally, Sister Regina Madonna said, "What's everyone laughing about? Share the joke! I know it's you, Bebe Buell!"

"No, no, not me," I said. Finally, she pulled up my dress and saw what was underneath. She said, "Okay, so you want to be a boy?" For the next two days, I had to be a boy. I had to wear my hair like a boy. It was the weirdest trip!

I was eleven when my mother remarried. Lester Edwin Johnson was a Marine Corps officer. He had a crew cut and crisp clothing. He said "Positive" and "Negative" instead of "Yes" and "No." My mom lost a lot of her sparkle when she got remarried. She no longer had that "Sister, we can do this without a man" attitude. She became a military wife. Lester had deficiencies as a human being. He was a control freak, he drank too much, and he smoked four packs of cigarettes a day. My mother got him off the cigarettes. Then he smoked a pipe. I just never felt that he liked me. I think he felt that I was a rebel, and he certainly was not. He was a military man and a conformist. I bitched about Vietnam. When he went there, I had no compassion. He had a very dominating, "in charge" personality, and he never encouraged my endeavours.

I was an incredible swimmer and a talented artist, but he never complimented me. He was hard on me. Whereas my mother would buy me an easel and say, "Paint, child!" And if I sat down and made a racket on the piano, my mother never discouraged me by telling me not to tinker. She would brag to all her friends that I could play songs by ear. So that was the big difference between them. When my stepfather came along, our life became more rigid and our bohemian lifestyle changed. My mother became more conscious of

Shooting hoops at Villa Maria Academy, 1966/BUELL PRIVATE COLLECTION

perfection. I wasn't as close to her as I had been before. She went from being a Democrat to a Republican—Kennedy to Nixon. I felt completely left out. I was a hyperactive child; like Liv, I suffered from attention deficit disorder, except we didn't know all that stuff back then. I was a ball of fire. I did everything to my mother that my daughter turned out to do to me! But by the time Liv was a child, we knew what it all meant, so I knew how to cope. She turned out the way she did because I was able to nurture the art within her, which found its fruition in the beautiful actress she became.

When my mother remarried, I was packed off to a Catholic boarding school, the Villa Maria Academy, in Lynchburg, Virginia. Here from sixth through eighth grades, I lived my early teenage years in tune with the explosive rock 'n' roll culture. At boarding school, I was the girl who knew about rock and roll. I knew all the cool songs. When I came back from vacation, I showed people how to move like Mitch Ryder. I sang "Devil with a Blue Dress On." I got a petition up in eighth grade to watch the Monkees' weekly TV show.

I was five nine by the time I was twelve, so I played basketball. By thirteen, I'd become a basketball star and the bad girl at school—just not bad enough to get expelled. I played forward on the basketball team. That's the star position—you make the baskets. The guards block you from making the baskets, or protect you when you are trying to make your baskets. I started as a guard because of my height, but I wasn't able to prevent people from making baskets. I didn't have it in me. I just loved watching people make baskets! To me, it didn't matter which side made them. The nuns decided that I should shoot baskets; they fostered that ability. I was unbelievable; I could shoot from halfway across the court. I'm still great at it. Being a tad bit obsessive-compulsive, getting balls in holes was right up my alley. And doing it well was like, Yeah! I got respect from the kids. But in terms of the success you are told you should get—scholastic overachiever, the girl who comes up with the brilliant science project—I wasn't any good. The only respect I got was because of my ability to shoot hoops.

The way I saw it, my parents got rid of me. I think Lester felt I needed disciplining. They thought I had been allowed to run free and do what I wanted. My mother got pregnant twice while married to Les. She lost two sets of twins. I almost had four brothers. That was a lot for her to put up with, but I was at boarding school and missed all of it.

One of my teachers, Mother Seraphin, had a profound love for me, which touched me deeply. She was short and stocky and meaner than the meanest rooster in the henhouse. If she cracked a smile, you really felt it meant something, because she always had a chip on her shoulder. Fast and stern, she walked, ate, and moved like a little bulldog. She crossed herself that way, too. When you were in trouble and had to be spanked, she'd take your hand and move you around in a circle while she pounded your ass with a ruler. My friends and I called it the "roundy roundy." While you were getting your ass pounded, you were also getting spun around until you were dizzy. Right before she got ready to hit, she pulled your pants down. It was more a humiliation than anything else.

Boarding school years–my first fan, Mother Seraphin, my mentor at Villa Maria Academy–1964-66, Grades 6-8/BUELL PRIVATE COLLECTION

We didn't have names for hyperactivity, inability to concentrate, and screaming matches with nuns. Mother Seraphin didn't expel me, because she knew that was what I wanted. I wasn't bad in her eyes. She thought I'd be a great achiever.

I played a tambourine in the choir. I developed quickly. I was the first person at school to wear a bra, but I was the last to start my period, and everyone thought that was freaky. The first time people told me I needed a bra, I was out at my neighbor's, bouncing on the trampoline, and all my friends really came down on me. They said, "Bebe, tell your mother to get you a trainer bra. This is terrible." So I went home and said, "Mom, everyone says I really need a bra."

"That's too bad," she said. "You don't need one yet." But my mother finally did get me the bra. I think she realized she had to.

———

I was one of millions of prepubescent and pubescent girls whose hearts and minds were invaded by the Beatles in 1964 and conquered by the Rolling Stones in 1966, so what made me stand out among them? What propelled me to dream of my own stardom? When people write about the British Invasion now, they treat it as if it was just a 1960s version of a contemporary trend, but at the time, it didn't just change music; it changed lives. I was very susceptible to it. Music for me was much more than just a girl liking songs and boys from afar. Music represented freedom, inspiration, rebellion. The British bands brought a whole new generation of British girls into the lime-light—Marianne Faithfull, Chrissie Shrimpton, Julie Christie, Patti Boyd, Linda Keith, Anita Pallenberg, and Hayley Mills, among others. The majority of my friends hated these competitors for their heroes' attention, but I was as infatuated with them as I was with the boys in the bands. When I was a young girl, I used to look at Marianne Faithfull and Anita Pallenberg and think those girls were gorgeous. I used to think, Jesus, they are so free. They are so wild-looking. These must be the girls that the guys write the songs about. These must be the girls that make the whole fucking thing tick. That was before they called girls "groupies."

When the Rolling Stones and the Who and the Beatles first became popular, the girls they hung around with were exceptional creatures. Then girls started hanging around like flies. It got cheap on a lot of levels, because girls started hanging out in alleyways like cats, wearing fishnet stockings and meowing at the boys. They were acting like prostitutes, instead of playing a real muse role, having real relationships.

And then it got down to which fan club you were in: the Beatles versus the Stones. You couldn't be both. Kids would get really up-pity—you had to pick. I don't think that just because you liked the Stones better you were a bad kid. Actually, I found the good little girls liked the Stones, and the bad little girls liked the Beatles—I think the good little girls had bigger imaginations. To me, Mick Jagger was the ideal male. When we first heard "Satisfaction," it would whip us into a frenzy. It was the dirtiest record on earth. You could only play it when your mom wasn't home.

I immediately realized that I was not going to be a conformist, and I was not going to be a normal girl. The Rolling Stones did

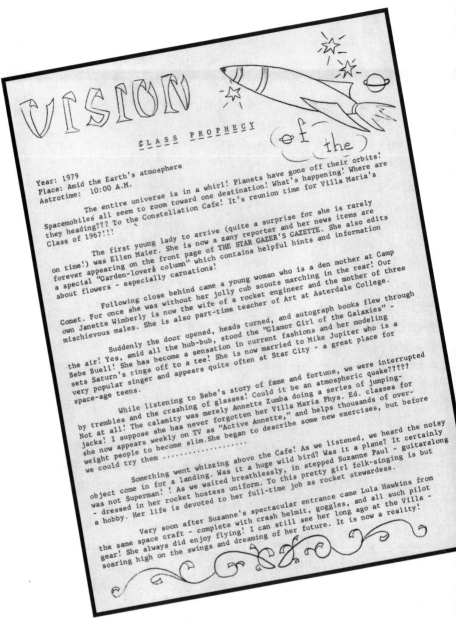

VISION

CLASS PROPHECY (of the)

Year: 1979
Place: Amid the Earth's atmosphere
Astrotime: 10:00 A.M.

The entire universe is in a whirl! Planets have gone off their orbits! Spacemobiles all seem to zoom toward one destination! What's happening! Where are they heading??? To the Constellation Cafe! It's reunion time for Villa Maria's Class of 1967!!!

The first young lady to arrive (quite a surprise for she is rarely on time!) was Ellen Maier. She is now a zany reporter and her news items are forever appearing on the front page of THE STAR GAZER'S GAZETTE. She also edits a special "Garden-lover's column" which contains helpful hints and information about flowers - especially carnations!

Following close behind came a young woman who is a den mother at Camp Comet. For once she was without her jolly cub scouts marching in the rear! Our own Janette Wimberly is now the wife of a rocket engineer and the mother of three mischievous males. She is also part-time teacher of Art at Asterdale College.

Suddenly the door opened, heads turned, and autograph books flew through the air! Yes, amid all the hub-bub, stood the "Glamor Girl of the Galaxies" - Bebe Buell! She has become a sensation in current fashions and her modeling sets Saturn's rings off to a tee! She is now married to Mike Jupiter who is a very popular singer and appears quite often at Star City - a great place for space-age teens.

While listening to Bebe's story of fame and fortune, we were interrupted by trembles and the crashing of glasses! Could it be an atmospheric quake????? Not at all! The calamity was merely Annette Zumba doing a series of jumping-jacks! I suppose she has never forgotten her Villa Maria Phys. Ed. classes for she now appears weekly on TV as "Active Annette," and helps thousands of over-weight people to become slim. She began to describe some new exercises, but before we could try them ....

Something went whizzing above the Cafe! As we listened, we heard the noisy object come in for a landing. Was it a huge wild bird? Was it a plane? It certainly was not Superman! ! As we waited breathlessly, in stepped Suzanne Paul - guitaralong - dressed in her rocket hostess uniform. To this pretty girl folk-singing is but a hobby. Her life is devoted to her full-time job as rocket stewardess.

Very soon after Suzanne's spectacular entrance came Lula Hawkins from the same space craft - complete with crash helmit, goggles, and all such pilot gear! She always did enjoy flying! I can still see her long ago at the Villa - soaring high on the swings and dreaming of her future. It is now a reality!

My eighth grade class prophecy, 1966/BUELL PRIVATE COLLECTION

something to me. The second I saw them, that was it. I knew I was going to go to New York to be a model. In my eighth-grade space-themed yearbook, they called me "the glamour girl of the galaxy." They said that my modeling set Saturn's rings off to a T and that I was going to marry Mick Jupiter. I used to tell my mother all the time, "I'm gonna marry Mick Jagger," and she'd say, "Well, that's nice, Bebe."

Starting in eighth grade, students got to live in the big house with the nuns. We slept in a long room, six to a side. My dorm was called Fatima and the sister dorm was called Lourdes. Each girl had a bed, a dresser, and part of a closet. I had a girlfriend, Robin Lewis, who looked just like Mick Jagger, so I called her "Mick." We made out, but we weren't lesbians. We were pretending, practicing. She looked more like Steven than Mick because she was Italian. She would be Mick and I would be Brian. Since I've started to analyze my life while writing this book, I realize that I wanted to *be* Mick Jagger and *fuck* Brian Jones. But I didn't know how to be Mick Jagger.

I loved Brian Jones in his pinstriped suit, playing the harmonica. That's the picture I rubbernecked to get. That's what I wanted. He was sexy playing the harmonica, because he was doing something different; he wasn't just standing there with his guitar. He was talented and brilliant. And my sexual desires went from this Mick thing to wanting Mick with a big brain, too. That's why I found Brian Jones to be the sexy one all of a sudden and why I ended up with a Todd Rundgren. It was also why I ended up with an Elvis Costello. The part of me that was intrigued about where the genius came from got really turned on by the whole essence of the artist. It really captured me. When I first saw the Stones, Mick was in the front, and seeing him was like finally coming face-to-face with a fantasy, but Brian was the one who drew me in. His essence screamed rock and roll. It screamed intelligence. And it screamed something different from the overt sexuality that Mick was oozing, or the stereotypical persona that Keith was emanating. I mean, if you touch Keith Richards, you will turn into rock—he *is* rock and roll. Whereas Brian took it to that deeper level. The gift, the music—where does it come from? I had to find out. I started to become a songwriter and a secret singer, and I realized that songs are gifts from heaven.

Rock and roll music was an environment. I loved the way it looked like those people were living—this wonderful freedom, the attitude of no restrictions, just being able to travel wherever you wanted.

When I was fourteen, my stepfather got stationed in Rhode Island

The summer I turned thirteen in Norfolk, Virginia. Also, the same summer I saw the Rolling Stones–July 1966/BUELL PRIVATE COLLECTION

and I transferred to St. Catherine's Academy in Newport.

I really started to look hot around ninth grade. I began to elongate and thin out. I was constantly told how beautiful I was. When I was thirteen or fourteen, my mom told me that I should be a model. She came from that world. She knew I would have the ability. People would say I was swanlike, willowy, a blond, blue-eyed beauty.

My mother had been reading about Eileen Ford, who had one of the most successful modeling agencies in New York. One article said her ideal model was the Nordic type. I fit the profile to a T. I started fantasizing about escaping and going to New York. I had my mother's *Vogue* magazines and an image of what New York City was like. Once on a drive from Rhode Island to Virginia, we passed through Manhattan on the West Side Highway. I started hyperventilating as I looked at the NYC skyline. I wanted to go there so bad! "Calm down. You'll be here," my mother told me. "You have to finish high school first."

Everybody wanted to go to California in the sixties. All my friends wanted to go to L.A. Not me. New York meant what I was seeing in *Vogue*. Andy Warhol. Nico. I had fantasies of my face flying across the pages of *Vogue*. I cut out pictures of the coolest model of 1970, Lauren Hutton, and stuck my head on them.

Apart from Paul Cowsill, I was terrified of dating. All the guys at school were animals. You sat down in their cars and they just went for it immediately. I didn't like that. I thought sex was something you did when you finally met someone who didn't hit on you like an animal. I felt most comfortable in my room with my rock magazines and my Rolling Stones records and my occasional Dave Clark Five or Monkees record. And I really did withdraw into that little room quite a bit.

I thought that the way that you met people like Mick Jagger was to be a fabulous model, a genius aristocrat, or a movie star. At the beginning of the seventies, there was a different kind of class structure in rock and roll. It was like an aristocratic club. I would look at *Vogue* and see David Bailey pictures and Jean Shrimpton and Twiggy, and it all made perfect sense to me and I wanted to be a part of it.

ACKNOWLEDGMENTS

For someone who has always had to keep secrets, writing my memoirs was a soul-searching experience and a revelation. *Liberating* would be an understatement. Life is a precious gift, and, as Oscar Wilde said, "Life is what you make it." It's been a bumpy ride, with highs and lows, love and loss, pain and growth. The one thing I've learned is that it is never too late to change, evolve, or take charge. You're never too old to rock—or to do anything, for that matter. There is no such thing as "too late." You can never have enough experiences. And with experience comes wisdom.

This book is a celebration of four decades of pop culture: my loves, my lessons, and my personal journey.

I want to thank the following:

New York City for always inviting me back with open arms and embracing my ventures as an artist; Portland, Maine, for keeping me sane; and London for always "getting it."

Todd Rundgren, for reasons even I don't understand.

My beautiful family—my mommy, Dorothea; Annie and Teddy; Julia, Harry, and Jim; Tom and Heather; and my dear partner, Jim Wallerstein and his entire family. My precious daughter, Liv, whose true understanding of me has given me strength and independence as a woman and fulfillment as a mother. You will always be the one true love of my lifetimes—past and future. Shine on, my sweetest angel. Royston and all Langdons.

My darling "real" friends who have loved me unconditionally and completely through thick and thin: Liz Derringer, Ivan Suvanjieff, Pam Turbov, Mark Bacine, David Croland, Don Crosby and the Crosby clan, Pip Walter, Bob and Elizabeth Gruen, Missy and Tom Sesto, Beth Blood, Beth Simkoff, Charles E. Hall, Elvis Costello, Steven Tyler, Ric Ocasek, Ginger Coyote,

Mort Todd, Mariah Aguiar, and Roger Friedman—your constant and devoted dedication has been unfailing. Victor Bockris for riding the roller coaster with me. The Rolling Stones for stimulating my libido. Clive Arrowsmith for opening my Third Eye.

Everyone at IMG—Chuck Bennett, Stewart Ross, Jan Planit and Jonathan Pang—for seeing my vision. Kurt J. Schoeppler for his excellent financial advice. The Huvane Brothers and Scott Landis for taking care of my baby girl. My agent, David Vigliano, for giving me confidence. St. Martin's Press and Sally Richardson for giving me the chance to shine on my own. Elizabeth Beier for her understanding and respect from the onset. Michael Connor for his assistance. Steve Snider for seeing beauty the same way I do. James Sinclair and Kathryn Parise for artistic symmetry. Gregg Sullivan, John Murphy, and Dori Weintraub for "press perfection!" Mick Rock for always having the "perfect light." Lynn Goldsmith for taking the shots that started it all.

My band—David Matos, Gregg Carey, and Tommy Furar, who have never wavered in their belief in me as an entertainer. Don Hill—my mentor. Hilly Kristal and Louise for "digging it" first, Danny Fields for being "Danny," and for all those about to rock, I salute you!

The "girls"—Debbie Harry, Chrissie Hynde, Joan Jett, Patti Smith, Marianne Faithfull, and Anita Pallenberg—you're still my "goddesses."

The "other girls"—Miss Guy, Mistress Formika, Michael Schmidt, Lily of the Valley, Sherry Vine, Dean Johnson, Michael Musto, Leee Black Childers, and Jayne County—thanks for the "tips" on everything and anything.

Robert and Katherine Altman for their warmth. Don Fleming for his belief in my songs. Stephen Davis, for anointing me "Eagle Woman." Hugh Hefner and *Playboy*, which changed my life completely. Cameron Crowe and Nancy Wilson for being so cool and perceptive, John and Mellow Lomba—thanks for the "comeback." Norah Lawlor for the wonderful parties.

All the photographers for your gorgeous images, which are such an important part of this book. Virginia from Starfile.

Dr. Donna Lewinter, Sirius Trixon, Mat Snow, and Stephanie Chernikowski for the phone and psychiatric sessions.

My most beloved animals—Furburger, Little Man, Raheena, Seymour, Chiquita, and Pancho—my little "spirit guides."

My angels, who have wrapped their warm wings around me more than once. My "other" angels, Jeanne Theis, Michelle Myer, Stiv Bators, J. T. Walsh, Johnny Thunders, John Lennon, and Mossy, for watching over me.

My higher power, for allowing me to do what I love most—playing loud, nasty, sexy, raw, and, most of all, *fun* rock 'n' roll.

At the time this book went to press, some new and interesting things have happened. I have made amends with Cyrinda Foxe and let go of any old, negative feelings. I want to send her my love and support. I also want to embrace anyone from my past—all the ups and downs—good and bad—right or wrong. At this point in my life journey, I have only positive feelings and wonderful memories. Even Lisa Robinson and I had a lovely chat at the Sony Records party last year. I realized she's really not so bad and actually kind of fun. And I adore Linda Stein—a real, original, dear person.

I'm excited to start working on my next book, *The Rock 'n' Roll Book of Etiquette: Inside Rock Society.* It's an idea I have had for twenty years, inspired by my darling mother, who is the founder of the Protocol School of Washington and the most polite person I have ever known. See how the girls in this family stick together? That's what family is all about—including my extended family and my rock 'n' roll family, of which I am blessed to be a part.

I Love You XXXX

Bebe Buell

NYC 2001

Joey Ramone, 1951-2001. RIP, Dear Angel/NORMAN BLAKE

DISCOGRAPHY

1981 *COVERS GIRL*

12-inch EP, 4 songs: "My Little Red Book," "Wild One Forever," "Little Black Egg," "Funtime." Rhino, United States, produced by Ric Ocasek and Rick Derringer.

"I would've made a record a long time ago, but I wanted to do it when people would accept me as a singer instead of somebody's girlfriend. Elvis heard me singing to an old Smokey Robinson song that was on the radio one day and he said I was incredible.

My first record for Rhino—a four-song EP produced by Ric Ocasek and Rick Derringer/RICHARD CREAMER

Ric and Bebe/BUELL PRIVATE COLLECTION

That was good enough for me." Bebe Buell, in *Creem*, October 1980.

"In February, Bebe went into the studio with old friends Derringer and Ocasek. 'Ric had heard me sing and he thought I should do it,' she said.

"The songs produced by

367

Derringer are the rocking 'Little Red Book,' originally done by Love, and 'Wild One Forever,' a ballad with lush, full backing. Written by Tom Petty.

"Ocasek and other members of the Cars play on 'Little Black Egg,' a funky-bumpy number which was 'a hit in Ohio' in the 1960s for the Night-crawlers, and a wild version of Iggy Pop's 'Funtime' with lots of Elliot Easton on guitar.

"Bebe is a smart, full-throated vocalist in the style of the Pretenders' Chrissie Hynde. She proved herself at ease with the variety of material on the demo tape and on rehearsal tapes with the B-Sides.

"Comprised of George Gordon on lead guitar, Don Crosby on rhythm, Beth Blood on bass, and Mike McInnis on drums, the B-Sides sound like a punchy powerful unit." Doug Warren, *Maine Sunday Telegram*, October 26, 1980.

" 'I've been around the music business for years,' said Miss Buell, a poised Virginian native who dated rock luminary Todd Rundgren from 1974 to 1977. 'I knew I wanted to get into music myself, so I was always learning, always observing.

" 'Sometimes people would stereotype me as someone who was just hanging around the rock scene, and I'd think to myself, "Hey, why do you think I'm here—to snag a husband? I want to do this myself." ' " Dyke Hendrickson, *Evening Express* (Portland, Maine), November 4, 1980.

"This was one of the strongest independent debuts to date, with more than one critic comparing her powerful voice to 'a rockin' Brenda Lee.' That pillar of taste, Motörhead's Lemmy, says she sounds like 'a teenage boy,' which, we believe, was meant as a big compliment." Bebe Buell Bio/Press release.

1982 "LITTLE BLACK EGG" (A SIDE)/"FUNTIME" (B SIDE)
7-inch single. Moonlight, England.

"American ex-model Bebe does have a great voice. The A side is unfortunately a bit dull. For some strange reason it makes me think of Carlene Carter. Not that she's dull of course, only the B side is so much better. It's Iggy Pop/David Bowie number 'Funtime' and it's great. Five stars for the B side." Paul Barney, *ZigZag*, August 1982.

British single

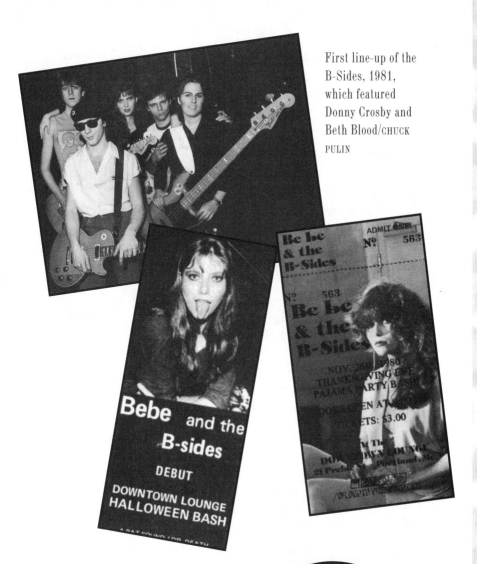

First line-up of the B-Sides, 1981, which featured Donny Crosby and Beth Blood/CHUCK PULIN

1984 *A SIDE OF THE B-SIDES*
12-inch EP, 3 songs: "Windy Words," "Battle Cry," "Mr. Never Forever," picture disk. Blue Flake, Canada, produced by Todd Rundgren.

"Bebe Buell, who's a great singer and a beautiful lady, has a country voice that'll knock you out—we sound really great together." Brian Setzer, *Guitar World*, May 1985.

Picture disc produced by Todd Rundgren, 1984

Performing with the B-Sides in NYC, 1982/
NORMAN BLAKE

The Gargoyles (*left to right*): Charles
Hall (bass), me, Steve Marshall (guitar),
and Todd Bricker (drums)/ALEXANDER
RYAN

1987 "JACUZZI JUNGLE" (A SIDE)/"13 WRONG TURNS" (B SIDE)

Bebe Buell and the Gargoyles, 7-inch single, Rt. One, United States.

"Bebe's been pursuing her musical ambitions directly, rather than vicariously, for the past eight years; first with the B-Sides, and now with the Gargoyles. She's now over here with her single 'Jacuzzi Jungle' in pursuit of a U.K. deal. And the music she writes and sings with the Gargoyles, well, Bebe would just call it rock 'n' roll, but it's lyrically sharp and bluesy. Pastiche-punk might be closer." Tony Mitchell, *Sounds*, March 21, 1987.

"For most of the 80s Bebe lived in Portland, Maine, bringing up Liv, her daughter, on whom she dotes, and putting together a succession of bands in which she sang her own raunchy, R&B-based leads. She has an impressive singing voice. Despite critical acclaim and the support of many of her loyal—and famous—fans, she found herself bedevilled by a record industry unable to see beyond its nose.

"None of the reviews her band has received in the last five years has referred to her as either a 'bimbo' or a 'supergroupie,' which she regards as a victory of sorts; and, anyway, she claims her family are all late bloomers. 'If you stick at something long enough, you will get there,' she says." Rodney Tyler, *You*, London, May 27, 1990.

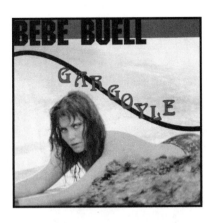

1993 "GARGOYLE" (A SIDE)/"BORED BABY" (B SIDE)
Single, Ultra Under Records, Cave Creek, Arizona.

"Bebe is back in the studio after having assembled a new line-up featuring Ratboy (formerly with L.A.'s 'Motorcycle Boy') and Coyote Shivers on guitars. These sessions have yielded her strongest, most exciting material to date and the resulting single of 'Gargoyle' and 'Bored Baby" is already commanding some major attention. A little melodic '60s psychedelic, some bump and grind crunch of early '70s hard rock, and the attitude/aggression of punk . . . all sung with a voice that can go from a sultry purr to a cardiac howl in the space of an instant. If you still love and miss the excitement of real rock 'n' roll, then Bebe Buell is for you. No bullshit, no hype, no empty promises . . . this is fun stuff that is so real you can taste it." Bebe Buell Bio/Press release.

1994 *RETROSEXUAL*
CD, Sky Dog International, France.

"The musical history of a gorgeous rebellious girl. Bebe truly combines the psychedelic melody of the '60s, the bump & grind crunch of the early '70s and the attitude aggression of punk. As she describes this CD: she tells you, 'It will hurt.' This sound is even more alive and living in the '90s than when it was recorded. A must." *Area*.

"Buell grabs center stage with tunes

My French CD, 1994

from the Thunders/Dead Boys/Patti Smith/early CBGB school of raunch. Songs like 'Bored Baby' and 'Cosmic Kiss' ring loud and true, with Bebe's clear alto purr cutting through the razor's edge guitar shrieks." S.L.D., *RIP*, December 1994.

"With the possible exception of Marilyn Monroe, Buell gets my vote for coolest Playmate, here creating an early punk sound as brutal and raw as anything by her famous ex-boyfriends Steven Tyler and Stiv Bators. Buell growls and screams with authentic intimidation as she looks back in anger (and hilarity) at a very full rock and roll life." Charles M. Young, *Playboy*, December 1995.

Back onstage after five years—feels so good—playing to a packed house at Don Hill's in NYC, 1999/BOB GRUEN

"Star Billing"/BUELL PRIVATE COLLECTION

372

INDEX

Note: Boldface page numbers denote photographs.

Photo of me and Liv, 1978, taken by my dear friend, Mark, who has always
been there for me–Thanks M.B.